Handbook of Pragmatics Highlights
语用学研究前沿丛书 7

社会与语言的使用
Society and Language Use

Edited by Jürgen Jaspers,
Jan-Ola Östman
and Jef Verschueren

上海外语教育出版社
SHANGHAI FOREIGN LANGUAGE EDUCATION PRESS

图书在版编目（CIP）数据

社会与语言的使用/雅斯佩斯（Jaspers J.）等编.
—上海：上海外语教育出版社，2014
（语用学研究前沿丛书）
ISBN 978-7-5446-3730-5

I. ①社… II. ①雅… III. ①社会语言学—英文
IV. ①H0

中国版本图书馆CIP数据核字（2014）第096485号

Original edition: *Society and Language Use* edited by Jürgn Jaspers, Jan-Ola Östman and Jef Verschueren © 2010 John Benjamins Publishing Company, Amsterdam/Philadelphia. Reprinted by permission for distribution in the People's Republic of China only.

本书由John Benjamins出版社授权上海外语教育出版社有限公司出版。
仅供在中华人民共和国境内销售。

图字：09-2013-421号

出版发行：**上海外语教育出版社**
（上海外国语大学内）　邮编：200083
电　　话：021-65425300（总机）
电子邮箱：bookinfo@sflep.com.cn
网　　址：http://www.sflep.com.cn　http://www.sflep.com
责任编辑：梁晓莉

印　　刷：上海信老印刷厂
开　　本：787×1092　1/16　印张21.75　字数362千字
版　　次：2014年7月第1版　2014年7月第1次印刷
印　　数：2 100 册

书　　号：ISBN 978-7-5446-3730-5 / H · 1347
定　　价：55.00 元

本版图书如有印装质量问题，可向本社调换

总　序

关注这套书已经很久了。2011年10月法兰克福书展开展时，约翰·本杰明斯出版公司（John Benjamins Publishing Company）的展台上已经摆出了9本，据其参展人员说，最后一本也将在年底前出版。因为是多年的合作伙伴，版权谈得很顺利。在图书即将引进出版之际，想杂七杂八说几句。

一、缘起

丛书的汉语名称最后定为"语用学研究前沿丛书"，是意译，英语原文为"Handbook of Pragmatics Highlights"，直译的话应该是"语用学手册选要"。要介绍本套丛书，先要从"语用学手册"（Handbook of Pragmatics）说起。

1986年，国际语用学协会（International Pragmatics Association, IPrA）成立。协会章程早期版本（Verschueren 1987）的III.1款表明，作为实现拟定目标的举措之一，协会准备组织编写一套"语用学手册"（以下简称"手册"），预计1989年完稿，并交由约翰·本杰明斯出版公司出版。为了更好地体现语用学不断发展的趋势，"手册"不是由一篇篇固定的文章组成的文集，而是采取一种可以不断扩充和修订的模式。此后，协会多次交流、协商，专门定期印发了工作文件，最后确定了"手册"的基本形式，即一本固定的指南（Manual）和一份每年更新的活页年册（Annual Installments）。

出于各种原因，"手册"的出版日期一推再推，第一版迟至1995年才露面。由于内容丰富、作者权威、形式新颖，"手册"面世后受到了广泛的欢迎。2003年，约翰·本杰明斯出版公司又推出了"手册"的网络版。网络版不仅避免了传统年册版的内容重复和纸张浪费，方便了更新，而且由于使用了先进的检索技术，查阅起来也更加顺手了。

从1995年出版的"手册"看，指南部分除了Jef Verschueren的一篇《语用学视角》（"The Pragmatic Perspective"）外，还收录了以下3个方面的文章：1. 语用学及相关学科的传统知识，如分析哲学（Analytical Philosophy）、应用语言学（Applied Linguistics）、认知科学（Cognitive Science）、内涵逻辑（Intensional Logic）、布拉格学派（the Prague School）、法位学（Tagmemics）等；2. 语言学方法，如对比分析（Contrastive Analysis）、解构主义（Deconstruction）、直觉与内省（Intuition and Introspection）等；3. 语言学的标注系统，如形式语义学的

标注（Notation in Formal Semantics）、口语标注系统（Transcription Systems for Spoken Discourse）等。

"手册"的第二部分，即1995年至今的活页年册所收录的条目主要有语用学的经典话题，如回指（Anaphora）、双语（Bilingualism）、语码转换（Code-switching）、衔接（Cohesion）、话语标记（Discourse Markers）、含义（Implicature）、大众传媒（Mass Media）、否定（Negation）、社会制度（Social Institutions）、招呼语（Terms of Address）；也有著名学者的介绍，如奥斯汀（Austin）、布勒（Bühler）、格莱斯（Grice）、莫里斯（Morris）、萨丕尔（Sapir）等。每个版次的活页年册的条目虽有少量增加，但主要变化还是体现在固有条目内容的定期调整和扩充上。为了便于检索，"手册"附有索引。经过多年滚雪球似的积累，"手册"目前已厚达5000余页。

鉴于"手册"体系庞大，内容复杂，两位总主编Jef Verschueren和Jan-Ola Östman决定从中精选出一批重要条目，以主题为线，分门别类，编成10册平装本。每册首篇为分册主编撰写的该领域的最新概览，主体部分为精选出来的12-20个条目。主编们希望各分册以精挑细选、主题突出、价格低廉的特点，更精准地走到读者的案头，同时也可以作为语用学相关课程的阅读资料。这10册精选出来的出版物就是我们看到的"语用学研究前沿丛书"（以下简称"前沿丛书"）。

二、语用视角

由于主编们起跑后快慢不一，"前沿丛书"各分册出版的年份有早有晚。为了探求两位总主编的编写思路，我们还是看看他们最初拟定的丛书内容和顺序（出版成书时的书名和排序根据实际情况有所调整，详见本书封三书单）：

1. 语用学的核心概念 Key Notions for Pragmatics
2. 语用学的哲学观点 Philosophical Perspectives
3. 语法、意义与语用 Grammar, Meaning and Pragmatics
4. 认知与语用 Cognition and Pragmatics
5. 社会与语言的使用 Society and Language Use
6. 文化与语言的使用 Culture and Language Use
7. 变异和演变的语用学 The Pragmatics of Variation and Change
8. 互动语用学 The Pragmatics of Interaction
9. 话语语用学 Discursive Pragmatics
10. 实用语用学 Pragmatics in Practice

粗看一下，感觉这10本语用学书包罗万象，把语言研究的全部内容都放进去了。为了把问题弄得更清楚，我们来看看另外一本著名的语用学手册，即Laurence R. Horn和Gregory Ward主编的 *The Handbook of Pragmatics*（Blackwell Publishing, 2005）。该手册分4个部分。第一个部分语用学的领地（The Domain of Pragmatics）仅6小块，即含义、预设、言语行为、指称、指示词和确定与不定。而信息结构、语境、回指、省略等则列入第二部分语用学和话语结构（Pragmatics and Discourse Structure）。语用学与语法、语义、词汇、习得等关系属于第三部分——语用学与其界面（Pragmatics and Its Interface）。最后一部分是语用与认知（Pragmatics and Cognition），涉及关联理论、认知语言学、构式语法等。从目录上看，Horn和Ward的手册基本上沿袭了我们所熟悉的Levinson（1983）的语用学框架（当然，增加了过去20年热门的认知语言学的内容），把语用学的核心研究领域限定在几个传统的议题上。这和Verschueren和Östman主编的"手册"内容形成了强烈的反差：前者研究领域狭窄、明确；后者研究领域则宽泛、模糊。

造成这种反差的因素主要是英美和欧洲大陆语用学研究的两种不同的传统，即模块论和视角论，这点后面将专门论及。这里我想重点谈谈Verschueren对视角论的发展和他特色鲜明的语用学顺应论，因为作为丛书编写的指导思想，这直接影响了"前沿丛书"内容的筛选。

国际语用学协会成立后，先后有过6任主席，分别是John Gumperz、Sandra Thompson、Ferenc Kiefer、Susan Ervin-Tripp、Sachiko Ide、Jan-Ola Östman。从协会章程和运作情况上看，主席选举产生，名誉的成分较大，真正负责协会日常工作的是设在比利时安特卫普大学（University of Antwerp）的秘书处，而自协会成立以来一直担任秘书长的正是Jef Verschueren。

作为国际语用学协会的发起人，Jef Verschueren的学术主张自20世纪70年代末以来一直有一条明晰的主线，即视角论和顺应论。应该说视角论是Haberland和Mey（1977: 5）最早提出来的。两位作者在 *Journal of Pragmatics* 创刊号的社论里提到，"语言的语用学应该提供一种视角俯瞰语言学所有的核心模块及其复合分支"，"语言的语用学可以表述为看待语言问题的新视角，而不是标出与其他学科的边界。"早在1978年，Verschueren就受Jacob Mey的影响，关注语用学理论的统一性。这个思想在Verschueren（1987）中基本定型，Verschueren（1999）则进一步将其系统化。收录在"前沿丛书"第一册的《语用学视角》一文则是Verschueren语用学思想的提炼和浓缩。

在Verschueren看来，语用学繁多的话题和芜杂的研究方法严重影响了学者间的交流和对学科研究的促进，因而有必要寻求一种系统的、统一的语用学理论，让针对同一语用现象的不同功能性研究成果有一个互相对比的框架。在批评分析了英美语用学理论把语用学作为一个模块和语音学、句法学、语义学并列的观点后，Verschueren提出了"语用学视角"的观点，即语用学是鸟瞰语言学各个模块，以及心理语言学、神经语言学、社会语言学、人类语言学等所谓复合（hyphenated）学科的一种视角，是语言使用的语言学。由于语言使用涉及认知的过程，发生在社会中、经受文化的限制，因而语用学视角主要是认知的、社会的、文化的。

所谓语言使用，不论对说话人还是对听话人来说，都是一种选择。要理清语言使用和人之间的关系，至少有3个概念非常重要。变化性（variability）指语言在各个层面上都有可供选择的一些结构。语言的这个特点为使用者提供了选择的目录。推敲性（negotiability）指没有固定的原则或规则来指导说话人的语言选择，因而选择是不确定的，不排除可能存在其他符合交际需要的选择。顺应性（adaptability）指语言的另外一个特点，即语言能够促使人类从众多可推敲的选择中确定一种选择来满足交际的需要。这3个概念互相关联，他们本身不是语用学研究的课题，而是语用学的研究课题——语言的功能性（the functionality of language）的3个特点。另外，3个概念不是平等的关系，顺应性的层级更高，因而在Verschueren语用学理论中占据了核心的地位。

从顺应性出发，Vershueren区分了语用学的4个任务（task），或者研究角度（angle of investigation）。第一个是"顺应性的语境关联"（Contextual Correlates of Adaptability），指我们传统意义上说的语言选择的语境。第二是"顺应性的结构对象"（Structural Objects of Adaptability），该任务是对语言选择本身的描述，指的是语言选择所面临的不同结构。第三个是"顺应性动力学"（Dynamics of Adaptability），其目的是解释语言使用中的各种原则和策略影响语言选择的动力机制。第四个是"顺应过程的凸显性"（Salience of the Adaptation Processes），指做出语言选择时人的意识上的努力程度（不是指语境因素的凸显程度）。这样，"语境关联"和"结构对象"构成了语用研究的处所，"动力学"研究顺应过程的运作机制，"凸显性"体现了运作的意识特点。Vershueren用这4大要素构筑了他自己的语用学理论大厦，并用来解释语言使用中意义的动态生产过程——用其本人的术语说，即"语言的意义生产机能"（the Meaningful Functioning of Language）。

三、内容

在Verschueren看来，语用学理论不再是针对某个具体的语言现象的描写和解释，而是面向所有语言使用的一个宏观视角。语用研究所涉及的范围也自然是"普天之下，莫非王土"了。

在10本"前沿丛书"中，《语用学的核心概念》是基础。里面除了传统的言语行为理论（Speech Act Theory）、预设（Presupposition）、指示词（Deixis）、语境和语境化（Context and Contextualization）外，还收录了Verschueren的顺应性（Adaptability）、信道（Channel）、隐含性（Implicitness）、非言语交际（Non-verbal Communication）、灵长类交际（Primate Communication）等等。

Verschueren的语用观不仅决定了"前沿丛书"第一本，即《语用学的核心概念》的词条选项，也决定了整套"前沿丛书"的总体布局和其他9本书的具体内容。

哲学是语用学的本源，因而《语用学的哲学观点》作为第二本紧随《语用学的核心概念》。该书人物词条有莫里斯（Charles Morris）、维特根斯坦（Ludwig Wittgenstein）、奥斯汀（J. L. Austin）、格莱斯（H. P. Grice）；哲学理论和流派有分析哲学—日常语言哲学（Analytic Philosophy – Ordinary Language Philosophy）、语境论（Contextualism）、认识论（Epistemology）、内涵逻辑（Intensional Logic）、模型理论语义学（Model-Theoretic Semantics）、语言哲学（Philosophy of Language）、心灵哲学（Philosophy of Mind）等。值得注意的是，通常情况下，内涵逻辑和模型理论语义学都被列入语义学，而不是语用学的范畴。除此之外，有些词条带有明显的欧洲大陆传统色彩，如巴赫金（Mikhail Bakhtin）、解构主义（Deconstruction）、福柯（Michel Foucault）、普遍语用学和超验语用学（Universal and Transcendental Pragmatics）等。

生成语义学（Generative Semantics）、构式分析（Constructional Analysis）、词序（Word Order）、布拉格学派（the Prague School）、否定（Negation）、心理空间（Mental Space）、象似性（Iconicity）等有的属于认知语言学，有的属于形式语言学，有的则属于功能语言学，有的属于语法学。在这些常见的研究领域里，一个共同的特点是意义会对句法结构产生影响，基于这一点，它们都作为条目被列入了第三本《语法、意义与语用》。同样被收入的还有控制（Control，指句法中主语对不定式或动名词的管辖）、框架分析（Frame Analysis，指与脚本（Script）、图式（Schema）有关的情景的类型）等。

前面提到，在Verschueren看来，语用学是对语言和交际的认知的、社会的、文化的研究。不难理解，接下来的3本书《认知与语用》、《社会与语言的使用》和《文化与语言的使用》就分别代表了语言在这3个侧面的研究。

Verschueren所理解的认知比较宽泛,除了认知科学(Cognitive Science)、实验(Experimentation)外,还包括认知语言学、计算机对认知的模拟以及心理语言学、语言学习等领域的范畴。由于认知语言学中的部分话题已经在《语法、意义与语用》中出现,《认知与语用》仅收录了范畴化(Categorization)、认知语法(Cognitive Grammar)。计算机对认知的模拟方面收录了人工智能(Artificial Intelligence)、连接主义(Connectionism)。心理语言学和语言学习方面的话题有语言交际中的大脑分工(Cerebral Division of Labour in Verbal Communication)、理解与生产(Comprehension vs. Production)、发展心理学(Developmental Psychology)、心理语言学(Psycholinguistics)、多语种词汇(The Multilingual Lexicon)、语言习得(Language Aquisition)等。

从主编Jürgen Jaspers的序言上看,《社会与语言的使用》可以算作具有欧洲大陆特点的社会语言学手册。除了社会语言学的传统概念如性别(Gender)、语码转换(Code-switching)、双语和多语(Bilingualism and Multilingualism)、言语社区(Speech Community)、社会制度(Social Institutions)之外,该书还收录了两类词条。一类是体现欧洲研究特长的一些研究领域,如"他者"的再现('Other' Representation)、马克思主义语言学(Marxist Linguistics)、主体与语言(Agency and Language)、语言意识形态(Language Ideology);另外一类是英美社会语言学界所忽视或回避的一些话题,比如语言统治和少数化(Language Dominance and Minorization)、语言权利(Language Rights)等。

第七本书名为《文化与语言的使用》,里面分量最多的理所当然地是与文化有关的语言学研究,例如文化(Culture)、文化脚本(Cultural Script)、民族志(Ethnography)、跨文化交际(Intercultural Communication)、敬语(Honorifics)等。另外,该书还收录了人类学领域的人类语言学(Anthropological Linguistics)、认知人类学(Cognitive Anthropology)以及马凌诺斯基(Bronislaw Kasper Malinowski)、萨丕尔(Edward Sapir)、沃尔夫(Benjamin Lee Whorf)、洪堡特(Wilhelm von Humboldt)等。而田野调查(Fieldwork)、提取(Elicitation)则属于社会科学里通用的研究方法。

《变异和演变的语用学》(实际成书时书名调整为《语用学视角下的变异与演变》,*Variation and Change: Pragmatic Perspectives*)收录的条目涉及语言的变异和演变。通常情况下,变异,包括方言、洋泾浜语、克里奥语,属于社会语言学的范畴,而演变则属于历史语言学的研究领域。借词(Borrowing)、方言(Dialect)、语域(Register)、语言接触(Language Contact)、历史语言学（Historical Linguistics）、历史语用学（Historical Pragmatics）等自然列入该书。另外，在变异和演变的标题下，该书还收录了中介语语用学（Interlanguage Pragmatics）、类型学（Typology）、行话（Jargon）等能够导致语音、句法、语义变化的其他因素。

传统上，与口语与书面语对应研究分别是对话分析（Conversational Analysis）和话语分析（Discourse Analysis）。"前沿丛书"专门列出了《互动语用学》和《话语语用学》两本书来展示这两方面的研究现状。《互动语用学》收录了对话分析（Conversational Analysis）、对话类型（Conversational Type）、常人方法学（Ethnomethodology）、韵律（Prosody）、话序（Sequence）、萨克斯（Harvey Sacks）、口语标注系统（Transcription Systems for Spoken Discourse）等。《话语语用学》中主要有衔接与连贯（Cohesion and Coherence）、批评语言学和批评话语分析（Critical Linguistics and Critical Discourse Analysis）、辞格（Figure of Speech）、话语类型（Genre）、语用标记（Pragmatic Markers）、文本语言学（Text Linguistics）以及具有欧洲大陆特色的研究课题，如复调（Polyphony）、互文性（Intertextuality）、言说：法国语用学方法（Énonciation: French Pragmatic Approach(es)）等。

语用学已经是研究使用中的语言了，那么"前沿丛书"的最后一本《实用语用学》有什么内容呢？分册主编Östman给出了4个的领域，即传统的日常语言的使用、语言与伦理、顺应中的语言使用以及语用学在相关学科的应用。收录的项目有读写能力（Literacy）、大众传媒（Mass Media）、语料库分析（Corpus Analysis）、对比分析（Contrastive Analysis）、语言与法律（Language and the Law）、翻译研究（Translation Studies）、错误分析（Error Analysis）、应用语言学（Applied Linguistics）、临床语用学（Clinical Pragmatics）等。从这些项目上看，"实用语用学"仍然是语用学与相关学科的跨学科研究，一部分属于一些大的跨学科研究所未及涉及的东西，另一部分收录了一些小的跨学科研究，可以看作"前沿丛书"收尾时的"拾遗"。

四、两个传统

早在30多年前，Levinson（1983:ix）就提到语用学研究的两个传统，在承认自己在书中追随了英美研究传统的同时，也指出欧洲大陆的语用学研究范围更为宽泛，包含了社会语言学的研究领域。近年来，黄衍（Huang 2010, 2012）致力于语用学的系统化梳理（systematizing pragmatics），明确地把两个传统描述为模块论和视角论。在黄衍看来，受20世纪分析哲学的影响，英美语用学传统试图通过使用（use）研究意义（meaning）。这些研究具体落实在含义、预设、言语行为、指示、指称等几个模块上，因而可以称作模块论。模块论与前面提到的Mey、Verschueren等学者倡导的视角论明显不同，后者把语用学看作凌驾于所有语言使用研究之上的一种理论角度。因此，我们看到，"前沿丛书"的内容有一个特点，即从各册目录上看，语用学囊括了语言学及应用语言学、语言学复合学科的所有研究领域，无论是它们语音的、语法的、语义的、形式的、功能的，还是认知的、文化的、社会的、历史的。

尽管两个传统有较大的差异，然而它们都没有背离Morris对语用学的定义，即语用学研究的是符号与解释者之间的关系。英美传统中的指示、指称、含义等语言现象理所当然地属于语用学的领域，因为其理解需要和解释者联系起来。欧洲大陆传统也名正言顺地属于这个权威定义下的语用学。Morris甚至明确地说，"语用学可以足够准确地描述为研究符号的生命特征，亦即符号运作中心理的、生物的、社会的现象"（1938: 108），这何尝不是对欧洲语用学研究宽泛的传统的准确预测？

造成两个传统"同宗同族，各奔前程"这个局面的原因是语用学在英美和欧洲大陆发展的土壤不同。具体说来，既有哲学传统的差异，也有语言学传统的分野。

20世纪英美分析哲学从Russel、前期维特根斯坦、维也纳学派再到Quine，在形而上学上坚持的是实在论（Realism），即认为客观世界独立于人而存在，哲学的任务之一就是确立语言与世界的对应关系。可是后来哲学家们发现，无论是自然语言还是逻辑语言的语义学都不能独立完成指称的任务，这就需要语用学以新模块的方式加入进来，协助完成。过去20年对语义学和语用学划界与分工的讨论和过去10年语境主义和极简主义争执的前提也是模块论。

从语言学的角度说，自Saussure区分了语言和言语后，英美传统更注重对语言的研究，结构主义所进行的语言描述的主要目的是发现语言系统，Chomsky更是关注语言能力（competence）和普遍语法（UG），把语言符号的运用排斥到自己的研究领域之外，而语用学这个垃圾桶则在需要的时候很好地起到了补充的作用。因此无论是从哲学的角度还是从语言学的角度看，英美传统中语用学都是作为一个模块，是对语义学的补充。

欧洲大陆则是一种完全不同的景象。Husserl的现象学承袭了Kant对现象（phenomena）重视，更关注经验和意识，而不在意客观实在（noumena）。而经验和意识是一种客观和主观的混合体，主观因其意向性（intentionality）而和客观结合起来。因此和英美实在论不同的是，现象学的世界不是客观世界，而是生活世界（lifeworld，或Lebenswelt）。人的因素，或者说人文性，不再是世界的某个模块，而是融合到世界的各个要素里面了。

在语言学上，欧洲大陆对Saussure的发展也走向了另外一个方向。在Benveniste看来，我们不能把语言系统看作一个完成的系统、把人看作一个完成的人，实际上人在不停地创造语言，语言也在不停地创造人，人和语言之间是一种密不可分的关系。因此，人和所有的语言要素都有关联。

不论是英美传统，还是欧洲大陆传统，语用学的研究都是从人对语言的解释的角度看待语言所受的影响和所反映的信息。两个传统的区别其实可以看作是对同一个领域的不同研究课题的兴趣。在英美传统看来，意义、指称、言语行为等问题是影响分析哲学理论基石的问题，对这些问题的理解决定了分析哲学的走向乃至成败。因而，有关这方面的研究比较深入，成果也多，形成了英美语用学的几个重要的研究模块。而在欧洲大陆，人们对语言系统与社会、文化的关系特别关注，对人在世界中的作用，即"人文性"有浓厚的兴趣，希望通过语言的语音、句法、篇章的分析，揭示人的本性与特点、人与自然的关系、人与社会的关系，进而加深对人的权力、自由、解放等问题的深入探讨。值得注意的是，两个传统并非泾渭分明的，在学术交流日趋频繁的今天，英美和欧洲大陆的学者也在互相学习，互相借鉴。

五、结语

总的说来，"前沿丛书"的主编们虽然立足欧洲，在选目上却也顾及了英美传统的语用学，展现了一种国际视野。因此，从两种研究传统均衡的角度来说，他们是客观的。长期以来，由于受语用学教育、欧洲语言障碍等因素的影响，我国语用学界对英美传统的研究较深入，而对欧洲大陆传统的引介较少，这套丛书的出版对我国语用学界拓宽视野来说无疑是个福音。

最近几年，语用学学科出版了多套百科全书式的手册。单卷本的除了前面提到的Horn和Ward主编的*The Handbook of Pragmatics*（Blackwell Publishing, 2005）外，还有Keith Allan和Kasia M. Jaszczolt主编的*The Cambridge Handbook of Pragmatics*（Cambridge University Press, 2012），黄衍（Yan Huang）主编的*The Oxford Dictionary of Pragmatics*（Oxford University Press, 2012）。多卷本的有Wolfram Bublitz, Andreas H. Jucker, Klaus P. Schneider主编的9卷本的*Handbooks of Pragmatics*（De Gruyter Mouton, 2010-2014）。虽然风格各异，然而无论从规模上还是从体例上说，还没有任何一种能和洋洋洒洒5000余页的"手册"比肩。我们

在感谢两位主编的同时,也不得不提提约翰·本杰明斯出版公司。

20世纪90年代初我在上外读研究生时,看到资料中心许多自己喜欢的语言学"新书"都是约翰·本杰明斯出版公司出版的,如John Haiman的*Iconicity in Syntax*(1985),Brygida Rudzka-Ostyn的*Topics in Cognitive Linguistics*(1988),以及*Pragmatics & Beyond*丛书中的好几本。留校进了上海外语教育出版社之后才知道,这是一家荷兰的家庭出版社,主要出版语言学、翻译学方面的图书,其书目中仅与语用学有关的就多达近300种。这几年John Benjamins先生年事已高,书展上,台前台后都是女儿女婿张罗,他自己则静静地端坐在展台一角。每次去法兰克福,我都乐意过去坐会儿,翻翻书,聊几句,心中充满了对这位出版老人深深的敬意。

孙玉
上海外国语大学
2014年春

参考书目:

Huang, Yan. (2010). Pragmatics: Anglo-American and European continental traditions. In L. Cummings (ed.) *The Pragmatics Encyclopedia*. New York: Routledge.

Huang, Yan. (2012). Re-systematizing Pragmatics.《外国语》,2:2-21.

Levinson, Steven. (1983). *Pragmatics*. Cambridge: CUP.

Haberland, Hartmut and Jacob Mey. (1977). Editorial: Linguistics and pragmatics. *Journal of Pragmatics*, 1:1-13.

Morris, Charles. (1938). *Foundations of the Theory of Signs*. Chicago: University of Chicago Press.

Verschueren, Jef. (1978). Reflections on presupposition failure: A contribution to an integrated theory of pragmatics. *Journal of Pragmatics*, 2: 107-151.

Verschueren, Jef. (1987). Pragmatics as a theory of linguistic adaptation (First working document drafted for the International Pragmatics Association in Preparation of a Handbook of Pragmatics). Antwerp: International Pragmatics Association.

Verschueren, Jef. (1999). *Understanding Pragmatics*. London: Arnold.

Society and Language Use

Edited by

Jürgen Jaspers
University of Antwerp

Jan-Ola Östman
University of Helsinki

Jef Verschueren
University of Antwerp

Handbook of Pragmatics Highlights (HoPH)

The ten volumes of *Handbook of Pragmatics Highlights* focus on the most salient topics in the field of pragmatics, thus dividing its wide interdisciplinary spectrum in a transparent and manageable way. Each volume starts with an up-to-date overview of its field of interest and brings together some 12–20 entries on its most pertinent aspects.

Since 1995 the *Handbook of Pragmatics (HoP)* and the *HoP Online* (in conjunction with the *Bibliography of Pragmatics Online*) have provided continuously updated state-of-the-art information for students and researchers interested in the science of language in use. Their value as a basic reference tool is now enhanced with the publication of a topically organized series of paperbacks presenting *HoP Highlights*. Whether your interests are predominantly philosophical, cognitive, grammatical, social, cultural, variational, interactional, or discursive, the *HoP Highlights* volumes make sure you always have the most relevant encyclopedic articles at your fingertips.

Editors

Jef Verschueren
University of Antwerp

Jan-Ola Östman
University of Helsinki

Volume 7

Society and Language Use
Edited by Jürgen Jaspers, Jan-Ola Östman and Jef Verschueren

Table of contents

Preface to the series   IX

Acknowledgements   XI

Introduction – Society and language use   1
Jürgen Jaspers
1. Linguistic antecedents   2
2. Antecedents in social theory   8
3. Late modern trends and issues   12

Accommodation theory   21
Nikolas Coupland
1. Overview   21
2. Speech accommodation theory   21
3. Conceptual developments   23
4. The accommodation model: Predictive or interpretive?   23
5. Discourse attuning   24

Agency and language   28
Laura M. Ahearn
1. Practice theory   31
2. Anthropological contributions to practice theory   33
3. Intentionality   34
4. The grammatical encoding of agency   37
5. Talk about agency – Meta-agentive discourse   41
6. Language in action, agency in language   44

Authority   49
John Wilson & Karyn Stapleton
1. Introduction   49
2. Authority and the self   51
3. Authority in each other   55
4. Authority in the world   57
5. Authority in (and through) God   58

6. Authority and gender 59
7. Authority in language 62
8. Authority 64

Bilingualism and multilingualism 71
Monica Heller & Aneta Pavlenko
1. Introduction 71
2. Four approaches to the study of bilingualism and multilingualism 72
   2.1 Neurolinguistic and psycholinguistic approaches to multilingualism 73
   2.2 Social psychological approaches 75
   2.3 Linguistic and sociolinguistic approaches 76
   2.4 Sociological and anthropological approaches 77
3. Conclusion 79

Code-switching 84
Peter Auer & Carol M. Eastman
1. Introduction 84
2. Terminological and methodological issues 85
3. Early studies 87
4. The meaning of code-switching 90
   4.1 The politics of code-switching 90
   4.2 Code-switching in interaction 95
5. Grammatical constraints on code-switching 101
6. Future directions in code-switching research 107

Cognitive sociology 113
Barry Saferstein
1. Historical overview 113
2. The interrelation of interactional sense-making processes and social organization 116
   2.1 Interaction 116
   2.2 Discourse 116
   2.3 Cognition 117
   2.4 Organizational activities and materials 117
3. Key concepts 117
   3.1 Interpretive procedures 117
   3.2 Expertise 118
   3.3 Social organization 118
   3.4 Inequality and stratification 119
   3.5 Organizational constraints 119
4. Methodology 119
5. A sample analysis 120

Contact 127
Li Wei
1. Language contact: Causes, processes and outcomes   127
2. Theoretical and methodological approaches to language contact   130
3. The pragmatics of language contact   135
4. Conclusion   138

Correlational sociolinguistics 140
Norbert Dittmar
1. Introduction   140
2. Concepts of linguistic variation   141
   2.1 Tradition and innovation   142
   2.2 Methodology   142
   2.3 Description   143
   2.4 Explanation   143
   2.5 Theory   143
   2.6 Application   144
3. Basic lines of argumentation: The corpus   144
4. Rules: How instances of usage are described   145
5. Language change: The perspective of explanations   148
6. Outlook   150

Gender 152
Robin Tolmach Lakoff
1. Language and gender   152
2. Pragmatic aspects of gender   153
3. The prehistory of language and gender research   153
4. The history of language and gender research   155
   4.1 The 1970s   155
   4.2 The 1980s   161
   4.3 The 1990s   164
   4.4 The 2000s: Some concluding remarks   166

Interactional sociolinguistics 169
Jef Verschueren
1. Background   169
2. Contributions   170
3. Program   173

Language dominance and minorization 176
Donna Patrick
1. Introduction 176
2. Linguistic hierarchy and nation-building 178
   2.1 Language and nationalism 179
   2.2 Official languages 180
   2.3 Other dominant language ideologies 181
3. Minorization 183
   3.1 International declarations of minority language rights 186
4. Conclusion 188

Language ideologies – Evolving perspectives 192
Paul V. Kroskrity
1. Introduction 192
2. The historical emergence of language ideologies 192
3. Some key concepts 195
4. Recent developments 201
5. Perspectives for future research 205

Language rights 212
Tove Skutnabb-Kangas
1. Introduction: Language rights, linguistic human rights, and (linguistic) assimilation or integration 212
2. Basic concepts, continua and dichotomies 215
   2.1 Who or what can have rights? 215
   2.2 Individual versus collective rights 215
      2.2.1 Individual rights 215
      2.2.2 Collective rights 216
      2.2.3 What is a minority? 217
   2.3 Negative versus positive rights 219
   2.4 Personal versus territorial rights 220
   2.5 Rights in 'hard law' versus 'soft law' 221
   2.6 Expressive versus instrumental rights 222
   2.7 LHR hierarchies 222
3. LHRs in education 223
   3.1 Are there any binding LHRs in education? 223
   3.2 Linguistic genocide 225
4. To conclude 228

Marxist linguistics 233
Niels Helsloot
1. Introduction 233
2. Marr vs. Stalin 234
3. Recent trends 235
4. Gramsci 236
5. Vološinov 236
6. Pêcheux 237
7. Marxist linguistics today 238

'Other' representation 241
Nikolas Coupland
1. On representation 242
2. On 'the other' 244
3. Discourse strategies in representations of 'the other' 248
   - 3.1 Homogenisation 248
   - 3.2 Pejoration 250
   - 3.3 Suppression and silencing 252
   - 3.4 Displaying 'liberalism' 252
   - 3.5 Subverting tolerance 253
4. Beyond minoritisation 254

Social institutions 261
Richard J. Watts
1. Introduction 261
2. The social constructivist approach to 'social institutions' 262
3. Social reproduction and the notion of symbolic resource 263
4. The discourse of social control: The reproduction of social institutions 264
5. Family discourse as a form of institutional discourse 266
6. Conclusion 272

Speech community 274
Ben Rampton 274
1. Community speech and speech community: Pragmatic vs. distributional perspectives 275
2. 'Speech community' at the interface of 'tradition and modernity' 278
3. Late modern discourse, language and community 282
4. Communities of practice 284
5. 'Community' as a semiotic sign 286

6. Language ideologies and the production of community   287
7. From the 'linguistics of community' to a 'linguistics of contact'   289
8. Community and discourse in the Information Age   292
9. Conclusion   296

Symbolic interactionism   304
Rod Watson

Index   315

Preface to the series

In 1995, the first installments of the **Handbook of Pragmatics (HoP)** were published. The HoP was to be one of the major tools of the International Pragmatics Association (IPrA) to achieve its goals (i) of disseminating knowledge about pragmatic aspects of language, (ii) of stimulating various fields of application by making this knowledge accessible to an interdisciplinary community of scholars approaching the same general subject area from different points of view and with different methodologies, and (iii) of finding, in the process, a significant degree of theoretical coherence.

The HoP approaches pragmatics as the cognitive, social, and cultural science of language and communication. Its ambition is to provide a practical and theoretical tool for achieving coherence in the discipline, for achieving cross-disciplinary intelligibility in a necessarily diversified field of scholarship. It was therefore designed to provide easy access for scholars with widely divergent backgrounds but with converging interests in the use and functioning of language, in the topics, traditions, and methods which, together, make up the broadly conceived field of pragmatics. As it was also meant to provide a state-of-the-art report, a flexible publishing format was needed. This is why the print version took the form of a background manual followed by annual loose-leaf installments, enabling the creation of a continuously updatable and expandable reference work. The flexibility of this format vastly increased with the introduction of an online version, the **Handbook of Pragmatics Online** (see www.benjamins.com/online).

While the HoP and the HoP-online continue to provide state-of–the-art information for students and researchers interested in the science of language use, this new series of **Handbook of Pragmatics** *Highlights* focuses on the most salient topics in the field of pragmatics, thus dividing its wide interdisciplinary spectrum in a transparent and manageable way. The series contains a total of ten volumes around the following themes:

- Key notions for pragmatics
- Pragmatics and philosophy
- Grammar, meaning and pragmatics
- Cognition and pragmatics
- Society and language use
- Culture and language use
- The pragmatics of variation and change

- The pragmatics of interaction
- Discursive pragmatics
- Pragmatics in practice

This topically organized series of paperbacks, each starting with an up-to-date overview of its field of interest, each brings together some 12-20 of the most pertinent HoP entries. They are intended to make sure that students and researchers alike, whether their interests are predominantly philosophical, cognitive, grammatical, social, cultural, variational, interactional, or discursive, can always have the most relevant encyclopedic articles at their fingertips. Affordability, topical organization and selectivity also turn these books into practical teaching tools which can be used as reading materials for a wide range of pragmatics-related linguistics courses.

With this endeavor, we hope to make a further contribution to the goals underlying the HoP project when it was first conceived in the early 1990's.

Jan-Ola Östman (University of Helsinki) &
Jef Verschueren (University of Antwerp)

Acknowledgements

A project of the HoP type cannot be successfully started, let alone completed, without the help of dozens, even hundreds of scholars. First of all, there are the authors themselves, who sometimes had to work under extreme conditions of time pressure. Further, most members of the IPrA Consultation Board have occasionally, and some repeatedly, been called upon to review contributions. Innumerable additional scholars were thanked in the initial versions of handbook entries. All this makes the Handbook of Pragmatics a truly joint endeavor by the pragmatics community world-wide. We are greatly indebted to you all.

We do want to specifically mention the important contributions over the years of three scholars: the co-editors of the Manual and the first eight annual installments, Jan Blommaert and Chris Bulcaen were central to the realization of the project, and so was our editorial collaborator over the last four years, Eline Versluys. Our sincerest thanks to all of them.

The Handbook of Pragmatics project is being carried out in the framework of the research program of the IPrA Research Center at the University of Antwerp. We are indebted to the university for providing an environment that facilitates and nurtures our work.

Jan-Ola Östman (University of Helsinki) &
Jef Verschueren (University of Antwerp)

Introduction – Society and language use

Jürgen Jaspers
University of Antwerp

> "The simplest and yet most important contribution of sociolinguistics [and similar disciplines willing to go under that flag] to social scientific knowledge is its insistence on recognizing the considerable variation in speech that exists within even the most homogeneous of societies. The second important contribution is the insistence that this variation is neither trivial nor a pale reflection of 'real' language, but that it is systematic and that the systematicity of linguistic variation is an imperative object of study in itself. Having recognized that different people talk differently, and that the same people talk differently at different times, a central problem of sociolinguistics is – or ought to be – to understand why people talk the way they do. It then becomes clear that the research questions of sociolinguistics are preeminently social questions."
> (Woolard 1985: 738)

Formulated a quarter of a century ago, Woolard's words have not lost their edge in emphasizing that the analysis of systematic linguistic variation is key to understanding the societies we live in. Undoubtedly the insistence underlying her words stems from the earlier paucity of attention given to social questions in much of linguistics, not unrivalled by the long-term neglect for language use in sociology. Indeed, it cannot be underestimated that fifty or sixty years ago, Woolard's words may very well have risked derision, indifference or swift oblivion. And beyond the limits of the academy today, sociolinguistic questions are still far from being viewed as social questions. In Flemish Belgium, for example, a region that can hardly be accused of indifference to linguistic issues given its history of fighting for Dutch linguistic rights (a fight which militant voices say still continues), it is not uncommon that sociolinguists are interviewed by public media about multilingualism as a primarily cognitive phenomenon affecting children in their personal and educational development. But as soon as attention turns to language as a socio-political issue of concern to adults, usually only politicians or political scientists are asked to comment on policy measures with regard to speakers of other languages on Flemish territory (such as, recently, making a willingness to learn Dutch or a competence in speaking it conditional to obtaining social housing, welfare benefits or information from local authorities). Hence, whatever sociolinguists may have to say about multilingualism as a social issue is effectively sidelined by such media preferences and preserves the acceptability of an emphatic monolingual policy. Also within the academy, it would probably be naive to presume that social and sociolinguistic questions now form a united front. In Flanders at least, some sociolinguists, accused of being over-tolerant of linguistic variation, maintain that their only concern is the neutral description of existing linguistic variation; yet at the same time they can also be heard reassuring their worried audiences repeatedly that they will not hesitate to send away students at exams if the latter use a substandard, 'inappropriate', Dutch variety. Clearly, however, these two concerns cancel each other out or depend on putting up a wall between one's practices as a sociolinguist and as an (authoritative) language user. Besides their edge, therefore, Woolard's words have neither lost their relevance.

This volume topicalizes the importance of addressing the mutually constitutive relation between society and language use. It highlights a number of the most prominent approaches of this relation and it draws attention to a selected number of topics that the study of language in its social context has characteristically brought to bear. Notwithstanding some of the theoretical and methodological differences between them, all chapters in this book assume that it is necessary to look at society and language use as interdependent phenomena, and that by attending to microscopic phenomena such as language use at a given moment (and to the phonological, morphological and other elements that together make up 'speech'), one is also keeping a finger on the pulse of broader, macroscopic social tendencies that at the same time facilitate and constrain language use. The study of 'society and language use' obviously covers a much broader terrain than can be covered in this highlights volume. And given the fairly recent nature of most of the contributions, I shall in this introduction provide a sketch of their intellectual antecedents in the volume's two 'mother disciplines', viz., linguistics and social theory (although admittedly these concepts sometimes draw neater boundaries around scientific practices than can often be found in actual fact) before pointing at recent common ground in the rising attention for discourse and what has come to be called late-modernity.

1. Linguistic antecedents

Attention for society and language use had to wrestle itself away in the 1950s and 1960s from under the hegemonic hold of 'formal' or 'Chomskyan' linguistics where consideration for the social context of language use was virtually non-existent. This neglect was not unreasoned. Chomsky's intention was to isolate language from its social surroundings in order to study its intrinsic generative creativity – humans' ability to make endless new sentences with only a limited set of verbal building blocks. In this frame, it made sense to work with an abstract notion of language, to strip those phenomena that were seen as unrelated to this capacity, and to ignore for whatever reasons humans would use language. Rather than denying linguistic heterogeneity and variation, therefore, Chomsky and his followers saw these phenomena as largely superficial and irrelevant outcomes of 'real' language, that is, a deeper-lying systematics in individual cognition. Even so, language use remained a necessary heuristic device to trace the underlying fundamentals that generated it and it was felt that an efficient description of these fundamentals would only be possible if the input was kept under control by reducing the noise and the other limitations of language use by specific speakers in specific socio-cultural contexts (such as interruptions, hesitations, lapses, muttering, etc.) – whence Chomsky's postulation of speakers and hearers in a completely uniform linguistic community (Chomsky 1965: 3). Consequently, in this view language users become mere "implementer[s] of language as it is" (Fishman 1972: 216) or "hosts for language" (Kroskrity, p. 194, this volume), rather than social agents who accomplish something by talking to others.

Chomsky's relegation of language use to the margins of serious study had been preceded by a part-European (de Saussure), part-American (Bloomfield, Boas, Sapir) structuralist tradition. This tradition itself ushered in a paradigm shift in linguistics, which in the closing decades of the 19th century had been dominated by the Neogrammarian hypothesis that strict laws could be formulated which described regular sound change within a particular language or language family. In contrast with this focus on the historical trajectory of individual sounds, structuralists insisted (1) that languages be approached as systems or structures where the relations between sounds prevail over the sounds themselves, ruling out the historical comparison of isolated sounds from different systems of relations; (2) that these systems needed to be studied first and foremost synchronically, before one would be able to study their change over time; (3) and that language systems be regarded as autonomous from so-called external (e.g. sociological, psychological) influences or human intervention. This autonomy principle motivated the distinction between an 'internal' linguistics, concerned with the language system proper, and an 'external' linguistics, of secondary importance, that would investigate the uses of language without a concern for, say, its hardware. Social and cultural meaning was thus generally considered an external, optional aspect of language that did not lend itself well to a truly empirical linguistics or which was merely derivative of the linguistic structure (Van de Walle et al. 2006). In sum, and passing over the major fissures between structuralist and Chomskyan approaches, mainstream 20th century linguistics up to the 1960s worked with an abstract notion of language and perceived systematicity only within language rather than in its use.

These assumptions were increasingly opposed in the 1960s and 1970s by Labov, Fishman, Gumperz, Halliday and Hymes, among others. These scholars questioned the exclusion of external factors as secondary or less empirically tameable elements and the idea of language use as a conceptual wastebasket for heterogeneity and variation; they had serious reservations about the assumption that systematicity implied or could be equated with linguistic synchronicity, and they disputed the postulation of linguistic homogeneity as either a methodological prerequisite in generative models or as a theoretical priority in structuralist thinking (where self-contained systems seemed to exclude the existence of contradictory norms belonging to the same system, implying that languages and communities were largely coterminous, cf. Voloshinov 1973: 56, cited in Meeuwis & Brisard 1993).

In a number of seminal studies, Labov managed to deliver a formidable blow to mainstream linguistics when he showed that synchronic linguistic heterogeneity is the basic origin of language change (e.g. Labov 1966). In drawing attention to the fact that minor sound differences were illustrative of social differentiation, that speakers were aware of the social value of these linguistic details and that as a result of this, some linguistic variants became more popular than others and gradually made their competitors become obsolete, he had found the key for the door between language internal and external analysis. Because as it appeared, the rising popularity of seemingly unimportant or superficial performance features started to influence the sound relations in the whole linguistic system, and eventually contributed to the emergence of a new, 'changed' code. Besides showing in this way that even seemingly homogeneous communities exhibit meaningful linguistic variation, he was able to point out that social meaning (in the form of evaluations of language) could not be reasonably kept out of the analysis. What is more, if sociolinguistic patterns allowed researchers to observe linguistic change in progress, there was no reason anymore to study languages synchronically first before attending to their diachronic evolution (cf. Weinreich, Labov & Herzog 1968; also see Dittmar, this volume).

No less effectively, Hymes, from a linguistic anthropological angle, critically approached Chomsky's failure to account for the various ways in which social and contextual exigencies continually influence the shape of utterance production, as well as his failure to address the fact that ungrammatical sentences may be quite acceptable, appropriate or even artful in actual social settings. In contrast with the central tenet in Chomskyan linguistics that "uses of language [are] everywhere essentially equivalent" (1996: 101), Hymes insisted that even if speakers' ability to produce grammatical sentences merits description, social life would be impossible if "anyone can say anything to anyone in any way" (ibid.; Fishman 1972: 3). In addition to acquiring a grammatical system or 'linguistic competence', Hymes argued that speakers must acquire a 'communicative competence', a system of use associated with the social environments and institutions they are part of and which constrains the range of possibilities while allowing for recognisable and artful behaviour within the system's limitations (cf. Gumperz 1972: 14; Johnstone & Marcellino 2010).

Besides the emphasis on the inevitable interpenetration of code and behaviour (cf. Halliday 1984: 7), there grew extensive opposition to mainstream linguistics' disregard for linguistic variation as a social fact and for the unintended consequences of building linguistic theory on an idealised linguistic community. Chomsky's focus on abstract monolingual language only helped to endorse, or was not very much concerned with negating, the idea that monolingualism can be considered a normal state of affairs; that, consequently, bilingualism, code-switching and language contact are only secondary phenomena; and it helped to strengthen the assumption that each language has a single standard, superior to dialects and vernaculars, and possessed by 'best users' whose intuition decides on grammaticality or acceptability (Hymes 1996: 95–96; cf. also Fishman 1972; Gumperz 1972; Haugen 1966). Even if these assumptions were unintentional collateral damage in the search for linguistic universals, it was argued that "the more one emphasizes universals, the more mysterious actual language becomes. Why are there more than one, or two or three? [...] [m]ost of language begins where universals leave off" (Hymes 1996: 29). In the same vein, Gumperz (1982) indicated that the Chomskyan paradigm at least implicitly seemed to assume that the role of language in communication was merely to signal referential and grammatical meaning, which failed to explain why grammatically identical varieties were perceived as dissimilar languages or grammatically separate ones as one language, or why speakers would care to convey referentially similar information in a different style, genre or register, unless because varieties or codes give off social/indexical meanings and "are (at least partly) the message" of what speakers want to say (Fishman 1972: 4).

These and other criticisms have consequently inspired the emergence of very productive research traditions and a glowing attention for a whole range of new topics. Labovian, 'correlational' or 'quantitative' sociolinguistics started to produce wide-scale distributional accounts of specific linguistic variables, Fishman's 'sociology of language' programme set out to examine the interaction between language use and the social organization of behaviour (1972: 1), while Gumperz and Hymes (1972) proposed an 'ethnography of communication', arguing that knowledge of what is communicatively and socially appropriate can only be obtained through long-term immersion in social settings, and via close observation of speech repertoires and the moment-by-moment unfolding of meaningful face-to-face interaction (see also Cicourel 1973). Increasingly inspired by the sociology of everyday encounters (see below), and against the thrust of (at that time already quite successful) correlational sociolinguistics, which he argued could not adequately address the complexities of face-to-face language use, Gumperz later called for an interactional sociolinguistics (Gumperz 1972: 13; 1982: 25; Verschueren, this volume). In their consideration for interaction, indexical meaning, implicitness and appropriateness, the latter two research traditions also found likeminded students working under the heading of 'linguistic pragmatics' and/or invited them to develop a 'pragmatics of (real-world) interaction' (cf. D'hondt et al. 2009).

Despite their serious methodological differences, these traditions developed a common interest in

1. the documentation of the largely unexplored field that mainstream linguistics had largely left lying fallow, viz., the terra incognita of practices beyond standard

languages (Hymes 1996, p.66ff.), the impressive amount of variation in 'monolingual' linguistic communities, bilingual and multilingual repertoires (cf. Heller and Pavlenko, this volume), the social conditions of variation and the meanings given to different linguistic resources (in terms of class, gender (cf. Lakoff, this volume), occupation, age, ethnicity, …), language use in specific settings and social institutions (cf. Watts, this volume), contact between and manipulation (switching, mixing) of different languages or varieties (cf. Auer and Eastman, this volume; Auer 1984; Blom & Gumperz 1972; Heller 1988; Li Wei, this volume); next to this, attention also turned to

2. the symbolic and indexical dimensions of language that make speakers display "overt behaviour toward language and toward language users" (Fishman 1972: 1), that inspire speakers to pay attention to what they say and style-shift (cf. Labov's work), or that allow speakers to produce communicatively (in)appropriate language, (dis)affiliate with other speakers, locate them socially, assign intentions and identities, and which allows them to economize on explicitness (Gumperz, Hymes);

3. a critical concern for the regularity and complexity of marginal, non-elite groups: by showing orderliness in so-called 'non-standard' speech, sociolinguists made clear it was necessary to look beyond 'elite' speech and in this way dignified non-elite speakers (e.g. Labov 1969). The latter came increasingly to be typified as 'different but equal' against earlier deficit or deprivation views (cf. Coupland 2001; Helsloot, this volume; Rampton, this volume) – a development that chimed in with and found support in the growth of educational-anthropological studies (Mehan 1979; McDermott 1974; Erickson 1982; Cazden, John & Hymes 1972; Heath 1983; Varenne & McDermott 1999). This socio-political dimension in addition encouraged a discussion of linguistic policy and planning, language dominance and minorization (Patrick, this volume), linguistic rights (Skutnabb-Kangas, this volume; also see May 2001), (standard) language ideologies (Milroy & Milroy 1985; Kroskrity, this volume), authority (Wilson and Stapleton, this volume), and gender (Lakoff, this volume; also see Eckert & McConnell-Ginet 2003, Cameron & Kulick 2003), not to mention the effects of these ideas in the field of language teaching methodology (e.g. communicative language teaching, cf. Widdowson 1979).

This proliferation of new lines of research, however, also brought along new problems. As attention shifted from speakers' linguistic faculty to their real-life uses of language, linguistic regularity was found predominantly in speakers' observance of social norms, and in the assumption that their competence derived from long-term participation in stable social networks. Rampton (this volume) indicates, however, that this idea of a deeply-ingrained communicative consensus alongside investigators' foregrounding of systematicity and orderliness within non-elite groups, allowed a notion of speech community to sediment which ultimately (and not unlike formal linguistic paradigms) tended to weed out or repress linguistic hybridity, irregularity and mixing, or which tolerated these phenomena only in the gap between separate socio-cultural groups rather than within these groups; at their margins, rather than at their core (cf. Ortner 1995; Pratt 1987: 56). A similar homogenizing tendency was couched in the idea that language change mainly involved the levelling of variation: by assuming that variation offered various possibilities for language change, and that change was complete when one variant had made the others become obsolete, variation itself appeared to be considered a functional yet intermediate phase separating stable stages of the language or stable stages of shared communicative competence (cf. Meeuwis & Brisard 1993: 38–41; Williams 1992). In spite of all the attention for linguistic variation, therefore, there remained a persistent impulse to unify social and linguistic worlds (Pratt 1987: 52).

In addition, language users' presumed reliance on social norms invited arguments as to whether and how sociolinguists (used here as a cover term) should engage with the explanation of social normativity and with social theory in general (Cameron 1997; Coupland 2001: 1–9; Romaine 1984). A number of them, mostly working in the correlational paradigm, would have certainly disagreed with Woolard's statement at the beginning of this introduction to insist that the primary aims ought to be improving linguistic theory, and developing insight into the nature of language (change) rather than the workings of society (Trudgill 1978; Hudson 1996; Labov 1994). Others, however, objected that such a stance left unanswered the question *why* people use language as they are found to do; or that the usual account for this endorsed the view that language reflected a society (an identity, attitude, category, or a group norm) that was closely connected to but essentially independent from it (Cameron 1997; Gumperz 1972: 14–15), which appeared to reinstate the a priori separation between language and society sociolinguistics had fulminated against. It was argued too that this discussion exemplified that sociolinguistics had already engaged with social theory, albeit implicitly and unreflectively, and that borrowing from, but not contributing to social theory was not an option as the borrowed notions themselves were the object of much sociological controversy.

These issues were exacerbated by the contemporaneously growing interest in language in sociology departments, where there was much more interest for indeterminacy and ambivalence, and for language use as a constructive part of (rather than a reflectively connected aspect of) the social, as a reaction to all too deterministic and consensus based explanations of social action. Not unlike linguists who had been trying to reconcile momentary language use and individual linguistic creativity with a stable structure that facilitates as well as constrains it, sociologists had been concerned with how to bring together individual action and an infinite diversity of (at times anti-social) interests with a stable and enduring social system. In general, their answers have moved from macro-social, so called 'constraint theories', to micro-social interactionist theories and again to integrationist or practice theories that try to transcend the macro/micro dichotomy. I will now offer a brief sketch of these evolutions and their relevance for the study of language in society (see Coupland 2001; Erickson 2004; Heritage 1984; Layder 1994; Ortner 2006; Sarangi 2001; Varenne & McDermott 1999; Williams 1992 for more elaborate treatment).

2. Antecedents in social theory

From the perspective of social theory, interest in language use and society emerged from increasing criticism in the 1950s and 60s of Talcott Parsons's influential theory of structural-functionalism (Parsons 1937, 1951). Parsons was centrally preoccupied with the question how one could account for the fact that people do not passively adapt to the external circumstances they encounter, but usually put in a lot of effort to alter these circumstances in ways they feel are more in keeping with the ideals they subscribe to. Against assumptions of earlier theories positing that this activity was driven by economic/material self-interest and conflict (such as classical marxism), and contra earlier traditions that conceived of social action as the result of biological make-up, environmental conditions or cultural ideals and essences, Parsons developed a 'voluntaristic theory of action'. It underlined people's capacity for acting on the basis of their own decisions and aspirations rather than on the obligations imposed by economic systems or other circumstances, and it posited that these actions were qualified by adherence to subjectively held norms and (systems of) values. People's espousal of these values was seen to keep egocentric tendencies in check while it would also diminish the need to police deviant behaviour. This espousal, however, was the theory's Achilles heel. For if people were more or less free to decide on their adherence to these values, their subsequent action could not be counted on to feed back into a more stable social structure, and this would drive an analytical wedge between the facts of concrete actions and the facts of society. To obviate this, Parsons suggested that adherence to values, and to the social roles and behaviours that are constitutive of them, is secured via (1) social actors' socialization processes, during which they are deeply inculcated with moral values, related behaviour patterns and/or situational road maps; and via (2) social actors' desire to live up to expected behaviour patterns, for fear of experiencing personal identity conflicts and missing out on others' positive support and trust. Thus, by positing that individuals are necessarily committed to seeking social gratification and conformity, Parsons claimed he had found a key to explaining the general orderliness of society that others appeared to take for granted or could not account for; while preventing, on the one hand, the elimination of the actual, recalcitrant conditions human beings are faced with, and, on the other, the fact that there is a value dimension to their actions (more simply, a subjective reason for prioritizing one line of action over another in pursuit of a certain end). Given Parsons's authority in social theory, his conception of normativity exerted a strong influence on sociolinguistic thought when it started to attend to communicative norms and shared evaluations of language.

Nonetheless, the greater the necessity for individuals to adhere to social norms, the more this proviso created a tension with the idea of voluntarism Parsons started off with, and the more his theory became vulnerable to the criticism that he introduced a new kind of determinism. Garfinkel (1967) pointed out that Parsons had, in contrast with his basic assumption that actors act on the basis of their own decisions, expertly eliminated actors' rationalities by equating rationality solely with scientific knowledge, and by consequently disqualifying actors' common-sense views in favour of internalized values – at the expense of portraying the actor as a human puppet, an unthinking acceptance seeker or judgemental dope (Heritage 1984: 24–27, 30–33; Layder 1994: 22). Similar objections were formulated about Parsons's failure to explain actors' ability to share knowledge of the actual situation, and to acquire a common perspective on the normative orientation of their subsequent actions, other than by assuming shared and deeply internalized cognitive standards/rules alongside a communication system that consisted of fixed, already established, sign-referent relations (given that actors' common-sense ability to determine the local meaning of signs, and the course of resulting action, had already been excluded from the analysis to preserve the systematicity and predictability of their actions). Clearly though, this left unanswered the question how communication actually unfolds, and at what point actors' perspectives converge and mutually shared meaning gets established.

If language had hitherto only been allowed to play a minor role in sociology, it now jumped on the scene as an essential aspect of the explanation of social life. Inspired by phenomenological thought (Husserl, Schütz) on perception and meaning construction as processes which are largely based on taken-for-granted knowledge and procedures, Garfinkel rejected radically the view that common-sense, approximate judgements were irrelevant to the analysis of social interaction. Instead, he argued that it was precisely people's practical considerations which had to be taken as central in the accomplishment of a stable social order, and that language use played an essential role in this as the way in which interactants accounted for their behaviour, established mutual knowledge and oriented to meaningful courses of action. Thus, against Parsons's external analysis Garfinkel pitted a treatment of social action which was seen to be intrinsic to members' experiences, and which called for an investigation of "the methods by which people make sense of the situations in which they find themselves and how they manage to sustain an orderliness in their dealings with others" (Layder 1994: 81). In this view norms were the routine product of interaction, rather than its prerequisite. The resulting 'ethnomethodology' (Firth in D'hondt et al. 2010) consequently acted as a muse in the development of Sacks's enthusiastically followed 'conversation analysis' or 'CA' (Sacks, Schegloff & Jefferson 1978), and it was also foundational to the development of a cognitive, discourse-based, sociology which was interested in the interrelation of interactional sense-making procedures and social organization, cf. Cicourel (1973), Saferstein (this volume).

Another muse for CA, and for many students of society and language use, was Goffman. Although he is often seen as a representative of the school of 'symbolic interactionism', Watson (this volume) indicates that his allegiance to symbolic interactionism is quite ambivalent; some of his early ethnographic work may also be difficult to reconcile with a symbolic interaction perspective. In the course of his career, Goffman started off with a primary interest in situational meaning but increasingly came to call attention to face-to-face communication as a distinct level of (ritual) organization, bridging the linguistic and the social as well as private and public spheres, and which therefore needed to be analysed in its own terms. But also in his later work which explicitly focused on 'forms of talk' (Goffman 1981), he recurrently pointed at the interplay between talk, movement, glances, situations and participation statuses (which is also present in some educational anthropologists' work, see, e.g. McDermott, Gospodinoff & Aron 1978). Goffman had a strong impact on students of language, most obviously on politeness theorists (Brown & Levinson 1987), but also on interactional sociolinguists (Auer 1992; Gumperz 1982; Rampton 1995), and accommodation theory (Coupland, this volume). As mentioned above, some of his interest in interaction was indebted to symbolic interactionism, which itself had emerged in the first decades of the 20th century from the philosophical writings of Mead (Watson, this volume). The latter asserted that meaning, rather than abstract social processes, needed to be seen as the glue that held people together socially, and that much of people's experiences and meaning was inextricably the result of their communicative, and thus language based, participation in social groups. Thus, also here, language entered the picture as an object of study in its own right, more precisely, as a bank of highly complex, shared symbols which allowed people to prefigure what effects their production might cause for others and for themselves (although, as in Parsons's theory of communication, the sharedness of these verbal symbols was presupposed rather than communicatively (re-)established).

Hence, in reaction to Parsons and to macro-social theories that were seen to neglect the meanings permeating people's lives and relations, several approaches to social action were developed that gave full precedence to the micro-level of individual agency and to face-to-face interaction – although symbolic interactionists are usually less radically seen to depart from a consideration of social structure than are ethnomethodologists. A shared premiss of these approaches is that social life must be studied in terms of the sense people themselves make of their social arrangements, and by and large these approaches endorse the assumption that society or institutions, and at its most radical, physical processes, do not exist outside of people's sense-making processes but emerge in and through interaction. These approaches in their turn received criticism however for their lack of theoretical consideration for the contexts in which interaction takes place, and for the wide-scale happenings and histories that precede and follow the here-and-now of actual practices (see e.g. Blommaert 1999, 2005; Comaroff & Comaroff 1992; Varenne & McDermott 1999). Methodologically, too, questions were asked about the rigidity of analytic procedures, as in CA, which exclude firmly any interpretation based on what conversationalists do not explicitly topicalize through their talk (Coupland 2001: 13–14; Billig 1999). After all, these not only implied the primacy of verbal communication over non-verbal semiotics, but they were difficult to square with the emphasis in linguistic pragmatics on how the production of meaning depends on the interplay between explicit words and largely implicit, extracommunicative knowledge (Levinson 1983; Verschueren 1999). In their focus on explicitness these sociological approaches of language likewise developed little attention for the symbolic and indexical dimensions of language that communication ethnographers were investigating.

In sum, micro-social approaches were criticized for over-emphasising the intricacies of social production at micro-level at the expense of explaining reproduction at macro-level, and for maintaining an oppositional relationship between structures and individuals' agency or creativity. Several authors, of which Bourdieu and Giddens are often seen as the most influential, subsequently took up the challenge of transcending this opposition by arguing for a dialectical relationship between these opposed notions. In principle, and omitting some important differences between them (see Erickson 2004; Layder 1994; Sarangi 2001 for insightful treatments; see also Ahearn, this volume, and Watts, this volume), integrationist theorists contend that individuals are neither an omnipotent creator of their own circumstances nor "a mere leaf in the social winds" (Varenne & McDermott 1999: 131), but actively and creatively (re)shape their societies anew in everyday practice. A crucial point however is that these practices do not take place in a social vacuum, but are streamlined by longer-standing and larger-scale habits (and power inequalities, see below) that restrict the range of possible new interactions. A potent motive for this is that habits provide recognisable frames, identities and relationships which assure participants' ontological security when they are reproduced. Yet, even though social interactions gravitate towards reproducing existing structures, their necessary actualization in interaction implies they are inevitably vulnerable for innovation and potential change (Voloshinov 1973). The idea is thus that there is a two-way connection between local happenings and larger-scale processes to the effect that the latter never totally determine what social actors can do but still allow for actions that deviate, resist, question, by-pass or negotiate these habits – although, as said, not all practice theorists usually included under this label are equally tolerant of individuals' agency (Bourdieu's notion of habitus echoes a

Parsonian internalization of values). But it is safe to point at the convergence in their views that practices and structures need to be attended to in the same analytical frame, and that it is crucial to try "to keep both person and [structure] alive, interactive and mutually constitutive" (Varenne & McDermott 1999: 165; Ahearn, this volume).

This 'grounding' of larger-scale processes in people's everyday relations (cf. Ortner 2006) clearly has much to recommend it, even if some theorists in this tradition do not always specify clearly what the exact role of language use is in people's structuring practices. But it is important to see that these developments have since the late 1980s increasingly become entangled with the arrival of what has been called 'late modernity', which has brought about a significant change in the shape and effects of large-scale processes themselves, and a growing epistemological introspection with regard to how these processes must or can be approached. These combined evolutions have fertilized a number of trends and issues in the study of society and language use that I will turn to in the following paragraphs.

3. Late modern trends and issues

Late-modernity (often preferred to a term as post-modernity for its suggestion that modernity itself has not faded away but continues to have a strong impact) is often seen as a set of quite recent and fast evolving socio-cultural conditions, viz., globalisation and its market-driven logic. Globalisation has caused huge flows of people, objects, money, information, images and ideas to cross national borders physically and audiovisually on an unprecedented scale (Bauman 1998). It has put nation-states to the test both economically and socio-culturally: some companies have annual revenues that exceed those of entire national economies, and accelerated by processes of economic deregulation, labour markets are increasingly susceptible to polarisation, leading to growing rather than declining social inequalities. Globalisation has also involved the nation-state's evaporating control over what gets produced at a cultural level: the bulk of artistic production (music, film) now largely obeys an international return-on-investment logic that does not linger over paying tribute to national identities, not to mention national languages. In the same vein, the proliferation of information media and communication means has hastened the demise of (the idea of) a shared, national public sphere, while the dissipating boundaries between private and public spheres have encouraged the contestation and transformation of the (linguistic) norms for public discourse (cf. Bauman 1998; Blommaert 2010; Coupland 2003; Giddens 1991; and see Gumperz 1982: 26 and Pratt 1987 for early accounts of this).

Alternatively, late-modernity has been conceived as the serious rethinking of a number of basic assumptions underpinning research in the social and cultural sciences as a result of the 'discursive turn' brought about by French post-structuralist or post-modern philosophy (see Sarangi 2001 for a detailed discussion, and see Helsloot, this volume). This 'turn' has mainly involved the conception of the social space as a 'discourse', a stable although never fully fixed set of meaningful, not exclusively textual, social practices. Discourse theory most importantly draws attention to the fact that discourses organize regimes of power and inequality, i.e. that they assist and reproduce differentially distributed opportunities for discourse participants to find (mis)recognition for their interests, voices and concerns. It is highlighted moreover that these unequal opportunities and the resulting social leverage and identity for its owners are fostered and legitimated through ideologies or widespread representations of, for example, what language is, which and whose language is best, and how it should be used appropriately (cf. Bauman & Briggs 2003; Blommaert 2005; Coupland (this volume 'other'); Kroskrity (this volume); Laclau & Mouffe 1985; Verschueren 2010). Not least, authors such as Foucault repeatedly stressed the historical nature of discursive practices, and in this way post-structuralists came to stress a number of notions which had hitherto not featured very prominently in social theory. In any case, the basic implication of this line of thinking was that if all social spaces are discursive, there can be no discourse-free or ideology-free perspective, hence the criticism of modernist notions of objectivity, neutrality, progress, beauty, appropriateness, educatedness, articulatedness, and so on, as ideologized and in principle particular (usually Western, male, white, capitalist, heterosexual) rather than universal or neutral representations.

These evolutions form the backdrop to a couple of trends I would like to point at in winding up. Firstly, a growing number of students is now taking the cosmopolitan or global city (Grillo 2000) as its scene of action and is committed to describing, often with much ethnographic detail, interaction in small-scale 'communities of practice' (Lave & Wenger 1991) rather than pre-defined and larger socio-linguistic units. In these practice communities, language use and identity are not described anymore as the result of thorough socialization in a relatively stable mono-ethnic setting, but as processes that need to be seen as constantly caught between the warp and woof of self- and other-ascripted identities, agentive and structural forces, local and established representations. In this description the focus likewise shifts from a dignifying account of systematic and complex difference, to how participants construct systematic difference or belonging in their daily interactions while orienting to larger-scale discourses. Notable here is the analysis of interaction at inner-city schools and other institutions, where most participants are increasingly multilingual and where a growing gap develops between monolingual institutional discourses on the one hand, and pupils' multilingual backgrounds as well as their adherence to the multi-modal semiotic resources of the world outside, on the other (cf. Blackledge & Creese 2009; Creese & Blackledge 2010, forthc.; Heller 1999; Jaspers 2005; Li Wei forthc.; Rampton 2006; Rymes 2003). Similarly notable is research into how experiences of diaspora and transnationalism impact on global city inhabitants' sense of belonging, identification and (bi)lingual practices (Bucholtz & Skapoulli 2009; Harris et al. 2002; Heller 2007; Keating & Solovova forthc.); into how the global spread of commodities such as hip hop interweaves with local languages and ethnicities and leads to new artistic products for new audiences and consumers (Alim et al. 2009; Bucholtz 1999; Cutler 1999, 2008); how, in the wake of the massively increased uses of the internet and its various applications, computer-mediated communication aids the construction and sharing of social-electronic identities (Androutsopoulos 2006; Georgakopoulou 2005); and there has been more and more notice, too, of how interaction among urban youth of diverse backgrounds has led to the development, spread and reworking of multi-ethnic, often working-class vernaculars or local youth languages and urban styles (see e.g. Auer 2007; Cornips & Nortier 2008).

Secondly, in line with the interest in practices that cross cultural, institutional or national boundaries, and in contrast with the earlier emphasis on regular, largely unconscious and authentic language use which was necessary for describing regularity and systematicity, there has emerged an interest for inauthentic, ludic, sardonic, eye catching, observer-paradoxed and non-routine language (cf. Rampton, this volume). These verbal objects are not only seen as highly informative of the routine expectations they breach, but also as particularly apt for attending to the complexities of a late-modern world. For if such a world entails a huge increase of situations where participants cannot presume a common ground or are intensely aware of social, cultural and linguistic differences, one can expect a corresponding increase of non-routine behaviour, as well as a heightened awareness of, reflection on and comment about others' social and linguistic practices. Given these metalinguistic qualities, inauthentic, self-conscious or stylised language use (Rampton 2006; Coupland 2007: 30) serves as an extremely fruitful starting point for investigating how utterances comment on the situation in which they are produced, how they are illustrative of participants' perceptions and how these perceptions can be reconciled with, or rather challenge, inflect and/or reconfigure ideologized representations of language and social behaviour, and with what results. Likewise, stylised language use is pinpointed as a useful entry for analysing the boost of reflexivity that accompanies late modernity, i.e. the fact that practices (of both self and others) are more and more mirrored back through the massive impact and availability of the media and communication technologies and consequently get inserted and recycled in face-to-face interaction (cf. Cameron 2000; Coupland 2007: 30). Unsurprisingly perhaps, adolescents often play a central role in the abovementioned work, given the easily accessible "efflorescence of symbolic activity" (Eckert 2000: 5) that accompanies their continuous and conspicuous experimenting with new social roles and behaviour (cf. Garrett et al. 2004).

Late-modern reflexivity has found an epistemological counterpart in the growing consideration for 'professional ideologies' and the politics of sociolinguistic research (cf. Kroskrity, this volume; see also Calvet 2006; Harris 1998; Jørgensen 2008;

Makoni & Pennycook 2006; Pratt 1987; Rampton, this volume). As already suggested above, post-structuralist thought led researchers of society and language use to re-think their confidence in the naturalness and omni-relevance of established identity categories and to look for how people in their everyday activities develop and sustain relationships and identifications that contest, rework or re-key social inheritances and the patterns of language use that are seen as characteristic of them (cf. Bucholtz & Hall 2004; Rampton 1995). But also language has come to be the object of reflection. Rather than empirically identifiable entities, languages and codes are recognized as problematic inventions, linguists' rather than speakers' distinctions (Auer and Eastman, this volume), useful but reductive fictions (Haugen 1972 in Calvet 2006; Harris 1998; Hymes 1996; Mühlhäusler 1996; Silverstein 1998), that need to be deconstructed or 'disinvented' in order to develop new ways of thinking about language while 'reconstituting' some of their undeniable real-world effects (Makoni & Pennycook 2006). This requires attention for the social, political and semiotic processes that lead to the naming of languages (e.g. Gal & Irvine 1995), for the reasons that languages are 'obviously' associated with certain groups and it firmly draws students of language use into the analytic picture as social-political actors rather than neutral observers (cf. Jaspers 2008; Helsloot, this volume). The latter point has also opened up reflection on the desirability of sociolinguists' impact on the social context they are working in, and what rapport can be established between scientific knowledge and ordinary speakers' conceptions of language and society (cf. Cameron 1995; Lippi-Green 1997; Mugglestone 2004). But as Coupland argues, next to resisting essentialising tendencies, we should also resist de-essentialising ones (Coupland 2001: 18). And in this vein, some authors are saying that in spite of globalisation's captivating charm, it would be unwise to "give up entirely any notion of system and boundary, any notion of constraint" (Heller 2007: 341) and to dismiss evidence of the *basso continuo* of older, modernist discourses on the social world "under the weight of a new form of social theorising about identity" (Coupland, this volume, p. 257; Rampton, forthc.). Hence the attention for how monolingual nation-states and social institutions (such as education, the health sector, administration, the judicial system) have (not always positively) reacted to cosmopolitan impulses (Collins & Slembrouck 2005; Jaspers 2006, forthc.; Jaspers and Verschueren, forthc.; Maryns 2005; Moyer, forthc.) or how advocacy of diversity and multilingualism can help legitimate unequally rewarding discursive regimes (cf. Meeuwis forthc.).

Thirdly and finally, in all of this discourse regularly crops up as a cover term or potential rallying ground for the diverse attempts at describing and explaining society and language use. At least if understood as more than the mere textual concept it has traditionally been in sociolinguistics as language use above sentence level (cf. Brown & Yule 1983). Blommaert (2005: 3) casts the net as wide as possible by proposing that discourse comprises "all forms of meaningful semiotic human activity seen in connection with social, cultural and historical patterns and developments of use". In this way, one would avoid a mono-disciplinary tunnel vision on what are in principle multi-semiotic data and develop "a social science that utilises linguistic technique to answer social-scientific questions" (Blommaert 2005: 237), a science which could in addition also speak to non-linguists, non-interactionists and produce analyses of *social* consequence. Some of the unifying potential of discourse is noticeable in recent disciplinary identity cards as 'interactional discourse analysis', conceptions of discourse as talk at micro-level as well as social structures at macro-level (cf. Gee's distinction between 'little d' discursive interaction and 'big D' discourses; Erickson 2004) as well as in how discourse plays a major role in various domains such as new literacy studies, discursive psychology, business studies, literary studies, political theory, psychiatry, and so on. Arguably, though, and if appropriately theorised, 'culture' could capture most of what is implied in discourse too (cf. Ortner 2006; Varenne & McDermott 1999; Williams 1977). Strong methodological disagreements also remain between discourse analysts of various stripes (see, e.g. Blommaert 2005; Verschueren 2001) as well as different orientations owing to disciplinary trainings and researchers' "identification with certain people and parts of the world" (Hymes 2000: 313). So perhaps more than whatever label is used, one can hope the basic message does not get overlooked, viz. that language use and variation need to be approached as more than a linguistic issue, but as an intrinsically social question, with attention for the rapport between the individual speaker, communicative networks and larger-scale events; and that one should insist on analysis of language use in investigations of the social world, or that social theoretic accounts ought to be tied down to the level of face-to-face interaction where fine-grained ethnographic analysis can function as a corrective power for hasty generalisations. In line with Woolard's programmatic statement above, it may help future students to have similar edgy things to say with regard to language and the social world.

References

Alim, S., I. Awad & A. Pennycook (eds) (2009). *Global linguistic flows*. Routledge.
Androutsopolous, J. (ed) (2006). Sociolinguistics and computer mediated communication. *Journal of Sociolinguistics* 10(4).
Auer, P. (1984). *Bilingual Conversation*. John Benjamins.
Auer, P. (1992). 'Introduction. John Gumperz' approach to contextualization', in P. Auer & A. Di Luzio (eds) *The contextualization of language*: 1–37. John Benjamins.
Auer, P. (ed) (2007). *Style and social identities*. Mouton De Gruyter.
Bauman, Z. (1998). *Globalisation. The human consequences*. Polity Press.
Bauman, R. & C. Briggs (2003). *Voices of modernity. Language ideologies and the politics of inequality*. Cambridge University Press.

Billig, M. (1999). Whose terms? Whose ordinariness? Rhetoric and ideology in conversation analysis. *Discourse and Society* 10(4): 543–558.
Blackledge, A. & A. Creese (2009). Meaning-making as dialogic process: official and carnival lives in the language classroom. *Journal of Language, Identity & Education* 8(4): 236–253.
Blom, J.P. & Gumperz J. J. (1972). Social meanings in linguistic structures. J. J. Gumperz & D. Hymes (eds), *Directions in sociolinguistics*: 407–434. Holt, Rinehart & Winston.
Blommaert, J. (ed) (1999). *Language ideological debates*. Mouton De Gruyter.
Blommaert, J. (2005). *Discourse. A critical introduction*. Cambridge University Press.
Blommaert, J. (2010). *The sociolinguistics of globalization*. Cambridge University Press.
Brown, P. & S. Levinson (1987). *Politeness*. Cambridge University Press.
Brown, G. & G. Yule (1983). *Discourse analysis*. Cambridge University Press.
Bucholtz, M. (1999). You da man. Narrating the racial other in the production of white masculinity. *Journal of Sociolinguistics* 3(4): 443–460.
Bucholtz, M. & K. Hall (2004). Language and identity. In A. Duranti (ed), *A companion to linguistic anthropology*: 369–394. Blackwell.
Bucholtz, M. & E. Skapoulli (eds) (2009). Youth language at the intersection. From migration to globalization. *Pragmatics* 19(1).
Calvet, L-J. (2006). *Towards an ecology of world languages*. Polity Press.
Cameron, D. (1995). *Verbal Hygiene*. Routledge.
Cameron, D. (1997). Demythologizing sociolinguistics. In N. Coupland & A. Jaworski (eds), *Sociolinguistics: a reader and coursebook*: 55–67. Palgrave.
Cameron, D. (2000). *Good to talk? Living and working in a communication culture*. Sage.
Cameron, D. & D. Kulick (2003). *Language and sexuality*. Cambridge University Press.
Cazden, C., V. John & D. Hymes (eds) (1972). *Functions of language in the classroom*. Teachers College Press.
Chomsky, N. (1965). *Aspect of the theory of syntax*. MIT Press.
Cicourel, A.V. (1973). *Cognitive sociology*. Penguin.
Collins, J. & S. Slembrouck (2005). Multilingualism and diasporic populations. Spatializing practices, institutional processes and social hierarchies. *Language & Communication* 25: 189–195.
Comaroff, J. & J. Comaroff (1992). *Ethnography and the historical imagination*. Westview Press.
Cornips L. & J. Nortier (eds) (2008). Ethnolects? The emergence of new varieties among adolescents. *International Journal of Bilingualism* 12(1–2).
Coupland, N. (2001). Introduction. Sociolinguistic theory and social theory. In N. Coupland, S. Sarangi & C. Candlin (eds), *Sociolinguistics and social theory*: 1–26. Longman.
Coupland, N. (ed) (2003). Sociolinguistics and globalisation. *Journal of Sociolinguistics* 7(4).
Coupland, N. (2007). *Style. Language variation and identity*. Cambridge University Press.
Creese, A. & A. Blackledge (2010). Translanguaging in the bilingual classroom. A pedagogy for learning and teaching? *Modern Language Journal* 94(1): 103–115.
Creese, A. & A. Blackledge (2010). Separate and flexible bilingualism in complementary schools. *Journal of Pragmatics*. Forthcoming.
Cutler, C. (1999). Yorkville crossing. White teens, hip hop and African American English. *Journal of Sociolinguistics* 3(4): 428–442.
Cutler, C. (2008). Brooklyn style: Hip-hop markers and racial affiliation among European immigrants in New York City. *International Journal of Bilingualism* 12(1–2): 7–24.
D'hondt, S., J.O. Östman & J. Verschueren (eds) (2010). *The pragmatics of interaction*. John Benjamins.
Eckert, P. (2000). *Linguistic variation as social practice*. Cambridge University Press.
Eckert, P. & S. McConnell-Ginet (2003). *Language and gender*. Cambridge University Press.

Erickson, F. (1982). Classroom discourse as improvization: relationships between academic task structure and social participation structure in lessons. In L.C. Wilkinson (ed), *Communicating in the classroom*: 153–181. Academic Press.

Erickson, F. (2004). *Talk and social theory*. Polity Press.

Gal, S. & J. Irvine (1995). The boundaries of languages and disciplines: how ideologies construct difference. *Social Research* 62(4): 967–1002.

Garfinkel, H. (1967): *Studies in ethnomethodology*. Prentice Hall.

Garrett, P., N. Coupland & A. Williams (2004). Adolescents' lexical repertoires of peer evaluation. In A. Jaworski et al. (eds), *Metalanguage*: 193–225. Mouton de Gruyter.

Gee, J.P. (2005). *An introduction to discourse analysis. Theory and method* (2nd edition), Routledge.

Georgakopoulou, A. (2005). Computer mediated communication. In J. Verschueren et al. (eds), *Handbook of pragmatics*.

Giddens, A. (1991). *Modernity and self-identity*. Polity Press.

Goffman, E. (1981). *Forms of Talk*. University of Pennsylvania Press.

Grillo, R. (2000). Plural cities in comparative perspective. *Ethnic and Racial Studies* 23(6): 957–981.

Gumperz, J. (1972). Introduction. In J. Gumperz & D. Hymes (eds), *Directions in sociolinguistics. The ethnography of communication*: 1–25. Holt, Rinehart & Winston.

Gumperz, J. (1982). *Discourse strategies*. Cambridge University Press.

Gumperz, J. & D. Hymes (eds) (1972). *Directions in sociolinguistics. The ethnography of communication*. Holt, Rinehart & Winston.

Fishman, J. (1972). *The sociology of language. An interdisciplinary social science approach to language in society*. Newbury House.

Halliday, M.A.K. (1984). Language as code and language as behaviour: a systemic-functional interpretation of the nature and ontogenesis of dialogue. In R.P. Fawcett et al. (eds), *The Semiotics of Culture and Language*: 3–35. Francis Pinter.

Harris, R. (1998). *Introduction to integrational linguistics*. Pergamon.

Harris, R., C. Leung & B. Rampton (2002). Globalisation, diaspora and language education in England. In D. Block & D. Cameron (eds), *Globalisation and language teaching*: 29–46. Routledge.

Haugen, E. (1966). *Language conflict and language planning. The case of modern Norwegian*. Harvard University Press.

Heath, S.B. (1983). *Ways with words: language, life and work in communities and classrooms*. Cambridge University Press.

Heller, M. (1988). *Codeswitching. Anthropological and sociolinguistic perspectives*. Mouton De Gruyter.

Heller, M. (1999). *Linguistic minorities and modernity*. Longman.

Heller, M. (ed) (2007). *Bilingualism. A social approach*. Palgrave Macmillan.

Heller, M. (2007). The future of bilingualism. In Heller (ed), *Bilingualism. A social approach*: 340–345. Palgrave Macmillan.

Heritage, J. (1984). *Garfinkel and ethnomethodology*. Blackwell.

Hudson, R. (1996). *Sociolinguistics*. Cambridge University Press.

Hymes, D. (1996). *Ethnography, linguistics, narrative inequality. Toward an understanding of voice*. Taylor & Francis.

Hymes, D. (2000). The emergence of sociolinguistics: a response to Samarin. *Journal of Sociolinguistics* 4(2): 312–315.

Jaspers, J. (2005). Linguistic sabotage in a context of monolingualism and standardization. *Language and Communication* 25(3): 279–297.

Jaspers, J. (2006). Stylizing Standard Dutch by Moroccan boys in Antwerp. *Linguistics and Education* 17(2): 131–156.

Jaspers, J. (2008). Problematizing ethnolects. Naming linguistic practices in an Antwerp secondary school. *International Journal of Bilingualism* 12(1–2): 85–103.

Jaspers, J. (2010). Talking like a zerolingual. Ambiguous linguistic caricatures at a secondary school. *Journal of Pragmatics*. Forthcoming.

Jaspers, J. & J. Verschueren (eds) (2010). *Multilingual structures and agencies*. Special issue of *Journal of Pragmatics*. Forthcoming.

Johnstone, B. & W.M. Marcellino (2010). Dell Hymes and the ethnography of communication. In R. Wodak, B. Johnstone & P. Kerswill (eds), *The Sage handbook of sociolinguistics*. Sage. (in press)

Jørgensen, J.N. (2008). Polylingual languaging around and among adolescents. *International Journal of Multilingualism* 5(3): 161–176.

Keating C. & O. Solovova (2010). Multilingual dynamics among Portuguese-based migrant contexts in Europe. *Journal of Pragmatics*. Forthcoming.

Labov, W. (1966). *The social stratification of English in New York city*. Center for Applied Linguistics.

Labov, W. (1969). *The logic of non-standard English*. Georgetown Monographs on Language and Linguistics.

Labov, W. (1994). *Principles of linguistic change. Volume 1: Internal factors*. Blackwell.

Laclau, E. & C. Mouffe (1985). *Hegemony and socialist strategy*. Verso.

Lave, J. & E. Wenger (1991). *Situated learning*. Cambridge University Press.

Layder, D. (1994). *Understanding social theory*. Sage.

Levinson, S. (1983). *Pragmatics*. Cambridge University Press.

Lippi-Green, R. (1997). *English with an accent. Language, ideology and discrimination in the United States*. Routledge.

Li Wei (2010). Creating and managing multilingual spaces through discursive practices. *Journal of Pragmatics*. Forthcoming.

Makoni, S. & A. Pennycook (eds) (2006). *Disinventing and reconstituting languages*. Multilingual Matters.

Maryns, K. (2005). *The asylum speaker. An ethnography of language and communication in the Belgian asylum procedure*. St. Jerome Publishing.

May, S. (2001). *Language and minority rights*. Longman.

McDermott, R. (1974). Achieving school failure: an anthropological approach to illiteracy and social stratification. In G.D. Spindler (ed), *Education and cultural process*: 82–118. Holt, Rinehart & Winston.

McDermott, R., K. Gospodinoff & J. Aron (1978). Criteria for an ethnographically adequate description of concerted activities and their contexts. *Semiotica* 24: 245–275.

Meeuwis, M. (2010). Bilingual inequality. Linguistic rights and disenfranchisement in late Belgian colonization. *Journal of Pragmatics*. Forthcoming.

Meeuwis, M. & F. Brisard (1993). *Time and the diagnosis of language change*. University of Antwerp (Antwerp Papers in Linguistics, 72).

Mehan, H. (1979). *Learning lessons. Social organization in the classroom*. Harvard University Press.

Milroy, J. & L. Milroy (1985). *Authority in language*. Routledge.

Moyer, M. (2010). What Multilingualism? Agency and unintended consequences of multilingual practices in a Barcelona health clinic. *Journal of Pragmatics*. Forthcoming.

Mugglestone, L. (2004). *Talking proper. The rise of accent as social symbol*. Oxford University Press.

Mühlhäusler, P. (1996). *Linguistic ecology*. Routledge.

Ortner, S.B. (1995). Resistance and the problem of ethnographic refusal. *Comparative Studies of Society and History* 37(1): 173–193.
Ortner, S. (2006). *Anthropology and social theory*. Duke University Press.
Parsons, T. (1937). *The structure of social action*. McGraw-Hill.
Parsons, T. (1951). *The social system*. Free Press.
Pratt, M.L. (1987). Linguistic utopias. In N. Fabb et al. (eds), *The linguistics of writing*: 48–66. Manchester University Press.
Rampton, B. (1995). *Crossing. Language and ethnicity among adolescents*. Longman.
Rampton, B. (2006). *Language in late modernity. Interaction at an urban school*. Cambridge University Press.
Rampton, B. (2010). Style contrasts, migration and social class. *Journal of Pragmatics* (forthcoming).
Romaine, S. (1984). The status of sociological models and categories in explaining linguistic variation. *Linguistische Berichte* 90, 25–38.
Rymes, B. (2003). Contrasting zones of comfortable competence: popular culture in a phonics lesson. *Linguistics and Education* 14(4): 321–335.
Sacks, H., E. Schegloff & G. Jefferson (1978). A simplest systematics for the organization of turn taking for conversation. In J.N. Schenkein (ed), *Studies in the organization of conversational interaction*: 7–55. Academic Press.
Sarangi, S. (2001). A comparative perspective on social theoretical accounts of the language-action interrelationship. In N. Coupland, S. Sarangi & C.N. Candlin (eds), *Sociolinguistics and social theory*: 29–60. Longman.
Silverstein, M. (1998). Contemporary transformations of local linguistic communities. *Annual Review of Anthropology* 27: 401–426.
Trudgill, P. (1978). Introduction: sociolinguistics and sociolinguistics. In P. Trudgill (ed), *Sociolinguistic patterns in British English*: 1–18. Edward Arnold.
Van de Walle, J., D. Willems & K. Willems (2006). Structuralism. In J. Verschueren et al. (eds), *Handbook of pragmatics*. John Benjamins.
Varenne, H. & R. McDermott (1999). *Successful failure. The school America builds*. Westview Press.
Verschueren, J. (1999). *Understanding pragmatics*. Edward Arnold.
Verschueren, J. (2001). Predicaments of criticism. *Critique of Anthropology* 21(1): 59–81.
Verschueren, J. (2010). *Engaging with language use and ideology. Pragmatic guidelines for empirical ideology research*. Forthcoming.
Voloshinov, V.N. (1973). *Marxism and the philosophy of language*. Seminar Press.
Weinreich, U., W. Labov & M.I. Herzog (1968). Empirical foundations for a theory of language use. In W.P. Lehmann & Y. Malkiel (eds), *Directions for historical linguistics. A symposium*: 95–188. University of Texas Press.
Widdowson, H.G. (1979). *Teaching language as communication*. Oxford University Press.
Williams, G. (1992). *Sociolinguistics. A sociological critique*. Routledge.
Williams, R. (1977). *Marxism and literature*. Oxford University Press.
Woolard, K.A.(1985). Language variation and cultural hegemony: toward an integration of sociolinguistic and social theory. *American Ethnologist* 12(4): 738–748.

Accommodation theory

Nikolas Coupland
Cardiff University

1. Overview

The term 'accommodation theory' identifies a research program that has developed since the early 1970s, very largely stimulated by the research of Howard Giles and his colleagues. Accommodation theory accounts for diverse contextual processes that impinge on the selection of sociolinguistic codes, styles and strategies and their interactional consequences. In its earliest forms, accommodation theory was a strictly socio-psychological model of speech-style modification, best represented in Giles and Powesland's (1975) account. Currently, accommodation theory has the status of a truly interdisciplinary model of relational processes in communicative interaction. In the view of some commentators (e.g. Bradac, Hopper & Wiemann 1989), accommodation theory is the predominant model at the interface of sociolinguistics, communication and social psychology. Studies across the disciplines, from various methodological and ideological perspectives, appear regularly.

Recent treatments (see Giles, Coupland & Coupland eds. 1991 for an overview) have begun the task of relating the key explanatory concepts of accommodation theory to local discursive processes in face-to-face interaction, particularly those that relate to achieving solidarity with, or dissociation from, a conversational partner and the social group with which she/he identifies. Extensions of this work could offer pragmatics the means of drawing on a very rich fund of conceptual and empirical data from the social psychology of language and social psychology in general.

This article briefly reviews the original concerns of 'speech accommodation theory' and traces its progressively broader involvement with communication strategies relevant to both individuals and social groups.

2. Speech accommodation theory

Consistent with the earliest emphases of social psychology itself, most of the early work establishing accommodation theory was laboratory-based and relatively insensitive to the descriptive linguistic characteristics of the speech varieties and styles that it researched. Giles (1973) demonstrated the phenomenon of accent convergence as a central option within his 'accent mobility' model. Speakers were said to converge sociolinguistically when they reduced the actual or apparent phonological differences between their respective speech styles. Coupland (1984), for example, reports data that show how one travel agency assistant adjusts the standardness of her pronunciation in ways that quite directly match the speech characteristics of her clients. Giles, Taylor and Bourhis (1973) provided empirical support for an association between the strategy of convergence and positive social evaluations of the converging speaker. They found that the more effort to converge that a speaker was thought to have made, the more favorably that person was evaluated, and the more listeners converged in return.

From this basis, speech accommodation theory (SAT) focused mainly on the social cognitive processes mediating people's perceptions of their environment and language use. Speech convergence was defined as a general strategy through which individuals adapt to each others' speech and non-verbal behaviors on many dimensions – including variation in speech-rate, pausal phenomena, utterance-length, segmental phonology, smiling, gaze and gesture, information density, response latency and self-disclosure (Coupland & Giles eds. 1990 is a collection of such studies; a detailed review of published work is available in Coupland, Coupland & Giles 1991: 7ff.).

Overall (and despite some findings which reported individual differences in this tendency, such as Natale 1975), speech convergence was shown to reflect a speaker's motivation to gain social approval and/or increase communication effectiveness. Convergence may be seen in an individual's behavior within an interaction, but also in a group's longer-term and normative shifts, for example if a minority group gradually adopts a style or code more similar to that of the dominant variety in a host community. Under these circumstances, the accommodation model gives an account for that group's progressive integration into the target community (see also Trudgill 1986 where 'accommodation' is developed as a central concept for explaining long-term change in dialect contact situations). Correspondingly, studies showed that perceived convergence does commonly bring the positive social benefits that speakers anticipate. Berger and Bradac (1982), for example, argued that speakers who sound similar to oneself are perceived to be more predictable and more supportive.

Divergence was the term used to refer to how speakers may accentuate speech and non-verbal differences between themselves and others. Speech divergence was established as a group-level phenomenon, reflecting speakers' motivations to dissociate themselves symbolically from the social group membership (ethnic, political, class, age or gender) of an interlocutor. Bourhis and Giles (1977) were able to demonstrate that groups of Welsh language learners broadened their accents of Welsh English when responding to questions posed by a very English-sounding speaker who challenged their reasons for learning what he called 'a dying language with a dismal future' (see also Bourhis, Giles, Leyens & Tajfel 1979 for some related Belgian data). In this regard, speech accommodation theory is deeply indebted to Tajfel's theorising of intergroup relations (e.g. Giles & Hewstone 1982; Tajfel 1974). Speech maintenance, the absence of detectable speech modification, was likewise found to reflect dissociative intents, supporting the view that a general tendency to accommodate is operative in pro-social interpersonal interaction.

3. Conceptual developments

Early formulations of convergence and divergence were resolutely mechanistic. Giles and Powesland (1975), for example, distinguished 'upward' from 'downward' accent/dialect convergence and divergence, terms which endorsed fundamentally linear conceptions of speech style modification. It was recognised that shifts in sociolinguistic styles could operate differently in respect of different speech variables, and so be 'multimodal' (Giles, Mulac, Bradac & Johnson 1987). But the model continued to develop through the testing of predictions about the co-variation of either speakers' social motives or listeners' social evaluations with dimensions of language behavior.

But the 1980s saw important developments specifically of the model's social psychological core. Thakerar, Giles and Cheshire (1982) argued it was crucial to distinguish 'subjective' from 'objective' accommodation. That is, our perceptions and beliefs about (our own and others') sociolinguistic behaviors are more directly relevant to our strategic initiatives and social evaluations than are the objective facts of selection and variation. Previous studies had already established that, for example, speakers labeled 'black' may be heard as more nonstandard than speakers labeled 'white' (Williams 1976). If such processes of 'behavioral confirmation' operate in face-to-face interaction, then we know that context can override actors' and analysts' readings of 'objective' conversational data.

The accommodation model has also stimulated significant research into the multiple meanings of communication strategies. In another experimental design, Bourhis, Giles and Lambert (1975) showed how accent/dialect shifts carry social costs as well as social advantages. A more standard-accented style can trigger judgements of low trustworthiness at the same time as judgements of greater intelligence, and so on. Again, studies within the accommodation paradigm have emphasized how communicators' readings of social norms will color their responses to communicative strategies. Convergence is likely to reap its relational rewards only if it is not normatively prescribed, and if listeners attribute its motives positively. Accommodative language is clearly to be distinguished from the accommodative 'state' of a speaker's adjudged disposition.

4. The accommodation model: Predictive or interpretive?

Until recently, summaries of accommodation research have been presented as a set of predictive axioms attempting to set out (a) the conditions under which convergence, divergence and maintenance will occur, and (b) their relational and evaluative consequences (e.g. Giles, Mulac, Bradac & Johnson 1987). This tendency was consistent with the overtly experimentalist tradition within which accommodation research was originally conceived. As empirical studies have raised ever more particular contextual considerations and caveats, it has become less feasible to predict specific accommodation processes and outcomes from taxonomies of situational configurations. The model has, in one sense, been a victim of its own success. In another sense, its own development has established the need for an alternative, non-experimentalist approach to language and social context, in order to appreciate local socio-psychological processes relevant to particular instances.

Social psychology itself has been reappraising its epistemological foundations. A significant body of researchers have raised doubts about the empiricist assumptions that have dominated social psychology, including accommodation theory (Giles & Coupland 1991; Potter & Edwards 1992; Potter & Wetherell 1987; Shotter & Gergen eds. 1989). This new climate of openness to qualitative research within social psychology, and greater emphasis on discursive approaches to language and context generally, have influenced recent theoretical discussions of accommodation theory.

5. Discourse attuning

Some discussions have begun to elaborate, in discursive terms, the concept that lies at the core of accommodation theory: what it means to 'be accommodative' in the contexts of interpersonal and intergroup communication. The strategies of convergence, divergence and maintenance have been shown to have a clear potential to mark and modify relationships. Coupland, Coupland, Giles and Henwood (1988) group them as 'approximation' strategies which deploy the indexical potential of degrees of similarity/difference between speakers' communication behaviors. In the way originally specified by SAT, a speaker can symbolise an 'accommodative' intent by reducing perceived dissimilarities in communicative styles. Convergence of styles is a viable metaphor, in social interaction, for converging of psyches and dispositions.

But speakers can achieve the same or similar affective results through strategies that have nothing to do with degrees of approximation between respective styles. For example, speakers may modify aspects of the interpretability of their talk, in relation to the familiarity of topics they establish, the weighting of given and new information, degrees of technicality or complexity, and so on. When speakers strategically focus on the interpretability of their talk, a further rich domain for discourse attuning (or counter-attuning) is opened up. Being discursively 'accommodating' includes regulating how interpretable our talk is, and is designed to be, for our hearers.

SAT has considered circumstances when speakers' overall framing of a discourse sequence will be adjudged either overaccommodative or underaccommodative (Coupland et al. 1988). The concept of overaccommodation provides one account of demeaning or patronising talk, where, on some specific dimension(s), a speaker may be deemed to have transcended a notionally 'appropriate' or 'well-attuned' behavioral standard. To take one clear instance, in the case of talk between a young adult and an elderly adult, the younger person may be perceived to have modified her/his way of speaking to a greater extent than the recipient judges to be appropriate. If vocal amplitude is in question, and the younger speaker rightly considers some speech-modification to be necessary, but is still heard to be shouting (cf. Coupland, Coupland & Giles 1991; Hamilton 1991, 1994), then the mismatch of intended and perceived strategies can be explained by the notion of overaccommodation. Parallel examples include the possibility that talk to older adults is restricted to 'safe' or age-salient conversation topics, such as talk about the past as discussed by Boden & Bielby (1986), or some carers' use of so-called 'secondary baby-talk' to elderly people in residential care, as discussed by Caporael and Culbertson (1986).

Dismissive ways of speaking (or avoiding speaking) may be characterized as under-accommodative – orientations to communication which betray insufficient engagement or consideration. Younger adults sometimes consider that older people show insufficient concern for their own priorities and interests – for example, when older adults are heard to be egocentric and to dwell on their own personal troubles (Coupland et al. 1991). Interpretability can again be a salient dimension for this assessment, if the means of being dismissive is to sustain talk on topics predictably beyond older people's domains of interest or knowledge (perhaps pop music, recent fashion, their own networks). But underaccommodation can also relate to domains of control, when speakers do not afford their listeners adequate rights or space in conversational interaction. One recently examined instance is nurses' deflecting of elderly people's complaints in residential nursing homes (Grainger, Atkinson & Coupland 1990).

Degrees and means of 'being accommodative' clearly pervade social interaction. For this reason, Coupland et al. (1988) suggested that degrees of attuning can be charted in an array of discourse management dimensions. SAT therefore needs to account for the extents to which speakers facilitate or inhibit a partner's contribution to on-going talk. Examples include offering adequate and timely turns at talk, eliciting disclosable information, avoiding or repairing problematical sequences, and generally working to redress positive or negative face-threats to a recipient. Again, supportive recipiency strategies, endorsing and accrediting a partner's contributions through positive back-channelling or more explicit approbatory moves can lead to judgements of positive attuning (see Hamilton 1991, 1994 for an extended study of these processes in conversations between a carer and an Alzheimer's patient).

This framework needs further development, and several possibilities suggest themselves. For example, theoretical research could explore the overlap between strategies relevant to discourse attuning and documented strategies of positive politeness

(Brown & Levinson 1987). Again, sociolinguistic discussions of cooperative or competitive language have relied on specific linguistic/behavioral indices, such as positive back-channelling and progressive topic development (see the discussion in Coates 1988) or, on the other hand, interruptions (Zimmerman & West 1975). These literatures could be strengthened if they are reframed to take into account the socio-psychological dimensions of context specified by SAT. Reciprocally, SAT will itself offer a more coherent explanation of relational and intergroup processes if, in future, its core concepts are better specified at the level of speech acts and realisations.

The relationship between characteristics of utterances and judgements of cooperativity, and over- and underaccommodation is context-sensitive. The particular contribution of SAT to date is to stipulate that utterances and forms of talk find their place in a complex, layered socio-psychological context, where intentions, strategic operations, attributions and social evaluations are concurrent, interconnected aspects of how social meanings are generated. These constructs are core elements of the SAT model. Attempts to reify discourse operations in a physical model (e.g. Giles, Coupland & Coupland eds. 1991: 40) will always be suspect if they are read as supposedly linear specifications of non-linear processes. However, the accommodation model has served as a useful check-list of the range of affective and strategic factors that are relevant to any context of face-to-face talk. One value of explicit modelling is that it imposes a set of imperatives for explanatory research. SAT seems set to continue to be of value to researchers in pragmatics and discourse analysis as a coherent statement of the socio-psychological constitution of face-to-face interaction.

References

Berger, C.R. & J.J. Bradac (1982). *Language and social knowledge.* Edward Arnold.
Boden, D. & D. Bielby (1986). The way it was. *Language and Communication* 6: 73–89.
Bourhis, R.Y. & H. Giles (1977). The language of intergroup distinctiveness. In H. Giles (ed.) *Language, ethnicity and intergroup relations*: 119–135. Academic Press.
Bourhis, R.Y., H. Giles & W.E. Lambert (1975). Social consequences of accommodating one's style of speech. *International Journal of the Sociology of Language* 6: 55–72.
Bourhis, R.Y., H. Giles, J-P. Leyens & H. Tajfel (1979). Psycholinguistic distinctiveness. In H. Giles & R. StClair (eds.) *Language and social psychology*: 158–185. Basil Blackwell.
Bradac, J.J., R. Hopper & J.M. Wiemann (1989). Message effects. In J.J. Bradac (ed.) *Message effects in communication science*: 294–317. Sage.
Brown, P. & S. Levinson (1987). *Politeness.* Cambridge University Press.
Coates, J. (1988). Gossip revisited. In J. Coates & D. Cameron (eds.) *Women in their speech communities*: 94–121. Longman.
Caporael, L. & G.H. Culbertson (1986). Verbal response modes of baby talk and other speech at institutions for the aged. *Language and Communication* 6 (1/2): 99–112.
Coupland, N. (1984). Accommodation at work. *International Journal of the Sociology of Language* 46: 49–70.

Coupland, N., J. Coupland & H. Giles (1991). *Language, society and the elderly*. Blackwell.
Coupland, N., J. Coupland, H. Giles & K. Henwood (1988). Accommodating the elderly. *Language in Society* 17: 1–42.
Coupland, N. & H. Giles (eds.) (1990). *Communicative accommodation*. Special issue of *Language and Communication* 8 (3/4).
Giles, H. (1973). Accent mobility. *Anthropological Linguistics* 15: 87–105.
Giles, H. & N. Coupland (1991). *Language: contexts and consequences*. Open University Press.
Giles, H., N. Coupland & J. Coupland (eds.) (1991). *Contexts of accommodation*. Cambridge University Press.
Giles, H. & M. Hewstone (1982). Cognitive structures, speech and social situations. *Language Sciences* 5: 187–219.
Giles, H., A. Mulac, J.J. Bradac & P. Johnson (1987). Speech accommodation theory. In M.L. McLaughlin (ed.) *Communication Yearbook 10*: 13–48. Sage.
Giles, H. & P.F. Powesland (1975). *Speech style and social evaluation*. Academic Press.
Giles, H., D.M. Taylor & R.Y. Bourhis (1973). Towards a theory of interpersonal accommodation through language. *Language in Society* 2: 177–192.
Grainger, K., K. Atkinson & N. Coupland (1990). Responding to the elderly. In H. Giles, N. Coupland & J. Wiemann (eds.) *Communication, health and ageing*: 192–212. Manchester University Press.
Hamilton, H.E. (1991). Accommodation and mental disability. In H. Giles, N. Coupland & J. Coupland (eds.): 157–86.
——— (1994). *Conversations with an Alzheimer's Patient*. Cambridge University Press.
Natale, M. (1975). Convergence of mean vocal intensity in dyadic communication as a function of social desirability. *Journal of Personality and Social Psychology* 32: 790–804.
Potter, J. & J. Edwards (1992). *Discursive psychology*. Sage.
Potter, J. & M. Wetherell (1987). *Discourse and social psychology*. Sage.
Shotter, J. & K.J. Gergen (eds.) (1989). *Texts of identity*. Sage.
Tajfel, H. (1974). Social identity and intergroup behaviour. *Social Science Information* 13: 65–93.
Thakerar, J.N., H. Giles & J. Cheshire (1982). Psychological and linguistic parameters of speech accommodation theory. In C. Fraser & K.R. Scherer (eds.) *Advances in the social psychology of language*: 205–255. Cambridge University Press.
Williams, F. (1976). *Explorations in the linguistic attitudes of teachers*. Newbury House.
Zimmerman, D.H. & C. West (1975). Sex roles, interruptions and silences in conversations. In B. Thorne & N. Henley (eds.) *Language and sex*: 105–129. Newbury House. [*See also*: Social psychology].

Agency and language*

Laura M. Ahearn
Rutgers University

Agency is an abstract concept that scholars often define inadequately, if at all, but it has nevertheless become a widely used term across the humanities and social sciences. Before attempting to define the term, it is worthwhile to ask why so many scholars in so many fields have become interested in the concept of agency. Ellen Messer-Davidow (1995: 23) poses this question directly, asking, "Why agency now?" While there are undoubtedly many answers to this question, one is that there is a clear connection between the emergence of interest in approaches that foreground practice on the one hand, and the social movements of the 1960s and 1970s on the other (Ortner 1984: 160). In addition, the social upheavals in central and eastern Europe in the late 1980s and early 1990s directly led many scholars to articulate more clearly their ideas about human agency and social structures (e.g. Sztompka 1991). As a result of witnessing or participating in actions aimed at transforming society, then, many academics began to investigate how linguistic and social practices can either reproduce or transform the very structures that shape them. I believe it is no coincidence that the recent agentive[1] turn, an outgrowth of the trends Ortner identified in 1984, follows on the heels not only of the social movements of the past few decades but also of postmodern and poststructuralist critiques within the academy that have called into question impersonal master narratives that leave no room for tensions, contradictions, or oppositional actions on the part of individuals and collectivities.

It is because questions about agency are so central to contemporary political and theoretical debates that the concept arouses so much interest – and why it is so crucial to define the term clearly. Let me therefore present a provisional definition: *Agency refers to the socioculturally mediated capacity to act.*

---

*Parts of this essay have been adapted and updated with permission from "Language and Agency," published in the *Annual Review of Anthropology* (Ahearn 2001b).

1. There is no unanimity in the choice of an adjectival form for "agency." While other writers use "agential" or "agentic," I prefer "agentive."

This barebones definition leaves a great deal unspecified, but it serves as a starting point for further elaboration of the concept. Scholars interested in the concept might ask the following kinds of questions in order to flesh out their particular usages more precisely:

1. Must all agency be human? Can nonhuman primates (Small 1993), machines (Pickering 1995), technologies (Dobres 2000), spirits (Keane 1997: 64–66), or signs (Colapietro 1989: 95–97; Kockelman 2007; Peirce 1955) exercise agency, as some researchers have suggested?
2. Must agency be individual, or can agency also be supra-individual – the property, perhaps, of families, faculties, institutions, or labor unions? Some scholars, such as Wertsch et al. (1993) and Latour (2005), advocate a non-individualistic notion of agency. Drawing on Vygotsky (1978, 1987) and paraphrasing Bateson (1972), they argue that agency "extends beyond the skin" because it is frequently a property of groups and involves "mediational means" such as language and tools (Wertsch et al. 1993: 352; cf. Latour 2005).
3. Conversely, can agency be sub-individual, as when someone feels torn within herself or himself – the property therefore of "dividuals," to borrow the term used by McKim Marriott, Val Daniel, Bonnie McElhinny, and others (Daniel 1984: 42; Marriott 1976; McElhinny 1998: 181)?
4. What does it mean to be an agent of *someone else*?
5. Must agency be conscious, intentional, or effective? What does it *mean* for an act to be conscious, intentional, or effective?

No matter how scholars choose to answer these questions, two oft-assumed synonyms for agency – "free will" and "resistance" – must immediately be ruled out if agency is understood as referring to the sociocultural capacity to act.

First, agency cannot be considered a synonym for free will because such an approach ignores or only gives lip service to the social nature of agency and the pervasive influence of culture on human intentions, beliefs, and actions. Even Charles Taylor, a philosopher whose writings on language and agency are extremely thought provoking, locates agency inside the mental processes of particular individuals rather than within broader social processes when he connects agency with "second-order desires," "strong evaluation," and "a vocabulary of worth" (Taylor 1985). Similarly, Ludwig Wittgenstein, the famous philosopher to whom linguistic anthropologists increasingly look for inspiration, fails to theorize adequately the sociocultural nature of language and action. While Wittgenstein (1958) recognizes the degree to which language and social forms are intertwined, he leaves the details of this interrelationship unexplained. Practice theorist Anthony Giddens notes this shortcoming in Wittgenstein's work on language and action, stating, "Wittgensteinian philosophy has not led towards any sort of concern with social change, with power relations, or with conflict in society" (1979: 50).

Second, agency should not be considered a straightforward synonym for resistance. Labeling as agency *only* those actions that resist the status quo is characteristic of the work of some anthropologists, many scholars in subaltern studies, and, until recently, most feminist theorists in a number of fields. According to these researchers, in order to demonstrate agency, a person must resist existing power differentials. While one can certainly understand the impulse behind equating agency with resistance, agency should not be reduced to it. **Oppositional agency is only one of many forms of agency.**

Cultural anthropologists and feminist theorists such as Saba Mahmood have recently been challenging this equation of agency with resistance. In her book on the women's mosque movement in Cairo, Egypt, Mahmood (2005) argues strongly for a notion of agency that does not unreflectively reproduce culturally specific western notions of personhood, oppression, and freedom. I agree entirely with Mahmood when she writes, "I am not interested in offering *a* theory of agency, but rather I insist that the meaning of agency must be explored within the grammar of concepts within which it resides" (2005: 34; emphasis in the original). Anything more precise than a barebones definition of agency runs the risk of over-generalizing notions that are actually culturally or linguistically specific.

It is therefore important for scholars to ask themselves how conceptions of agency may differ from society to society, and how these conceptions might be related to notions of personhood and causality. Andrew Pickering suggests that "within different cultures human beings and the material world might exhibit capacities for action quite different from those we customarily attribute to them" (1995: 245). Robert Desjarlais presents an illustration of this within the United States itself in his study of a homeless shelter in Boston, in which he argues that the forms of agency he observed among the shelter's residents emerged out of a specific sociocultural context. Agency did not exist prior to that context, Desjarlais maintains, but arose from within the social, political, cultural, and linguistic dynamics of the homeless shelter during a particular time period (Desjarlais 1997: 204). Claudia Strauss (2007) offers another example of varying ideas about responsibility and agency in the wake of the 1999 Columbine High School shooting in Colorado, in which two students killed twelve other students, a teacher, and themselves. Strauss demonstrates that "the cultural model of persons as autonomous agents, while certainly very important in the contemporary United States, is just one of a number of cultural models Americans use to explain human action" (Strauss 2007: 807–808).

Among the many social theories that attempt to do exactly this – explain human action – practice theory presents the most promising approach, though as I indicate in the next section, it is not without its weaknesses and critics.

1. Practice theory

Consider Karl Marx's famous words in "The Eighteenth Brumaire of Louis Bonaparte":

> Men make their own history, but they do not make it just as they please; they do not make it under circumstances chosen by themselves, but under circumstances directly found, given and transmitted from the past. The tradition of all the dead generations weighs like a nightmare on the brain of the living (Marx 1978[1852]: 595).

How can we reconcile the fact that, as Marx noted almost a century and a half ago, individuals appear to create society even as they are created by it? Peter L. Berger and Thomas Luckmann turn this question into a trilogy of paradoxical statements in their famous book, *The Social Construction of Reality*: "*Society is a human product. Society is an objective reality. Man is a social product*" (Berger & Luckmann 1966: 61; emphasis in the original). On attempt to reconcile these seemingly contradictory statements is practice theory, which Sherry Ortner (1989: 11, 1984) defines as, "a theory of the relationship between the structures of society and culture on the one hand and the nature of human action on the other." The emphasis in practice theory is on the social influences on agency; human actions are central, but they are never considered in isolation from the social structures that shape them.

Anthony Giddens is perhaps the central figure in the debate about agency and structure and is considered one of the founders of practice theory (Giddens 1979, 1984; Archer 1988; Burns & Dietz 1994; Karp 1986). Explicitly drawing on the insights of ethnomethodologists such as Harold Garfinkel and interactionist sociologists such as Erving Goffman, Giddens attempts to breathe life into social structures and bring social structures into contact with human actions (Giddens 1979: 57, 68, 83; Bryant & Jary 1991; Sewell 1992). Unlike scholars who treat agency as a synonym for free will or resistance, Giddens consistently links agency to structure through his discussion of rules and resources. Central to Giddens' theory of structuration is the understanding that people's actions are shaped (in both constraining and enabling ways) by the very social structures that those actions then serve to reinforce or reconfigure. Given this recursive loop consisting on the one hand of actions influenced by social structures, and on the other hand by social structures (re-)created by actions, the question of how social change can occur is crucial and will be taken up below in the context of other practice theorists.

Some sociologists prefer to use the term "practice" or "praxis" (drawing on and redefining the Marxist term) in addition to, or instead of, "agency" (Giddens 1979: 56; Sztompka 1994). Piotr Sztompka, for example, distinguishes the two terms in the following manner: "Agency and praxis are two sides of the incessant social functioning; agency actualizes in praxis, and praxis reshapes agency, which actualizes itself in changed praxis" (Sztompka 1994: 276; emphasis in the original). Thus, agency can be considered the socioculturally mediated capacity to act, while praxis (or practice) can be considered the action itself.

Aside from Giddens, the most influential theorist within practice theory is Pierre Bourdieu, a professor of sociology who conducted ethnographic fieldwork in Algeria. Bourdieu borrows and redefines the term "habitus," first used in anthropology by Marcel Mauss to refer to a habitual condition, particularly of the body (Farnell 2000: 399). Bourdieu's definition refers to a generative process that produces practices and representations that are conditioned by the "structuring structures" from which they emerge. These practices and their outcomes – whether intended or unintended – then reproduce or reconfigure the habitus (Bourdieu 1977: 78). The recursive nature of this process mirrors that found in Giddens' theory of structuration. The habitus generates an infinite but bounded number of possible actions, thoughts, and perceptions, each one of which is imbued with the culturally constructed meanings and values embodied by the habitus. These actions, thoughts, and perceptions in turn then recreate and/or challenge the culturally constructed meanings and values.

With this analysis of agency, Bourdieu moves us far from the concept of free will. Although he defines the habitus as "an endless capacity to engender products," Bourdieu emphasizes dispositions in order to preclude any assumption of absolute free will on the part of actors, repeatedly pointing out how far removed his concept of the habitus is from a creation of unpredictable novelty. What prevents the creation of unpredictably novel sociocultural products are the (pre-)dispositions the habitus embodies in its many forms and structures. Of the infinite thoughts, meanings, and practices that the habitus can produce at any given historical moment, there is only a minimal probability that any will ever be thought or practiced because individuals will be predisposed to think and act in a manner that reproduces the existing system of inequalities.

As necessary and helpful as his reminders are of the constraints on individuals' actions and thoughts, Bourdieu, like Giddens, faces the dilemma of explaining how social reproduction becomes social transformation (Sewell 1992). Bourdieu emphasizes the reproductive tendencies of the habitus, which, because it is sturdy and well-rooted, located in the physical environments containing actors and embodied mentally and physically within the actors themselves, can be applied in new as well as familiar situations to reinforce the status quo. Despite the theoretical possibility of social transformation resulting from actions generated by the habitus, Bourdieu's framework leaves little room for resistance or social change.

The microprocesses of resistance are taken up in the *Practice of Everyday Life*, written by another theorist commonly associated with practice theory, historian Michel de Certeau. De Certeau encourages other scholars to attend to the actions of ordinary people, especially when they engage in "la perruque" (literally, "the wig"), a French idiomatic expression that refers to the work one does for oneself in the guise of work done for an employer (de Certeau 1984: 25). De Certeau uses the trope of "la perruque" to describe how individuals use strategies and tactics to carve out a semi-independent domain of practice within the constraints placed upon them by the powerful.

Although de Certeau, Bourdieu, and Giddens offer us theories with significant explanatory power in regard to the persistence of deeply embedded relations of inequality, they give insufficient attention to the question of how any habitus or structure can produce actions that fundamentally change it. In an attempt to understand more fully how social change occurs, let us look at the writings of other practice theorists working within anthropology.

2. Anthropological contributions to practice theory

In his *Historical Metaphors and Mythical Realities*, Marshall Sahlins sets for himself the task of understanding how an attempt at social reproduction can become social transformation (Sahlins 1981; cf. Obeyesekere 1992). Sahlins, unlike Bourdieu, attends closely to the processes of social transformation and emphasizes the importance of history in his historical and ethnographic account of the transformation that Hawaiian society underwent in the wake of Captain Cook's arrival and his subsequent murder. Noting (perhaps too perfunctorily) that such transformations can occur even without intercultural collisions, Sahlins nevertheless focuses on how these cross-cultural contacts may speed or facilitate unprecedented change. When individuals bring their cultural understandings, as derived from structural principles (what Bourdieu would call their habitus), to bear on new situations, the dynamics of practice – what Sahlins calls "the structure of the conjuncture" (Sahlins 1981: 35) – can cause unintended outcomes. What starts as an attempt to reproduce social structure may end in social transformation. By interweaving history and structure in this manner, Sahlins not only highlights the importance of agency and its often unintended consequences, but throws into question the concept of resistance as conscious activity. Nevertheless, because Sahlins' work, like Bourdieu's, evinces traces of its structuralist roots, the processes of social reproduction/transformation he posits are rather mechanistic, and his "permanent dialectic of structure and practice" (Sahlins 1981: 54) has little room in it for tensions inherent within social structure itself.

Addressing this very issue, Sherry Ortner (1989) builds on the theories of both Sahlins and Bourdieu in *High Religion: A Cultural and Political History of Sherpa Buddhism*. In her elucidation of the terms practice, structure, actor, and history, Ortner sets out the four cornerstones on which her ethnography is built, thereby sidestepping the dualistic, mechanistic formulations of Bourdieu and Sahlins. Practice for Ortner entails the recognition of asymmetry and domination in particular historical and cultural settings, along with an awareness of the cultural schemas and constraints within which individuals act. Departing from both Bourdieu and Sahlins, Ortner emphasizes the existence of inherent structural contradictions that keep a simple reproduction of the hegemonic social order from being a foregone conclusion. As Raymond Williams (1977: 113) notes, "The reality of any hegemony, in the extended political and cultural sense, is that, while by definition it is always dominant, it is never either total or exclusive." Because of the tensions and contradictions inherent in the habitus, actors are neither free agents nor completely socially determined products. Instead, Ortner (1989: 198) suggests that they are "loosely structured." The central question for practice theorists, then, is determining how such loosely structured actors manage at times to transform the systems that produce them.

Such loose structuring can occur linguistically as well as socioculturally. Speakers of a given language are constrained to some degree by the grammatical structures of their particular language, but they are still capable of producing an infinite number of grammatically well-formed utterances within those constraints. Moreover, languages, like cultures, change over time through drift and contact despite their supposedly self-reproducing structures. It is therefore helpful to look closely at language (both its grammatical structures and its patterns of use) in order to gain a more thorough understanding of how people reproduce and transform both language and culture.

3. Intentionality

A central dilemma for theorists who want to define agency more precisely than the bare-bones definition of "the socioculturally mediated capacity to act" is the question of intentionality. If intentional, goal-directed action is added to this skeletal definition, then the question arises as to what it means to intend to do something. Giddens, for example, recognizes intentionality as a key element of the concept of agency, but he advocates what Ortner (2006: 134–135) calls a "soft" definition of agency – one that acknowledges the role of intentionality in human agency but considers intentionality to be a continuous process rather than a set of discrete goal-directed intentions. Agency, too, is similarly a continuous process rather than a set of discrete acts. Thus Giddens writes:

> 'Action' or agency, as I use it, thus does not refer to a series of discrete acts combined together, but to *a continuous flow of conduct*. We may define action…as involving a 'stream of actual or contemplated causal interventions of corporeal beings in the ongoing process of events-in-the-world. (1979: 55; emphasis in the original)

Intentionality comes into play in Giddens's conception of agency in the form of what he calls "practical consciousness." Humans constantly engage in a largely unconscious or only partly conscious reflexive monitoring of their own and others' conduct, and this reflexive monitoring, he argues, "refers to the intentional or purposive character of human behavior: it emphasizes 'intentionality' *as process*. Such intentionality is a routine feature of human conduct and does not imply that actors have definite goals consciously held in mind during the course of their activities" (1979: 56; emphasis in the original). This practical consciousness is, Giddens continues, "tacit knowledge that is skillfully applied in the enactment of courses of conduct, but which the actor is not able to formulate *discursively*" (1979: 57; emphasis mine). Indeed, he goes on to say that the reasons that people supply for their actions after the fact often "stand in a relation of some tension" to the actions themselves (1979: 57). In other words, people's retroactively stated reasons for their behavior may or may not bear any resemblance to their actual reasons at the time – if indeed such actual reasons could ever be identified and articulated.

Three other theorists have recently taken stands on the role of intentionality in defining agency: Sherry Ortner, Alessandro Duranti, and Paul Kockelman. Ortner criticizes "soft" definitions of agency that either sidestep the whole question of intentionality, as my barebones definition does, or treat intentionality as a process, as Giddens's definition does. Although Ortner recognizes that intentions are often "after-the-fact rationalizations," that unconscious processes are important in any theory of action, and that "most social outcomes are in fact unintended consequences of action," her main reason for wanting to retain a stronger notion of intentionality as central to the definition of agency is that "if one is too soft on intentionality, one loses a distinction that I think needs to be maintained, between routine practices on the one hand, and 'agency' seen precisely as more intentionalized action on the other" (2006: 135). Ortner posits a continuum between routinized practices on the one end and "agentive acts that intervene in the world with something in mind (or in heart)" on the other, and asserts that it seems important to maintain the distinction at the two ends of the spectrum even if the middle is full of grey areas (2006: 136).

Alessandro Duranti (2006) has also written an essay noting the centrality of intentionality. In his earlier work in Samoa, however, Duranti (1988) had commented upon how reticent Samoans were to attribute intentions to others. "In engaging in interpretation," Duranti wrote, "Samoans are not so much concerned with knowing someone else's intentions, as much as with the implications of the speaker's actions/words for the web of relationships in which his life is woven" (1988: 27). The fact that a society can "carry on a great deal of complex social interaction without much apparent concern with people's subjective states" of mind, Duranti notes (1988: 30), poses a challenge to social theorists interested in intentionality, interpretation, and agency.

In his 2006 essay, Duranti takes up that challenge directly and suggests that social theorists must find a way of reconciling a notion of human action as goal-oriented with the fact that not all societies emphasize or even recognize intentions as being central to explaining human behavior. The solution, he argues, involves distinguishing a narrow, culturally specific understanding of intention in the sense of "a determination to do a specified thing" (2006: 34) from a universally applicable concept of intentionality that resembles that of Giddens and draws on philosophers Franz Brentano and Edmund Husserl in that it is the "'aboutness' of our mental and physical activity, that is, the property that our thoughts and embodied actions have to be directed toward something… This property of being directed does not presuppose that a well-formed thought precedes action" (2006: 36). Sometimes, Duranti asserts, it might be possible to identify the "directionality" of particular communicative acts without being able to specify whether the speakers did or did not have the narrow intention to communicate what is being attributed to them by their listeners (2006: 36). But at other times we might in fact be able to identify these kinds of narrower intentions – and this is exactly the role of the ethnographer, Duranti argues, one that is made possible by a basic notion of universal human intersubjectivity.

While intentionality is not mentioned per se in the definition of agency that Duranti proposes in his 2004 "Agency in Language" essay in the *Companion to Linguistic Anthropology* volume, Duranti does explain that intentionality in the universal "aboutness" sense is closely related to the first of his three proposed properties of agency: control over one's own behavior. Duranti's full definition of agency is as follows:

> Agency is here understood as the property of those entities (i) that have some degree of control over their own behavior, (ii) whose actions in the world affect other entities' [actions] (and sometimes their own), and (iii) whose actions are the object of evaluation (e.g. in terms of their responsibility for a given outcome) (Duranti 2004: 453).

In contrast to Duranti's definition, Paul Kockelman, another linguistic anthropologist, defines agency as follows: "Agency might initially be understood as the relatively flexible wielding of means toward ends" (2007: 375). Given the centrality of means and ends in Kockelman's definition, intentionality clearly plays an important role in his understanding of agency. Indeed, Kockelman discusses intentions and intentionality at length in his response to the comments on his article by other researchers, and in that response he distinguishes among *intentional statuses*, *intentional roles*, and *intentional attitudes*, all from a perspective that draws on the work of Charles Sanders Peirce (Kockelman 2007: 395–396).

Many of the scholars who have written about agency have attempted to subdivide agency into different types or categories. Ortner, for example, proposes two different but closely interrelated types of agency: (1) the agency of (unequal) power; and (2) the agency of projects. The first kind of agency involves domination or resistance to domination and is therefore to a large degree defined by the terms of the dominant group, while the second kind of agency "is about (relatively ordinary) life socially organized in terms of culturally constituted projects that infuse life with meaning and purpose" (2006: 147). In agency of projects, Ortner directs us to look for how people attempt to sustain their own culturally constituted projects, often in the face of overwhelming power differentials in the form of colonialism or racism. Kockelman (2007) also identifies two types of agency: "residential agency" (involving power and choice) and "representational agency" (involving knowledge and consciousness). Likewise, Duranti (2004) has identified two different dimensions of agency in language: the performance of agency (which he subdivides further into "ego-affirming" and "act-constituting") and the grammatical encoding of agency.

All of these attempts to define, subdivide, and categorize types of agency are very useful for scholars interested in analyzing language. Duranti's second dimension, the grammatical encoding of agency, is particularly important to understand, as it is central to questions of agency in language, and so we turn now to this topic.

4. The grammatical encoding of agency

Any discussion of agency and language must consider how grammatical categories in different languages distinguish among types of subjects, actors, or agents, for such categories, "to the extent that they are obligatory and habitual, and relatively inaccessible to the average speaker's consciousness, will form a privileged location for transmitting and reproducing cultural and social categories" (Hill & Mannheim 1992: 387). While each language has its own set of linguistic resources that can be used to exercise, attribute, or deny agency, there are also some features that seem to be present in every language (Comrie 1981). According to R.M.W. Dixon (1994: 6), for example, all languages work in terms of three basic relations – *S, A,* and *O* – defined as follows:

S – *S*ubject of an intransitive verb (e.g. ***Sita*** went to Kathmandu);
A – *A*gent, or subject, of a transitive verb (e.g. ***Parvati*** loves Shiva); and
O – *O*bject of a transitive verb (e.g. Maya ate ***rice***).

Semantically, there are various roles the subject of a sentence can take, such as the following (Duranti 1994: 122–123; cf. Duranti 2004: 460; Keenan 1984):

Agent	**Pabi** read the book.
Actor	**Shiva** danced.
Perceiver	**Tika** heard the news.
Instrument	**The stone** broke the window.
Patient/Undergoer	**The old woman** died.

These semantic roles can be treated in various ways grammatically. Defining the linguistic subject in a way that applies to all languages turns out to be a challenging and controversial topic over which linguists differ (Comrie 1981: 98–101). In the majority of languages, including most of the languages of Europe, the subjects of transitive and intransitive verbs are treated the same way grammatically, while the object of a transitive verb is treated differently. This pattern is known as **accusativity**. In about a quarter of the world's languages, however, a complementary pattern obtains in which the subject of an intransitive verb and the object of a transitive verb are treated the same way syntactically, while the subject of a transitive verb is treated differently. This pattern is known as **ergativity** (Bittner & Hale 1996; Dixon 1994).[2] In ergative languages, there is usually a grammatical marker that distinguishes Agents (of transitive verbs) from Subjects (of intransitive verbs) and Objects (of transitive verbs). Consider the following examples, taken from Duranti (1994: 122), in which the ergative marker *e* is present only in (1), before the Agent – *'e le tama'* ('the boy') – of the transitive verb, and not before the Subject – *'le tama'* ('the boy') – of the intransitive verb in (2):

(1) 'ua fa'atau *e* *le* *tama* le suka.
    TA[3] buy ERG ART boy ART sugar
    <u>The boy</u> has bought the sugar.

(2) 'ua alu *le* *tama* 'i le maketi.
    TA go ART boy to ART market
    <u>The boy</u> has gone to the market.

Some languages have "split" grammatical systems in which speakers follow an accusative pattern in some cases and an ergative pattern in other cases. In standard Nepali, for example, the ergative marker *le* is obligatorily used with the Agents of transitive verbs in the past tense only – not in the present or future tense. In the dialect of Nepali spoken in the village of Junigau, Nepal, however, where I have conducted long-term field work, people use the ergative marker *le* in non-obligatory ways in the present and future tenses when they want to place emphasis on the Agent, as can be seen in the following example taken from a Junigau woman's narrative of marriage:

(3) *mai* *le* pani mān garchhu.
    I ERG too respect do
    <u>I</u>, too, respect [my husband].

A related sort of split appears in languages that have grammatical systems in which the subjects of some intransitive verbs are categorized with transitive subjects, while the subjects of other intransitive verbs are categorized with intransitive subjects. In Guaraní, for example, the word for 'I' used with more agentive intransitive verbs, such as 'go' and

---

2. Languages in which the subjects of transitive and intransitive verbs are treated the same way syntactically while the transitive object is treated differently are also called "nominative-accusative." Languages in which the subjects of intransitive verbs and the objects of transitive verbs are treated the same way syntactically are also called "ergative-absolutive" (cf. Duranti 2004: 460ff). I follow Dixon (1994) in shortening these terms to "accusativity" and "ergativity," respectively, in order to emphasize which case is being treated uniquely. With accusativity, Objects are placed in the accusative case and are treated differently from Subjects and Agents, whereas with ergativity, Agents are placed in the ergative case and are treated differently from Subjects and Objects.

3. The abbreviations used in the interlinear glosses have the following meanings: TA refers to a marker of verb tense or aspect; ERG refers to an ergative marker; ART refers to an article (Duranti 1994: 177–178).

'get up', is the same word for 'I' used with the transitive verb 'bring' (Mithun 1991: 511). A completely different word for 'I' is used with less agentive intransitive verbs, such as 'to be' – the same word that is used for the direct object pronoun 'me'. In these languages, attributions of agency are built right into syntactic, semantic, and pragmatic practices.

Let me emphasize, however, that in none of these cases is it possible to draw a simplistic connection between the presence of ergative case markings and "more" or "less" agency.[4] Nevertheless, ergative languages present researchers with a valuable tool they can use to explore notions of subjectivity and action in other cultures.

While languages may encode agency differently in their grammatical categories, there are some universal patterns that can be discerned regarding the types of nouns most likely to appear in the Agent position. Drawing on linguistic data from Chinook and Dyirbal, both of which are split ergative systems that use an ergative pattern of case-marking for certain types of noun phrases and an accusative pattern for other types of noun phrases, Michael Silverstein (1976: 116–122) proposes an Animacy Hierarchy that predicts where on the spectrum of noun phrases the split between ergativity and accusativity will occur.

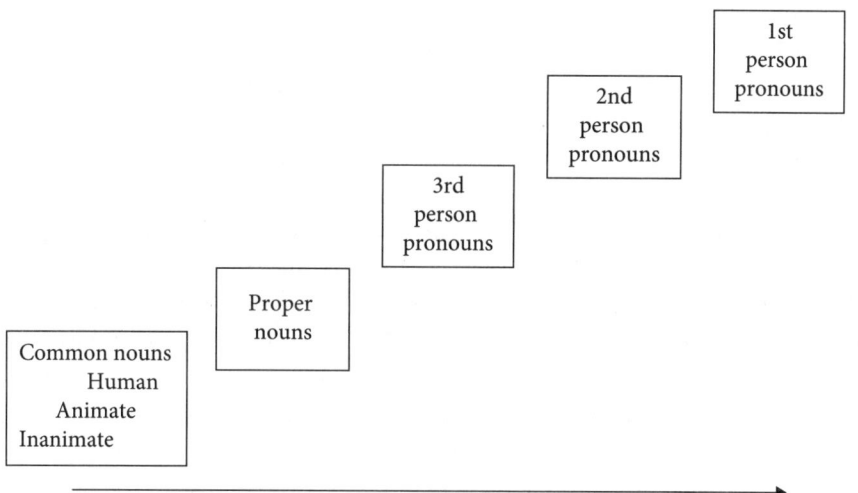

Increasingly likely to be in Agent position rather than in Object position

Figure 1. The animacy hierarchy (based on Dixon 1994: 85; Foley 1999: 210; revised from Silverstein 1976: 122; reproduced from Ahearn 2001b: 123)

---

4. It is not useful, in my opinion, to talk of having "more," "less," or even "no" agency. As I hope I have demonstrated in this essay, agency is not a quantity that can be measured. Rather, researchers should focus on delineating different kinds of agency, or different ways in which agency is socio-culturally mediated in particular times and places.

Dixon generalizes from Silverstein's Animacy Hierarchy, a revised version of which is shown in Figure 1, arguing that in all languages, the items toward the right of the spectrum are more likely to be in the Agent function, and the items to the left of the spectrum are more likely to be in the Object position. Dixon (1994: 84) summarizes this important linguistic universal as follows:

> Put very roughly, a speaker will think in terms of doing things to other people to a much greater extent than in terms of things being done to him. In the speaker's view of the world, as it impinges on him and as he describes it in language, he will be the quintessential agent.[5]

In other words, it appears that the universal grammatical principles underlying all languages identify the speaker ('I') as the "most salient person" in a linguistic interaction (Foley 1999: 210). The second most salient person is the addressee, 'you.' Both 'I' and 'you' are more salient, and therefore more likely to be found in the Agent position, than the absent participants in the interaction, ranked in the following order: third person pronouns, proper nouns, common nouns referring to humans, common nouns referring to animate non-humans, and common nouns referring to inanimate objects. While there have been some challenges and revisions to this model (cf. Dixon 1994: 83–94), the implications of a possibly universal tendency regarding the attribution of linguistic agency are worth considering. **Note carefully, however, that we are talking about grammatical, not social, definitions of agency here.** There are times when the grammatical and social categories of Agent will overlap, but this remains to be determined in each particular context (cf. Duranti 1994: 124).

How can the grammatical details regarding Agent, Subject, and Object in particular languages be relevant to scholars interested in the social aspects of agency? As DuBois (1987) notes, ergativity originates in discourse itself – in other words, in naturally occurring conversations. Derbyshire (1987: 319), for example, reports that in many Amazonian languages, when a noun phrase describing a highly ranked person is the subject in a transitive clause, the accusative pattern is followed, whereas when a noun phrase describing the higher ranked person is the object (a more marked, or unexpected, occurrence), the ergative pattern is followed. In English, LaFrance (1992) has shown that when subjects are asked to supply plausible scenarios of events that might have preceded and followed a set of sentences alternating male and female subjects and objects, they demonstrate a linguistic bias against women that she calls "the disappearing agent effect." Her findings indicate that if a sentence is phrased such that a

---

5. Dixon's use of the masculine generic demonstrates yet another example of how grammatical categories predispose speakers to attribute agency more often to certain kinds of subjects. See McConnell-Ginet (1979), Silverstein (1985), and Waugh (1982) for analyses of markedness in the use of masculine and feminine pronouns.

female is described as doing something or feeling something, especially with respect to a male, then she fades from causal view, but when she is on the receiving end of someone else's actions, then the subject or source of these events, rather than she herself, is highlighted (LaFrance 1992: 341). While these responses were elicited rather than taken from naturally occurring conversations, an ethnographically informed investigation of this phenomenon would demonstrate exactly how these linguistic usages reflect, reinforce, and sometimes reconfigure agency and status hierarchies in the society.

Alessandro Duranti's *From Grammar to Politics: Linguistic Anthropology in a Western Samoan Village* (1994) provides just such an ethnographically rich example of how attention to what may seem like highly technical, esoteric grammatical forms can shed light on human agency (see also Duranti & Ochs 1990). Duranti maintains that the Samoans' use of ergative markers reveals how they attribute agency socially, especially in cases of praise or blame. Powerful individuals are more likely to use the ergative marker when they want to accuse someone of a malicious act, whereas less powerful individuals try to resist such accusations by suggesting alternative linguistic definitions of events. Duranti's "grammar of praising and blaming" demonstrates how agency is expressed in, and shaped by, the linguistic forms that a socially and linguistically embedded speaker uses. Through this sort of close linguistic analysis, the links between micro and macro levels of power and agency become evident.

5. Talk about agency – Meta-agentive discourse

Another way of analyzing agency in language is to look for how people **talk about agency** – how they talk about their own actions and others' actions, how they attribute responsibility for events, how they describe their own and others' decision-making processes. I call this kind of talk about agency "meta-agentive discourse," piggybacking onto the term "meta-pragmatic discourse," as used by Michael Silverstein (1976, 1993, 2001), Debra Spitulnik (2001), and others. Such talk about agency can be found in everyday mundane conversations, in narratives and life stories, in politicians' speeches, and in many other oral and written genres, including Nepali love letters, which I will discuss further below. Meta-agentive discourse can also be found in scholars' own writings (this piece included, of course).

Analyzing meta-agentive discourse can provide insight into people's own theories of agency. An example of such work can be found in Christopher McCollum's (2000) study of two different kinds of narratives he elicited from middle-class couples in the U.S. – (1) how they ended up with their current romantic partners, and (2) how they ended up in their current career. In the first type of narrative, people often presented the process by which they met and fell in love with their current romantic partners as one involving fate or chance. They just happened to go to a singles bar or answer a personal ad, they claimed, even though they had not been looking to get involved with anyone. In the second type of narrative, in contrast, the same individuals presented themselves as much more agentive in the process of arriving at their current professional position. They told of making active choices to major in a particular subject or apply for a certain job, even though there may have been at least some degree of luck or privilege involved in who mentored them, where they went to school, and how they happened to be hired at one place rather than another. A close analysis of meta-agentive discourse can thus bring to light differences in people's theories of agency in various areas of their lives.

Another example of how a study of meta-agentive discourse, combined with a grammatical analysis and grounded in long-term ethnographic research, can provide a deeper understanding of people's conceptualizations of their own and others' actions comes from my own work on love letter writing in Nepal (Ahearn 2001a, 2008a, 2008b). Love letter writing only became possible in the Nepali village of Junigau in the 1990s because it was during that decade that most of the young women became literate – and they put their literacy skills to an unexpected use: writing love letters.[6] The letters were about much more than love, however; they were saturated with "development discourse" (cf. Escobar 1995; Pigg 1992, 1996). The practice of sending and receiving of love letters came to be interpreted by Junigau residents in the 1990s as indexing a certain kind of person – a "developed" (*bikāsī*) person as opposed to a "backward" (*pichhyāDī*) person (and they used these exact terms).

Many social, economic, and political changes were taking place in Nepal in general and Junigau in particular during the 1990s. For our purposes here, the most relevant changes came in the ways that people conceptualized causality or responsibility for events – in other words, their theories of agency. To oversimplify quite a bit but to give a basic idea of the trend, more and more Junigau residents in the 1990s attributed events to particular individuals rather than to fate. This trend was not unidirectional, nor was it without complexities, but the trend was very evident, both to villagers themselves, who commented explicitly on the change and to me during the years I lived in the village.

The trend also had gendered dimensions. In a close analysis I conducted of the love letters of a woman named Shila and a man named Vajra, I found a difference in their conceptions of their own and others' actions – both in their explicit talk about agency in their letters and in their implicit grammatical choices (Ahearn 2008b). While they both mixed individualistic and fatalistic notions of action in their letters, Shila tended

---

6. Love-letter writing turned out to be a short-lived literacy practice, as I discovered during fieldwork conducted in 2010, when it became apparent that young villagers were no longer communicating with potential marriage partners through writing but instead were talking (not texting) on their new mobile phones.

to emphasize more fatalistic notions, claiming that it was not possible to achieve what one wanted to achieve in life. Vajra, on the other hand, often stated that any and all obstacles could be overcome. Here are just a few examples of the many that contain meta-agentive discourse in their love letters – first, an example from a letter written by Shila[7] in July 1990 (Letter #18, 2047-4-8):[8]

> But what to do? A person probably doesn't get to survive just because s/he says, 'I will survive,' and a person probably doesn't get to die just because s/he says, 'I will die.' And so, even though I've said, 'I'm an unfortunate one; I'll die,' I haven't been able to die. How very, very much suffering and sadness, how many thousands of troubles and difficulties, how many thousands of obstacles I've borne! And even though they have burnt up this heart/mind inside me and turned it into ashes and stones, I find that I'm obliged to go on living in this human world……..? Let's see what this human world will be, ……..., I write. If whatever one said became true, I would……..you today. What to do? It seems to me that whatever one says does not necessarily become true.

And here is another excerpt from a letter written by Shila in September 1990 (Letter #27, 2047-6-12):

> I find that the world is like this: how many wishes, how many desires, how many interests, how many hopes there keep on being, but – what to do? – because of conditions and obstacles they get lost by themselves. And yet I find that it's necessary to go on living. You'll probably say, "What kinds of conditions and obstacles are there, after all?" you'll probably say, but – what to do? – it's not possible to cut one's chest open to show the obstacles and conditions that have arisen.

And indeed, Vajra writes frequently of being able to overcome all obstacles and of his belief that nothing was impossible. Here is an excerpt from a letter that he wrote in June 1990 (Letter #12, 2047-3):

> Because one is human, one has to do all kinds of things – one has to walk, one has to talk. Why wouldn't all kinds of circumstances befall one in whatever group/class?? In that way, one has to be able to become part of one's family/race/group. That alone is called a

---

7. In keeping with anthropological conventions, these names are pseudonyms, and I obtained informed consent from all of the letter writers to share their letters with scholarly and non-scholarly audiences. A complete translation of Shila and Vajra's entire love letter correspondence, and all of the love letters written by another man who eventually married a woman from Junigau, are available online at the University of Michigan Press's website: http://www.press.umich.edu/pdf/0472097849-appa.pdf and at http://www.press.umich.edu/pdf/0472097849-appb.pdf.

8. The Nepali calendar differs from our own. Each year starts in mid-April, and the year is roughly 56 years ahead of ours. This notation indicates the date on which the letter was written – on the 12th day of the 6th month of the year 2047 – correlating approximately to the end of September, 1990.

> human life. Whoever can mold time and circumstances during one's own lifetime – that alone is the human condition.
>
> These days nothing is impossible in this world. A person can do anything. I offer a prayer today to Shree Pashupatibaba that just as our love develops more and more fully, so too may it grow and develop fully in the future, may it be able to blossom and blossom. I also say today that love is for the purpose of spending one's whole life together forever; [I don't say that love is] for the purpose of separation.

And here are excerpts from two different letters that he wrote in August 1990 (Letter #21, 2047-4-15; and Letter #22, 2047-4-25):

> It seems to me that if anyone challenges us, we shouldn't retreat/run away; rather, after we show that person, s/he will give up. To laugh and to talk is in the nature of human beings. In the face of pure love, any power in the world must go down to defeat in the end, as much love as there is.
>
> Whenever doing anything some obstacles will always arise, but just because those obstacles arise, should we not do it? It will be necessary to complete the work with a lot of effort in order to overcome those obstacles. After beginning any kind of work, it will certainly be completed in the end; it shouldn't be left off in the middle. It must be completed. With any kind of work, what kind of circumstance is it if one talks and talks about it, then leaves it off in the middle without finishing it? Looking at what kind of manner that is, [it looks] so bad.

In Vajra's letters, therefore, we see a theory of agency that leans toward attributing to people in general and certainly to himself and Shila the ability to achieve their goals and to overcome any obstacles that arise. In Shila's letters, in contrast, there are more mentions of limitations, constraints, and fate. Many of the statements of both Vajra and Shila are gendered in very interesting ways. Although this is a partial analysis, what is clear is that there is a definite difference in Shila and Vajra's meta-agentive discourse in the letters.

6. Language in action, agency in language

As linguistic anthropologists and other scholars increasingly treat language use as a form of social action, the task of developing a theoretically sophisticated understanding of agency becomes ever more urgent. Much as Susan U. Philips (2001) has proposed for the relationship between language and power, I would argue that the relationship between language and agency can be studied from three quite different but interrelated perspectives. First, there is agency as encoded in, and shaped by, **linguistic structure**, such as ergativity or pronouns, for example. Second, there is agency as embedded within large-scale **socio-historical processes**, such as the ones that Judith Irvine and

Susan Gal (2000) identify in their influential discussion of the semiotic processes of linguistic differentiation (iconization, fractal recursivity, and erasure). Language ideologies at this macro level can affect, for example, which speech varieties are labeled as languages and which as dialects, thereby both shaping and being shaped by the agency of individuals. The social theories of scholars such as Pierre Bourdieu, Sherry Ortner, and Anthony Giddens are helpful in understanding these large-scale social, political, and historical processes. And finally, there is agency as emerging from *discourse*, both in the sense of micro-level face-to-face interactions and also in Foucault's broader sense of discourse as a form of power to which we are all subordinated. Meta-agentive discourse can operate at both these levels.

In conclusion, it is essential that researchers interested in studying language in actual social contexts carefully consider which concept(s) of agency they are employing in their scholarship, lest they allow unsophisticated, possibly contradictory conceptions of action, causality, and responsibility to underpin, and possibly undermine, their work. A deeper understanding of social theory, especially practice theory, can help scholars develop insightful analyses of linguistic and social practices.

References

Ahearn, L.M. (2001a). *Invitations to Love: Literacy, Love Letters, and Social Change in Nepal*. University of Michigan Press.

—— (2001b). Language and Agency. *Annual Review of Anthropology* 30: 109–37.

—— (2008a). Fateful Literacy: New Meanings, Old Ideologies, and Some Unexpected Consequences of Nepali Love Letter Writing. In M. Prinsloo & M. Baynham (eds.) *Literacies: Global and Local*: 93–116. John Benjamins.

—— (2008b). From Grammar to Love?: Agency and Ergativity in Nepali Love Letters. Invited colloquium presentation at the Center for Language, Interaction, and Culture (CLIC) at UCLA, 2 April 2008.

Archer, M.S. (1988). *Culture and Agency: The Place of Culture in Social Theory*. Cambridge University Press.

Bateson, G. (1972). *Steps to an Ecology of Mind: A Revolutionary Approach to Man's Understanding of Himself*. Ballantine.

Berger, P.L. & T. Luckmann (1966). *The Social Construction of Reality: A Treatise in the Sociology of Knowledge*. Doubleday.

Bittner, M. & K. Hale (1996). Ergativity: Toward a Theory of a Heterogeneous Class. *Linguistic Inquiry* 27(4): 531–604.

Bourdieu, P. (1977). *Outline of a Theory of Practice*. Cambridge University Press.

Bryant, C.G.A. & D. Jary (eds.) (1991). *Giddens' Theory of Structuration: A Critical Appreciation*. Routledge.

Burns, T.R. & T. Dietz (1994). Introduction to the Series. In P. Sztompka (ed.) *Agency and Structure: Reorienting Social Theory*. International Studies in Global Change, vol. 4: vii–xiv. Gordon & Breach.

Colapietro, V.M. (1989). *Peirce's Approach to the Self: A Semiotic Perspective on Human Subjectivity*. SUNY Press.
Comrie, B. (1981). *Language Universals and Linguistic Typology: Syntax and Morphology*. Basil Blackwell.
Daniel, E.V. (1984). *Fluid Signs: Being a Person the Tamil Way*. University of California Press.
De Certeau, M. (1984). *The Practice of Everyday Life* (trans. S. Rendall). University of California Press.
Derbyshire, D.C. (1987). Morphosyntactic Areal Characteristics of Amazonian Languages. *International Journal of American Linguistics* 53: 311–326.
Desjarlais, R. (1997). *Shelter Blues: Sanity and Selfhood Among the Homeless*. University of Pennsylvania Press.
Dixon, R.M.W. (1994). *Ergativity*. Cambridge University Press.
Dobres, M.-A. (2000). *Technology and Social Agency: Outlining a Practice Framework for Archaeology*. Blackwell.
Dubois, J. (1987). The Discourse Basis of Ergativity. *Language* 63: 805–855.
Duranti, A. (1988). Intentions, Language, and Social Action in a Samoan Context. *Journal of Pragmatics* 12: 13–33.
—— (1994). *From Grammar to Politics: Linguistic Anthropology in a Western Samoan Village*. University of California Press.
—— (2004). Agency in Language. In A. Duranti (ed.) *A Companion to Linguistic Anthropology*: 451–473. Blackwell.
—— (2006). The Social Ontology of Intentions. *Discourse Studies* 8(1): 31–40.
Duranti, A. & E. Ochs (1990). Genitive Constructions and Agency in Samoan Discourse. *Studies in Language* 14(1): 1–23.
Escobar, A. (1995). *Encountering Development: The Making and Unmaking of the Third World*. Princeton University Press.
Farnell, B. (2000). Getting Out of the *Habitus*: An Alternative Model of Dynamically Embodied Social Action. *Journal of the Royal Anthropological Institute* 6: 397–418.
Foley, W.A. (1999). Information Structure. In K. Brown, J. Miller (eds.) & R.E. Asher (consulting ed.) *Concise Encyclopedia of Grammatical Categories*: 204–213. Elsevier.
Giddens, A. (1979). *Central Problems in Social Theory: Action, Structure and Contradiction in Social Analysis*. University of California Press.
—— (1984). *The Constitution of Society: Outline of the Theory of Structuration*. University of California Press.
Hill, J.H. & B. Mannheim (1992). Language and World View. *Annual Review of Anthropology* 21: 381–406.
Irvine, J.T. & S. Gal (2000). Language Ideology and Linguistic Differentiation. In P.V. Kroskrity (ed.) *Regimes of Language: Ideologies, Polities, and Identities*: 35–83. School of American Research Press.
Karp, I. (1986). Agency and Social Theory: A Review of Anthony Giddens. *American Ethnologist* 13(1): 131–37.
Keane, W. (1997). Religious Language. *Annual Review of Anthropology* 26: 47–71.
Keenan [Ochs], E.L. (1984). Semantic Correlates of the Ergative/Absolutive Distinction. *Linguistics* 22: 197–223.
Kockelman, P. (2007). Agency: The Relation between Meaning, Power, and Knowledge. *Current Anthropology* 48(3): 388–389.
La France, M. (1992). When Agents Disappear: How Gender Affects the Implicit Causality of Interpersonal Verbs. In K. Hall, M. Bucholtz & B. Moonwomon (eds.) *Locating Power: Proceedings*

of the Second Berkeley Women and Language Conference, April 4&5, 1992: 338–343. Berkeley Women and Language Group.

Latour, B. (2005). *Reassembling the Social: An Introduction to Actor-Network-Theory.* Oxford University Press.

Mahmood, S. (2005). *The Politics of Piety: The Islamic Revival and the Feminist Subject.* Princeton University Press.

Marriott, M. (1976). Hindu Transactions: Diversity Without Dualism. In B. Kapferer (ed.) *Transaction and Meaning: Directions in the Anthropology of Exchange and Symbolic Behavior:* 109–142. Institute for the Study of Human Issues Publications.

Marx, K. (1978). [1852] The Eighteenth Brumaire of Louis Bonaparte. In R.C. Tucker (ed.) *The Marx-Engels Reader*, 2nd ed.: 594–617. Norton.

McCollum, C.C. (2000). The Cultural Patterning of Self-Understanding: A Cognitive-Psychoanalytic Approach to Middle-Class Americans' Life Stories. Ph.D. dissertation, Duke University.

McConnell-Ginet, S. (1979). Prototypes, Pronouns, and Persons. In M. Mathiot (ed.) *Ethnolinguistics: Boas, Sapir, and Whorf Revisited*: 63–83. Moulton.

McElhinny, B. (1998). Genealogies of Gender Theory: Practice Theory and Feminism in Sociocultural and Linguistic Anthropology. *Social Analysis* 42(3): 164–189.

Messer-Davidow, E. (1995). Acting Otherwise. In J. Kegan Gardiner (ed.) *Provoking Agents: Gender and Agency in Theory and Practice*: 23–51. University of Illinois Press.

Mithun, M. (1991). Active/Agentive Case marking and its Motivations. *Language* 67(3): 510–46.

Obeyesekere, G. (1992). *The Apotheosis of Captain Cook: European Myth-Making in the Pacific.* Princeton University Press.

Ortner, S.B. (1984). Theory in Anthropology Since the Sixties. *Comparative Studies in Society and History* 26(1): 126–66.

——— (1989). *High Religion: A Cultural and Political History of Sherpa Buddhism.* Princeton University Press.

——— (2006). Power and Projects: Reflections on Agency. In S.B. Ortner *Anthropology and Social Theory: Culture, Power, and the Acting Subject*: 129–153. Duke University Press.

Peirce, C.S. (1955). *Philosophical Writings of Peirce* (ed. J. Buchler). Dover.

Philips, S.U. (2001). Power. In A. Duranti (ed.) *Key Terms in Language and Culture*: 190–192. Blackwell.

Pickering, A. (1995). *The Mangle of Practice: Time, Agency, and Science.* University of Chicago Press.

Pigg, S.L. (1992). Inventing Social Categories through Place: Social Representations and Development in Nepal. *Comparative Studies in Society and History* 34(3): 491–513.

——— (1996). The Credible and the Credulous: The Question of 'Villager's Beliefs' in Nepal. *Cultural Anthropology* 11(2): 160–201.

Sahlins, M. (1981). *Historical Metaphors and Mythical Realities: Structure in the Early History of the Sandwich Islands Kingdom.* University of Michigan Press.

Sewell Jr., W.H. (1992). A Theory of Structure: Duality, Agency, and Transformation. *American Journal of Sociology* 98(1): 1–29.

Silverstein, M. (1976). Hierarchy of Features and Ergativity. In R.M.W. Dixon (ed.) *Grammatical Categories in Australian Languages*: 112–171. Australian Institute of Aboriginal Studies.

——— (1985). Language and the Culture of Gender: At the Intersection of Structure, Usage, and Ideology. In E. Mertz & R.J. Parmentier (eds.) *Semiotic Mediation: Sociocultural and Psychological Perspectives*: 19–59. Academic.

——— (1993). Metapragmatic Discourse and Metapragmatic Function. In J. Lucy (ed.) *Reflexive Language: Reported Speech and Metapragmatics*: 33–58. Cambridge University Press.

—— (2001). The Limits of Awareness. In A. Duranti (ed.) *Linguistic Anthropology: A Reader*: 382–401. Blackwell.
Small, M.F. (1993). *Female Choices: Sexual Behavior of Female Primates*. Cornell University Press.
Spitulnik, D. (2001). The Social Circulation of Media Discourse and the Mediation of Communities. In A. Duranti (ed.) *Linguistic Anthropology: A Reader*: 95–118. Blackwell.
Strauss, C. (2007). Blaming for Columbine: Conceptions of Agency in the Contemporary United States. *Current Anthropology* 48(6): 807–832.
Sztompka, P. (1991). *Society in Action: The Theory of Social Becoming*. University of Chicago Press.
—— (1994). *The Sociology of Social Change*. Blackwell.
Taylor, C. (1985). *Human Agency and Language: Philosophical Papers*, vol. 1. Cambridge University Press.
Vygotsky, L.S. (1978). *Mind in Society: The Development of Higher Psychological Processes* (ed. M. Cole, V. John-Steiner, S. Scribner & E. Souberman). Harvard University Press.
—— (1987). *Thinking and Speech* (ed. and transl. N. Minick). Plenum.
Waugh, L.R. (1982). Marked and Unmarked: A Choice Between Unequals in Semiotic Structure. *Semiotica* 38: 299–318.
Wertsch, J.V., P. Tulviste & F. Hagstrom (1993). A Sociocultural Approach to Agency. In E.A. Forman, N. Minick & C.A. Stone (eds.) *Contexts for Learning: Sociocultural Dynamics in Children's Development*: 336–356. Oxford University Press.
Williams, R. (1977). *Marxism and Literature*. Oxford University Press.
Wittgenstein, L. (1958). *Philosophical Investigations*, 2nd ed. (transl. G.E.M. Anscombe). Blackwell.

Authority

John Wilson & Karyn Stapleton
University of Ulster

1. Introduction

Since the publication of the original version of this article (Wilson 1996), the field of Pragmatics has not seen major developments specifically in the study of authority. This might be due to the way 'authority' is commonly conceptualised in relation to power. From a standard social psychology perspective, authority is one form (or sub-set) of power. The widely cited taxonomy developed by Raven and Rubin (1983), for example, lists six different bases of social power (reward, coercion, expertise, legitimacy, reference, and information), within which authority derives from the legitimacy source. Hence, authority is often seen simply as 'legitimate power' and, for this reason, it might reasonably be assumed that the topic is covered within the burgeoning literature on 'language and power'. Certainly, the relationship between language and power has been extensively addressed within the overlapping fields of pragmatics, sociolinguistics, discourse analysis, conversation analysis and linguistic social theory (e.g., Cameron 1998; Edley & Wetherell 1997; Erickson 2004; Gal 1993; Harris 1995; Heller 2001; Lemke 1995; Mayr 2004; Simpson & Mayr 2009; Thornborrow 2002; Talbot, Atkinson & Atkinson 2003; Thomas & Wareing 1999; Wilson 2006; Wilson & Stapleton 2007). In addition, research in Critical Discourse Analysis (CDA) is centrally concerned with the ways in which power relationships are enacted and perpetuated (or resisted/transformed) through linguistic and discursive practices (e.g., Fairclough 1989, 1992, 1995, 2000; Wodak & Meyer 2001; Wodak et al. 1999).

However, the concept of 'authority' is more complex than being simply a sub-set of power, and for this reason, it needs to be studied in its own right. For example, some forms of commonly referenced authority are not necessarily legitimated in a formal or institutional sense (e.g., authority of the self in relation to claims about one's body or physical experiences; see below). On the other hand, formally granted authority may be challenged or rejected by others (e.g., Phillips & Hardy 1997). A teacher, for instance, who has formal authority over his pupils, may find that the pupils challenge his position and refuse to cooperate with his directions. Now, in a formal or legitimated sense, the teacher's authority is still intact. However, he has not affected or controlled the pupils' behaviour in the way he would wish; hence, from a performative perspective, he has failed to work out his authority claims in the form of social power. Crucially, he has failed to gain consent for these claims from his interactional partners. Looked at in this way, the relationship between authority and power is, arguably, reversed, in that, rather than authority being a form of power, power may be seen as a potential outcome of authority.

Authority will be defined here, then, as a form of legitimation that comes to be worked out on an interactional, social, and cultural level. The most obvious example of authority as legitimation is the law itself. The police, the courts, the judiciary are said to have a legal authority. This is also manifested, however, on many other levels of interaction. Parents, for instance, have a legal responsibility, at a number of levels, for their children; in institutions and hospitals doctors will have, again at different levels, responsibility for their patients, and in the classroom teachers operate with a legal authority in relation to their pupils. These are examples of institutional and social allocations of authority in law, and hence legitimation seems an appropriate term.

Outside of the strict legal domain we would argue that authority may also be seen as legitimated, in this case in relation to other dimensions such as personal or cultural knowledge (see Bourdieu 1986, 1992). We say, for instance, that John is an authority on linguistics, meaning that he has an immense knowledge of this area. Or we say that the Talmud is the guiding authority for Jewish behaviour in that it is accepted as a normative set of principles by those of the faith (Billig 1991). Equally, we might accept if I have a pain in my stomach, for instance, that this is something personal to me. The knowledge of my pain cannot normally be legitimately challenged by others since it is my pain, and in this sense I am the authority of my own body ('I should know; it's my stomach'). On an interpersonal level there is a sense in which authority becomes communicatively negotiated, from the very construction of meaning itself (Habermas 1995; Mead 1962) to the choice of who talks when and about what, in both formal and informal contexts (Campion & Langden 2004; Eelen 1993; Ford et al. 2002; Giles & Coupland 1991; Houtkoop-Steenstra 2002; Hutchby 1996; Sacks et al. 1974). And at a social and historical level, the authority claims of what is knowledge, what it is that we know, how we define what we believe and understand, becomes legitimated in what Foucault (1972) has called 'discourse formations' (see Goodrich 1987; Lynch & Woolgar 1990).

Defined as a form of legitimation, legally, culturally, and interactionally constructed, authority comes to be worked out within everyday life as linguistic, pragmatic, practice. In this sense authority issues in pragmatics are much more pervasive than is normally acknowledged. As discussed above, it is power which often gains attention (see Erickson 2004; Fairclough 1992, 2000; Foucault 1972; Lakoff 1992; Mayr 2004; Mumby 1988; Sarangi & Slembrouck 1996; Thornborrow 2002; Watts 1995; Wodak 1996) rather than a recognition that power is frequently the linguistic working out of particular authority claims (see e.g., Verwey 1990 on authority and power in radio talk shows). There is frequently an implicit recognition of this claim in that one often finds the terms power and authority used together (see Bourdieu 1992), and for some scholars the two seem almost synonymous (Reynolds 1990). For us, the argument is that the language of law, medicine, and education emerges from selectional choices that are employed in establishing relationships of power and status against a background of conventional authority claims. Consider the following:

- No Smoking
- No person under the age of 18 is permitted to enter
- All claims for expenses will be set at a limit of £10
- Trespassers will be prosecuted
- Danger. Keep away
- Smoking can damage your health

All of these reflect an authority in their production. Their potential for controlling our actions is reflected not simply in their pronouncement, but in our assumptions or knowledge of the base of their authoritative claims. In a classic speech act sense of appropriate conditions, the voice behind each of these examples is a recognised and appropriate voice of authority (Searle 1969). If we come across a *No smoking* sign in the Underground or at the Airport, we assume that the injunction is projected by the Underground and Airport authorities. In the case of *Trespassers will be prosecuted*, we sometimes see *by order of the police*, where the authority for the injunction is clear. In the case of *Smoking can damage your health*, this is found on the side of cigarette packets and has the voice of the Government's Surgeon General. Here, then, we have the forces of government appeal and medical advice, both authoritative in their own right. What is authoritative is what is accepted as legitimated within different domains through different but appropriate voices. In order to understand authority, therefore, we need to reflect on the various ways in which it comes to be worked out, how it comes, that is, to be legitimated in different contexts.

2. Authority and the self

Perhaps the clearest example of authority in the case of the individual self is personal experience and personal knowledge. Now, of course, there is a sense in which one might argue that the authority of the individual does not exist. What we come to know and believe is interpersonally or socially constructed (Antaki & Widdicombe 1998; Benwell & Stokoe 2006; Billig 1987; Bucholtz & Hall 2005; Habermas 1995; Potter & Wetherell 1987; Shotter & Gergen 1989; Wittgenstein 1953). Mead's work attempts to show how communication as symbolic rule-following only emerges where one takes meaning to be established from the mediated process of understanding oneself and one's actions in terms of the other's reactions as meaning and interpretation; what Mead calls 'taking the attitude of the other', in a more social sense, the 'generalised other' (cf. Habermas 1995: 44). One might suggest, therefore, that access to specific linguistic forms and processes is institutionally and culturally constrained so that the emergent self is seen as grammaticalised in language (see Bucholtz & Hall 2005; Harré 1985, 1989, 1998; Harré & Gillet 1994; Shotter 1993). In this construction of self, interactional, social, and cultural dimensions converge. At one level the 'other' generates a normative basis of authority claims for action and interaction, and the self becomes a construction from within a range of authority claims. Nevertheless, on a more mundane level of what we claim to know as individuals, there is still a primary sense of experience that we present within a framework of cultural assessment, and it is at this primary level that we begin.

At this more basic pragmatic level we can highlight the self and its working out as linguistic practice. In a sense, while one might argue that what we understand from what we see, smell, taste, or touch, is a negotiated social and cultural construction, there is still a core difference between such evidential formulations and those of what we believe or imagine, or that which we are told or given. Here we are in the linguistic realms of evidentiality. This is a primary basis for understanding the authority of our own and others' knowledge of the world and of one another.

Evidentiality is pervasive within the world's languages (see the papers in Chafe & Nichols 1986) and normally signals the morphological marking of evidence types. In English, evidentiality is centrally marked in modality (see Coates 1987; Palmer 1979, 1986). Although modality is, in some respects, difficult to define, paraphrasing Palmer (1986), it is related to the way in which a speaker's subjective attitude or opinion is marked within a sentence (*John may be at home; John could be at home; John might be at home*) and in relation to epistemics (*It is possible that John is at home; I think John is at home; I know that John is at home*). In terms of evidential choice, selection is also differentially marked in terms of the type of evidence one has for one's claims. Sensory experience is particularly important here (*John is at home, I heard/saw him come in*).

There are two senses in which evidentiality is relevant to the pragmatics of authority. The first is the linguistic choice of evidential marking in purely epistemological terms; and the second is the way in which epistemology is affected by the context of production.

In the first case, certain types of evidence receive more acceptance or attention than others; or, in our terms, they are more authoritatively received. For example, if you ask me how much money I have, I might say any of the following:

- Five pounds
- I have five pounds
- I think I have five pounds
- Maybe five pounds
- Some

In each case, differential choice affects the strength of what is said and, equally, the responsibility, or authority claims, in relation to knowledge in the world. If I state

I have five pounds, then I am held strongly to the truth of this fact; *Maybe five pounds* is less strongly implicated, and so on.

Now, not only do we expect speakers to provide us with degrees of evidence (authority) for what they know, but where that evidence or knowledge proves incorrect, we hold the speaker responsible as in *You lied to me*, or *You claimed X was the case*, or *You assured me that Y was the case*, or *You told me P*. Hence speakers are very sensitive to personal epistemological responsibility inherent in what they say. As a result when speakers are not sure of some information they wish to convey, or have been asked to convey, then they might 'hedge' (see Chafe 1986; Holmes 1995; Lakoff 1975; O'Barr 1982) by referring to the statement as a belief, a general thought, an imagined possibility and so on. Equally, if one wishes to increase the strength and positive authority of statements one may mark them in terms of their sensory evidence: *John is at home – I saw him*; *I heard you say X*; *I know how I feel*, and so on. Such types of evidence are considered to be forms of authoritative validation. We are more likely to believe what we have seen with our own eyes, or heard with our own ears. Equally, we are more likely to believe others where they offer such forms of sensory evidence for their claims (although the differing strength of sensory experience as opposed to other forms of experience such as imagination or dreaming will be affected by culture; see papers in Chafe & Nichols 1986).

These options indicate degrees of authority in what we say relative to our knowledge of the world and the evidence we have for that knowledge. The fact that we are held responsible for our epistemological claims, and, further, that these claims may be challenged results in a range of pragmatic practices which assist in negating such challenges and mitigating selected responsibility claims.

One obvious place for the operation of both actions may be found in politics. Politicians' claims are frequently challenged and we are all keen to see politicians held responsible for their claims where these prove unreliable or untrue (Van Dijk 2003). Equally, however, we expect our politicians to be leaders, to know that is what they are doing, to have a directness and strength of purpose. In this sense, an overuse of certain modal forms or limited evidence types may prove problematic (see below for an extension of the same point in relation to the courtroom). It may be for this reason that the general distribution of evidentials within parliamentary debate, for instance, is lower than that found in either conversation or academic writing. Chafe (1986) notes that evidentials occur at a rate, on average, of sixty per thousand words in conversation and sixty-four per thousand in academic writing. Wilson (1995), on the other hand, has found that in parliamentary debate they occur at a rate of only forty per thousand words. A lower rate of evidentials here indicates a higher ratio of bald statements, which are generally given a stronger confidence rating, i.e., they are seen as indicating a greater degree of speaker knowledge in terms of their claims. This distribution of evidentiality types will also vary, however, relative to the context of production (and in relation to culture). The scores for politicians within interviews and speeches, where claims are frequently more prospective and less clearly delimited in terms of evidence, may approximate more closely to the norms of conversation or academic writing. There is a range of other techniques which politicians employ in order to delimit individual responsibility claims: the manipulation of factive and other presuppositional forms (see Epstein 1982) the differential use of personal pronouns (Goffman 1981; Gruber 1993; Maitland & Wilson 1987; Urban 1986; Chilton 2004) and the marking of contextual constraints of time, context, and general limitation; e.g., *at this time*; *in the present fiscal environment*; *we're doing all within our power* (see Eelen 1993).

Another context where individual epistemological responsibility proves pragmatically significant is the courtroom, and indeed in other legal contexts (see Shuy 2001). O'Barr (1982) has shown that 'hedging' may result in negative interpretations of the speakers who use hedging devices. O'Barr distinguishes between powerful and powerless styles, with hedging forming an element within a powerless style. Such powerless styles may be viewed less positively, which means that speakers who adopt such styles may become less convincing or even less believable. This may be understood in terms of authority as to what we as individuals know. If our evidence is marked by hedges, it may be seen as uncertain or limited rather than as a reflection of stylistic choice. If we mark a statement as uncertain in any way, or as based on weaker (e.g., indirect information such as hearsay) rather than stronger evidence (direct sensory experience), then the assumption may be that we are not sure of what we say. In a general Gricean sense (Grice 1975, 1989; see also Sperber & Wilson 1996), there should not be a problem with hedging on evidence; indeed, in some senses, it might be expected (remember Grice's maxims: 'do not say that which is false, or that for which you lack adequate evidence'). It would seem, however, that in the courtroom (and, we would argue, other formal contexts such as debates, teaching, committee meetings and so on), modifiers of our limited understanding are not seen in a Gricean way as an individual doing the best they can with limited information, but, rather, as a sign of weakness, or a lack of authority in one's own knowledge.

Individual authority also seems to be affected by context and audience in the medical encounter. The medical encounter has been studied in detail from an interactional perspective (e.g., Atkinson 1995; Heritage & Maynard 2006; Roberts & Sarangi 2003; Sarangi & Roberts 1999; Silverman 1990) and underlying most of the work is an assumption that the doctor's knowledge gives them power. This is true, but like all knowledge the doctor's information is affected by the context of the interaction. It has been shown that while doctors might say to patients *You have an X problem*, this may become reworked if the doctor is talking to a colleague of similar status as *I think he/she has got X*; or in talking to a superior this might become *I believe from the evidence I have that it's X*. The knowledge statements frequently expressed by doctors (and indeed other professionals) are never as exact or precise as they may seem to the patient. Traditionally, the patients' ignorance and acceptance of the doctor's knowledge as authority has meant that they are not in a position to challenge any medical claims (but see below). Other professional doctors are in such a position, however. Hence, the authority of professional medical knowledge (and other areas of professional knowledge) is interactionally affected by the level of relevant knowledge held by the interlocutor. This reflects the way in which individual knowledge claims become constrained by the context of relative authority in interaction (in both institutional and knowledge terms).

Also, knowledge as authority is rarely static. In the case of doctors we must remember why we approach them in the first place; it is because we believe they have access to information and skills of specific relevance to our own needs. In this sense we recognise the doctor's authority within the medical domain. The boundaries of this domain may vary depending on how far we believe the doctor's authority reaches. With evergrowing use of the Internet, today's patients can access a wealth of medical knowledge from their own homes/offices. This potentially challenges the doctor's traditional authority by placing the doctor-patient relationship on a more equal footing (Broom 2005; Nwosu & Cox 2000). In addition, there is a real sense in which the patient is the ultimate authority on his/her bodily sensations and experiences (e.g., pain; see above) and, hence, on his/her 'symptoms'. This point is not often foregrounded within the medical framework, but it becomes apparent when, for example, a patient's symptoms cannot be medically diagnosed. Here, the 'infallibility' of the patient's knowledge contrasts with the doctor's imperfect knowledge, thereby shifting the authority relationship in favour of the patient (Peters et al. 1998).

In recent times, doctors and other health practitioners (in conjunction with governments) have gone beyond the domain of medical consultation, and actively encouraged and supported the propagation of particular life styles. This preventive medical perspective moves beyond the waiting room to attempt to control the way we live. Authority claims in this broader domain are, however, more controversial, since agreement on what is and what is not possible for a healthy life varies from specialist to specialist. General public reaction to such authority claims are accordingly much more varied and muted.

3. Authority in each other

There are a number of levels on which one might consider authority in interpersonal relations. At the simplest level there is a sense in which the pragmatic structure of talk in interaction is designed to distribute authority in specific structural ways. The turn-taking system (Sacks et al. 1974) distributes authority through its rules about who speaks when (turn initiator vs. turn recipient); and adjacency pairs constrain who has the right and authority to respond to particular first-pair parts, and they constrain what kinds of second-pair parts are legitimate (questions normally receive answers, for example). As these structures become worked out in context, they contribute directly to the definition and creation of social structure itself. The social structure of formal encounters such as teaching, medical diagnoses, legal trials, business meetings, news interviews and so on, is in part delimited by authority claims to questions, turns, topics etc. (Boden 1994; Boden & Zimmerman 1991; Clayman & Heritage 2002; Dingwall 2000; Heritage 2003; Heritage & Greatbatch 1991; Hutchby 1996, 2005; Schegloff 1991; Travers & Manzo 1997). As mentioned above, doctors control not only the quantitative distribution of questions, but also the limits of response. West (1990) has shown, for instance, that while patients do ask doctors questions, doctors rarely answer these questions, and where they do, they rarely answer them directly (although, as indicated above, developments in electronic information access are increasingly challenging the conventional doctor-patient relationship). In the classroom, teachers control not only the range of topics and the distribution of questions, but they also define the limits of what is seen as legitimate responses to questions. Further, Buzzelli & Johnston (2001) highlight the ways in which concepts of *morality* are played out in relation to the teacher's authority within classroom discourse. In the courtroom, the barrister/lawyer has very specific authority rights to questions, questioning techniques and formulations of events. To this extent, the courtroom becomes a site in which lawyers and barristers can legitimately construct particular versions of events (see, e.g., Ehrlich 1999). Moreover, through the conventions and constraints of courtroom discourse, professional legal identities are constructed, challenged and/or maintained (Bogoch 1999).

Outside these standard and formal contexts, authority is also being worked out interpersonally in more informal interaction. Eelen (1993) claims that what is talked about in general social relations is negotiated in terms of the authorities speakers create ('hierarchical relationships') through the interaction itself. This may be seen at two ends of the interpersonal spectrum. Initial encounters are defined, in part, in relation to strategies of self-disclosure, the information one provides about oneself. Self-disclosure acts, according to Berger (1979), as a form of reduction of uncertainty. Language acts as a tool for accessing information and creating predictability and complementarity. Control of information, along with the authority of when and how to use it, resides with each individual. If we wish to reveal information, but limit its distribution, we may mark the information as limited (*confidentially speaking; I wouldn't say this outside this room; between you and me*). When participants have achieved a high level of complementarity, as in intimate relationships (Duck 1982), authority over knowledge domains becomes more relaxed. Couples involved in an intimate relationship offer up to each other almost all domains of knowledge held by the individual self. Interestingly, in this respect, Hopper (1981) has argued that the indication of a relationship decline is that control of information and limitation of involvement in certain topics increases. This is not to say that relationship development is simply the reverse of relationship decline (this is an area of some controversy; see Baxter 1985; Duck 1982), but in authority terms, rights of access are clearly opened up and closed down relative to the degree of intimacy in a relationship.

Within interpersonal interaction there are a host of dimensions within which one might explore authority claims. Access to talk in general, or topics, or narratives or specific styles, and so on, are not only affected by such things as sex, age, ethnic or religious affiliation but actively contribute to their social construction (Benwell & Stokoe 2006; Bucholtz & Hall 2005; Coates 1996; Cameron 1995; Giles & Coupland 1991). Since it is agreed that constraints on talk (topic, turns etc.) within informal contexts are negotiated (as opposed to institutionally displayed, as in the courts, or in the classroom; although see Giddens 1984), there is an assumption, as with any negotiation, that different parties have some say on how the interaction should proceed. In the informal context (and many institutional contexts), we always have the right to withdraw (through silence, or by closing down the encounter). In this process all of us have a degree of authority in the interaction, and the relative distribution of this authority interacts with, and in the process socially constructs, features such as gender, class, and status.

4. Authority in the world

What we know about our external world has been dominated and driven by authority claims about that world, as they are given back to us via areas such as science, medicine, history, and so on. There is a sense in which knowledge of the world outside of the self and interpersonal domains (but still being affected by and interacting with these) is legitimated in society via normative processes of education and behaviour. The dominance of scientific and other forms of knowledge in this century has been clearly documented (e.g., Foucault 1972; Lynch & Woolgar 1990; Lyotard 1984). Nevertheless, in more recent analyses, claims founded on such externalised knowledge have been challenged. A Wittgensteinian inspired ordinary language analysis has revealed the way in which so-called 'representation devices' (devices for describing an independent external world such as maps, machine readings and so on; Tibbets 1990) are interpreted and understood not within some context-free objective environment, but in relation to forms of linguistic practice. Foucault (1972) has been particularly clear on the way in which knowledge is grounded within specific discourse formations; and within social constructionism (Harré 1985, 1998; Shotter 1993), the rhetoric of a positivistic world is deconstructed and laid bare.

As an influential example of this approach, Discursive Psychology (Edwards 1997; Edwards & Potter 1992; Potter 1996, 2000; Potter & Wetherell 1987) has shown us how the authority of the experimental perspective within human interaction may be replaced by the real world of pragmatic production in everyday practice. The authority for one's own memory, for example, or for how one accounts for one's actions, is taken out of the range of objective measures and placed back where it belongs, where it came from; i.e., from real people in a real world of interaction. In addition, work in the Sociology of Scientific Knowledge (e.g., Gilbert & Mulkay 1984; Latour & Woolgar 1986) has shown how scientific accounts are constructed within different discursive repertoires (of commitment, belief, empiricism, contingency) and so on, depending on the context and purpose of production (see also Jasanoff et al. 2002; Potter 1996). On another level, Critical Discourse Analysis has been central in bringing forward a critical linguistic view of socially received information, challenging the cultural and ideological authority claims operative within a range of social institutions.

5. Authority in (and through) God

When religion and state are coterminous, aspects of religious talk take on not simply religious authority, but also legal authority. This may be seen in the blasphemy laws of various countries where comment on specific deities or aspects of these deities may be prosecuted under the law; or, less contentiously, in such things as marriage rites, christenings, and burials, which are completed through the use of the authority of the Church, as represented by ordained priests and ministers.

The issue of the language of religion has always contained a tension regarding who or what is the authorial voice. When Moses, for example, delivers the Ten Commandments to the Israelites they are literally the word of God, words therefore of ultimate authority. More indirectly, many of the Old Testament prophets claimed to be speaking their message from God. Hence, the authority of what they said was not in them, but through them, in God; they were literally 'the mouth of God'. This notion was further developed following the death of Jesus, as debates emerged regarding the Gospels. Were these descriptive accounts, provided by disciples who were with Jesus or did they have some form of divine authority? Indeed, in John 1: verse 1, it is stated that *In the beginning was the word and the word was with God, and the word was God.*

The emergence and development of Christianity required administration and organisation. The early Christian communities required leaders who "shall instruct the congregation in the works of God he shall love them as a father loves his children and shall carry them in his distress like a Shepherd does his sheep" (Vermes 2000, cited in Freeman 2005: 124). Such a role would be taken by the Bishops, who developed as a specific elite community charged by God to provide institutional authority in the Church, through sacraments and interpretation of the scriptures. This authority of interpretation meant that only in the Bishops could it be decided what was the word of God. In the Roman Catholic Church, to the present day, the Pope continues to be seen as 'infallible', insofar as he is seen as the earthly representative of God.

Of course, Christianity is only one perspective on religious authority. The 21st century is witnessing a clash between the western Christian view and the view of Islam, which is partly evidenced in the claims to authority over what one might say. For instance, in 1989, the Iranian ruler, Ayatollah Ruhollah Khomeini, issued a fatwa (or Islamic legal ruling), calling for the assassination of the British-Indian writer, Salman Rushdie, following the publication of Rushdie's novel, *The Satanic Verses*. This novel was based on a controversial and highly contested account of the life of the prophet Muhammad, and was seen as offensive, indeed blasphemous, by many Muslims worldwide. A more recent example is the controversy over the 'Muhammad cartoons', first published by a Danish newspaper in September 2005 and later reprinted by newspapers in more than fifty countries. Seen as blasphemous and insulting, the cartoons led to intense and sometimes violent protests by Muslims worldwide.

Similarly, as part of his rhetoric on the second Iraq war, President G.W. Bush has, on occasion, referred to a 'crusade' against terrorism, gesturing at the moral and religious basis not only of his own faith, but also of the actions of the USA. This, in turn, has inspired radical Islamic leaders to talk of a holy war against the Islamic faith. Sheikh Ahmed Yassin described the actions of the west as "a crusader's aggression, a crusader's war, and an occupation" (Greene 2003: 2). Indeed, since the 9/11 attacks in New York, President Bush has constructed a sustained discursive and rhetorical framework in which 'good' and 'evil' are moral absolutes, and in which the US and its often faceless enemies are pitted against each other in a 'war on terror' (see, e.g., Coe et al. 2004; Smith 2005). In this way, President Bush calls upon a moral authority through which the actions of the US are not only justified, but beyond reproach as part of 'the good fight'. Graham et al. (2004) see this discursive move as a defining feature of historical and present-day 'calls to arms'. Having examined four such speeches, they identify four generic features, which characterise the discourse: (i) an appeal to an external legitimate power source, which is seen as both legitimate and 'good'; (ii) an appeal to the historical significance of 'our' culture; (iii) the construction of the enemy as inherently evil; and (iv) an appeal to unify 'behind the legitimating external power source'. Graham et al. claim that such appeals are generally made when there is a crisis of political legitimacy, serving as a means of (re)legitimising the present government and its actions. In the present case, and in many others, the legitimating external power source is God. Hence, the moral absolutes, linked rhetorically in this way, can be seen as an attempt by President Bush and other political leaders to effect their own political authority through an alignment with the highest moral authority of God.

6. Authority and gender

Much has been written about the relationships between gender, language/discourse and power. Research in Language and Gender (L&G) has shown how gender hierarchies are both codified within language itself and enacted in everyday linguistic interaction (e.g., Cameron 1990; Coates 1993, 1998; Crawford 1995; Holmes & Meyerhoff

2003; Lakoff 1975; Litosseliti & Sunderland 2002; Mills 1995; Pauwels 1998; Romaine 1999; Spender 1980). Early work on 'women's language' suggested that women's speech was 'powerless' and deferent, thereby both reflecting and maintaining their subordinate position in society (e.g., DeFrancisco 1991; Fishman 1983; Lakoff 1975). Others have suggested that male and female speech are 'culturally' different from one another, with women being oriented towards relationships, emotions and intimacy and men towards tasks, facts and status (see Tannen 1990).

Today, most L&G research is conducted within a broadly social constructionist framework (see Stapleton 2001). Such approaches recognise that, in any culture, there are gendered speech styles (i.e., styles which, at an ideological level, are associated with either men or women), but that, in reality, these styles are not limited to either gender, and can be used by any speaker to create a particular type of (gender) identity (e.g., Bergvall et al. 1996; Cameron 1998; Hall & Bucholtz 1995; Romaine 1999). However, these identities are presented and constituted within particular contexts of interpretation. In their highly influential application of 'communities of practice' to sociolinguistics, Eckert and McConnell-Ginet (1992, 1999) have proposed that identities are constituted through specific sets of practices (e.g., ways of talking, hand gestures, style of dress, beliefs and values), which emerge within particular, mutually engaged, communities (e.g., a sports team, a family, a professional occupation) and are simultaneously located within the wider social and cultural context. These practices both help to define the community itself and offer members the means of constituting themselves *as* community members.

Perceptions and expectations of gendered speech clearly have implications for the enactment of authority by men and women. Women have traditionally had less participation than men in public, formal contexts, i.e., those that emphasise status differentials and task performance. This historical fact is, perhaps, reflected in notions of 'feminine' speech styles, which are typically seen as more indirect, polite, other-oriented, egalitarian and collaborative (Coates 1996; Holmes 1995, 2000; Holmes & Schnurr 2006; Kendall & Tannen 1997). In positions of authority, then, women are more likely to adopt face-saving strategies, such as mitigating directives/orders and using indirect means of obtaining compliance (Tannen 1994; Wodak 1995). Many studies have shown that, when appropriately contextualised, such strategies are, in fact, highly effective on a 'task' level; for example, in terms of female doctors gaining compliance from their patients (West 1990, 1995) and female managers from their workers (see Holmes et al. 2003). Nonetheless, normative expectations (of both 'women's speech' and formal/authoritative language) mean that women are often perceived to be less suited to or less competent in positions of authority. Crawford (1995), for example, points to the many assertiveness programmes aimed specifically at women (see also Cameron 1995), while Coates (1995: 13) proposes that "gender-differentiated language use may play a significant role in the continued marginalisation of women in the professions". Indeed, a range of empirical studies have shown that women can face very real struggles to maintain authority in male-dominated institutional contexts, due to such things as interruptions, task-divergent talk and struggles over the conversational floor; see Conefrey's (1997) conversation analytic and ethnographic study of laboratory interactions; Bergvall and Remlinger's (1996) CDA study of university classroom discourse; and Bogoch's (1999) quantitative and qualitative analyses of courtroom interaction in the US, which showed how the professional competence of female judges and lawyers was challenged and undermined through frequency and type of directives, interruptions, address terms, challenging interjections and, in the case of lawyers, judges' takeover of examinations.

However, in many cases, women working within institutional or business contexts – particularly in traditionally male-dominated domains – simply adopt a more 'masculine' speech style in line with the institutional norms and culture (Coates 1995). McElhinny (1998), in her study of female police officers, argues that by converging to the male norm in this way, women are not necessarily trying to present a more masculine identity, but rather to forge a credible and professional identity, as interpreted within the institutional culture. Other studies support this claim. Bogoch (1997), for example, found little difference between male and female lawyers' interactions with clients, and concluded that female lawyers' talk is 'role behavior rather than gendered behavior'. (Incidentally, this study also showed that both male and female clients showed more deference to the male lawyers.) However, given the strength of prevailing expectations about feminine speech, research has shown that women who do adopt a more direct and forceful speech style are often judged negatively by their colleagues, being seen as, for example, 'pushy', domineering or aggressive (see Holmes et al. 2003; Kendall & Tannen 1997; Walsh 2001). In the world of politics, Shaw (2000) has shown that in Westminster parliamentary debates, female MPs who successfully adopt the aggressive conventions and techniques of this genre are judged negatively by their peers. In contrast, male MPs who master this style are seen as successful politicians. Such perceptions, then, do not provide a good basis for legitimating authority claims; and, indeed, in this study, Shaw demonstrates how women MPs continually struggle to compete on equal terms with their male colleagues. Other studies, however, have shown that women *can* successfully negotiate the twin demands of 'doing authority' and 'doing femininity'. Holmes & Schnurr (2006), in their analyses of workplace interactions, demonstrate that 'femininity', as constituted in discursive and interactional practice, *is* accepted as both 'normal' and effective in many workplace contexts. They also highlight the fact that, in such contexts, women perform 'multiple femininities', through their use of normative and non-normative strategies of talk and interaction.

In summary, then, the relationship between gender, language and authority is a complex one, which fully highlights the interplay between linguistic, social, cultural and contextual factors.

7. Authority in language

Language is an area where authority claims arise in the form of both prescriptions and descriptions. Linguistics frequently defines itself in this distinction, with prescription being seen as negative and normative comment on what speakers should do, as opposed to a positive descriptive approach in relation to what speakers actually do. As Cameron (1995) has perceptively pointed out, linguists' descriptions are themselves frequently couched in a formal format, which by its very nature is an injunction to follow a rule. (In this vein, Verschueren (1999) has discussed the ways in which Pragmatics, itself, has become institutionalised as a discipline; and how academic authority is established and maintained within this discipline.) What we have, then, in the prescription/description distinction is a clash of different authority claims (see Bex & Watts 1999). What is possible and not possible in language becomes formulated in different ways and in different styles of argument, depending on the authority one draws upon. Linguistics attempts to avoid forms of social influence/bias (i.e., specific subjective comments) on what is defined as acceptable or unacceptable speech (grammatical vs. ungrammatical) because of linguistics' affiliation with the objective processes of science (in most textbooks linguistics is described as 'the science of language'). The normative claims of the prescriptivists are various, but they reside in the maintenance of difference, inequality and domination (Cameron 1995; Edwards 1989; Hymes 1996). While stating how language should be used for the benefit of all members in society, prescriptivists, by their very claims, deny automatically the rights of all those in society whose education, experience and culture is different from the standard.

Prescription is seen as the appeal to an authority in language such as a dictionary, a grammar, a standard dialect (see Milroy & Milroy 2005). Indeed, such appeals frequently reference a specific, named authority (e.g., Webster, Fowler, the Oxford English Dictionary). In recent years, we have seen a renewed interest in prescriptivist ideas within popular culture. Lynne Truss's book *Eats, Shoots and Leaves* (2003) is one prominent and fashionable example of the call for greater adherence to prescriptions of grammar and punctuation. Such prescriptions assume certain predefined standards in language use, particularly those found in the written form, but also in terms of spoken standards in accent as well (see Lippi-Green 1997; Mugglestone 2003). The history and nature of prescription has been well charted in recent times (Cameron 1995; Milroy & Milroy 2005; Mugglestone 2003; Wright 2006). In general it is interconnected with processes of standardisation, and the emergence of particular attitudes to language. It is at this level of attitude that the pragmatics of authority seems particularly relevant. In terms of what Mey (1993) has called 'societal pragmatics', where particular linguistic choices become more powerful and dominant, while others are denigrated and rejected. This is not merely a judgement of whether one uses the correct style or grammar, but such choices become tied to ideological motivations above and beyond language itself. Consider the following quotes (cited in Cameron 1995: 94):

The overthrow of grammar coincided with the acceptance of the equivalent of creative writing in social behaviour. As nice points of grammar were mockingly dismissed as pedantic or irrelevant, so was punctiliousness in such matters as honesty, responsibility, property gratitude and so on. (John Rae, *The Observer* 7th February 1982).

If you allow standards to slip to the stage where good English is no better than bad English, where people turn up filthy at school ... all of these things tend to cause people to have no standards at all, and once you lose standards then there is no imperative to stay out of crime.(Norman Tebbit, MP Radio 4, 1985).

In these examples a drop in grammatical standards correlates with a decline in societal standards. Natural dialects which deviate from the standard do not become associated simply with variation, but with dishonesty, filth and crime. Such claims are, to use Cameron's words, 'baffling'. But they are, nonetheless, influential; and the authority of a correct standard in language is something found in most cultures (see Hymes 1996). What it has meant in Britain is a continual cycle of arguments of decline in the English language followed by a push for the problem to be solved through proper educational standards in the teaching of English in schools (Cameron & Bourne 1989). This generally means the domination of one particular dialect of English (Standard English) over all other dialect possibilities (Bex & Watts 1999; Wright 2006).

Such outcomes, then, follow from a symbolic and moral association with authority as hierarchy. Membership of particular groups in society is defined most readily by language (see Clement 1996; Labov 1972; Milroy 1985; Wright 2006). Those in positions of power adopt particular styles because they believe these have a natural authority of correctness; and, therefore, any deviations from these are not only wrong, but mark others as outside the establishment and acceptance of this authority. This is readily evidenced in numerous studies of language attitudes towards standard and non-standard speech. To take one example: Dixon et al. (2002) found, in a matched guise test, that a male criminal suspect who spoke with a non-standard dialect (in this case, Birmingham or 'Brummie') was judged to be 'significantly more guilty' than a counterpart who spoke with a standard accent. Looking specifically at gendered social/linguistic judgements, Gordon (1997) found that New Zealand women who spoke with a non-standard accent were judged not only as socially or intellectually inferior to their 'standard' counterparts, but as likely to be *morally* inferior as well. Hence, dialects become disempowered and, in modern society, those without access to the standard, or who refuse to use it, become disenfranchised in accessing their rights in areas such as welfare; and in negotiating a position for themselves and their children within employment and education (Sarangi & Slembrouck 1996; Soukup 2001; Wilson & Haugh 1995).

At another level of linguistic organisation, i.e., language planning, language selection within emerging or established nation states may operate in a very similar way (see Blommaert 1996). Who speaks which language and where, and which language is used for education or business may become politically driven. And this takes us back to where we began. We are back to legitimation in the context of legal and constitutional rights; in this case, the right to determine, from among a range of options, the language of the state (Su Hwi 1996). Clearly, this selection may be driven, as in the case of dialects, by social rather than linguistic forces. This need not be the case, however, and language planning influenced by linguistic practice may offer up a more rational approach to national issues of linguistic selection. Nevertheless, we must bear in mind that for language planners, like linguists in general, formulations are rule-, or theory-based; and such rules and theories, to extend Cameron's point, offer themselves as a form of authority for action or, in some cases, inaction.

In the modern communication context, new and emerging issues are also being prescribed, if not in the explicitly defined manner of 'correct' vs. 'incorrect' language judgements. Baron (2002), for example, analyses stylistic conventions in email communication as, partly, prescriptively derived from other social contexts of language use. Specifically, she considers the extent to which the individual has freedom to negotiate these prescriptions within this emergent language medium. Cameron (2000) critically discusses the current emphasis on communication as inherently beneficial (literally, 'good to talk'). Referencing genres such as sales encounters, call centres and talk shows, she demonstrates that a prevailing discourse across these (and many other) domains is the 'discourse of therapy'. This carries its own specific prescriptions about what constitutes good (or successful/skilled/effective) communication; e.g., British Telecom's suggestions for achieving more effective conversations. Thus, Cameron shows how this 'technologized' and scripted approach to talk represents a particular version of language stylisation, standardisation and regulation/surveillance within the (post)modern context.

8. Authority

We have touched on a broad range of domains within which authority may be said to operate. Taking legitimation as both a formal and negotiated concept, authority is the legitimation of certain linguistic practices within social life. In this sense it is more widespread than we have normally been willing to consider. There is an argument, however, that the lack of attention to authority has been because where it has worked, it produces other outcomes than itself: e.g., power, status, class, gender, law, government. In this sense, authority has been widely studied within pragmatics, but not always by that name.

References

Antaki, C. & S. Widdicombe (1998). *Identities in Talk*. Sage.
Atkinson, P. (1995). *Medical Talk and Medical Work*. Sage.
Baron, N.S. (2002). Who sets email style? Prescriptivism, coping strategies, and democratizing communication access. *The Information Society* 18(5): 403–413.
Baxter, L.A. (1985). Accomplishing relationship disengagement. In S. Duck & D. Perlmann (eds.) *Understanding Personal Relationships*: 243–265. Sage.
Benwell, B. & E. Stokoe (2006). *Discourse and Identity*. Edinburgh University Press.
Berger, C.R. (1979). Beyond initial interaction. Uncertainty understanding and the development of interpersonal relationships. In H. Giles & R.N. St Clair (eds.) *Language and Social Psychology*: 122–144. Blackwell.
Bergvall, V.L., J.M. Bing & A.F. Freed (1996). *Rethinking Language and Gender Research*. Longman.
Bergvall, V.L. & K.A. Remlinger (1996). Reproduction, resistance and gender in educational discourse: The role of Critical Discourse Analysis. *Discourse and Society* 7(4): 453–480.
Bex, T. & R.J. Watts (eds.) (1999). *Standard English: The Widening Debate*. Routledge.
Billig, M. (1987). *A Rhetorical Approach to Social Psychology*. Cambridge University Press.
——— (1991). Ideology Rhetoric and Opinions. London. Sage.
Blommaert, J. (1996). The politics of multilingualism and language planning: Introduction. In J. Blommaert (ed.) *The Politics of Multilingualism and Language Planning. Antwerp Papers in Linguistics* 87: 3–26.
Boden, D. (1994). *The Business of Language*. Polity Press.
Boden, D. & D.H. Zimmerman (1991). *Talk and Social Structure*. Polity Press.
Bogoch, P. (1997). Gendered lawyering: Difference and dominance in lawyer-client interaction. *Law and Society Review* 31(4): 677–712.
——— (1999). Courtroom discourse and the gendered construction of professional identity. *Law and Social Inquiry* 24(2): 329–375.
Bourdieu, P. (1986). The forms of capital. In J. Richardson (ed.) *Handbook of Theory and Research for the Sociology of Education*: 241–258. Greenwood Press.
——— (1992). *Language and Symbolic Power*. Polity Press.
Broom, A. (2005). Medical specialists' accounts of the impact of the Internet on the doctor/patient relationship. *Health* 9(3): 319–338.
Bucholtz, M. & K. Hall (2005). Identity and interaction: A sociocultural linguistic approach. *Discourse Studies* 7(4/5): 585–614.
Buzzelli, C.A. & A. Johnston (2001). Authority, power and morality in classroom discourse. *Teaching and Teacher Education* 17(8): 873–884.
Cameron, D. (1995). *Verbal Hygiene*. Routledge.
——— (1998). 'Is there any Ketchup, Vera?': Gender, power and pragmatics. *Discourse and Society* 9(4): 437–455.
——— (2000). *Good to Talk? Living and Working in a Communication Culture*. Sage.
——— (ed.) (1990). *The Feminist Critique of Language*. Routledge.
Cameron, D. & J. Bourne (1989). No common ground: Kingman, grammar and the nation. *Language and Education* 2(3): 147–160.
Campion, P. & M. Langdon (2004). Achieving multiple topic shifts in primary care medical consultations: A conversation analysis study in U.K. general practice. *Sociology of Health & Illness* 26(1): 81–101.

Chafe, W. (1986). Evidentiality in English conversation and academic writing. In W. Chafe & J. Nichols (eds.): 261–273.
Chafe, W. & J. Nichols (eds.) (1986). *Evidentiality: The Linguistic Coding of Epistemology*. Ablex.
Chilton, P. (2004). *Analysing Political Discourse*. Routledge.
Clayman, S. & J. Heritage (2002). *The News Interview: Journalists and Public Figures on the Air*. Cambridge University Press.
Clement, R. (1996). The Social Psychology of Intergroup Communication. *Journal of Language and Social Psychology* 15(3).
Coates, J. (1987). Epistemic modality and spoken discourse. *Transactions of the Philological Society*: 110–131.
—— (1993). *Women, Men and Language*, 2nd ed. Longman.
—— (1995). Language, gender and career. In S. Mills (ed.): 13–30.
—— (1996). *Women Talk*. Blackwell.
—— (1998). *Language and Gender: A Reader*. Blackwell.
Coe, K., D. Domke, E.S. Graham, S.L. John & V.W. Pickard (2004). No shades of gray: The binary discourse of George W. Bush and an echoing press. *Journal of Communication* 54(2): 234–252.
Conefrey, T. (1997). Gender, culture and authority in a university life sciences laboratory. *Discourse and Society* 8(3): 313–340.
Crawford, M. (1995). *Talking Difference: On Gender and Language*. Sage.
DeFrancisco, V. (1991). The sound of silence: How men silence women in marital relationships. *Discourse and Society* 2(4): 413–424.
Dingwall, R. (2000). Language, law and power: Ethnomethodology, Conversation Analysis and the politics of law and society studies. *Law and Social Inquiry* 25(3): 885–911.
Dixon, J.A., B. Mahoney & R. Cocks (2002). Accents of guilt? Effects of regional accent, 'race' and crime type on attributions of guilt. *Journal of Language and Social Psychology* 21(2): 162–168.
Duck, S. (1982). A topography of relationship disengagement and dissolution. In S. Duck (ed.) *Personal Relationships 4: Dissolving Relationships*: 141–162. Academic Press.
Eckert, P. & S. McConnell-Ginet (1992). Think practically and look locally: Language and gender as community-based practice. *Annual Review of Anthropology* 21: 461–490.
—— (1999). New generalisations and explanations in language and gender research. *Language in Society* 28(2): 185–201.
Edley, N. & M. Wetherell (1997). Jockeying for position: The construction of masculine identities. *Discourse and Society* 8(2): 203–217.
Edwards, D. (1997). *Discourse and Cognition*. Sage.
Edwards, D. & J. Potter (1992). *Discursive Psychology*. Sage.
Edwards, J. (1989). *Language and Disadvantage*. Cole & Whurr.
Eelen, G. (1993). Authority in international political discourse: A pragmatic analysis of United Nations documents on the Congo Crisis. *Text* 13(1): 29–63.
Ehrlich, S. (1999). Communities of practice, gender and the representation of sexual assault. *Language in Society* 28(2): 239–256.
Epstein, J.P. (1982). The grammar of a lie. In R.J. De Pietro (ed.) *Language and the Professions*: 133–143. Ablex.
Erickson, F. (2004). *Talk and Social Theory*. Polity Press.
Fairclough, N. (1989). *Language and Power*. Longman.

—— (1992). *Discourse and Social Change*. Polity Press.
—— (1995). *Critical Discourse Analysis: The Critical Study of Language*. Longman.
—— (2000). Discourse, social theory and social research: The discourse of welfare reform. *Journal of Sociolinguistics* 4(2): 163–195.
Fishman, P. (1983). Interaction: The work women do. In B. Thorne, C. Kramarae & N. Henley (eds.) *Language, Gender and Society*: 89–101. Newbury House.
Ford, C.E., B.A. Fox & S.A. Thompson (eds.) (2002). *The Language of Turn and Sequence*. Oxford University Press.
Foucault, M. (1972). *The Archaeology of Knowledge*. Tavistock Publications.
Freeman, C. (2005). *The Closing of the Western Mind*. Vintage.
Gal, S. (1993). Diversity and contestation in linguistic ideologies: German speakers in Hungary. *Language in Society* 22(3): 337–359.
Giddens, A. (1984). *The Constitution of Society: Outline of a Theory of Structuration*. Polity Press.
Gilbert, G.N. & M. Mulkay (1984). *Opening up Pandora's Box: A sociological Analysis of Scientists' Discourse*. Cambridge University Press.
Giles, H. & N. Coupland (1991). *Language Contexts and Consequences*. Open University Press.
Goffman, E. (1981). *Forms of Talk*. Basil Blackwell.
Goodrich, P. (1987). *Legal Discourse*. MacMillan.
Gordon, E. (1997). Sex, speech and stereotypes: Why women use prestige forms more than men. *Language in Society* 26(1): 47–63.
Graham, P., T. Keenan & A.M. Dowd (2004). A call to arms at the end of history: A discourse–historical analysis of George W. Bush's declaration of war on terror. *Discourse and Society* 15(2/3): 199–221.
Greene, D.L. (2003). Bush turns increasingly to language of religion. *Common Dreams News Center* 1–4 (www.commondreams.org/headlines, 2006).
Grice, H.P. (1975). Logic and conversation. In P. Cole & J.L. Morgan (eds.) *Syntax and Semantics Vol. 3: Syntax and Semantics*. Academic Press.
—— (1989). *Studies in the Ways of Words*. Harvard University Press.
Gruber, H. (1993). Political language and textual vagueness. *Pragmatics* 3(1): 1–28.
Habermas, J. (1995). *The Theory of Communicative Action*. Cambridge University Press.
Hall, K. & M. Bucholtz (eds.) (1995). *Gender Articulated: Language and the Socially Constructed Self*. Routledge.
Harre, R. (1985). The Language Game of Self Ascription: a note In K.J. Gergen & K.E. Davis (eds.) *The Social Construction of The Person*: 259–265. Springer-Verlag.
—— (1989). Language games and texts of identity. In J. Shotter & K. Gergen (eds.) *Texts of Identity*: 20–36. Sage.
—— (1998). *The Singular Self: An Introduction to the Psychology of Personhood*. Sage.
Harre, R. & G. Gillet (1994). *The Discursive Mind*. Sage.
Heller, M. (2001). Undoing the macro/micro dichotomy: Ideology and categorisation in a linguistic minority school. In N. Coupland, S. Sarangi & C.N. Candlin (eds.) *Sociolinguistics and Social Theory*: 212–235. Longman.
Heritage, J. (2003). Designing questions and setting agendas in the news interview. In P. Glenn, C.D. LeBaron & J. Mandelbaum (eds.) *Studies in Language and Social Interaction: In honor of Robert Hopper*: 57–90. Lawrence Erlbaum.
Heritage, J. & D. Greatbatch (1991). On the institutional character of institutional talk: the case of news interviews. In D. Boden & D.H. Zimmerman (eds.) *Talk and Social Structure*: 93–138. Polity Press.

Heritage, J. & D.W. Maynard (eds.) (2006). *Communication in Medical Care: Interaction Between Primary Care Physicians and Patients.* Cambridge University Press.
Holmes, J. (1995). *Women, Men and Politeness.* Longman.
—— (2000). Women at work: Analysing women's talk in New Zealand workplaces. *Australian Review of Applied Linguistics* 22(2): 1–17.
Holmes, J. & M. Meyerhoff (eds.) (2003). *The Handbook of Language and Gender.* Blackwell.
Holmes, J. & S. Schnurr (2006). 'Doing femininity' at work: More than just relational practice. *Journal of Sociolinguistics* 10(1): 31–51.
Holmes, J., L. Burns, M. Marra, M. Stubbe & B. Vine (2003). Women managing discourse in the workplace. *Women in Management Review* 18(8): 414–424.
Hopper, P. (1981). The taken for granted. *Human Communication Reserach* 7: 195–211.
Houtkoop-Steenstra, H. (2002). Questioning turn format and turn-taking problems in standardized interviews. In D.W. Maynard, H. Houtkoop-Steenstra, N.C. Schaeffer & J. van der Zouwen (eds.) *Standardization and Tacit Knowledge: Interaction and Practice in the Survey Interview:* 243–261. John Wiley.
Hutchby, I. (1996). Power in discourse: the case of arguments on a British talk radio show. *Discourse and Society* 7(4): 481–499.
—— (2005). *Media Talk: Conversation Analysis and the Study of Broadcasting.* Open University Press.
Hymes, D. (1996). *Ethnography, Linguistics, Narrtive Inequality: Toward an Understanding of Voice.* Taylor & Francis.
Jasanoff, S., G.E. Merkle, J.C. Peterson & T.J. Pinch (eds.) (2002). *Handbook of Science and Technology Studies.* Sage.
Kendall, S. & D. Tannen (1997). Gender and language in the workplace. In R. Wodak (ed.) *Gender and Discourse*: 81–105. Sage.
Labov, W.A. (1972). The logic of non standard English. In W.A. Labov (1972) *Language in The Inner City: Studies in the Black English Vernacular.* University of Philadelphia Press.
Lakoff, R. (1975). *Language and Women's Place.* Harper.
—— (1992). *Talking Power.* Sage.
Latour, B. & S. Woolgar (1986). *Laboratory Life: The Construction of Scientific Facts,* 2nd ed. Princeton University Press.
Lemke, J.L. (1995). *Textual politics: Discourse and Social Dynamics.* Taylor & Francis.
Lippi-Green, R. (1997). *English with an Accent: Language, Ideology and Discrimination in the United States.* Routledge.
Litosseliti, L. & J. Sunderland (eds.) (2002). *Gender Identity and Discourse Analysis.* John Benjamins.
Lynch, M. & S. Woolgar (1990). *Representation and Scientific Practice.* Mass. MIT Press.
Lyotard, J.F. (1984). *The Postmodern Condition: A Report on Knowledge.* Manchester University Press.
Maitland, K. & J. Wilson (1987). Ideological conflict and pronominal resolution. *Journal of Pragmatics* 11: 495–512.
Mayr, A. (2004). *Prison Discourse: Language as a Means of Control and Resistance.* Palgrave Macmillan.
McElhinny, B. (1998). 'I don't smile much anymore': Affect, gender and the discourse of Pittsburgh Police Officers. In J. Coates (ed.): 309–327.
Mead, G.H. (1962). *Mind Self and Society.* Chicago University Press.
Mey, J. (1993). *Pragmatics.* Blackwell.
Mills, S. (1995). *Language and Gender: Interdisciplinary Perspectives.* Longman.
Milroy, L. (1985). *Language and Social Networks.* Blackwell.
Milroy, J. & L. Milroy (2005). *Authority in Language,* 3d ed. Taylor & Francis.

Mugglestone, L. (2003). *Talking Proper: The Rise of Accent as Social Symbol*, 2nd ed. Oxford University Press.
Mumby, D.K. (1988). *Communication and Power in Organisations. Discourse Ideology and Domination*. Ablex, Norwood.
Nwosu, C.R. & B.M. Cox (2000). The impact of the Internet on the doctor- patient relationship. *Health Informatics Journal* 6(3): 156–161.
O'Barr, W. (1982). *Linguistic Evidence*. Academic Press.
Palmer, F. (1979). *Modality and the English Modals*. Longman.
—— (1986). *Mood and Modality*. Cambridge University Press.
Pauwels, A. (1998). *Women Changing Language*. Longman.
Peters, S., I. Stanley, M. Rose & P. Salmon (1998). Patients with medically unexplained symptoms: Sources of patients' authority and implications for demands on medical care. *Social Science and Medicine* 46(4/5): 559–565.
Phillips, N. & C. Hardy (1997). Managing multiple identities: Discourse, legitimacy and resources in the UK refugee system. *Organization* 4(2): 159–185.
Potter, J. (1996). *Representing Reality: Discourse, Rhetoric and Social Constructionism*. Sage.
—— (2000). Post-cognitive psychology. *Theory and Psychology* 10(1): 31–37.
Potter, J. & M. Wetherell (1987). *Discourse and Social Psychology*. Sage.
Raven, B.H. & J.Z. Rubin (1983). *Social Psychology*. Wiley.
Reynolds, M. (1990). Classroom power: some dynamics of classroom talk. In R. Clark et al. (eds), *Language and Power*: 122–136. BAAL and CILT.
Roberts, C. & S. Sarangi (2003). Uptake of discourse research in interprofessional settings: Reporting from medical consultancy. *Applied Linguistics* 24(3): 338–359.
Romaine, S. (1999). *Communicating Gender*. Lawrence Erlbaum.
Sacks, H., E. Schegloff & G. Jefferson (1974). A simplest systematics for the organization of turn taking in conversation. *Language* 50(4): 696–733.
Sarangi, S. & C. Roberts (eds.) (1999). *Talk, Work and Institutional Order: Discourse in Medical, Mediation and Management Settings*. Mouton de Gruyter.
Sarangi, S. & S. Slembrouck (1996). *Language, Bureaucracy and Social Control*. Longman.
Schegloff, E.A. (1991). Reflections on talk and social structure. In D. Boden & D.H. Zimmerman (eds.): 44–71.
Searle, J.R. (1969). *Speech Acts*. Oxford University Press.
Shaw, S. (2000). Language, gender and floor apportionment in political debates. *Discourse and Society* 11(3): 401–418.
Shotter, J. (1993). *Cultural Politics of Everyday Life*. Open University Press.
Shotter, J. & K.J. Gergen (eds.) (1989). *Texts of Identity*. Sage.
Shuy, R. (2001). Discourse Analysis in the Legal Context. In D. Shiffrin, D. Tannen & H. Hamilton (eds.) *The Handbook of Discourse Analysis*: 437–452. Blackwell.
Silverman, D. (1990). Communication and Medical Practice. Social Relationships within the Community. Sage.
Simpson, P. & A. Mayr (2009). *Language and Power*. Routledge.
Smith, C.A. (2005). President Bush's enthymeme of evil. *American Behavioral Scientist* 49(1): 32–47.
Soukup, B. (2001). 'Y'all come back now, y'hear?' Language attitudes in the United States towards Southern American English. *Vienna English Working Papers* 10(2): 56–68.
Spender, D. (1980). *Man Made Language*. Routledge.
Sperber, D. & D. Wilson (1996). *Relevance*. Blackwell.
Su Hwi, T. (1996). A critical review of sociolinguistic engineering in Singapore. In J. Blommaert (ed.): 107–142.

Stapleton, K. (2001). Constructing a feminist identity: Discourse and the community of practice. *Feminism and Psychology* 11(4): 459–491.
Talbot, M., K. Atkinson & D. Atkinson (2003). *Language and Power in the Modern World*. Edinburgh University Press.
Tannen, D. (1990). *You Just Don't Understand: Men and Women in Conversation*. Morrow.
——— (1994). *Talking from 9 to 5: Women and Men at Work*. Morrow.
Thomas, L. & S. Wareing (1999). *Language, Society and Power*. Routledge.
Thornborrow, J. (2002). *Power Talk: Language and Interaction in Institutional Discourse*. Longman.
Tibbets, P. (1990). Representation and the realist-constructivist debate. In M. Lynch & S. Woolgar (eds.): 69–85.
Travers, M. & J. Manzo (1997). *Law in Action: Ethnomethodological and Conversation Analytic Approaches to Law*. Ashgate-Dartmouth.
Truss, L. (2003). *Eats, Shoots and Leaves: The Zero Tolerance Approach to Punctuation*. Profile Books.
Urban, G. (1986). Rhetoric of a war chief. Working Papers and Proceedings of the Centre for Psychosocial Studies 5: 1–27.
Van Dijk, T. (2003). Knowledge in Parliamentary debates. *Journal of Language and Politics* 1(2): 93–129.
Vermes, G. (2000). *The Changing Faces of Jesus*. London.
Verschueren, J. (1999). Whose discipline? Some critical reflections on linguistic pragmatics. *Journal of Pragmatics* 31(7): 869–879.
Verwey, N. (1990). *Radio Call-Ins and Covert Politics*. Gower.
Walsh, C. (2001). *Gender and Discourse: Language and Power in Politics, the Church and Organisations*. Pearson.
Watts, R. (1995). *Language and Power in the Family*. Mouton.
West, C. (1990). Not just 'Doctors' Orders': Directive-response sequences in patients' visits to women and men physicians. *Discourse and Society* 1(1): 85–113.
——— (1995). Women's competence in conversation. *Discourse & Society* 6(1): 107–131.
Wilson, J. (1995). Linguistic Forms of Political Life. Unpublished ms.
——— (1996). Authority. In J. Verschueren, J.O. stman, J. Blommaert & C. Bulcaen (eds.) *Handbook of Pragmatics*. John Benjamins.
——— (2006). Power. In K. Brown (ed.) *Encyclopedia of Language and Linguistics*. LALI 00339: 1–3. Elsevier.
Wilson, J. & B. Haugh (1995). Collaborative modelling and talk in the classroom. *Language and Education* 9(4): 265–283.
Wilson, J. & K. Stapleton (2007). The discourse of resistance: Social change and policing in Northern Ireland. *Language in Society* 36: 3.
Wittgenstein, L. (1953). *Philosophical Investigations*. Blackwell.
Wodak, R. (1995). Power, discourse and styles of female leadership in school committee meetings. In D. Corson (ed.) *Discourse and Power in Educational Organizations*: 31–54. Hampton Press.
——— (1996). *Disorders of Discourse*. Longman.
Wodak, R., R. De Cillia, M. Reisigl & K. Liebhart (1999). *The Discursive Construction of National Identity*. Edinburgh University Press.
Wodak, R. & M. Meyer (eds.) (2001). *Methods of Critical Discourse Analysis*. Sage.
Wright, L. (ed.) (2006). *The Development of Standard English 1300–1800*. Cambridge University Press.

Bilingualism and multilingualism

Monica Heller & Aneta Pavlenko
University of Toronto & Temple University

1. Introduction

Studies of bilingualism and multilingualism have a long history, yet the reason why these phenomena have been taken as objects of scrutiny is not because they have been central to dominant social and political ideologies, but rather because of the challenge they have presented to prevailing ideologies. Indeed, whenever monolingualism has been central to imperial expansion or the construction of nation-states, multilingualism has been consequently seen as a problem to be understood (through scientific description) and thereby controlled.

European inquiry into multilingualism is often said to have begun with the surveys of the Abbé Grégoire in France during the Revolution, surveys designed to chart the dimensions of knowledge of French among the populace in preparation for the development of tools to foster the acquisition and use of the newly emerging national language (Balibar & Laporte 1974; Grillo 1989). For Grégoire, French monolingualism was central to the implementation of the revolution's goals, specifically the guarantee of universal access to equality and liberty and the fostering of solidarity against both internal and external enemies, as well as to the political consolidation of revolutionary structures of power. Grégoire thus serves as an early and influential example of the ways in which scientific studies of multilingualism serve the interests of nationalisms in which monolingualism plays a central role, or, on the contrary, are part of efforts to resist such forms of control (wherever the specific politics of specific movements may be on the political spectrum in any given place at any given time).

By casting studies of multilingualism in this social and political light, we want to emphasize the links between interests in the cognitive, social and political dimensions of language practices and the social and political ideologies prevalent in Europe and North America over the last 200 years or so. Our position is that arguments about whether bilingualism is good or bad for you as an individual, about whether it makes you confused or instead is the mark of an exceptional intelligence, are linked to arguments about whether or not monolingualism should be (or simply is) the natural, normal order of things for political entities. Interest in individual bilingualism cannot be divorced from interest in the bilingualism of the body politic.

It is not surprising then that in the 19th and the early 20th century individual bilingualism was approached with a double standard in both Europe and North America.

Elite bilingualism, that is bilingualism of the upper and middle classes, was viewed as a positive phenomenon and encouraged in the children of the elite (Pavlovitch 1920; Ronjat 1913). In contrast, bilingualism and multilingualism of immigrants and linguistic minority members was associated with split identities, moral inferiority, and mental retardation (e.g. Saer 1924). In Germany, with the rise of the Nazi regime, bilingualism became associated with Jews and other ethnic minorities and identified as one of the causes of their intellectual deterioration, pathological inner split, and 'mercenary relativism' (e.g. Sander 1934). It is only after World War II that bilingualism emerged as a proper object of study, in part in the wake of new migratory movements and later in connection with struggles for national liberation on the part of ethnolinguistic minorities.

Current research on bilingualism and multilingualism raises a number of questions central to linguistic enquiry. What does multilingualism tell us about linguistic structure and about the physiological dimensions of the human capacity for language? Why do people use more than one language? How do people become multilingual?

In the following section we will outline some of the major work in each of these areas of enquiry beginning with the studies which are the clearest foundations of the current construction of the field, in terms of the delineation of interest in cognitive, social psychological, sociolinguistic and sociological or anthropological dimensions of multilingualism. Examinations of the cognitive dimensions of multilingualism, centered in neurolinguistic and psycholinguistic approaches, have focused on issues of language processing and language acquisition. Social psychological studies have explored language attitudes and psychological motivations for multilingual language practices. Sociolinguistic analysis has addressed the systematicity of multilingualism, linking multilingual practices in social interaction to cognitive constructions of the world and to language learning processes. Sociological and anthropological approaches used the study of multilingualism to understand important social processes, such as the definition and establishment of personal and political power, and social inequality. The final section of this chapter will focus on ways in which studies of multilingualism have facilitated linkages between cognitive, interactional-pragmatic, sociolinguistic and sociological or anthropological areas of concern and outline some opportunities that an integrated approach may present, not only for the development of theory but also for public policy and practice.

2. Four approaches to the study of bilingualism and multilingualism

The 1950s and 1960s saw the publication of seminal work on multilingualism in Europe and North America. Basing themselves on a dialectological tradition which orthodoxly focused on the purest and most 'conservative' speech, several scholars set out to examine the extent to which multilingualism could also be described in the same terms. Weinreich's (1953) *Languages in contact* was a major contribution to the structural analysis of the linguistic systems of bilinguals. At the same time, Haugen (1953) published a detailed study of Norwegian as spoken in the United States in the aftermath of one of the major migratory movements between Europe and North America in the late 19th and early 20th centuries. This was followed by a broader survey of bilingualism in the Americas (Haugen 1956). Together, these works underlie an important sociolinguistic research tradition, devoted to demonstrating the systematic nature of what at first blush appear to be disorganized, mixed, heterogeneous forms – forms which are often taken as degraded and contaminated variants of a true original. In the late 1950s, Gumperz (see Gumperz 1971) began to explore the social correlates of the kind of heterogeneity that Weinreich and Haugen had described, examining the social organizational basis for linguistic variability in India. This work launched a prolific research tradition devoted initially to tracing the social functional dimensions of bilingualism and later to exploring the ways in which language use is profoundly implicated in the evolution of social organization and social relations.

Together, these early studies provided a basis for a general awakening of interest in the social and psychological dimensions of language. This development can be understood historically in a number of ways. First, it can be seen as a reaction to structural and generative approaches which isolate language from its use and its users and which seek to understand language as an invariant, ideal form. In this respect, studies of multilingualism form but one part of a generalized interest in linguistic variability. Second, this development accompanies social movements characterized by bi- or multilingualism: mass migration and the politicization of ethnic minorities. It is clear that both these social processes take as their point of departure the legitimacy of a monolingual vision of the nation-state, claiming rights to autonomy on the basis of internal linguistic homogeneity. Nonetheless, such political efforts required that the *de facto* bilingualism of many of the individuals and political entities involved be confronted. It is in this context that the main threads of research on multilingualism take shape: the cognitive, social psychological, sociolinguistic and sociological-anthropological. We will now leave the historical structure of the narrative, in order to consider each of these domains in turn.

2.1 Neurolinguistic and psycholinguistic approaches to multilingualism

Neurolinguistic and psycholinguistic approaches are commonly used to examine representation and processing of multiple languages in a single mind/brain as a window onto the overall language architecture and the relationship between language and thought. Pioneering research in this area was conducted in the late 19th and early 20th century by clinicians who noted that multilingual patients suffering from aphasia may lose (and recover) their respective languages in different ways and at different rates, and tried to locate regularities in the recovery patterns (Bychowski 1919; Minkowski 1928; Pitres 1895; Ribot 1881). In the second half of the 20th century the research on the neurolinguistics of bilingualism has expanded from individuals with impairments, such as bilingual aphasia, to healthy individuals whose brain functioning is examined through recording of eye-movements and event-related potentials (ERPs), positron emission tomography (PET), and functional magnetic resonance imaging (fMRI) (Abutalebi et al. 2005; Fabbro 1999; Gullberg & Indefrey 2006; Paradis 2004).

From the mid-20th century onwards, studies with healthy bi-and multilinguals have also used psycholinguistic tasks, such as lexical decision, semantic categorization, semantic and sentence priming, picture-naming, translation, and the Stroop interference task to examine the relationship between forms and meanings of respective languages in the bi/multilingual mind (Kroll & De Groot 2005). Second language (L2) acquisition and first language (L1) attrition scholars have also used additional tasks, such as grammaticality judgments, verbal fluency and word association tasks, and speech elicitation, as well as a variety of analyses of spontaneous speech (Jarvis & Pavlenko 2008; Schmid & Köpke 2009).

Recent research in the field has advanced our understanding of such diverse aspects of multilingual experience as representation, processing, and crosslinguistic influence in the bilingual mental lexicon (Jarvis & Pavlenko 2008; Kroll & De Groot 2005; Pavlenko 2009), age effects in L2 acquisition (Birdsong 2005), affective aspects of individual bilingualism and L2 learning (Pavlenko 2005, 2006, 2008), L1 attrition (Schmid 2002; Schmid & Köpke 2009), bilingual autobiographical memory (Schrauf 2000, 2009), gesture use by multilingual speakers (Gullberg 2009), and bilingualism and bimodalism among the deaf (Grosjean 2008). At the same time, neurolinguistic and psycholinguistic research continues to experience conceptual and methodological problems that involve selection of study participants, tasks, and stimuli, interpretation of the study results, and modeling of bilingual processing and representation (Grosjean 2008). Future studies also need to address concerns about ecological validity of laboratory research and engage with the multimodal and integrative nature of multilingual language processing in context, that is with ways in which several types of linguistic information are integrated on-line with nonlinguistic input (Gullberg 2009; Marian 2009). An emerging agreement in the field is that optimal information will come from converging evidence, that is from triangulation of data from clinical, neuroimaging, and experimental studies with the data from analyses of spontaneous verbal and nonverbal performance.

To date, neurolinguistic and psycholinguistic approaches to the study of bilingualism focus on two main areas of inquiry. First, multilingualism provides a useful case for testing hypotheses about the physiological processes involved in language production, processing and acquisition, and more generally about the relationship between language and cognition. Secondly, the kinds of enquiries referred to here permit the exploration of the nature of bilingual proficiency, a nature which appears to be (appropriately) fairly heterogeneous. In order to explain this heterogeneity researchers are making links with other approaches to multilingualism, whether linguistic, pragmatic or sociolinguistic.

2.2 Social psychological approaches

Social psychological approaches, particularly popular in the 1960s and 1970s, aim to uncover speakers' psychological motivations for language learning, language choice and code-switching in multilingual settings, that is, to provide answers to questions about multilinguals' language learning and use.

The seminal work in this area was conducted by Canadian researchers Gardner and Lambert. Their studies of sociopsychological variables in L2 learning (Gardner & Lambert 1959, 1972) demonstrated that a positive, statistically significant, relationship can be established between motivation, positive attitudes towards the L2 and its speakers, and the mastery of those aspects of the L2 that are less susceptible to conscious manipulation, such as phonology.

Lambert and colleagues' (1960) study of French and English in Montreal introduced the matched guise test, in which bilingual speakers recorded passages in each of their languages, and members of each language group listened to these recordings, but were not told that they were made by the same person. Participants were then asked to rate the speakers on a variety of social and personality attributes (e.g. intelligence, wealth, warmth). The design of the study made it possible to attribute the evaluations to the values accorded to the language varieties alone, since all other aspects of the situation, including speaker identity, were the same. By discovering the value accorded to each language variety in the community repertoire by members of each group, it was possible to draw conclusions about what might motivate speakers to choose one language over another in any given situation. Lambert and colleagues noted that minority group members frequently shared majority group attitudes towards languages on dimensions having to do with power, but not on dimensions having to do with solidarity (so everyone would agree that majority group members were likely to be wealthier and more intelligent, say, while minority group members still liked co-members better than they did majority group members, finding them nicer and warmer).

Since then, the matched guise test has been frequently used by researchers to explore precisely these kinds of issues (e.g. Ryan & Giles 1982; Woolard 1989). The ways in which evaluations fall out along the dimensions of power and solidarity, and how groups align themselves in terms of social categories, help reveal the nature of relations of power among groups in a multilingual setting and the boundaries between groups. Such findings go a long way towards uncovering the social norms regulating intergroup relations and influencing motivations for language learning, among other things, although they cannot of course explain the origins or bases of those norms, nor the way they operate in social interaction.

Over the years, social psychological approaches have generated several theories and models aiming to explain the influence of sociopsychological factors on L2 learning outcomes (Gardner & Lambert 1972; Schumann 1978), the relationship between ethnic group membership and L2 learning and use (Tajfel 1974), and ethnolinguistic vitality of minority languages (Giles et al. 1977). Giles and colleagues (e.g. Giles 1984; Sachdev & Giles 2004) have developed the Communication Accommodation Theory, which argues that speakers are motivated by desires either to accommodate their interlocutor's perceived language preferences or to distance themselves from their interlocutor through divergent language choices. This approach depends on the simulation of social interaction, and elicits from subjects their evaluative reactions to specific language choices made by speakers in the simulated interaction.

While social psychological analyses of language learning, choice, and use have provided valuable insights, they have been criticized on a number of grounds. From a theoretical point of view, these studies offer interesting descriptive data but fail to illuminate historical and social processes that shape particular attitudes, motivations, and beliefs. From a methodological viewpoint, they rely on limited data collection techniques, such as questionnaires or simulated speech events, both of which explore language use out of context. Nonetheless, the questions raised by these studies regarding the value accorded to language varieties and language choice practices are important ones, and remain central to research on multilingualism.

2.3 Linguistic and sociolinguistic approaches

One of the major incentives to linguistic and sociolinguistic work on multilingualism has to do with questions about the extent of systematicity of any form of linguistic variability. A great deal of work can be said to flow directly from this concern, first in terms of documenting the linguistic regularity of multilingual language practices and then in terms of explaining the observed regularity.

Multilingual practices, and in particular code-switching, have been at the heart of this inquiry. The documentation of the regularity of multilingual language practices has touched not only on the structural dimensions already noted, but also on the functions of multilingualism in everyday social interaction. Following Gumperz's accounts of language choice and code-switching, in the 1970s and early 1980s, in North America, there was an initial burst of interest in establishing typologies of language forms and language functions (e.g. Blom & Gumperz 1972; Gumperz 1971, 1982; Poplack 1980). Eventually it became clear that multilingual practices were often part of rapidly changing social situations and hence rarely stable enough to permit detailed typologies. Instead, researchers adopted the notion that such practices could cover a wide variety of communicative functions. Analysts of multilingual language practices were able to demonstrate regular patterns, but had to confront the susceptibility of those patterns to the creativity of speakers. In other words, only under certain circumstances was it possible to describe routine, conventionalized patterns, since frequently the practices observed were part of an on-going process of negotiation and re-negotiation of conventions of interaction in the context of changing intergroup relations (Heller 1982). Thus one important current of sociolinguistic work on multilingual language practices focuses on the pragmatic dimensions which reveal the multiply embedded ways in which those practices serve as contextualization devices to build social meaning and stylistic significance, to manage social relationships (for example through the management of conversational processes such as turn-taking) and to frame discourse.

Yet interactional practices are only one of many strands of linguistic and sociolinguistic inquiry into multilingualism. In addition to multilingual interaction and code-switching (Auer 1984, 1998; Milroy & Muysken 1995; Muysken 2000), this inquiry has provided invaluable insights into linguistic aspects of language contact (Clyne 2003; Myers-Scotton 2002), bilingual first language acquisition and language development of multilingual children (Bialystok 2001; Genesee 2001; Lanza 1997; Paradis 2007; Verhoeven & Strömqvist 2001), L2 learning (Butler & Hakuta 2004; Dewaele 2007), L2 pragmatic development (Bardovi-Harlig & Hartford 2005; Kasper & Rose 2002), and bilinguals' identity performance (Koven 2007).

These studies showed that specific patterns vary not only from setting to setting but also from situation to situation and speaker to speaker. This has raised an important question of what underlies this type of variability, and what it can tell us about differences in the social dimensions of multilingualism. It is the latter question that sociological and anthropological studies of multilingualism have set out to address.

2.4 Sociological and anthropological approaches

The earliest work in this vein sought to link multilingual patterns to forms of social organization. In addition to the work of Gumperz cited above, it is important to note Ferguson's (1959) and Fishman's (1967) seminal articles on diglossia and Fishman's (1972a, b; Fishman et al. 1971) contributions to macro-sociological descriptions of language contact situations. All focused on social functional dimensions of multilingualism, pointing out the ways in which differences in language varieties corresponded to differences in social situations in which the varieties were used, and the related differences in values accorded to language varieties along the same dimensions. Such an approach, however, failed to account for how this relationship between form, situation and value could become established, nor did it explain how the relationship might change.

Building on the central insight of the early work that language varieties were key elements of social organization, more recent work has used the analysis of language practices to answer questions about social relations and examined the role of language in the development of social structures and social processes. In particular, researchers have been interested in exploring the definition of social boundaries, identities and relations of power and solidarity, and the links between social and linguistic practices and language ideologies (Blommaert 1999; Hill & Hill 1986; Kulick 1992; Schieffelin et al. 1998; Woolard 1985).

In order to do so, it has been necessary to confront the problem of how to relate the way language is used in social interaction in everyday life to broader social, economic and political processes. Gal (1988) has argued for an approach based on political economy, in which the kind of fine-grained analysis developed in interactional sociolinguistics serves as the basis for comparisons across settings and over time and for linkages between local interactional practices and community members' access to valued social, economic and political resources. She showed that individual bilingual (Hungarian-German) repertoires in a border village in Austria must be understood in terms of the ways those languages are bound up in the economic activities on the basis of which people make a living, and in the social networks which allow them to do so (Gal 1979). The conditions which sustain those activities and networks, however, change over time because of the particular place of this village in regional and ultimately global economic and political structures (the most important of which in this century have been the collapse of the Habsburg Empire, the rise and fall of the Nazi Regime, and industrialization and its role in globalizing economic networks).

An individual's linguistic repertoire is, then, tied to the position he or she has with respect to the arenas where different languages in circulation in the community are spoken. The ability to do different things with more than one language is therefore likely to be unequally distributed. The value they have for any speaker is also tied to the investment he or she has in any zone of a linguistic marketplace (to use Bourdieu's terms; cf. Bourdieu 1977) and the risks and benefits of using and learning languages in the community repertoire. Those kinds of consequences derive from the social, economic and political conditions which support the functioning of the marketplace, but which can at the same time in individual practices reinforce or challenge those conditions (Heller 1992, 1995).

This line of enquiry has led in two directions. First, increased attention has been paid to the role of language ideologies as a way to address how language practices come to have conventional values, and how those values serve the interests of specific groups in any community (Blommaert 1999; Hill 1985; Schieffelin et al. 1998). In other words, the construction of language ideologies is taken as a window onto the exercise of power and the establishment of hierarchical social relations; they are seen as a place where power (and potentially resistance) happen, and a domain which links specific instances of language use with social structural constraints and consequences.

Second, researchers have increasingly moved away from an initial focus on the relationship between groups to explore internal differences within groups under conditions of language contact. As it has become clear that language practices differ among members of a group (for example, between men and women, or between members of different class or occupational groups, as well as across generations) it has become important to understand the dynamics of cross-cutting relations of inequality and solidarity. In other words, a simple 'we-they' dichotomy cannot always hold, because groups can form ties across language boundaries and construct internal social – and ultimately linguistic – boundaries on either side of a major language boundary.

To date, sociological and anthropological studies of multilingual communities provided valuable insights in such diverse areas as language socialization of multilingual children (Garrett 2007), social underpinnings of language maintenance and shift (Gal 1979; Kulick 1992), and the role of language in nation-building and in the new economy (Heller 2003, 2007a,b). These insights in turn provided the basis for development of theories of language policy (Ricento 2006), minority language rights (May 2001), bilingual education (Baker 2006), and globalization and commodification of multilingualism (Heller 2003, 2007a,b).

Sociological and anthropological approaches to the study of multilingualism are thus increasingly concerned with addressing problems of social inequality and understanding both how power is wielded and how it is resisted. They are also concerned with exploring the complexity of the language boundaries which intersect with and form part of social boundaries of all kinds, in order to understand the role language plays in the evolution of social processes and social structures. They attempt to use fine-grained ethnographic and sociolinguistic analyses as an empirical basis for such theoretical aims. Generalizations are arrived at in two ways, either through comparisons across settings and across time, or through the ethnographic establishment of linkages among interactions and between interactions and documented institutional and historical practices. Here the study of multilingualism also contributes generally to the theoretical and methodological interface between sociolinguistic and social theory.

3. Conclusion

Studies of bilingualism and multilingualism, having started from a point of view which constructed these phenomena as counterexamples to the monolingual norm, have moved to a point of view in which multilingualism as a form of linguistic variability is taken as part of the normal human condition, a necessary dimension of differentiated societies (see e.g. Auer & Li Wei 2007). Having made that move, multilingualism becomes interesting for a host of reasons.

First, it is a privileged site for understanding the nature and consequences of that differentiation, and allows researchers to link up the individual's experience and practice of it to the social structural dimensions of social difference and social inequality. This necessitates thinking across disciplinary lines, and indeed studies of multilingualism increasingly aim for a theoretical and methodological integration of insights from the disciplines which have traditionally taken the individual as their object of study as well as from those which focus on groups, and from disciplines concerned with the physiological, psychological, structural, interactional and social dimensions of language competence and language use. Indeed, the kind of disciplinary integration that is emerging in this field challenges the very distinction between competence and performance that has been so central to linguistics in the 20th century.

Second, the emerging central concern of studies of multilingualism is connected to other important areas of activity, notably to questions of language policy in countries which are struggling with the collapse of the notion of the monolingual nation-state, and to related questions of language learning and language teaching (e.g. Block & Cameron 2002). New political ideologies and structures must take multilingualism into account, both in terms of what it reveals about social relations in any given community as well as across communities, and in terms of how it can be turned to advantage. In turn, studies of multilingualism have to come to grips with the political significance of their questions. Language teaching and learning often play an important role in these processes, as strategies for regulating the distribution of valued linguistic capital. From this point of view, language teaching and learning are becoming less and less considered as technical matters, and are more and more being understood as social processes (see also Baker 2006).

The pragmatics of multilingualism represents these emerging ways of recasting a well-known and long-studied phenomenon. It constitutes an attempt to use multilingualism as a way of understanding how we use language to link up the cognitive organization of our world with our organization of our social relations, and with the ways that organization constrains our possibilities for action and the ways our action affects that organization. It allows us to grasp the underpinnings and consequences of the politics of multilingualism. Finally, it contributes an empirical basis to social and cognitive theory and their applications in language teaching and language policy.

References

Abutalebi, J., Cappa, S. & D. Perani (2005). What can functional neuroimaging tell us about the bilingual brain? In J. Kroll & A. De Groot (eds.) *Handbook of bilingualism: Psycholinguistic approaches*: 497–515. Oxford University Press.

Auer, P. (1984). *Bilingual conversation*. Benjamins.

——— (ed.) (1998). *Code-switching in conversation: Language, interaction, and identity*. Routledge.

Auer, P. & Li Wei (eds.) (2007). *Handbook of multilingualism and multilingual communication*. Mouton De Gruyter.
Baker, C. (2006). *Foundations of bilingual education and bilingualism*. 4th ed. Multilingual Matters.
Balibar, R. & D. Laporte (1974). *Le Francais national*. Hachette.
Bardovi-Harlig, K. & B. Hartford (eds.) (2005). *Interlanguage pragmatics: Exploring institutional talk*. Lawrence Erlbaum.
Bialystok, E. (2001). *Bilingualism in development: Language, literacy, and cognition*. Cambridge University Press.
Birdsong, D. (2005). Interpreting age effects in second language acquisition. In J. Kroll & A. De Groot (eds.) *Handbook of bilingualism: Psycholinguistic approaches*: 109–127. Oxford University Press.
Block, D. & D. Cameron (eds.) (2002). *Globalization and language teaching*. Routledge.
Blom, J.-P. & J. Gumperz (1972). Social meaning in linguistic structure: Code-switching in Norway. In J. Gumperz & D. Hymes (eds.) *Directions in sociolinguistics*: 407–434. Holt, Rinehart & Winston.
Blommaert, J. (ed.) (1999). *Language ideological debates*. Mouton De Gruyter.
Bourdieu, P. (1977). L'économie des échanges linguistiques. *Langue française* 34: 17–34.
Butler, Y. & K. Hakuta (2004). Bilingualism and second language acquisition. In T. Bhatia & W. Ritchie (eds.) *The handbook of bilingualism*: 114–144. Blackwell.
Bychowski, Z. (1919). Über die Restitution der nach einem Schädelschuss verlorenen Umgangssprache bei einem Polyglotten. *Monatschrift für Psychologie und Neurologie* 45: 183–201.
Clyne, M. (2003). *Dynamics of language contact*. Cambridge University Press.
Dewaele, J.-M. (2007). Becoming bi- or multi-lingual later in life. In P. Auer & Li Wei (eds.): 102–130.
Fabbro, F. (1999). *The neurolinguistics of bilingualism: An introduction*. Psychology Press.
Ferguson, C. (1959). Diglossia. *Word* 15: 325–340.
Fishman, J. (1967). Bilingualism with and without diglossia; diglossia with and without bilingualism. *Journal of Social Issues* 23 (2): 29–38.
———— (1972a). Domains and the relationship between macro- and microsociolinguistics. In J. Gumperz & D. Hymes (eds.) *Directions in sociolinguistics*: 435–453. Harper & Row.
———— (ed.) (1972b). *Readings in the sociology of language*. Mouton.
Fishman, J., R. Cooper et al. (1971). *Bilingualism in the Barrio*. Indiana University Press.
Gal, S. (1979). *Language shift*. Academic Press.
———— (1988). The political economy of code choice. In M. Heller (ed.) *Codeswitching*: 245–264. Mouton de Gruyter.
Gardner, R. & W. Lambert (1959). Motivational variables in second-language acquisition. *Canadian Journal of Psychology* 13: 266–272.
———— (1972). *Attitudes and motivation in second language learning*. Newbury House.
Garrett, P. (2007). Language socialization and the (re)production of bilingual subjectivities. In M. Heller (ed.) *Bilingualism: A social approach*: 233–256. Palgrave.
Genesee, F. (2001). Bilingual first language acquisition: Exploring the limits of the language faculty. *Annual Review of Applied Linguistics* 21: 153–168.
Giles, H. (1984). The dynamics of speech accommodation. *International Journal of the Sociology of Language* 46: 1–55.
Giles, H., R. Bourhis & D. Taylor (1977). Toward a theory of language in ethnic group relations. In H. Giles (ed.) *Language, ethnicity, and intergroup relations*. Academic Press.
Grillo, R.D. (1989). *Dominant languages*. Cambridge University Press.

Grosjean, F. (2008). *Studying bilinguals*. Oxford University Press.
Gullberg, M. (2009). Why gestures are relevant to the bilingual lexicon. In A. Pavlenko (ed.) *The bilingual mental lexicon: Interdisciplinary approaches*: 161–184. Multilingual Matters.
Gullberg, M. & P. Indefrey (eds.) (2006). *The cognitive neuroscience of second language acquisition*. Blackwell.
Gumperz, J. (1971). *Language in social groups*. Stanford University Press.
—— (1982). *Discourse strategies*. Cambridge University Press.
Haugen, E. (1953). *The Norwegian language in America*. University of Pennsylvania Press.
—— (1956). *Bilingualism in the Americas*. University of Alabama, American Dialect Society.
Heller, M. (1982). Negotiations of language choice in Montreal. In J. Gumperz (ed.) *Language in social interaction*: 108–118. Cambridge University Press.
—— (1992). The politics of code-switching and language choice. *Journal of Multilingual and Multicultural Development* 13(1/2): 123–142.
—— (1995). Code-switching and the politics of language. In L. Milroy & P. Muysken (eds.) *One speaker, two languages*: 158–174. Cambridge University Press.
—— (2003). Globalization, the new economy and the commodification of language and identity. *Journal of Sociolinguistics* 7 (4): 473–492.
—— (ed.) (2007a). *Bilingualism: A social approach*. Palgrave.
—— (2007b). Multilingualism and transnationalism. In P. Auer & Li Wei (eds.): 539–553.
Hill, J. (1985). The grammar of consciousness and the consciousness of grammar. *American Ethnologist* 12(4): 725–737.
Hill, J. & K. Hill (1986). *Speaking Mexicano*. University of Arizona Press.
Jarvis, S. & A. Pavlenko (2008). *Crosslinguistic influence in language and cognition*. Routledge.
Kasper, G. & K. Rose (2002). *Pragmatic development in a second language*. Blackwell.
Koven, M. (2007). *Selves in two languages: Bilinguals' verbal enactments of identity in French and Portuguese*. Benjamins.
Kroll, J. & A. De Groot (eds.) (2005). *Handbook of bilingualism: Psycholinguistic approaches*. Oxford University Press.
Kulick, D. (1992). *Language shift and cultural reproduction*. Cambridge University Press.
Lambert, W., R. Hodgson, R. Gardner & S. Fillenbaum (1960). Evaluative reactions to spoken language. *Journal of Abnormal and Social Psychology* 60: 44–51.
Lanza, E. (1997). *Language mixing in infant bilingualism: A sociolinguistic perspective*. Oxford University Press.
Marian, V. (2009). Audio-visual integration during bilingual language processing. In A. Pavlenko (ed.) *The bilingual mental lexicon: Interdisciplinary approaches*: 52–78. Multilingual Matters.
May, S. (2001). *Language and minority rights: Ethnicity, nationalism, and the politics of language*. Longman.
Milroy, L. & P. Muysken (1995). *One speaker, two languages: Cross-disciplinary perspectives on code-switching*. Cambridge University Press.
Minkowski, M. (1928). Sur un cas d'aphasie chez un polyglotte. *Revue Neurologique* 49: 361–366.
Muysken, P. (2000). *Bilingual speech: A typology of code-mixing*. Cambridge University Press.
Myers-Scotton, C. (2002). *Contact linguistics: Bilingual encounters and grammatical outcomes*. Oxford University Press.
Paradis, J. (2007). Early bilingual and multilingual acquisition. In P. Auer & Li Wei (eds.): 15–44.
Paradis, M. (2004). *A neurolinguistic theory of bilingualism*. Benjamins.
Pavlenko, A. (2005). *Emotions and multilingualism*. Cambridge University Press.

—— (ed.) (2006). *Bilingual minds: Emotional experience, expression, and representation.* Multilingual Matters.

—— (2008). Emotion and emotion-laden words in the bilingual lexicon. *Bilingualism: Language and Cognition* 11(2): 147–164.

—— (ed.) (2009). *The bilingual mental lexicon: Interdisciplinary approaches.* Multilingual Matters.

Pavlovitch, M. (1920). *Le langage enfantin: Acquisition du serbe and du français par un enfant serbe.* Champion.

Pitres, A. (1895). Etude sur l'aphasie chez les polyglottes. *Revue de Médecine* 15: 873–899.

Poplack, S. (1980). Sometimes I'll start a sentence in Spanish y termino en español: Towards a typology of code-switching. *Linguistics* 18: 581–618.

Ribot, T. (1881). *Les maladies de la mémoire.* G. Baillère.

Ricento, T. (ed.) (2006). *An introduction to language policy: Theory and method.* Blackwell.

Ronjat, J. (1913). *Le développement du langage observé chez un enfant bilingue.* Champion.

Ryan, E. & H. Giles (eds.) (1982). *Attitudes towards language variation.* Arnold.

Sachdev, I. & H. Giles (2004). Bilingual accommodation. In T. Bhatia & W. Ritchie (eds.) *The handbook of bilingualism*: 353–378. Blackwell.

Saer, D. (1924). The effect of bilingualism on intelligence. *British Journal of Psychology* 14: 25–38.

Sander, F. (1934). Seelische Struktur und Sprache: Stukturpsychologisches zum Zweitsprachenproblem. *Neue Psychologische Studien* 12: 59.

Schieffelin, B., K. Woolard & P. Kroskrity (eds.) (1998). *Language ideologies: Practice and theory.* Oxford University Press.

Schmid, M. (2002). *First language attrition, use, and maintenance: The case of German Jews in anglophone countries.* Benjamins.

Schmid, M. & B. Köpke (2009). L1 attrition and the mental lexicon. In A. Pavlenko (ed.): 209–238.

Schumann, J. (1978). The acculturation model for second language acquisition. In R. Gingras (ed.) *Second language acquisition and foreign language teaching*: 27–50. Washington, DC, Center for Applied Linguistics.

Schrauf, R. (2000). Bilingual autobiographical memory: Experimental studies and clinical cases. *Culture & Psychology* 6(4): 387–414.

—— (2009). The bilingual lexicon and bilingual autobiographical memory: The neurocognitive basic systems view. In A. Pavlenko (ed.): 26–51.

Tajfel, H. (1974). Social identity and intergroup behavior. *Social Science Information* 13: 65–93.

Verhoeven, L. & S. Strömqvist (eds.) (2001). *Narrative development in a multilingual context.* Benjamins.

Weinreich, U. (1953). *Languages in contact: Findings and problems.* Linguistic Circle of New York.

Woolard, K. (1985). Language variation and cultural hegemony. *American Ethnologist* 12(4): 738–748.

—— (1989). *Double talk.* Stanford University Press.

Code-switching

Peter Auer & Carol M. Eastman[†]
University of Freiburg

1. Introduction

Whereas humans have doubtlessly been switching codes for as long as there have been bilinguals, the phenomenon of code-switching has only received substantial attention in linguistics in the second half of the last century (Alvarez Cáccamo 1998 traces the first mention of the term back to Vogt 1954), and large-scale research on code-switching did not start before the 1970s. Of course it had not escaped previous research on language contact that speakers switch between languages (cf. Hermann Paul's chapter on 'language mixture', 1898: 365–377); however, this was considered an externally induced mishap due to negative psychological or social factors (incompetence, laziness, lack of education, migration, conquest) which did not merit linguistic investigation and was, in any case, temporary ('man wird von der Zweisprachigkeit wieder zur Einsprachigkeit gelangen' ['from bilingualism one will arrive at monolingualism in the end'], as Paul 1898: 366 put it). In light of this neglect, we can doubtlessly discover a monolingual bias which was characteristic of linguistics for a long time: The beginnings of the discipline (in the early nineteenth century) coincided – not by chance – with the triumph of the nation state and its ideology of 'one nation one language'. In this ideology, multilingual language use had no place (Auer 2007; Heller 2007; Pujolar 2007), even though forms of language contact did (borrowing in particular, but also pidgin and creole formation). The enormous interest code-switching and related practices have found in linguistics over the last three decades is at least in part (i.e. in addition to internal developments in linguistics) due to the demise of the monolingual national language ideologies which have become less and less realistic in the age of globalization, transnationalism, and migration. Today, multilingual practices are an undisputed everyday phenomenon, even in the European nation states which hitherto considered themselves to be monolingual (see Stroud 2007 for a view beyond Europe).

As with most other linguistic activities, code-switching can be seen from a number of different angles. Code-switching is the most striking surface manifestation of bilingualism and as such can be investigated from the point of view of speech production; it can be seen as a particularly interesting outcome of language contact in grammar; it can be treated as (part of) a sociolinguistic style which has identity-related functions; it can be investigated in the context of bilingual first language acquisition; it may be a sign of (imminent) structural convergence between two languages, or a sign of language attrition; and it may be treated as a linguistic activity or practice in its own right.

In the following sections, we will first discuss some terminological and methodological issues (Section 2), followed by a brief historical overview of the genesis of the field of code-switching studies (Section 3). Next, we will discuss in greater detail the social and interactional meaning of code-switching as it emerges from sociolinguistic studies and how it can be analyzed in interactional (conversation-based) terms (Section 4). Section 5 is devoted to grammatical constraints on code-switching. By way of conclusion, we will suggest a number of areas for future research (Section 6).

2. Terminological and methodological issues

In general, code-switching is a phenomenon of *language contact*, usually observable in multilingual (and often urban) surroundings, which is noteworthy because it "violates a strong expectation that only one language will be used at any given time" (Heller 1988: 1). The "strong expectation", however, is often only present in the eyes of the (monolingual) outsider. For bilinguals, code-switching is often a natural way of speaking.

In the literature on language use, there have been a number of definitions of code-switching, and Gumperz's view – that it is "the juxtaposition within the same speech exchange of passages of speech belonging to two different grammatical systems or sub-systems" (1982: 59) – seems to be the most widely accepted. The lower level of code-switching (i.e. what counts as a "passage") is debatable, however. For instance, some researchers have argued that – contrary to borrowing – code-switching/-mixing is not possible word-internally (Poplack's free morpheme constraint, 1980), while others have argued against this restriction (e.g. Berruto 2005). It may even be argued that there are cases where a shift of prosody or the ad hoc use of a foreign sound segment (such as a 'French' uvular fricative /R/ in the coda by a speaker of Italian who usually has apical /r/) may have all the functional qualities of code-switching (Alvarez Cáccamo 1998). However, such a wide notion of code-switching has not seen general use in linguistics.

Gumperz's definition covers the alternating use of languages, dialects, and styles. In practice, however, scholars often intuitively restrict themselves to shifts between clearly identifiable *languages* (e.g. French/Dutch, French/English, English/Swahili) or clearly perceivable contrasts between standard and substandard variants of the same language. Work on stylistic or genre-based code-switching is rare. Similarly, authors often restrict themselves to discussing *one* form of variation only: between language A and language B, or between variant A and variant B of the same language. It is equally rare to encounter research on 'layered' code-switching, in which, besides a contrast between two languages, a number of (stylistic) contrasts within the contrasted languages are also significant (for an example, see Meeuwis & Blommaert 1998).

The focus on identifiable languages or language variants is an 'objective' analytic stance, which hides substantial methodological problems. Do speakers identify the 'languages' observed by the linguist as separate 'languages'? Or do they perceive them as parts of one repertoire from which they can select elements of speech, regardless of the 'objective' distinction between 'languages'? To put it more generally: Are the distinctions introduced by the linguist, and held to be relevant under all circumstances (e.g. the difference between two 'languages'), relevant for the speakers, or do the speakers have their own unique perceptions and criteria for assessing what they do when speaking? Auer (1988; also cf. Gafaranga & Torras 2001) argues that the speakers' perceptions should be the decisive factor. This means that Gumperz's definition has to be rephrased as follows: *Code-switching is the juxtaposition within the same speech exchange of passages of speech belonging to two different grammatical systems or subsystems which participants perceive as such.*

It is notoriously difficult to distinguish *borrowing* from code-switching. There can be no doubt that established borrowings (often called loanwords) – which can be found in dictionaries and are used and/or known by monolingual speakers as well – do not constitute switches in the above sense. However, there is considerable disagreement whether single, ad hoc insertions of lexical material from language B into a language A frame should be considered code-switching (for a summary of arguments against this, see Poplack 2004). Ad hoc ("nonce") borrowings may become established borrowings in the long run if they are used repeatedly and eventually passed on from the bilinguals to monolinguals. Since this process is inherently gradual, it is impossible to decide whether each individual borrowed token is ad hoc or established. Semantic criteria – above all the question of whether there is a corresponding non-borrowed word with approximately the same meaning available in variety B, or whether the borrowing fills a lexical gap – may influence whether a word becomes an established loan, but cannot indicate where the word is on the integration scale at a given moment. Structural integration of the borrowed element into the matrix language seems like a good criterion, but upon closer examination it leads to inclusive results as well: Phonetic integration is in itself gradual, and morphological integration is often absent since ad hoc borrowings into morphologically-rich varieties characteristically do not receive morphological marking ('bare forms'; cf. Budhzak-Jones & Poplack 1997; in contrast, cf. Poplack 2004 for a summary of sophisticated grammatical context analyses which describe the – gradual – process of borrowing). It may therefore be difficult or even impossible to define an exact break-off point between loanwords and borrowed words.

Another terminological distinction which often leads to misunderstandings is that between *code-switching* and *code-mixing*. The latter term is often used to refer to sentence-internal switching, while code-switching is reserved for cases of language alternation within independent syntactic units. Auer (e.g. 1999) propagates a different definition which captures a more fundamental difference. Here, the term "code-switching" is reserved for cases in which the individual juxtaposition of two codes (languages) is perceived and interpreted as a locally meaningful action by participants. The term "mixing" is used for cases in which the use of two languages is only meaningful (to participants) as a recurrent pattern, but not in each individual case. The fact that code-switching is more common between full syntactic units falls out naturally in this approach, since linguistic activities usually require larger grammatical units (such as 'sentences') to become recognizable. Frequent code-switching may be the first step towards a mixed speaking style (as argued by Myers-Scotton 1988, 1999 and Auer 1999).

A final question to be raised in this introductory section may come as a surprise: Do code-switchers have to be bilinguals? The answer obviously depends on what is meant by bilingualism. But it is clear that code-switching is possible with very little bilingual ability. Speakers can signal affiliation with a bilingual group by using token elements from a language in which they have only minimal proficiency (cf. e.g. Kelly-Holmes' "token bilingualism", 2005), and in certain forms of 'crossing' speakers may mimic or imitate other speakers by using what they think is typical of them, without being bilingual themselves (see Auer 2006 and Quist & Jørgensen 2007 for further references). These forms of code-switching have only moved into the focus of sociolinguistic research quite recently, but they are powerful interactional strategies (see below).

3. Early studies

Among the first studies of code-switching/-mixing, we find both pragmatic and structural investigations. Most important among the latter is Stolt's pioneering work on code-switching between Early New High German and Latin in Martin Luther's *Tischreden* (Stolt 1964) in which she distinguishes between *Umschaltung* (alternation) and *Einschaltung* (insertion) – a distinction which has played a role ever since (for instance in Muysken's 2000 typology). Among the first pragmatic analyses, Rubin (1962) relates code-switching to Brown and Gilman's (1960) work on terms of address, suggesting a parallel between code-switching and the way e.g. French and German speakers decide whether to use *tu/Du*, or *vous/Sie* respectively as pronouns of address in conversational interactions. Where the choice of a familiar or formal pronoun has implications for relationships of power and solidarity among French and German speakers in their respective speech communities, the choice of Spanish or Guaraní may be seen as having the same effect in Paraguay. That is, code-switching is a linguistic strategy available to bilinguals to reflect interpersonal relationships.

Blom & Gumperz's (1972) seminal paper on code-switching in Norway marked the beginning of new efforts to discern types of code-switching and their meaning throughout the world. Blom and Gumperz introduced a distinction between *situational* and *metaphorical* code-switching. Situational code-switching occurs where different linguistic varieties symbolize certain "social situations, roles and statuses and their attendant rights and obligations, expectations and assumptions" (Heller 1988: 5). Where a code is used out of context, it may evoke the aspects of the situation in which it would normally be expected, thus becoming meaningful as a metaphor of that situation. Where "situational switching involves change in participants and/or strategies, metaphorical switching involves only a change in topical emphasis" (Blom & Gumperz 1972: 409).

The frame of reference introduced by Blom and Gumperz spurred research on the discourse functions of code-switching. Timm (1975), for instance, found that a switch to Spanish from English was a way to show "such personal feelings as affection, loyalty, commitment, respect, pride, challenge, sympathy, or religious devotion". Spanish was also the code choice when the topic was related to life in Mexico or in the barrios. English, used for topics considered Anglo-American, was the language used to express "detachment, objectivity, alienation, displeasure, dislike, conflict of interest, aggression, fear or pain" (Timm 1975: 475). In essence, this kind of Spanish-English code-switching is often metaphorical in nature. The same pattern was found in other cases of switching in minority contexts as well, which led to a view of code-switching being meaningful because the minority language ('we code'; Blom & Gumperz 1972) is associated with the first set of feelings enumerated by Timm, and the dominant language ('they code') with the second set. Auer (1984a) calls approaches like the "we/they-code" model *semantic* because they build on the presupposition that the codes have a meaning which is independent of the local context in which they are used. This meaning is then channelled into the interaction and becomes relevant in it. In the unmarked case, i.e. where the situation 'fits' the language, no further inference is required. In the marked case, i.e. when language choice and the type of situation diverge, meanings are created on the basis of situation-specific inferences ('metaphorical' code-switching).

Since 1972, scholars have recognized that neither topics nor situations *per se* motivate code-switching. Instead of considering code-switching to be situational or metaphorical, Gumperz himself (1982) came to see it as a 'contextualization cue' – a way of generating meaning by putting a linguistic action into some kind of context – fulfilling a large number of interactional speech functions. Code-switching can be used to quote someone else, to direct an utterance to a particular individual, to emphasize a point, to elaborate, to establish either intimacy or social distance, etc. (cf. Gumperz 1976; Valdés-Fallis 1976; McClure 1977; Zentella 1981 for similar typologies of code-switching functions). In Auer ([1983] 1984b), these approaches are integrated into a model which distinguishes between discourse- vs. participant-related code-switching on the one hand, and insertional ('transfer') vs. alternational switching on the other. This model presents a more generalized way of dealing with code-switching functions than the previous listings. He also argues that the interactional relevance of code-switching can only be described adequately by subjecting its investigation to the strict methodological standards of sequential analysis (sequential analysis became available through conversation analysis around the time of those publications). The notion of participant-related code-switching made it possible to include cases in which code-switching is not a feature of the situation which is redefined (as in discourse-related switching), but in which certain attributes are ascribed by the participants to each other (including competence and incompetence in, or preference for one or the other language).

Another question already raised as early as 1969 by Gumperz and Hernandez-Chavez was whether different groups of speakers within a community switch in different ways. This differential approach was further pursued in quantitative studies on code-switching within a Labovian variationist framework, as pioneered by Shana Poplack (e.g. Sankoff & Poplack 1981; Poplack 1980, 1981). For this purpose, code-switching had to be broken down into different types (such as emblematic vs. intrasentential vs. intersentential; Poplack 1980, or 'clean' vs. 'ragged'; cf. di Pietro 1977). This eventually paved the way to an understanding of code-mixing (in the above terminology) as distinguished from code-switching. The results of these differential analyses showed a certain correlation of code-switching patterns with social networks, generational structure, and integration into the host society (in the case of immigrants).

Early studies on code-switching (such as the ones referred to in this section) usually also commented on grammatical constraints on code-switching in the community under investigation. For instance, Timm (1975) looked at the speech of bilingual Mexican-Americans in a number of domains and found that the "syntactic integrity" of each language was, for the most part, preserved. For example, Spanish *yo fui* and English *I went* are acceptable in each language while **I fui* or **yo went* would be seen as ridiculous in either. Likewise, switches are blocked between finite verbs and their infinitival complements such that e.g. **(they) want a venir* for *they want to come* is unacceptable. The use of auxiliaries with main verbs seems to be restricted to single language utterances, and verb negation is thought not to cross language boundaries. English *I don't want* cannot appear in a Spanish/English utterance as **I don't quiero*. A further prohibition involves noun phrases. English *his favorite spot* is unacceptable as Spanish/English **su favorito spot, su favorite lugar* or any permutation thereof. Such intersentential restrictions, Timm noted, "ensure the ultimate integrity and independence of each of the languages involved" (1975: 481).

In the subsequent development of the field, claims to universal constraints were made (most prominently, and first in a long series, by Poplack 1980). The long (and to the present day unfinished) discussion that followed is summarized in its early phase by Clyne (1987; also see Section 5 below).

Empirical psycholinguistic studies on code-switching were rare, although Clyne's 1967 study on the triggering of code-switching (for instance, through cognates preceding it) doubtlessly follows a psycholinguistic line of thought since it is concerned with the production side of (largely involuntary) switching.

4. The meaning of code-switching

4.1 The politics of code-switching

Whether code-switching occurs in a bilingual group of speakers, which form it takes, and how it is evaluated, is largely a result of political, economic, and historical forces at work. In discussing these factors, much emphasis is placed on the unequal distribution of linguistic resources in societies, and the regulatory role of institutions such as the education system in these distribution processes. Code-switching can index social class consciousness, political-ideological or ethnic affiliations and preferences, and so on.

An example of this kind of code-switching is Campus Swahili, a variety of Swahili used by the academic staff at the University of Dar es Salaam and by other members of the intellectual elite in Tanzania. Blommaert (1992) described how, although Campus Swahili is not the only urban Swahili variety in which Swahili is mixed with English, it is an exclusive, elite way of speaking due to the grammatical and semantic 'correctness' of English switches embedded into an equally 'high' variant of Swahili. Consider this example (Blommaert 1992: 66):

(1) *Shule   zilikuwa   nationalized karibu zote*
     schools they were nationalized nearly all
     'Almost all schools were nationalized.'

The English loan *nationalized* is correctly inflected, lexical-semantically intact, and harmoniously integrated in the syntactic string of inflected copula + past participle. It is the *quality* of these switches which sets Campus Swahili speech apart as an elite variant from other English-sprinkled Swahili speech in urban Dar es Salaam. The reason for this is the fact that 'good' English (and to a lesser degree, good Swahili) can usually only be obtained through – tightly controlled access to – higher education, since English is the language of instruction in secondary and post-secondary education. Only the small minority of Tanzanians who reach post-primary education are profusely exposed to 'high' varieties of English. Thus, university staff members speaking Campus Swahili exclude people who have not obtained the same degree of mastery in the two languages (1992: 67). The interplay here, too, reveals vestiges of a dual colonial past, such that the loanword *shule* ('school') has become fully incorporated into Swahili from German, while English is involved in the switch. Similarly, Campus Kiswahili represents a user effort to display a sense of superiority, to create the idea that one has knowledge others lack. It thus becomes part of the symbolic repertoire by means of which members of the intellectual elite enact and reproduce their elite membership. Such exclusive use of language is referred to by Myers-Scotton (1993b) as *elite closure*, a process whereby one group of speakers uses language to keep others out and thus deny them access to power.

To understand the pragmatic uses of code-switching, some scholars consider the diachronic aspects which have given rise to code-switching contexts. Susan Gal (1988) examines what she refers to as the *political economy of code choice*. It is her view that "to explain variation in code-switching, an integration of conversational, ethnographic and social historical evidence is required" (1988: 247). Given that code-switching is used conversationally to include and exclude others, to negotiate social identities, and to invoke sets of social rules and obligations, it must be recognized that the conversations involving code-switching index intergroup relations which "are the result of specific historical forces which produce different social and linguistic results at different times and places" (1988: 248). The factors that are responsible for code-switching, Gal suggests, may be used to examine the "symbolic aspects of power: how relations of domination, having a cultural component, are reproduced and sometimes resisted through local cultural practices" (1988: 249). Different forms of code-switching may correlate with different social and historical positions associated with ethnicity and class. Gal provides examples of how "the past and present structural position of a group can be used to understand its current code-switching practices" (1988: 251). Furthermore, such a perspective allows comparisons to be made elsewhere in the world. For example, suggests Gal, one may compare the Catalan situation in Barcelona with that of German in Transylvania. Both Catalans and Germans were politically and economically dominant in Spain and Transylvania (Romania), respectively. Significantly, they were dominant at a time when both Spain and Transylvania were relatively underdeveloped and peripheral within Europe. Both Catalan and German were long able to maintain prestige and authority over Castilian in Barcelona and Romanian in Transylvania for years, despite vast political and economic changes in their milieu. As late as the 1970s, intragroup code-switching among Catalans in Barcelona and Germans in Transylvania was rare, occurring occasionally to invoke humor.

Monica Heller (1992) examines French and English in Ontario and Quebec (Canada) between 1978–1990 to show how code-switching is a matter of socially constrained individual communicative repertoires. Given the availability of both linguistic and material resources, code choice is a political strategy used to regulate access to community resources. Scholars who take a political-economic perspective on code-switching and see it in an ever-changing historical context view language as a form of "symbolic capital" (in the sense of Bourdieu 1977) with situations of language use as "symbolic marketplaces" (Heller 1992: 124). Code-switching is a way in which people make claims to resources. With regard to the way French and English are used in Canada, Heller found that some people do not code-switch because they lack the requisite linguistic resources to do so. English speakers in Ontario and French speakers in Quebec who have not had contact with French and English are examples. Some people, on the other hand, opt not to code-switch in order to reinforce ethnic boundaries. English-rights activists in Quebec and Francophones in Ontario are examples. Still, some consider code-switching as a way to level ethnic differences. Among these are Anglophones in Quebec who send their children to French schools so their children will be able to compete in the French-dominant Quebec marketplace as adults. Heller's point is that code-switching behavior cannot be understood without an understanding of the social conditions underlying the fact that, within a community, people have different linguistic repertoires. The historical context of Canada, which has resulted in some people being monolingual and others not, needs to be seen as a factor in the linguistic strategies people use. To code-switch or not makes sense for some but not for others (cf. also Heller 1994).

Treffers-Daller's (1994) study of French-Dutch code-switching in Brussels found that only people belonging to the older generation in Brussels currently associate themselves with both Dutch and French and that French-Dutch code-switching seems to be disappearing. This situation contrasts with that found in Canada by Heller, where more and more people are availing themselves of the ability to choose French and English. What is happening in Brussels also contrasts with the situation in urban areas in parts of Africa where code-switching is increasingly becoming the norm and where standard forms are invoked primarily in the interest of asserting privilege. In Brussels, both standard Dutch and standard French are replacing the Brussels variety of each. The desire of speakers to maintain separateness works against the development of an urban language in this instance.

Swigart (1992) described the linguistic usage and attitudes of bilingual Dakar residents. Dakar, like a number of urban areas in post-colonial Africa, has an elite population of colonially educated people and a government that largely adopted the form of rule of the prior colonial regime. In such urban contexts, people speak a mixed urban form of language which, to an outsider, may appear to be bilingual (i.e. the outsider thinks people are speaking both a local language and a colonial language with numerous loanwords in each). For insiders, however, this urban code is variously seen as a corruption of the local language (Swahili in East Africa, Wolof in Senegal, etc.) or a reduced form of the colonial tongue (English or French). The way Wolof and French mix in Dakar has resulted in a form of speech which is the preferred (and 'normal') mode of communication for Senegalese city-dwellers. It is a linguistic manifestation of a more general "sociocultural creolization" evidenced in music, cinema, media, and fashion as well (Swigart 1992: Ch. 7: 4). Swigart's data are a case in point for the question of whether distinctions taken for granted by the outsider have equal relevance for insiders.

This urban mode of communication is, however, not homogeneous. Swigart found that older women spoke Wolof with the least amount of mixing while older men would code-mix or (depending on their ability) speak French. Similarly, younger women would use Wolof-only more than younger men would, with young men having evolved a mixed Wolof/French code among themselves as a kind of age-group argot. In addition to an age- and gender-based distinction, Swigart also found patterned disparity with regard to the way people feel about Urban Wolof. Most feel that it is somehow inferior, despite being widespread and the usual or expected mode of communication in their Dakar community. Swigart argues that sociohistorical circumstances are responsible for the emergence of this kind of mixing in Dakar. She suggests that future studies of code-mixing similarly be done on a community-wide basis, taking into consideration both synchronic language use as well as the diachronic conditions which created the urban milieu where mixed languages occur.

All these studies approach code-switching/-mixing (and bilingualism in general; cf. Heller 2007) as a symptom of something larger: political developments, language ideologies, social stratification, a particular history of migration or power distribution among various groups of speakers, and so on. On the other hand, recent studies also show that code-switching/-mixing is a way by which speakers actively *construct* their social identities within the larger macrosociological context, which at the same time constrains these construals (cf. Bailey 2007; Bierbach & Birken-Silverman 2007), thereby drawing both on local and global resources (cf. Sebba & Wootton 1998; Sebba & Tate 2002; Hinrichs 2006 on Jamaican/English code-switching). There is growing awareness that as a bilingual act of identity, code-switching/-mixing not only occurs in neatly defined bilingual communities (such as the traditional immigrant communities). Rather, code-switching/-mixing may also contest established correlations between languages and social roles and show a considerable degree of ambivalence and multiplicity (cf. Woolard 1999). For instance, Stroud (1998) shows how the traditional correlation between femininity and Taiap, and masculinity and Tok Pisin, respectively, is questioned by a female speaker who switches between Taiap and Tok Pisin in a small village in Papua New Guinea.

Most importantly, code-switching may both activate and contest *ethnic* (self- and other-) categorizations through what is known as *crossing* (Rampton 1995). Crossing is a particular kind of code-switching in which speakers 'transgress' into a language or variety which, in the social world in which the speakers act, is not generally thought to 'belong' to them. Keim (2002) gives the following example in which a Turkish-German bilingual girl brought up and living in Germany crosses into *Gastarbeiterdeutsch* (a fossilized learner variety typical of first-generation work migrants, i.e. a group of speakers who the daughter neither objectively belongs to nor wants to be affiliated with but to which the mother belongs):

(2) (from Keim 2002; German/Turkish/*Gastarbeiterdeutsch*; *Gastarbeiterdeutsch* underlined, Turkish in bold-face)

((participants: German interviewer IN, mother FU, daughter TE. They are talking about the new apartment into which the family of seven children and the parents are going to move. Will TE and her sister be willing to share a room? This is a question of concern to the mother.))

```
    01  IN   gehst mit hitace zusammen ins zimmer
                will you share a bedroom with Hitace ((her sister))
    02  TE   nee
                no
    03  IN:  net?
                no?
    04  TE   ⟨⟨p⟩ mid = der do = ned⟩
                not with this one
    05  IN   ((laughs [a little))
    06  TE              [ich will keins
                         I don't want any
    07  FU   ⟨⟨mf⟩ sieben kinder alle willen alle extra zimmer⟩
                seven children all want extra bedroom
    08  IN   die wollen' [jedes will n [zimmer
                they want each of them wants a bedroom of her own
    09  FU                 [isch'  [isch was machen?
                            I       what I do?
→10  TE   ⟨⟨f, imitating voice⟩ !JA :! was machen?
    11         hier sitzen wohin gehen?⟩ (-)
    12  FU   çadır ne kız almanca?
                what does tent mean in German, girl?
    13         çadırın adı [ne?
                what's the word for tent?
    14  TE              [zelt is gud
                         tent is good
    15  IN   ⟨⟨laughing⟩ zelt is gut (-) alle ins zelt⟩
                         tent is good (-) everybody into a tent
    16  FU:  ja ja he he
```

For the daughter, speaking *Gastarbeiterdeutsch* is a transgression into a variety which does not 'belong' to her but typifies another social group (that of first-generation *Gastarbeiter* such as her co-present mother), is clearly antagonistic: She uses language in order to erect a social boundary between her mother and herself which, in the context of the interaction at hand, serves to criticize the mother's point of view and, even more so, her lamenting style.

Crossing was first described by Ben Rampton (1995) in his study on the use of London Jamaican Creole and other immigrant varieties in the UK (Punjabi and Indian English) by 'white' English adolescents in the UK, which in turn built on previous sociological work by Hewitt (1986). Rampton observed crossing not in interactions between entitled and non-entitled users of the codes, but rather in intragroup situations where the 'crossers' were among themselves. (Hewitt 1986 in fact reports sanctions by Creole speakers when 'whites' used it, which explains this finding.)

4.2 Code-switching in interaction

A large number of studies of code-switching have been done from an interactional-sociolinguistic, discourse- or conversation-based standpoint. Among them, two main groups can be identified. The first group of studies aims at explaining the individual act of code-switching by reference to the social roles it symbolizes or evokes. A second group of studies argues that the conversational structure of code-switching represents a relatively independent third domain or type of orderliness between the macro-sociolinguistic and the grammatical order which, although sensitive to social factors, needs to be described in its own terms (Auer 1995).

Both approaches to the interactional meaning of code-switching stand in the tradition of Gumperz's interactional sociolinguistics which claims that the proper level of analysis of code-switching is the level of practice, as opposed to the level of grammar or community (Gumperz 1982: 41). Gumperz also emphasizes the importance of ethnographic, 'rich' data and detailed conversation-analytical analysis, because the intricate dynamics of contextualization can only be detected when data contain a maximum of contextual information and are subject to rigorous scrutiny.

The first group of discourse-oriented studies on code-switching treat code-switching as indexical of social relations. Myers-Scotton (1993a) is a coherent theoretical model of this kind (also cf. Myers-Scotton 1988, 1999). In her model of "code-switching as rational choice", she focuses on the individual speaker rather than on the 'situation' in the sense of an externally given determinant of language choice. In addition, an idea already foreshadowed in Blom and Gumperz (1972) becomes prominent in this model: An interactional exchange is characterized by a specific *set of rights and obligations* which are indexed by certain languages and evoked by their use. These rights-and-obligation sets are derived from the situation (Myers-Scotton 1999: 1263). Myers-Scotton differentiates various types of code-switching, two of which are reminiscent of Blom and Gumperz's distinction between situational and metaphorical switching. *Code-switching as a (sequentially) unmarked choice* occurs when speakers respond to a change in situation, from which a different set of rights-and-obligations derives, for which in turn a different language choice serves as an index. *Code-switching as a marked choice* occurs when speakers intentionally flout the maxim "choose the form of your conversational contribution such that it symbolizes the set of rights and obligations which you wish to be in force between speaker and addressee for the current exchange" (Scotton 1983: 116). This type of code-switching of course recalls Gumperz's "metaphorical code-switching", but there is a difference: For Myers-Scotton, a speaker wishes to renegotiate the rights-and-obligations balance between him/herself and the coparticipant(s) by code-switching in a situation in which this is not appropriate. For Gumperz, metaphorical code-switching activates an overlay of the metaphorical meaning on the rights-and-obligations-set evoked by the situation at hand.

It is not always easy to distinguish marked choices from unmarked choices due to a change of situation. Marked code-switching is of course only possible if the situational parameters strongly and unequivocally prescribe language choice. Some of Myers-Scotton's well-known examples take place in a bus in Nairobi, where Swahili is the unmarked choice for interactions with the conductor. In the following example, however, the passenger in the final exchange switches into English:

(3) (from Scotton & Ury 1977: 16–17, reprinted in Myers-Scotton 1988: 168)
(Swahili/ English code-switching, English underlined)

01 Passenger: *Nataka kwenda posta.*
                I want to go to the post office.
02 Conductor: *Kutoka hapa mpaka posta nauli ni senti hamsini.*
                From here to the post office, the fare is 50 cents.
03 ((Passenger gives the conductor a shilling from which there should be 50 cents in change.))
04 Conductor: *Ngojea change yako.*
                Wait for the change.
05 ((Passenger says nothing until a few minutes have passed and the bus nears the post office where the passenger will get off.))
06 Passenger: *Nataka change yangu.*
                I want my change.
07 Conductur: *Change utapata, Bwana.*
                You'll get your change, mister.
08 Passenger: <u>I am nearing my destination</u>.
09 Conductor: <u>Do you think I could run away with your change?</u>

Surely the choice of English in line 08 can be interpreted as a rhetorical strategy by which the passenger tries to renegotiate his and the conductor's rights and obligations. He tries to establish a hierarchical relationship in which he can claim superior status on grounds of education (higher education being symbolized by access to English). The conductor responds by also switching into the 'power code', thereby maintaining a balance of rights-and-obligations, although these rights and obligations have changed now. A renegotiation of the relationship between conductor and passenger has taken place, which leads to – and is indexed by – a renegotiation of the language-of-interaction. But it may be asked whether the difference between a situational renegotiation like in this example and a case of clearly unmarked code-switching is really so big. The main difference does not seem to be whether one language is 'predictable', but whether the renegotiation is successful and achieved in collaboration by both parties. This is not the case in (3), since the rights-and-obligations set the passenger wants to enact by switching into English is not accepted by the conductor, who insists on his authority and role-related professional integrity, and refuses the hierarchical relationship which the passenger wants to install.

In addition to code-switching as a marked or (sequentially) unmarked choice, Myers-Scotton's model provides further types. For instance, she argues that marked code choices may be unproblematic (and not invite further inferences) if they express deference (i.e. the speaker accommodates the co-participant's language choice, even though it is marked), or if one of the participants is not competent enough to speak the situationally unmarked language. In some situations, the unmarked language – and therefore the rights and obligations linked to the two codes – may not be easy to identify, since there are no trans-episodically stable associations of a language with this situation, and, as a consequence, language choice is open to negotiation. In these cases, the speaker may select one language and immediately switch into the other in order to keep the code choice open (*exploratory code-switching*). Finally, Myers-Scotton introduces a type of code-switching (or, in the terminology used in this paper, code-mixing) in which bilingual talk itself is the unmarked choice. Here, the situation does not change at all; rather, bilingual talk is the expected option. She explains these cases in terms of identities and assumes that "when the speaker wishes more than one social identity to be salient in the current exchange, and each identity is encoded in the particular speech community by a different linguistic variety, then those two or more codes constitute the unmarked choice" (1988) In this sense, she argues, speakers "have two such identities" at the same time, and want to make two different rights-and-obligations sets at relevant the same time (1988).

The second group of interactional studies approach code-switching from a conversation-analytic point of view. According to Auer (1984b, 1999), code-switching may be described as follows:

a. Code-switching occurs in a sociolinguistic context in which speakers orient towards a preference for one language at a time; i.e. it is usually possible to identify the language-of-interaction which is valid at a given moment, and when the switch itself occurs;
b. By departing from this established language-of-interaction, code-switching signals 'otherness' of the upcoming contextual frame and thereby achieves a change of 'footing'. The precise interpretation of this new footing needs to be 'filled in' in each individual case, a process in which previous experiences may be brought to bear on the interpretation of the case at hand;
c. Nonetheless, the mechanisms by which code-switching generates meaning can be described in a general way. Contexts are innumerable, as are the interactional meanings of code-switching; however the ways these meanings are constructed remain constant from one community to the next;
d. Code-switching may be a personal or group style. As a group style, its use may be subject to normative constraints valid within a speech community; however, it is not a variety in its own right;

e. Most code-switches occur at major syntactic and prosodic boundaries (at the clause or sentence level).[1] Since switching is activity-related, the utterance units affected by the switch must be large enough to constitute such an activity. For this reason, code-switching provides little interesting data for syntactic research;

f. Although code-switching bilinguals may be highly proficient in both languages, balanced proficiency is by no means a prerequisite. Indeed, code-switching is possible with a very limited knowledge of the 'other' language.

Conversational code-switching ("discourse-related code-switching" in the terminology of Auer 1995) has been attested widely in many bilingual groups of speakers. The data all prove that code-switching can be used as a cue by which speakers contextualize their utterances, rendering them meaningful in their conversational context (cf., among many: Auer 1984b; Gafaranga 2007; Gumperz 1982; Li Wei 1994, 2002; Sebba & Wootton 1998; Alfonzetti 1998; Guerini 2006; Jonsson 2005: Ch. 6; Bani-Shoraka 2005: Chs. 8 and 9). Several sub-types suggest themselves, such as:

– The distinction between switches that are closely linked to the 'machinery' of conversational exchanges, such as turn-taking, repair work, sequence organization, preference organization or participant constellation, beginning or ending a story, and switches that may be called stylistic, such as the contextualization of a different modality (joking/serious, fake/true, fantasy/reality) and of interpersonal intimacy vs. distance, expressivity vs. neutrality, etc.

– The distinction between turn-external and turn-internal switching. Turns may be composed of various units which represent different (minor or major) linguistic acts. Speakers may use code-switching to create turn-internal structure, for instance to set off reported speech from their own voice, statements from evaluations/assessments, topic from comment, turn-initial responsive elements, etc. (see Karrebaek 2003: 431–433 for examples).

– The distinction between alternational and insertional code-switching. Alternational switching (as in example (3) above) always questions the established language of interaction, if only for a temporary side-activity. It seems to be much more frequent than the insertional code-switching of single or complex units of B-talk into undisputed A-talk; still, the latter also occurs and can serve discourse-related functions, such as establishing coherence across utterances or turns (Angermeyer 2002; Guerini 2006: 203–216).

---

1. Exceptions are insertional code-switches (somewhat misleadingly called transfers in Auer 1984b in which a single word is inserted into an other-language frame to achieve a conversational effect; see Auer (1998: 6–7) for the discussion of an example.

- The distinction between structural contrast and interpersonal divergence. Code-switching capitalizes on the contrast between A-talk and B-talk. This contrast may be of a purely structural nature, or it may express a divergence between the speakers involved, i.e. their opinions, stances, or attitudes. This may happen, for instance, when a speaker diverges from an established language-of-interaction in order to express disagreement. The following example – a recording of members of the Chinese population in the UK – is a case in point:

(4) (from Li Wei 1994: 166) (Cantonese in simple italics, English underlined)
(Two young women are looking at new dresses.)

A: *nau, ni goh.*
 this one.
B: *ho leng a.*
 very pretty
A: *leng me?* (1.5)
 pretty?
 → very expensive.
B: *guai m gaui a?*
 expensive or not?
A: *hao guai.*
 very expensive.

The only departure from the established language-of-interaction (Cantonese) is A's English evaluative term *very expensive* in the arrowed line. B does not pick up on it; she continues to speak Cantonese. The language-of-interaction seems for a short moment to be in danger of dissolving. It is easy to see why this is so – and what conversational effect is achieved by it – if the sequential context is taken into consideration. Just prior to the switch, B had given an assessment of a dress identified by A in her first utterance. The assessment is positive. A first replies with a question repetition, which functions as an other-repair initiator. B, however, does not step back from her opinion (cf. the pause of 1.5 sec); at this point, A explicitly disagrees with B, at the same time abandoning the language-of-interaction. The disagreeing, negative assessment is given in the other language.

While discourse-related code-switching has received a lot of attention, and many conversational functions have been described, it must not be overlooked that there are other forms of bilingual talk that qualify as code-switching according to the definition given above. They are called participant-related in Auer (1984b). Often, they tell us less about the structure of the interaction than about the identities of the participants; in this sense, they close the gap between identity-related and conversational explanations in the investigation of the meaning of code-switching. Nevertheless, their sequential position is decisive for their interpretation. Many instances of such participant-related code-switching occur in language negotiation sequences in which co-participants negotiate the language for the conversation which is just about to begin, or renegotiate this language after situational shifts (see the examples in Guerini 2006: 106–120). Such preference-related switches can, additionally, have a discourse-related meaning. Each code-switch can endanger the established language-of-interaction; initiating and maintaining a language negotiation sequence can therefore be disaffiliative, but 'giving in' in such a sequence can also be affiliative.

Code-switching may also display a speaker's (relative and temporary) incompetence in one language or ascribe such (relative and temporary) incompetence to the conversational partner (competence-related code-switching). It is often forgotten that bilingual participants in interaction are seldom bilingual to the same degree; rather, they constantly display to each other their relative competence in one code vis-à-vis the other and thereby turn bilingual competence into a visible matter. This is partly done through code-switching which is then strongly linked to face-work: It can either be condescending or helpful to switch into the stronger language of one's partner. On the part of the speaker, a switch into one's stronger language can simply be a request for help from the co-participant or a way of gaining time to look for the right word, as in the following example:

(5) (from: Auer & Rönfeldt 2002) (F, a second-generation Italian/German bilingual immigrant girl in Germany, and a bilingual, non-immigrant, German-dominant adult woman, B; German underlined; topic: the visit of a TV team in the family's home; capitals represent stress)

    F: *siamo: andati n cuGIna,=*
           we went into the kitchen
    B: *nhn,=*
    F: *=volvavano (loro) vedere: äh:: i MMUri; (-)*
           they wanted to see the walls;
→   *perche sono tutti NE:ri e un po FEUCHT,*
           because they are all black and a little humid
    B: *ahha,=*
    F: *=un po UMmido:, (-)*
           a little humid
    B: *hn[hn,*
    B: *[e: hanne intervissatto, oppure Ie dovevo: (.) stare in cuCIna: a fare qualcossa.*
           and they interviewed (us), or I had to stay in the kitchen and do something

The speaker inserts a German word (*feucht*) into the arrowed utterance without any hedging (often, competence-related insertional switches as in this example are introduced by hesitation markers). However, despite the fact that her recipient signals understanding, she retrospectively self-repairs *feucht* and replaces it with the Italian counterpart *umido*. The self-repair first of all displays the speaker's basic competence in the two languages, but at the same time German is displayed as the language which comes to her mind first and is therefore dominant (cf. Auer 1997). By self-repairing the

German word in an Italian utterance, the speaker makes it clear that she orients her linguistic behavior towards a rule of 'one language at a time', in this case Italian (a language she sometimes struggles with, cf. the numerous dialectal interferences as well as the use of *volvavano* for standard Italian *volevano*). This also makes it possible to see the insertion of *feucht* as a competence-related switch, not as an unmarked case of mixing.

Code-switching and -mixing as conversational activities that display identities and contextualize speech can also be subject to sociolinguistic investigation in the more narrow sense of the word, i.e. by looking into whether, how, and how often different groups of speakers code-switch or -mix. Li Wei (Li Wei, Milroy & Pong Sin Ching 1992; Li Wei 1994) worked in northeast England among Chinese/English speakers and demonstrated how a social network approach to code-switching can be used to account for patterns of language choice in conversations more reliably than paying attention strictly to variables such as age, occupation, gender and so forth. A similar study combining ethnographic network analysis and code-switching was presented by Gal in her work on the German/Hungarian bilingual community in Oberwart, Austria (Gal 1979).

5. Grammatical constraints on code-switching

Based on work with Spanish/English data from Puerto Ricans living in New York, Poplack (1980, 1981) suggests that code-switching within sentences is constrained by the grammars of the respective languages involved. For example, the morphological structure of each language must be maintained within a word, e.g. the language cannot change between a stem and a suffix. Poplack refers to this as the *free morpheme constraint*. As argued in Poplack (2004), this constraint must be understood in the framework of a specific approach to code-switching which excludes most instances of single word insertions which are classified as "nonce borrowings". A second constraint – the *equivalence constraint* – operates such that the word order of the two languages involved in code transitions is homologous where the transition occurs. To illustrate, consider the following example (Poplack [1980] 2007: 219, Spanish/English, Spanish underlined):

(6) he was sitting down   <u>en la cama, mirandonos peleando,</u>
                          in the bed, watching us fighting
    <u>y</u>   I don't remember   <u>si el nos separo</u>
    and   if he separated us

The utterance consists of two grammatical units (here marked by different lines). In the first unit, the transition from English into Spanish occurs after the preposition, and since both Spanish and English prepositional phrases have the same structure (Prep + Det + N), they are homologous and transition into the other language is possible. In the second unit, conjoined with the first by the conjunction *y* which is also structurally homologous to *and*, the speaker returns to English after the conjunction, and again switches back into Spanish after the matrix verb of the first clause (the verbum sentiendi *remember*), which governs the complement clause introduced by *si*; English and Spanish matrix clause constructions are again homologous, and the mixed structure is therefore well-formed. In contrast, the constraint would have been violated in a mixed utterance like **si el us separated* since object pronouns precede the Spanish verb, but follow the English verb.

While Poplack's constraints have often been discussed as claims to universality, it seems more adequate to regard them as characteristic of a particular kind of code-mixing: Poplack presents a surface-oriented, incremental model of alternational mixing which is typical for some bilingual speakers and communities. In contrast, and more adequate for different data sets, Myers-Scotton (e.g. 2002) has developed a derivational model which assumes that each clause ('complementizer phrase') is associated with one matrix language only, which determines its overall structure.[2] Into this matrix, other-language elements can be inserted as *embedded language* elements. The model was originally developed on the basis of East African data, but has subsequently been applied to other bilingual situations as well (cf. Amuzu 2005; Finlayson et al. 1998; Owens 2005; Türker 2000; on a more critical note: Boumans 1998; Ziamari 2003; Muhamedowa 2006).

The selection of the matrix language imposes restrictions on the clause as a whole: The morpheme order must be that of the matrix language, and certain system morphemes must come from it. In the most recent version of the model (2002: 73–76), these morphemes are so-called late system morphemes whose selection depends on information from outside their immediate maximal projection (such as agreement markers or case). The embedded language may provide content morphemes, so-called early system morphemes (such as plural markers or determiners) whose form depends on the heads of their maximal projection but need no information from outside it, and so-called bridge system morphemes (morphemes linking content morphemes without needing information from their head; examples are genitive morphemes and suppletive morphemes).

Straightforward examples of insertional mixing according to the model are single content morpheme insertions such as the following:

(7) (Türker 2000: 70, Turkish/Norwegian in Oslo, Turkish underlined)

geç-en sene serie-de-ydi-k
pass-PART/SUBJ year league-LOC-bePAST-1PL
'last year we were in the league'

---

2. It should be noted that the terms 'matrix' and 'embedded' language are defined in purely grammatical terms in Myers-Scotton's later work. The idea expressed in her earlier papers, that the matrix language of a clause is also the language-of-interaction, i.e. the situationally adequate language, was later abandoned.

(8) (Myers-Scotton 2002: 89, Swahili/English in Nairobi, English underlined)
ile m-geni, hata si-ku-*comment*.
DEM/CL9 Ch/S-visitor, even 1SG.NEG-PST.NEG-comment
'that visitor, I did not even comment'

In the first case, it is the Norwegian word *serie* which is embedded into a Turkish frame; in the second case, it is the English verb (stem) *comment*. Both are treated as if they were words of the matrix language.[3] Note that due to the different morphological structure of the languages, no homology exists on the surface level.

An example of a bridge morpheme which is inserted into a Turkish matrix is the German preposition *mit* in the N *mit* N- construction:

(9) (Treffers-Daller 1995: 254; German/Turkish, German underlined)
Pilav mit pirinç yap-ıl-ır
Boiled-rice with unboiled-rice make-PASS-AOR
'Boiled rice is made with unboiled rice'

The special status of early system morphemes is responsible for the frequently observed double marking of the same grammatical category both with the early system morphemes of the embedded and the matrix language, as in:

(10) (Backus 1992: 90; Turkish/Dutch in the Netherlands, Dutch underlined)
Pol-en-lar-a Holanda-ca ders ver-di
pole-PL-PL-DAT Dutch-SUFF ders give-PAST
'he taught Dutch to Poles'

Here, the plural is marked both by the Dutch suffix *-en* and the Turkish suffix *-lar* (the matrix language suffix must be more peripheral than the embedded language suffix). The opposite also occurs, i.e. inserted words may appear as bare forms, with no morphological/grammatical marking at all. In the following example, the inserted Dutch noun *bibliotheek* in a Moroccan Arabic matrix clause should receive both a prepositional clitic /l/ and a definite prefix /l-/ if it were to conform to the grammar of the matrix language; however, it is inserted with neither of them. Note that the Dutch preposition is also lacking. According to Boumans (1998: 218), omission is particularly frequent after verbs of motion, where the role of the object can easily be reconstructed from the semantics of the verb and the object noun:

(11) (Boumans 1998: 218; Moroccan Arabic/Dutch in the Netherlands, Dutch underlined)
ġadi-n ne-mši-w [ ][ ] *bibliotheek*
FUT-PL 1-go-PL library
'We'll go to the library'

---

3. This is why researchers like Poplack do not speak of insertional mixing, but of borrowing here.

Myers-Scotton (1993c, 2002) argues that bare forms are used when the structures of the two languages are not compatible (2002: 119–27; also cf. Nortier 1990; Muysken 2000: 83). In the same way, Myers-Scotton accounts for another way in which the dominance of the matrix language over the embedded language can be avoided, i.e. the insertion of internally complex 'islands' which follow the grammar of the embedded language instead of the matrix language. These islands may be inflected words in the embedded language, as in:

(12) (Stolt 1964: 69; Latin/Early New High German)

omnes gentes, quae non habent religionem, muss-en ***superstitio-nem***
　　　　　　　　　　　　　　　　　　　　　must-1PL superstition-ACC.SG.
hab-en (371)
have-INF
'all people who don't have a religion, must have a superstition'

Islands can also be larger units, such as the modified noun phrase *humanum cor* in the following example:

(13) (Stolt 1964: 81; Latin/Early New High German)

<u>Human-um</u>　　　　　　<u>cor</u>　　　　　　kann　es　nit　fass-en
human-NEUTR.NOM.SG　heart- NEUTR.NOM.SG　can-3SG　it　not　seize-INF
'the human heart cannot grasp it'

The model is able to deal with a large amount of insertional mixing data. However, there are also numerous cases in which the neat division between matrix and embedded language presupposed by the model is not maintained. Thus, it is possible that the embedded language influences the structure of the matrix language (against the prediction of the model). In the following example, Early New High German (the matrix language) converges toward the embedded language (Latin) (more examples in Auer & Muhamedova 2005):

(14) (Stolt 1964: 71; Latin/Early New High German)

obschon [ ] <u>peccator-es</u> izt sind …
although sinner-PL now be-3PL.PRES
'although they are now sinners…'

Early New High German, like modern German, needs an overt subject and is therefore not a pro-drop language. In Latin, information about the subject is fully encoded in the finite verb, and no overt subject pronoun is necessary.

German:　*obschon sie Sünder sind*
Latin:　　*quamquam [ ] peccatores sunt*

In the example, the transference of the embedded language structure to the matrix language leads to the omission of the subject pronoun.

More frequently, we find the opposite, i.e. the structure of a complex embedded language island does not follow the grammar of the embedded language completely but converges towards the matrix language (a case which is also acknowledged by Myers-Scotton 2002: 102–105). For instance, there is strong evidence that in Kazakh/Russian code-mixing in Almaty (Muhamedowa 2006; Auer & Muhamedova 2005), Russian as an embedded language loses the gender category (as well as number), although this grammatical category is preserved in monolingual Russian discourse produced by the same speakers.

(15) (Auer & Muhamedova 2005; Russian/Kazahk in Almaty; Russian in Cyrillic writing)
Уже *anau* **стар-ый площадь**-*ti ne-ler-di žönde-di*
already this old-? square-?-ACC thing-PL-ACC renovate-PAST
'there the old square and so on were already renovated'

Apart from the initial adverb, the sentence is Kazakh, which is clearly the matrix language. The crucial issue is the inserted Russian island which fails to comply with the grammar of monolingual Russian since there is no gender agreement: *площадь* is a feminine noun, and the adjective modifying it should agree with it: *старая*. The use of the masculine form regardless of the gender of the nominal head in a large number of cases suggests that due to the influence of Kazakh (which has no gender), the Russian used as an embedded language structurally converges towards the matrix language.[4]

Finally, there are examples of *mutual* convergence between matrix and embedded language, such as in Hungarian/German code-mixing by German minorities in Hungary as discussed in Szabó (2008). In this old bilingual community, we find utterances such as the following:

(16) (Szabó 2008: 313; Hungarian/German dialect; Hungarian underlined)
do de ötlet war gut de mama ihre.
PART DET idea was good DET mum hers
'mum's idea was good'

den fogad immer el
that-AKK.MASC. take-? always VERB.PREF
'they always accept it.'

---

4. A similar case of gender neutralization is reported for Malinche Mexicano/Spanish mixing by Hill and Hill (1986: 266ff).

The second line of the utterance is remarkable for various reasons. First, German dialect seems to underlie the sentence, since the use of a separable verb prefix (*fogad...el* from the verb *el-fogad* 'to accept') does not conform to Hungarian grammar.[5] Rather, it seems to be modelled after the German pattern of separable verb particles (as in *nehmen... an* from the verb *an-nehmen*). It is difficult, however, to call *fogad ... el* an island, since its two elements are discontinuous and do not follow Hungarian morphology: The verb *fogad* receives no person and number marking as would be required in Hungarian (and German), i.e. it is a bare form. On the other hand, Hungarian has an impact on the sentence beyond that of providing lexical material which is inserted into a German sentence pattern. The subject pronoun is deleted, which is possible in Hungarian but not in German. Both languages seem to have converged and neither of them is used in a monolingual way, but it is difficult to say which one is the matrix language and which one the embedded language.

In sum, there is ample evidence that code-mixing creates specific forms of convergence which may not be present in the monolingual speech of the same bilingual speakers. These cases do not seem to be restricted to sociolinguistic situations of language attrition and shift, as Myers-Scotton (2002: 105) claims for 'composite code-switching'. In composite code-switching, "the abstract morphosyntactic frame derive[s] from more than one source language" and it is therefore impossible to identify a single matrix language.

While Poplack's and Myers-Scotton's theories of how the mixing of two languages is constrained have arguably been the most debated ones, there are other theories which are often formulated with reference to a specific version of generative grammar (such as Joshi 1985; Mahootin 1993; Di Sciullo, Muysken & Singh 1986), most of which do not stand the test of corpus-based studies, however. Some recent studies inspired by the Minimalist Programme argue that there should be no separate constraints on code-mixing at all other than the lexically encoded grammars of the languages involved (MacSwan 2004; Chan 1999). In all these studies, the claim is that the proposed constraints are universal.

As in the case of pragmatic theories of code-switching, grammatical differences can also be used to differentiate social groups (for instance, generations of immigrants), as has been shown by Backus (e.g. 1996).

---

5. While the separation of particle and verb in German is exclusively determined by the syntactic pattern of the sentence (in which the verb provides the left bracket, i.e. second position, and the particle the right bracket, i.e. final position), Hungarian separable verb prefixes are used to mark focus. In the present context, no separation is possible.

6. Future directions in code-switching research

The field of code-switching and code-mixing research is rapidly developing, and new aspects and perspectives are appearing. We can only mention some of these burgeoning fields here. For instance, there is a considerable interest in code-mixing and -switching in small children (cf. Meisel 1989; Köppe 1997; Tracy 2000) focusing around the issue of whether early mixed utterances are evidence of a fused system or whether the child is from the very start in a position to keep the two languages functionally apart. An important issue is whether the child's mixing is influenced by the input it receives from the parents, who may or may not follow a strategy of 'one parent – one language' (Lanza 1997). These are mostly longitudinal single case studies in middle class contexts. Bilingual interactions among older children and in a community setting are much less frequently investigated (but cf. Zentella 1997, particularly Ch. 10), and language acquisition in young and very young children in immigrant and lower class contexts is hardly ever studied. Code-switching in the classroom has received some attention in educational linguistics (cf. Dirim 1998; Martin-Jones 2000), and so has mixing and switching among adult second language learners (Lüdi 2003).

Another burgeoning area is psycholinguistic studies on the production and perception of code-mixing, although it seems that the methodological difficulties of experimentally testing linguistic activities which are typical of spontaneous speech still hamper the development of this approach (see Grosjean 1997 for a summary). The prevalent theme in psycholinguistic studies on bilingual speech production still seems to be the effect of the language *not* used (which in many models needs to be actively suppressed) on the language used, not on the alternating use of two languages (Costa 2004). The models of bilingual speech which have been proposed (such as Green 1986; de Bot's 1992 adaptation of Levelt's 1989 speaking model; or Myers-Scotton 2002 and Clyne 2003 from the linguists' side) are more deductive or based on indirect evidence from spontaneous speech than tested empirically.

Finally, there is the big but unresolved question of whether and how switching and mixing contribute to language change (cf. Muysken 2000, Ch. 9). Bilingual talk may not only reflect convergence between two languages, but also actively contribute to it, making the two languages more compatible than they used to be. There is also an ongoing debate about the status of full-fledged languages which involve surface alternations of two ancestor languages (so-called mixed or fused languages). One way of explaining the emergence of such languages is to think in terms of the sedimentation of frequent code-mixing (cf. Muysken 2007 for a discussion).

References

Alfonzetti, G. (1998). The conversational dimension in code-switching between Italian and dialect in Sicily. In P. Auer (ed.) *Code-Switching in Conversation. Language, Interaction and Identity*: 180–214. Routledge.

Alvarez Cáccamo, C. (1998). From 'switching code' to 'code-switching': Towards a reconceptualisation of communicative codes. In P. Auer (ed.) *Code-Switching in Conversation. Language, Interaction and Identity*: 29–50. Routledge.

Amuzu, E.K. (2005). Revisiting the classic codeswitching and composite codeswitching distinction: a case study of nonverbal codeswitching. *Australian Journal of Linguistics* 25 (1): 127–151.

Angermeyer, P. (2002). Lexical cohesion in multilingual conversation. *International Journal of Bilingualism* 6 (4): 361–393.

Auer, P. (1984a). On the meaning of conversational code-switching. In P. Auer & A. di Luzio (eds.) *Interpretive Sociolinguistics: Migrants – Children – Migrant Children*: 87–112. Narr.

—— [1983] (1984b). *Bilingual conversation*. John Benjamins.

—— (1988). A conversation analytic approach to code-switching and transfer. In M. Heller (ed.) *Code-switching*: 187–213. Mouton de Gruyter.

—— (1995). The pragmatics of code-switching: a sequential approach. In L. Milroy & P. Muysken (eds.) *One Speaker, Two Languages*: 115–135. Cambridge University Press.

—— (1997). Members' assessments and ascriptions of (in-)competence in bilingual conversation. In J.R. Dow & M. Wolff (eds.) *Languages and Lives* (F.S. W. Enninger): 121–136. Peter Lang.

—— (1998). 'Bilingual Conversation' revisited. In P. Auer (ed.) *Code-Switching in Conversation. Language, Interaction and Identity*: 1–24. Routledge.

—— (1999). From code-switching via language mixing to fused lects: toward a dynamic typology of bilingual speech. *International Journal of Bilingualism* 3 (4): 309–332.

—— (2006). Sociolinguistic crossing. In K. Brown (ed.) *Encyclopedia of Language and Linguistics 11*, 2nd ed.: 490–492. Elsevier.

—— (2007). The monolingual bias in bilingualism research or: why bilingual talk is (still) a challenge for linguistics. In M. Heller (ed.) *Bilingualism – A Social Approach*: 319–339. Palgrave.

Auer, P. & R. Muhamedova (2005). 'Embedded Language' and 'Matrix Language' in insertional language mixing: some problematic cases. *Italian Journal of Linguistics/Rivista di linguistica* 17 (1): 35–54.

Auer, P. & B. Rönfeldt (2002). Erinnern und Vergessen. Erschwerte Wortfindung als soziales und interaktives Problem. In M. Schecker (ed.) *Wortfindung und Wortfindungsstörungen*: 77–108. Narr.

Backus, A. (1992). *Patterns of Language Mixing: A Study of Turkish-Dutch Biligualism*. Harrassowitz.

—— (1996). *Two in One: Bilingual Speech of Turkish Immigrants in the Netherlands*. Tilburg University Press.

Bailey, B. (2007). Language alternation as a resource for identity negotiations among Dominican American bilinguals. In P. Auer (ed.) *Style and Social Identities*: 29–56. Mouton de Gruyter.

Bani-Shoraka, H. (2005). *Language Choice and Code-Switching in the Azerbaijani Community in Teheran*. Acta universitatis Upsaliensis/Studia Iranica Upsaliensia 9, Uppsala University Library.

Berruto, G. (2005). Dialect/standard convergence, mixing, and models of language contact: the case of Italy. In P. Auer, F. Hinskens & P. Kerswill (eds.) *Dialect Change*: 81–95. Cambridge University Press.

Bierbach, C. & G. Birken-Silverman (2007). Names and identities, or: How to be a hip young Italian migrant in Germany. In P. Auer (ed.) *Style and Identities*: 121–154. Mouton de Gruyter.

Blom, J.P. & J. Gumperz (1972). Social meaning in linguistic structures: code-switching in Norway. In J. Gumperz & D. Hymes (eds.) *Directions in Sociolinguistics*: 407–434. Holt, Rinehart and Winston.

Blommaert, J. (1992). Codeswitching and the exclusivity of social identities: Some data from Campus Kiswahili. *Journal of Multilingual and Multicultural Development* 13: 57–70.

Boumans, L. (1998). *The Syntax of Codeswitching. Analysing Moroccan Arabic/Dutch Conversation (Studies in Multilingualism* 12). Tilburg University Press.

Bourdieu, P. (1977). The economics of linguistic exchanges. *Social Science Information* 16: 645–668.

Brown, R. & A. Gilman (1960). The pronouns of power and solidarity. In T.A. Sebeok (ed.) *Style in Language*: 53–276. MIT Press.

Budzhak-Jones, S. & S. Poplack (1997). Two generations, two strategies: The fate of bare English-origin nouns in Ukrainian. *Journal of Sociolinguistics* 1: 225–258.

Chan, B. (1999). *Aspects of the Syntax, Production and Pragmatics of code-switching with special reference to Cantonese-English*. Ph.D. dissertation. University College, London.

Clyne, M. (1967). *Transference and Triggering. Observations on the Language Assimilation of Postwar German-speaking Migrants in Australia*. Mouton.

—— (1987). Constraints on code switching: how universal are they? *Linguistics* 25: 739–764.

—— (2003). *Dynamics of Language Contact*. Cambridge University Press.

Costa, A. (2004). Speech production in bilinguals. In T.K. Bhatia & W.C. Ritchie (eds.) *The Handbook of Bilingualism*: 201–223. Blackwell.

De Bot, K. (1992). A bilingual production model: Levelt's 'speaking' model adapted. *Applied Linguistics* 13: 1–24.

Di Pietro, R.J. (1977). Code-switching as a verbal strategy among bilinguals. In D.J. Paradis (ed.) *Aspects of Bilingualism* (4th Lacus Forum): 275–282. Hornbeam Press.

Di Sciullo, A.-M., P. Muysken & R. Singh (1986). Government and code-mixing. *Journal of Linguistics* 22: 1–24.

Dirim, I. (1998). *'Var mI lan Marmelade?' Türkisch-deutscher Sprachkontakt in einer Grundschulklasse*. Waxmann.

Finlayson, R., K. Calteaux & C. Myers-Scotton (1998). Orderly mixing and accommodation in South African codeswitching. *Journal of Sociolinguistics* 2 (3): 395–420.

Gafaranga, J. (2007). Code-switching as a conversational strategy. In P. Auer & Li Wei (eds.) *Handbook of Multilingualism and Multilingual Communication*: 279–313. Mouton de Gruyter.

Gafaranga, J. & M.-C. Torras (2001). Language vs. medium in the study of bilingual conversation. *International Journal of Bilingualism* 5: 195–219.

Gal, S. (1979). *Language Shift. Social Determinants of Linguistic Change in Bilingual Austria*. Academic Press.

—— (1988). The political economy of code choice. In M. Heller (ed.) *Code-switching. Anthropological and Sociolinguistic Perspectives*: 245–264. Mouton de Gruyter.

Green, D.W. (1986). Control, activation and resource: a framework and a model for the control of speech in bilinguals. *Brain and Language* 27: 210–233.

Grosjean, J. (1997). Processing mixed languages: issues, findings and models. In A.M.B. de Groot & J.F. Kroll (eds.) *Tutorials in Bilingualism: Psycholinguistic Perspectives*: 225–254. Lawrence Erlbaum.

Guerini, F. (2006). *Language Alternation Strategies in Multilingual Settings*. Peter Lang.

Gumperz, J. (1976). The sociolinguistic significance of conversational code-switching. In J. Cook-Gumperz & J. Gumperz (eds.) *Papers on Language and Context* (Working Paper No 46): 59–99. Berkeley.

―― (1982). *Discourse Strategies*. Cambridge University Press.

Gumperz, J.J. & E. Hernandez-Chavez (1969). *Cognitive aspects of bilingual communication*. (Language Behavior Research Laboratory Research Paper no.28). Berkeley.

Heller, M. (1988). Introduction. In M. Heller (ed.) *Code-switching*: 1–24. Mouton de Gruyter.

―― (1992). The politics of codeswitching and language choice. *Journal of Multilingual and Multicultural Development* 13 (1–2): 123–142.

―― (1994). *Crosswords*. Mouton de Gruyter.

―― (2007). Bilingualism as ideology and practice. In M. Heller (ed.) *Bilingualism – A Social Approach*: 1–22. Palgrave Macmillan.

Hewitt, R. (1986). *White talk black talk*. Cambridge University Press.

Hill, J. & K. Hill (1986). *Speaking Mexicano*. University of Arizona Press.

Hinrichs, L. (2006). *Codeswitching on the Web*. John Benjamins.

Jonsson, C. (2005). *Code-switching in Chicano Theater*. University of Umeå, Institutionen för moderna språk, Skrifter No 17.

Joshi, A.K. (1985). Processing of sentences with intrasentential code-switching. In D.R Dowty, L. Karttunen & A.M. Zwicky (eds.) *Natural Language Processing*: 190–205. Cambridge University Press.

Karrebæk, M.S. (2003). Iconicity and structure in codeswitching. *International Journal of Bilingualism* 7 (4): 407–441.

Kelly-Holmes, H. (2005). *Advertising as Multilingual Communication*. Palgrave Macmillan.

Keim, I. (2002). Bedeutungskonstitution und Sprachvariation. Funktionen des 'Gastarbeiterdeutsch' in Gesprächen jugendlicher Migrantinnen. In A. Deppermann & Th. Spranz-Fogasy (eds.) *Be-deuten. Wie Bedeutung im Gespräch entsteht*: 134–157. Stauffenburg.

Köppe, R. (1997). *Sprachentrennung im frühen bilingualen Erstspracherwerb Französisch/Deutsch*. Narr.

Lanza, E. (1997). *Language Mixing in Infant Bilingualism: A Sociolinguistic Perspective*. Clarendon Press.

Levelt, W.J. (1989). *Speaking*. MIT Press.

Lüdi, G. (2003). Second language acquisition by migrants in Europe. In R. Posner & J. N. Green (eds.) *Trends in Romance Linguistics and Philology*: 495–534. Mouton de Gruyter.

Macswan, J. (2004). Code switching and linguistic theory. In T.K. Bhatia & W.C. Ritchie (eds.) *The Handbook of Bilingualism*: 283–312. Blackwell.

Mahootian, S. (1993). *A Null Theory of Codeswitching*. Unpublished doctoral dissertation. Northwestern University.

Martin-Jones, M. (2000). Bilingual classroom interaction: A review of recent research. *Language Teaching* 33: 1–9.

McClure, E. (1977). Aspects of code switching among Mexican-American children. In M. Saville-Troike (ed.) *Linguistics and Anthropology*: 93–115. Georgetown University Press.

Meisel, J. (1989). Early differentiation of languages in bilingual children. In K. Hyltenstam & L. Obler (eds.) *Bilingualism Across the Lifespan*: 13–40. Cambridge University Press.

Meeuwis, M. & J. Blommaert (1998). A monolectal view of code-switching: Layered code-switching among Zairians in Belgium. In P. Auer (ed.) *Code-Switching in Conversation. Language, Interaction and Identity*: 76–100. Routledge.

Muhamedowa, R. (2006). *Untersuchungen zum kasachisch-russischen Code-mixing (mit Ausblicken auf den uigurisch-russischen Sprachkontakt)*. Lincom.

Muysken, P. (2000). *Bilingual Speech: A Typology of Code-Mixing*. Cambridge University Press.
—— (2007). Mixed codes. In P. Auer & Li Wei (eds.) *Handbook of Multilingualism and Multilingual Communication*: 315–340. Mouton de Gruyter.
Myers-Scotton, C. (1988). Code switching as indexical of social negotiations. In M. Heller (ed.) *Code-switching*: 151–186. Mouton de Gruyter.
—— (1993a). *Social Motivations for Codeswitching*. Oxford University Press.
—— (1993b). Elite closure as a powerful language strategy: the African case. *International Journal of Sociology and Language* 103: 149–163.
—— (1993c). *Duelling languages: grammatical structure in codeswitching*. Clarendon Press.
—— (1999). Explaining the role of norms and rationality in codeswitching. *Journal of Pragmatics* 32: 1259–1271.
—— (2002). *Contact Linguistics. Bilingual Encounters and Grammatical Outcomes*. Oxford University Press.
Nortier, J. (1990). *Dutch-Moroccan Arabic Code-switching among Young Moroccans in the Netherlands*. Foris.
Owens, J. (2005). Hierachicalized matrices: codeswitching among urban Nigerian Arabs. *Linguistics* 43 (5): 957–993.
Paul, H. (1898). *Prinzipien der Sprachgeschichte*. Niemeyer.
Poplack, S. [1980] (2007). Sometimes I'll start a sentence in English y termino en espanol. Toward a typology of code-switching. In Li Wei (ed.) *The Bilingualism Reader*, 2nd ed.: 213–243. Routledge.
—— (1981). Syntactic structure and social function of code-switching. In R.P. Durán (ed.) *Latino Language and Communicative Behaviour*: 169–184. Ablex.
—— (2004). Code-switching. In U. Ammon, N. Dittmar, K.J. Mattheier & P. Trudgill (eds.) *Soziolinguistik. An International Handbook*. 2nd ed.: 589–596. de Gruyter.
Pujolar, J. (2007). Bilingualism and the nation-state in the post-national era. In M. Heller (ed.) *Bilingualism – A Social Approach*: 71–110. Palgrave Macmillan.
Quist, P. & J.N. Jørgensen (2007). Crossing – negotiating social boundaries. In P. Auer & Li Wei (eds.) *Handbook of Multilingualism and Multilingual Communication*: 371–390. Mouton de Gruyter.
Rampton, B. (1995). *Crossing*. Longman.
Rubin, J. (1962). Bilingualism in Paraguay. *Anthropological Linguistics* 4 (1): 52–58.
Sankoff, D. & S. Poplack (1981). A formal grammar for code-switching. *Papers in Linguistics* 14: 3–45.
Scotton, C. (1983). The negotiation of identities in conversation: a theory of markedness and code choice. *International Journal of the Sociology of Language* 44: 115–136.
Scotton, C. & W. Ury (1977). Bilingual strategies: the social functions of code-switching. *International Journal of the Sociology of Language* 13: 5–20.
Sebba, M. & S. Tate (2002). 'Global' and 'local' identities in the discourses of British-born Caribbeans. *International Journal of Bilingualism* 6 (1): 75–89
Sebba, M. & T. Wootton (1998). We, they and identity: sequential versus identity-related explanation in code-switching. In P. Auer (ed.) *Code-Switching in Conversation. Language, Interaction and Identity*: 262–289. Routledge.
Stolt, B. (1964). *Die Sprachmischung in Luthers Tischreden. Studien zum Problem der Zweisprachigkeit*. Almqvist and Wiksell.
Stroud, C. (1998). Perspectives on cultural variability of discourse and some implications for code-switching. In P. Auer (ed.) *Code-Switching in Conversation. Language, Interaction and Identity*: 321–348. Routledge.

—— (2007). Multilingualism in ex-colonial countries. In P. Auer & Li Wei (eds.) *Handbook of Multilingualism and Multilingual Communication*: 509–538. Mouton de Gruyter.

Swigart, L. (1992). *Practice and Perception*. Ph.D. Diss., University of Washington.

Szabó, C. (2008). *Language Shift und Code-Mixing: Deutsch-ungarisch-rumänische Mehrsprachigkeit in einer dörflichen Gemeinde in Nordwestrumänien*. Unpublished Ph.D. Thesis, University of Freiburg.

Timm, L.A. (1975). Spanish-English code-switching. *Romance Philology* 28 (4): 473–481.

Tracy, R. (2000). Language mixing as a challenge for linguistics. In S. Döpke (ed.) *Cross-linguistic Structures in Simultaneous Bilingualism*: 11–36. John Benjamins.

Treffers-Daller, J. (1994). *Mixing Two Languages*. Mouton de Gruyter.

—— (1995). Les effets contrastants de l'emprunt et de l'interférence: similitudes et dissimilitudes entre Bruxelles et Strasbourg. *Plurilinguismes* 9/10: 101–124.

Türker, E. (2000). *Turkish-Norwegian Codeswitching*. University of Oslo, Faculty of Arts, Dissertation Series No. 83.

Valdés-Fallies, G. (1976). Social interaction and code-switching patterns: A case study of Spanish/English interaction. In G.D. Keller, R.V. Tetschner & S. Viera (eds.) *Bilingualism in the Bicentennial and Beyond*: 53–85. Bilingual Review.

Vogt, H. (1954). Language contact. *Word* 10 (2/3): 365–374.

Wei, Li (1994). *Three Generations, Two Languages, One Family. Language Choice and Language Shift in a Chinese Community in Britain*. Multilingual Matters.

—— (2002). What do you want me to say? On the conversation analysis approach to bilingual interaction. *Language and Society* 31: 159–180.

Wei, Li, L. Milroy & Pong Sin Ching (1992). A two-step sociolinguistic analysis of code-switching and language choice. *International Journal of Applied Linguistics* 2 (1): 63–80.

Woolard, K. (1999). Simultaneity and bivalency as strategies in bilingualism. *Journal of Linguistic Anthropology* 8 (1): 3–29.

Zentella, A.C. (1981). 'Hablamos los dos. We speak both'. Growing up biligual in El Barrio. Unpublished Ph.D. thesis, University of Pennsylvania.

Zentella, A.C. (1997). *Growing up Bilingual*. Blackwell.

Ziamari, K. (2003). *Le Code switching intra-phrastique dans les conversations des étudiants marocains de l'ENSAM: approche linguistique du duel entre l'árabe marocain et le français*. Thèse de doctorat, INALCO-Fès.

Cognitive sociology

Barry Saferstein
California State University San Marcos

1. Historical overview

Cognitive sociology applies ethnographically informed analysis of everyday social interaction, including problem solving in organizational contexts, in order to examine the role of social interpretive processes in the production and reproduction of authority structures. It develops longstanding sociological concerns about the relation between social organization, collective activity, and mind: e.g. individuals' understandings of their relationships to collectivities (Durkheim 1933); the relation between class consciousness and domination (Marx & Engels 1970); sociocultural influences on concepts of social order (Weber 1958); the relation of action to societal norms (Parsons 1937). In this regard, a principal finding of cognitive sociological research is that cognition is inherently social and cultural – not merely in terms of people sharing the topics and results of their interactions, but in terms of the interpretive practices through which people constitute the topics and results of their interactions. The study of this interrelationship of interaction, social organization, and cognition explicates the nature of order and power in particular social settings.

Cognitive sociology also shares a number of concerns with other disciplines and research traditions. These include:

1. The interactional production of social organization through practical sensemaking activities, particularly language (cf. ethnomethodology, conversation analysis, frame and dramaturgical analysis).
2. Social aspects of cognition: i.e. the relation of environment and interaction to the distribution of knowledge and organization of memory (cf. cognitive anthropology, cognitive psychology, cognitive science).
3. How knowledge relevant to a particular setting or activity is developed and conveyed through language (cf. discourse analysis).
4. Patterns of language use as components of cultural differences and similarities (cf. linguistic anthropology, ethnography of communication).
5. Language as a form of action, and epistemological stance as a consequence of language use in a particular context (cf. philosophy of language).
6. The epistemological consequences of human actions and their tangible results (cf. phenomenology, pragmatism).

These strands of social theory and research were brought together in an approach to cognitive sociology that emphasizes research methods and theory consistent with pragmatics and discourse analysis by Aaron V. Cicourel in *Cognitive sociology: Language and meaning in social interaction* (1973). Cicourel found that the cognitive processes indexed in contemporary linguistic theories involve social activities of meaning production that are also central to social organization. Integrating studies in sociology, linguistics, and cognition, he pointed out that interactionally developed understandings of social settings function not as norms rigidly prescribing appropriate behavior, but as triggers for modes of expression that sustain interaction and help people to define and solve problems. Thus, the study of language acquisition and language use elucidates the processes by which people constitute the patterns of action and constraint that we index as social structure (cf. Lemert 1979: 170–83; Manning 1992: 66–69). Cicourel addressed contextual aspects of language use. He criticized and provided an alternative to the approaches of theoretical linguists, psycholinguists, and cognitive psychologists of the Chomskyan school, who generally ignored the local ethnography or the way social organization impinges on discourse.

Cicourel's approach is aligned with that of linguistic anthropologists who find that a clear understanding of the ethnographic context of language use is necessary in order to analyze actual talk. Therefore, Cicourel advocates direct observation of behavior in actual settings prior to analysis of recorded interaction. He addresses a major problem in the human sciences – i.e. lack of attention to the way coding devices transform observations into a disembodied set of 'data' that does not express or account for the understanding that the observer had when making observations and recordings (cf. Cicourel 1964). He finds that, without such ethnographic context, analysts cannot identify relevant aspects of talk, except by imagining a social structure in which such talk could be understood. However, the experiential and cognitive bases of this imagined social structure are not independently studied by discourse scholars who ignore ethnography (Cicourel 1973) or by ethnographers who do not analyze discourse.[1]

Cicourel's cognitive sociology differs from linguistic anthropology by emphasizing that, in order to understand discourse processes, researchers must also understand

---

1. The notion of context is in dispute within approaches to the analysis of language use. The issue of how to evaluate both the meanings participants attribute to naturally occurring utterances and the effects of those meanings on social activity is a point at which cognitive sociology diverges from ethnomethodology and conversation analysis (cf. Hilbert 1990; Schegloff 1992). This is a key difference between cognitive sociology and conversation analysis. Many conversation analysts do not consider the study of participants' shared knowledge, relating to past and current social settings, to be essential for understanding the structure of talk and its consequences (cf. Cicourel 1980; Schegloff 1992). Thus, conversation analysts generally do not elaborate ethnographic context to explicate the semantic aspects of conversational interaction.

that the human mind is limited in the processing of information 'on-line' (i.e. during any moment of activity and perception). This limitation is revealed by studies of routine interaction as well as research on human memory and its organization. Due to this limitation, the organization and recall of memory is dependent on external representations in the environment (e.g. artifacts that are culturally created and interpreted). Cicourel uses the term 'cognition' to index how observable social activities reflexively relate to external representations of information and knowledge stored within peoples' minds.

A key finding of research which has developed this cognitive sociological perspective is that understandings and preferences related to social action do not result primarily from an evaluation of clear alternatives within the mind of an individual. Rather, they result from the social processes of interpretation related to the resources and constraints of particular settings (Cicourel 1973, 1982, 1990; Corsaro 1985, 2005; Knorr-Cetina 1981, 1999; Mehan 1979, 1991a; Minami 2007; Saferstein 1992, 1994, 2007, forthcoming). Cognitive sociology emphasizes that social organization is constituted through the social processes of interpretation central to interaction, not merely by the results of interaction (e.g. plans, artifacts, or symbols). Such emphasis on examining the linguistic, nonverbal, and pragmatic components of the interactions that constitute social organization and their reflexive relationship with culture is a key difference between cognitive sociology and the sociology of knowledge (e.g. Cicourel 1995; Corsaro 2005; Knorr Cetina 1999; Saferstein 2007, forthcoming).[2]

---

2. The recognition of the social aspects of cognition during the years since Cicourel first published *Cognitive Sociology* has contributed to some blurring of the distinction between cognitive sociology and the sociology of knowledge as categorical distinctions for specialisms within sociology. Strydom (2007) discusses various research approaches that may currently be identified as having cognitive sociological aspects. A number of these approaches do not emphasize the pragmatic and sociolinguistic examination of components of interaction, but focus on the dissemination and use of the symbolic cultural artifacts that result from interaction. Such approaches examine and expose how power coalesces around certain symbolic artifacts or epistemological positions. This differs from the cognitive sociological approach discussed here, which examines the production of authority and meaning during routine interaction in organizational settings in order to understand where interventions to change power relations can take place in the activities and settings that produce decisions, policies, and ideologies (e.g. Fisher 1995; Maseide 2006; Mehan et al. 1986; Saferstein 1994, 2007, forthcoming). This approach emphasizes the social cognitive processes that result in plans, symbols, and policies, rather than symbolic artifacts or epistemological positions and explicit contests over them, which have traditionally been emphases of the sociology of knowledge and semiotics (cf. Mannheim 1936; Barthes 1972, 1974).

2. The interrelation of interactional sense-making processes and social organization

Cognitive sociological studies examine the systematic practices through which people make sense of and organize their environment. Such practices for routine problem solving have gross features that can be typified as rules or norms, but are in fact constituted through moment-to-moment interaction. Through interactional interpretive processes we develop and express understandings of previous activities, materials at hand (e.g. notes, documents, recorded plans, tools, and artifacts), and objectives for future activities (Cicourel 1973, 1990; Corsaro 1985, 1992; Knorr-Cetina 1981, 1999; Mehan 1979, 1983; Mehan et al. 1986; Saferstein 1992, 1994, 2007).

2.1 Interaction

As people interact, they develop and display both tacit and explicit knowledge of patterns of interaction that pertain to certain settings and to certain types of activities. Analysis of interaction shows that the meanings of actions and utterances are, in practice, indeterminate and that understanding is constructed through social interpretive procedures. In order to participate in social settings, people rely on transient, incomplete meanings to trigger their knowledge of the interaction patterns central to communicating and acting. Such interpretive activities are accessible to empirical study through comparative ethnography and discourse analysis (Cicourel 1973; Corsaro 1981, 1988, 1992; Corsaro & Molinari 2000; Grimshaw 1982, 1989; Mehan 1979; Saferstein 2004).

2.2 Discourse

The analysis of everyday discourse is central to cognitive sociology. The approach to discourse includes attention to paralinguistic and nonverbal aspects of communication. Patterns of talk among participants are linked to activities common in a particular setting. Concern with the organization of utterances is linked to the pragmatic, semantic and performative aspects of discourse (Cicourel 1980, 1985, 1987; Corsaro 1981; Grimshaw 1987; Mehan 1991a; Saferstein 2004).

Research applying pragmatics often has both methodological and theoretical relevance, since it also deals with the relation of meaning to context and to participants' daily experience with discourse (cf. Casanovas 1990; Fillmore 1982; Halliday 1974; Streeck 1984; van Dijk 1972). Studies drawing on cognitive sociology find that both meanings and forms of expression are negotiated during interaction. Such interpretive activities set agendas for forms of representation (e.g. Mehan & Wills 1988; Molotch & Boden 1985; Saferstein 2007; Sarangi & Clarke 2002).

2.3 Cognition

Based on their ethnographic and sociolinguistic studies of social problem solving, decision making, and interpretive processes, cognitive sociologists always maintain the primary importance of social interaction and social constraint to the individual's cognition – both developmentally and in everyday activities (Cicourel & Mehan 1985; Corsaro 1992; Saferstein 1994; Knorr-Cetina 1981, 1999). Some cognitive sociologists (e.g. Cicourel 1974, 1985; Saferstein 2007, forthcoming) have found useful comparisons of their findings with studies of memory, individual cognitive functioning, language acquisition, and distributed cognition in the fields of anthropology, psychology, neuro physiology, and computer science (e.g. Bobrow & Norman 1975; D'Andrade 1989; Hutchins 1991; Norman 1969; Piaget 1952; Rumelhart & Norman 1981; Schank & Abelson 1995; Simon & Holyoak 2002; Winograd 1975). Such comparisons reinforce the interrelationship of interaction, cognition, and social organization.

2.4 Organizational activities and materials

Much of the research drawing on cognitive sociology has focused on activities in organizational settings. Materials such as plans, notes, records, schedules, and memos are both sources of ethnographic data and resources for interaction among the participants in an organizational setting. In the latter capacity, they link individuals' understandings of roles, objectives, and work procedures to an institutional context. For example, interaction to interpret plans, records, and notes plays a prominent part in the work discourse of routine organizational meetings and consultations. This activity constrains the duration and degree of attention to other substantive concerns, thereby affecting the social organization of the enterprise (Anspach 1993; Cicourel 1982, 1985, 1995, 2004; Fisher 1984, 1991; Fisher & Groce 1990; Grimshaw 1982, 1989; Mehan 1991b; Molotch 2003; Molotch & Mcclain 2008; Knorr-Cetina & Amann 1990; Saferstein 1992, 2007; Saferstein & Souviney 1998).

3. Key concepts

3.1 Interpretive procedures

Cicourel (1973) examines interactional practices and finds a number of regularities in the ways participants go about making sense of utterances and activities. These regularities are interpretive procedures – i.e. "[…] properties or principles which allow members to assign meaning or sense to substantive rules called social norms" (Cicourel 1973: 52; cf. Corsaro 1985: 67–69; Grimshaw 1987, 1989: 4–6). Researchers themselves use such interpretive procedures to make sense of the settings and interactions they study. By self-consciously taking into account these interpretive procedures, researchers can identify the interactional processes of social organization indexed by the vocabularies commonly used to describe or explain activities and settings (Cicourel 1986, 2006, 2009; Grimshaw 1987; Mehan 1983; Saferstein 2004).

Since Cicourel's initial discussion of interpretive procedures, researchers drawing on cognitive sociology have identified various social aspects of sense-making activities (e.g. Cicourel 1987, 2006; Corsaro 1988; Corsaro & Nelson 2003; Fisher & Groce 1990; Mehan 1991a, 1991b; Saferstein 1992, 2007, forthcoming; Saferstein & Sarangi 2010). These studies point out both interpretive procedures (interactionally developed and activated skills of individuals) and interpretive processes (sets of interpretive procedures and interactional conventions specific to particular settings and activities). Interpretive processes shape the social organization of particular settings, enterprises, and institutions by linking types of settings, shared knowledge, and the coordinated actions of individuals (Anspach 1993; Fisher 1993, 1995; Saferstein 1994).

3.2 Expertise

Analysis of interaction reveals the knowledge and interpretive skills relevant to moment-to-moment judgments and actions in a particular setting (Anspach 1993; Cicourel 1986, 1990, 2004; Fisher 1995; Knorr-Cetina 1999; Knorr-Cetina & Amann 1990; Maseide 2003; Molotch & Mcclain 2008; Saferstein 1992, 2007, forthcoming). In organizational settings, participants' specialized occupational knowledge and their pragmatically crafted elicitation procedures affect the organization of work and the nature of objectives. Participants in organizational activities develop, display, and apply occupational expertise (both their tacit and declarative knowledge) through discourse processes.

The interaction related to communicating across domains of expertise becomes a constraint on problem solving and other work activities (Cicourel 1982, 1987, 1990; Fisher 1986; Fisher & Groce 1990; Knorr-Cetina 1981, 1999; Maseide 2006; Mehan 1991a; Mehan et al. 1986; Saferstein 1994, forthcoming). As such, it affects power relations as well as organizational and institutional structures. Expressions of expertise, confidence, and appropriate action regarding work objectives have multiple meanings for the participants who interact to interpret such expressions in the context of their different, variable organizational capacities (Cicourel 1990; Grimshaw 1989; Mehan 1979; Saferstein 1992, 1994). The interpenetration of such communicative contexts affects interaction and its outcomes (Cicourel 1987).

3.3 Social organization

A number of studies applying cognitive sociological research methods have examined how interactional processes simultaneously affect and are affected by the formal structures of enterprises, institutions, and political entities (Anspach 1987, 1993; Candlin & Candlin 2002; Cicourel 1973, 1990, 2004; Cicourel et al. 1974; Corsaro 1988; Fisher & Groce 1990; Knorr-Cetina 1981, 1999; Mehan et al. 1986; Molotch 2003; Saferstein 1992). Through the analysis of interaction, the cognitive sociological perspective reframes conventional notions of social structure in terms of the local processes of social organization (Corsaro & Molinari 2000; Fisher 1986; Grimshaw 1989; Knorr Cetina & Bruegger 2005; Mehan & Wills 1988; Molotch & Boden 1985; Saferstein 1994).

3.4 Inequality and stratification

Many studies drawing on cognitive sociology have examined how a confluence of locally managed interactional processes, organizational constraints, and types of expertise affect stratification by gender, ethnicity, occupation, economic resources, etc. Such studies indicate that systems of social stratification in institutional settings are produced and reproduced through the context-specific processes of interpretation constituting interaction (e.g. Anspach 1993; Cicourel 1995; Cicourel & Mehan 1985; Cicourel et al. 1974; DeNora 1996; Fisher 1986, 1991, 1995; Grimshaw 1989; Mehan 1979; Mehan et al. 1986; Mehan 2005).

3.5 Organizational constraints

Power, authority, and material resources are not controlling functions determined by structures that exist independently of interaction. Rather, they are organizational constraints that both shape and are shaped by work interaction. Studies of activities in organizations show that there are a number of ways for participants to deal with authority, power, and resources (Anspach 1991; Cicourel 1995, 2004; Cicourel et al. 1974; Fisher 1984, 1991, 1995; Knorr-Cetina 1981, 1999; Maseide 1991; Mehan 2005; Molotch 2003; Saferstein & Souviney 1998). The expression of authority and the allocation of resources are subject to routine interpretive processes. The scope of the interpretive activities of a particular work event is affected by the amount of interaction participants devote to developing representations and practices related to authority and resources. Such representations and practices become interactional resources that affect the agenda of topics and forms of expression guiding subsequent work activities (Candlin & Candlin 2002; Saferstein 1994, 2007; Sarangi & Clarke 2002).

4. Methodology

Although transcription conventions vary among researchers applying a cognitive sociological approach, the propositional content of discourse is a key concern – i.e. the negotiation and construction of meaning through situated interaction. Therefore, integration of ethnography with discourse analysis is central to methodology. The ethnographic aspect of the research involves observation and participation in the settings studied. It also involves discussions of activities with participants and extensive recording (video or audio) of interaction (Cicourel 1973, Corsaro & Molinari 2000). Organizational records, documents, and work materials are also examined, since they result from and mediate interaction. Such recordings and organizational materials not only become data for discourse analysis, but are also presented to and discussed with participants (Cicourel 1973: 124, 128–129; Corsaro 1985: 48–49, 140–41; Mehan 1979: 16–18). This approach to ethnography (indefinite triangulation) provides researchers with an understanding of the activities and constraints faced by participants. It also provides researchers with opportunities to examine their own sense-making processes, which affect their findings about settings and subjects. To this end, researchers also consider the circumstances through which they gain access to and pursue observations in field settings in regard to the social organization of those settings (cf. Anspach & Mizrachi 2006; Cicourel 1974; Corsaro 1981, 1985; Corsaro & Molinari 2008).

In cases where researchers obtain and analyze informal interviews, they consider the constraints of elicitation frames, cognitive processing, and memory: e.g. rather than questioning respondents about a particular observed activity, researchers mention the ethnographic setting and let the respondents reconstruct and recount their activities (Cicourel 1974, 1988). Analyses of interviews also include explanations of the interviewer's intent and the conversational context of questions (Cicourel 1974; Minami 1993).

Such methodology provides information relevant to assessing ecological validity, i.e. the degree to which data reflect the systematic aspects of the social activity in a particular type of environment. By acknowledging and examining the processes of gathering and analyzing data, researchers can avoid turning them into measurements that merely reflect a priori assumptions about power and order (cf. Cicourel 1964, 1973, 1974, 1986, 1995; Corsaro 1985; Gobo 2001; Knorr-Cetina 1981). Saferstein (2004) examines the use of digital video technologies for recording, viewing, and organizing data in regard to the relationship between technologies and analytical frameworks. Features of digital video technology offer researchers the potential to modify analytical frameworks and procedures in ways that increase attention to nonverbal aspects of interaction.

5. A sample analysis

The following example demonstrates the interrelation of ethnographic research and discourse analysis featured in cognitive sociology (the example is taken from a more detailed discussion in Saferstein 1992). This case examines the collaborative processes that constitute much of the work of television production. The work discourse analyzed below occurred at the program *Hill Street Blues* during a production phase in which the participants observe and discuss an unfinished version of a television episode in order to clarify and enhance it by adding and changing sounds and dialogue. Through their work interaction, the participants develop interpretations of the scene they view, models of work objectives, and plans for subsequent activities to accomplish those objectives. The participants in this segment of the discussion are an associate producer, who supervises sound production, and one of the sound editors, who is involved in enhancing background voices and dialogue. Analysis of the ambiguity that they work to resolve in their discourse, points to the differing contexts in which they exercise their administrative capacities. Knowledge of the organizational and occupational contexts of their work is essential for the analyst as well as for the participants in order to make sense of their discourse. Thus, valid analysis of the recorded data requires ethnographic study within the work settings, which provides the analyst with the opportunity to encounter such information.

Television Production

28   editor: we gonna get this ??. We don't
29   associate producer: No, I think we'll get it
30   editor: We're doing our own scream…so
31   associate producer: The scream's on tape. I'll check to see if we have to do it ??

[key: . = pause of one second or less; ? = unclear word]

The participants' ambiguous communication here is due to their differing occupational expertise, as well as to the dual administrative and creative aspects of their work. For instance, in lines 28 and 30, the editor indicates that he begins to conceptualize the recording of a scream as work to be done at a recording session. Both for the administrative purpose of scheduling the sound recording session, and for the creative purpose of enhancing the television episode, the editor must acquire specific information that he can understand and act upon in terms of his work procedures. Such procedures include: (1) scheduling the actors who will be involved in the recording session; (2) documenting and preparing the recorded scenes that will be modified there.

The associate producer also has administrative concerns which affect the discussion. For example, he has access to materials and records which the editor has not seen. He suggests, in lines 29 and 31, that a recorded scream may already exist among unused material recorded during the filming of the episode. In this case, a new scream would not have to be created at the recording session.

Such patterns of work discourse (e.g. digressions as in lines 28–31) show how the participants' activities affect the social organization of industries and occupations. These discourse patterns occur throughout the production processes of many enterprises, constituting institutionalized opportunities for collaborative problem solving. For example, the difference between using a previously recorded scream, and producing a scream at a recording session has a number of administrative implications related to the participants' knowledge of the organization of production. Each of these activities would involve different teams of people, different work processes, and different worksites (indexed in (1) by forms of 'we get' and 'we do') – all of which have to be scheduled and coordinated. Furthermore, the sound editor and ADR editor are employed by a company specializing in post-production sound recording and editing, which had been contracted by the production company employing the associate producer. Thus, the relevant expertise of the sound editor, ADR editor and associate producer, which they index by 'we get' and 'we do', includes practical knowledge of their multiple activities and responsibilities in the different settings where they work to create the television program.

The participants' recall and display of such relevant information is related to the social interpretive activities of their immediate interaction. Knowledge of organizational constraints (such as the need to coordinate the work of two phases of production) prompts participants to mention certain aspects of projected work activities in order to develop objectives. The topics they mention and the interaction related to interpreting those topics also shape the collaborative event and its products, affecting work activities that constitute subsequent phases of production. Thus, the interpretive processes of interaction contribute to shaping the organization of work, the relative power of participants, the structure of the enterprise, and the nature of the product. Cognitive sociology examines this interplay between interaction, routine problem solving, and social structure.

References

Anspach, R.R. (1987). Prognostic conflict in life-and-death decisions: the organization as an ecology of knowledge. *Journal of Health and Social Behavior* 28: 215–231.
—— (1991). Everyday methods for assessing organizational effectiveness. *Social Problems* 38: 1–19.
—— (1993). *Deciding who lives*. University of California Press.
Anspach, R.R. & N. Mizrachi (2006). The field worker's fields: Ethics, ethnography, and medical sociology *Sociology of Health and Illness* 28(6): 713–731.
Barthes, R. (1972). *Mythologies*. Hill & Wang.
—— (1974). *S/Z*. Hill & Wang.
Bobrow, D.G. & D.A. Norman (1975). Some principles of memory schemata. In D.G. Bobrow & A.M. Collins (eds.) *Representation and understanding*. Academic Press.
Candlin, C.N. & S. Candlin (2002). Discourse, expertise, and the management of risk in health care settings. *Research on Language and Social Interaction* 35(2): 115–137.

Casanovas, P. (1990). Toward a sociopragmatics of legal discourses. In B. Jackson (ed.) *Oñati proceedings* (special issue). International Institute for the Sociology of Law.

Cicourel, A.V. (1964). *Method and measurement in sociology*. Free Press.

––––– (1973). *Cognitive sociology*. Penguin.

––––– (1974). *Theory and method in a study of Argentine fertility*. Wiley-Interscience.

––––– (1980). Three models of discourse analysis. *Discourse Processes* 33: 101–132.

––––– (1982). Language and belief in a medical setting. In H. Byrnes (ed.) *Contemporary perceptions of language*: 1–41. Georgetown University Press.

––––– (1985). Text and discourse. *Annual Review of Anthropology* 14: 159–185.

––––– (1986). Social measurement as the creation of expert systems. In D.W. Fiske & R.A. Shweder (eds.) *Metatheory in social science*: 246–270. University of Chicago Press.

––––– (1987). The interpenetration of communicative contexts. *Social Psychology Quarterly* 50(2): 217–226.

––––– (1988). Elicitation as a problem of discourse. In H. Ammon, N. Dittmar & K.J. Mattheier (eds.) *Sociolinguistics*: 903–910. Walter de Gruyter.

––––– (1990). The integration of distributed knowledge in collaborative medical diagnosis. In J. Galegher, R.E. Kraut & C. Egido (eds.) *Intellectual teamwork*: 221–242. Erlbaum.

––––– (1995). *The social organization of juvenile justice*. Wiley.

––––– (2004). Cognitive overload and communication in two healthcare settings. *Communication & Medicine* 1: 35–43.

––––– (2006). Cognitive/affective processes, social interaction, and social structure as representational re-descriptions: their contrastive bandwidths and spatio-temporal foci. *Mind & Society* 5: 39–70.

––––– (2009). John Rawls on two concepts of rules: Some speculations about their ecological validity in behavioral and social science research. *Journal of Classical Sociology* 9(4): 371–387.

Cicourel, A.V., K.A. Jennings, S.H.M. Jennings, K.C.W. Leiter, R. MacKay, H. Mehan & D. Roth (1974). *Language use and school performance*. Academic Press.

Cicourel, A.V. & H. Mehan (1985). Universal development, stratifying practices, and status attainment. In V.R. Robinson (ed.) *Research in social stratification and mobility*. JAI Press.

Corsaro, W.A. (1981). Communicative processes in studies of social organization. *Text* 1: 5–63.

––––– (1985). *Friendship and peer culture in the early years*. Ablex.

––––– (1988). Routines in the peer culture of American and Italian nursery school children. *Sociology of Education* 61: 1–14.

––––– (1992). Interpretive reproduction in children's peer cultures. *Social Psychology Quarterly* 55: 160–177.

––––– (2005). Collective action and agency in young children's peer cultures. In J. Qvortrup (ed.) *Studies in modern childhood: society, agency and culture*: 231–247. Palgrave Macmillan.

––––– (2006). Qualitative research on children's peer relations in cultural context. In X. Chen, D. French & B. Schneider (eds.) *Peer relations in cultural context*: 96–119. Cambridge University Press.

Corsaro, W.A. & L. Molinari (2000). Priming events and Italian children's transition from preschool to elementary school: representations and action. *Social Psychology Quarterly* 63: 16–33.

––––– (2008). Entering and Observing in Children's Worlds: A Reflection on a Longitudinal Ethnography of Early Education in Italy. In P. Christensen & A. James (eds.) *Research with children: perspectives and practices,* 2nd ed.: 239–259. Routledge.

Corsaro, W.A. & E. Nelson (2003). Children's collective activities and peer culture in early literacy in American and Italian preschools. *Sociology of Education* 76: 209–227.

D'andrade, R.G. (1989). Cultural cognition. In M.I. Posner (ed.) *Foundations of cognitive science*: 745–830. MIT Press.

Denora, T. (1996). From physiology to feminism reconfiguring body, gender and expertise in natural fertility control. *International Sociology* 11(3): 359–383.

van Dijk, T.A. (1972). *Some aspects of text grammars*. Mouton.

Durkheim, E. (1933). *The division of labor in society*. Free Press.

Fillmore, C.J. (1982). Ideal readers and real readers. In D. Tannen (ed.) *Proceedings of the 32nd Georgetown Roundtable on Languages and Linguistics*: 248–270. Georgetown University Press.

Fisher, S. (1984). Institutional authority and the structure of discourse. *Discourse Processes* 7: 201–224.

——— (1986). *In the patient's best interest*. Rutgers University Press.

——— (1991). A discourse of the social: medical talk/power talk/oppositional talk? *Discourse & Society* 2: 157–182.

——— (1993). Doctor talk/patient talk: How treatment decisions are negotiated in doctor-patient communication. In S. Fisher & A. Todd (eds.) *The social organization of doctor-patient communication*, 2nd ed.: 161–182. Ablex.

——— (1995). *Nursing wounds: nurse practitioners, doctors, women patients, and the negotiation of meaning*. Rutgers University Press.

Fisher, S. & S.B. Groce (1990). Accounting practices in medical interviews. *Language in Society* 19: 225–250.

Gobo, G. (2001). Best Practices: Rituals and Rhetorical Strategies in the "Initial Telephone Contact". *Forum: Qualitative Social Research* 2(1). http://www.qualitative-research.net/fqs-texte/1-01/1-01gobo-e.htm (September 25, 2006).

Grimshaw, A.D. (1982). Comprehensive discourse analysis. *Language in Society* 11: 15–47.

——— (1987). Disambiguating discourse: Members' skill and analysts' problem. *Social Psychology Quarterly* 50(2): 186–204.

——— (1989). *Collegial discourse*. Ablex.

Halliday, M.A.K. (1974). *Learning how to mean*. Arnold.

Hilbert, R.A. (1990). Ethnomethodology and the micro-macro order. *American Journal of Sociology* 50: 794–808.

Hutchins, E. (1991). Organizing work by adaptation. *Organization Science* 2(1): 14–39.

Knorr-Cetina, K. (1981). *The manufacture of knowledge*. Pergamon Press.

——— (1999). *Epistemic cultures: How the sciences make knowledge*. Harvard Edition World.

Knorr-Cetina, K. & K. Amann (1990). Image dissection in natural scientific inquiry. *Science, Technology, and Human Values* 15(3): 259–283.

Knorr Cetina, K. & U. Bruegger (2005). Global microstructures: the virtual societies of financial markets. *American Journal of Sociology* 107(4): 905–995.

Lemert, C.C. (1979). *Sociology and the twilight of man*. Southern Illinois University Press.

Mannheim, K. [1936] (1997). *Ideology and utopia*. Routledge.

Manning, P. (1992). *Organizational communication*. Aldine de Gruyter.

Maseide, P. (1991). Possibly abusive, often benign, and always necessary. On power and domination in medical practice. *Sociology of Health and Illness* 13(4): 545–561.

——— (2003). Medical talk and moral order: Social interaction and collaborative clinical work. *Text* 23(3): 369–403.

——— (2006). The deep play of medicine: Discursive and collaborative processing of evidence in medical problem solving. *Communication & Medicine* 3(1): 43–54.

Marx, K. & F. Engels (1970). *The German ideology*. International Publishers.

Mehan, H. (1979). *Learning lessons*. Harvard University Press.
—— (1983). Social constructivism in psychology and sociology. *Sociologie et Sociétés* 14: 77–96.
—— (1991a). Oracular reasoning in a psychiatric exam. In A.D. Grimshaw (ed.) *Conflict talk*. Cambridge University Press.
—— (1991b). The school's work of sorting students. In D. Boden & D.H. Zimmerman (eds.) *Talk and social structure*: 71–90. Polity Press.
—— (2005). Commentary: The changing but underrealized roles of state education agencies in school reform. *Journal of Education for Students Placed at Risk* 10: 139–146.
Mehan, H., A. Hertweck & J.L. Meihls (1986). *Handicapping the handicapped*. Stanford University Press.
Mehan, H. & J. Wills (1988). MEND: A nurturing voice in the nuclear arms debate. *Social Problems* 35: 363–383.
Minami, Y. (1993). Growing up in two cultures: the educational experiences of Japanese students in America and their return to Japan. Dissertation: UCSD.
—— (2007). Discourse of change among young Japanese sojourners: A case of "I've changed." *The Seijo Bungei: The Seijo University Arts and Literature Quarterly* 200: 278–256. http://weblab.seijo.ac.jp/yminami/site00.html
Molotch, H. (2003). *Where stuff comes from*. Routledge.
Molotch, H. & D. Boden (1985). Talking social structure. *American Sociological Review* 50: 273–288.
Molotch, H. & N. McClain (2008). Things at work: Informal social-material mechanisms for getting the job done. *Journal of Consumer Culture* 8(1): 36–67.
Norman, D.A. (1969). *Memory and attention*. Wiley.
Parsons, T. (1937). *The structure of social action*. McGraw-Hill.
Piaget, J. (1952). *The language and thought of the child*. Routledge & Kegan Paul.
Rumelhart, D.A. & D.A. Norman (1981). Analogical processes in learning. In J.R. Anderson (ed.) *Cognitive skills and their acquisition*: 335–359. Erlbaum.
Saferstein, B. (1992). Collective cognition and collaborative work. *Discourse & Society* 3: 61–86.
—— (1994). Interaction and ideology at work. *Social Problems* 41: 316–345.
—— (2004). Digital technology and methodological adaptation: Text on video as a resource for analytical reflexivity. *Journal of applied linguistics* 1(2): 197–223.
—— (2007). Process narratives, grey boxes, and discourse frameworks: Cognition, interaction, and constraint in understanding genetics and medicine. *European Journal of Social Theory* 10(3): 424–447.
—— (Forthcoming). *Understanding and interaction in medical and educational settings*. Equinox.
Saferstein, B. & S. Sarangi (2010). Mediating modes of representation in understanding science: The case of genetic inheritance. In P. Prior & J. Hengst (eds.) *Exploring semiotic remediation as discourse practice*. Palgrave Macmillan.
Saferstein, B. & R. Souviney (1998). Secondary science teachers, the internet, and curriculum development: The Community of Explorers Project. *The Journal of Educational Technology Systems* 26(2): 113–126.
Sarangi, S. & A. Clarke (2002). Zones of expertise and the management of uncertainty in genetics risk communication. *Research on Language and Social Interaction* 35(2): 139–171.
Schank, R.C. & R.P. Abelson (1995). Knowledge and memory: The real story. In R.S. Wyer, Jr. (ed.) *Knowledge and memory: The real story*: 1–85. Lawrence Erlbaum.
Schegloff, E. (1992). In another context. In A. Duranti & C. Goodwin (eds.) *Rethinking context*: 193–227. Cambridge University Press.

Simon, D. & K.J. Holyoak (2002). Structural dynamics of cognition: From consistency theories to constraint satisfaction. *Personality and Social Psychology Review* 6(6): 283–94.

Streeck, J. (1984). Embodied contexts, transcontextuals, and the timing of speech acts. *Journal of Pragmatics* 8: 113–137.

Strydom, P. (2007). A cartography of contemporary cognitive social theory. *The European Journal of Social Theory* 10(3): 339–356.

Weber, M. (1958). *The Protestant ethic and the spirit of capitalism.* Scribner's.

Winograd, T. (1975). Frame representations and the declarative/procedural controversy. In D.G. Bobrow & A.M. Collins (eds.) *Representation and understanding*: 185–210. Academic Press.

Contact

Li Wei
University of London

Contact is an important factor in language use, language maintenance, language variation, and language change. There is a cliché in linguistics that language is a living thing. But a moment's thought makes it clear that it is the user who gives language life. Language grows as the user grows; it varies and changes as the user varies and changes; it also dies as the user dies. Language contact is therefore contact between users of different languages.

There is a diversity of approaches to language contact. Some researchers regard contact as primarily a socio-historical issue and investigate the various causes of contact between speaker groups; others focus on the structural aspects of specific contact phenomena such as lexical borrowing, pidgins and creoles, and contact induced linguistic change. The purpose of this article is to provide an overview of language contact as a field of enquiry. I will first outline the key causes, processes and outcomes of language contact. I will then discuss the various theoretical and methodological approaches to language contact. Finally, I will outline the central issues of the pragmatics of language contact.

1. Language contact: Causes, processes and outcomes

Users of different languages get into contact with each other for different reasons and in different ways. Some do so out of their own choosing, while others are forced by circumstances. Key external factors contributing to language contact include (Baker & Prys Jones 1998; Li Wei 2007) the following.

- *Politics:* Political or military acts such as colonisation, annexation, resettlement and federation can have immediate linguistic effects. People may become refugees, either in a new place or in their homeland, and have to learn the language of their new environment. After a successful military invasion, the indigenous population may have to learn the invader's language in order to prosper. Colonisation is exemplified by the former British, French, Spanish, Portuguese and Dutch colonies in Africa, Asia and South America, most of which achieved independence in the nineteenth century. A modern example of annexation can be found in the absorption of the Baltic republics – Lithuania, Latvia and Estonia – into the Soviet Union after the Second World War. In the latter part of the twentieth century military conflicts in Central Africa and in the former Yugoslavia have seen the

resettlement of people of different ethnic backgrounds. Examples of federations where diverse ethnic groups or nationalities are united under the political control of one state include Switzerland, Belgium and Cameroon.
- *Natural disaster:* Famine, floods, volcanic eruptions and other such events can be the cause of major movements of population. New language contact situations then emerge as people are resettled. Some of the Irish and Chinese resettlements in North America were the result of natural disasters.
- *Religion:* People may wish to live in a country because of its religious significance, or to leave a country because of its religious oppression. In either case, a new language may have to be learned. The Russian speakers in Israel are a case in point.
- *Culture:* A desire to identify with a particular ethnic, cultural or social group usually means learning the language of that group. Minority ethnic and cultural groups may wish to maintain their own languages, which are different from the languages promoted by the governing state or institution. Nationalistic factors are particularly important.
- *Economy:* Very large numbers of people across the world have migrated to find work and to improve their standard of living. This factor accounts for most of the linguistic diversity of the US and an increasing proportion of the bilingualism in present-day Europe.
- *Education:* Learning another language may be the only means of obtaining access to knowledge. This factor led to the universal use of Latin in the Middle Ages, and today motivates the international use of English.
- *Technology:* The availability of information and communication technologies (ICT), such as the internet, has led to a further expansion of the use of English across the world. The vast majority of ICT users are non-native speakers of English.

From the above list we can see that one does not have to move to a different place to come into contact with people speaking a different language. There are plenty of opportunities for language contact in the same country, the same community, the same neighbourhood or even the same family. Indeed, globalization has made it easier for people from different parts of the world to experience different cultures, life styles and languages. The usual consequence of language contact is bilingualism, or even multilingualism, which is most commonly found in an individual speaker.

Yet, there are many different types of bilingual and multilingual language users, precisely because the different socio-historical causes lead to different processes of language contact, i.e. individuals and groups of language users getting into contact with each other in different ways. For instance, at an individual level, some people may become bilingual or multilingual because they are born into bilingual or multilingual families and are exposed to multiple languages simultaneously from birth, while others learn and acquire additional languages at a later age in life due to schooling or changes in life experience. Romaine (1995), extending the typology by Harding and Riley (1986), identifies six different processes whereby children can become bilingual or multilingual – cf. Table 1.

Table 1. Processes of bilingual acquisition (based on Romaine 1995)

	Parent	Community	Strategy
1. One Person One Language	The parents have different native languages with each having some degree of competence in the other's language.	The language of one of the parents is the dominant language of the community.	The parents each speak their own language to the child from birth.
2. Non-Dominant Home Language/ One Language One Environment	The parents have different native languages.	The language of one of the parents is the dominant language of the community.	Both parents speak the non-dominant language to the child, who is fully exposed to the dominant language only when outside the home, and in particular in nursery school.
3. Non-Dominant Home Language without Community Support	The parents share the same native language.	The dominant language is not that of the parents.	The parents speak their own language to the child.
4. Double Non-Dominant Home Language without Community Support	The parents have different native languages.	The dominant language is different from either of the parents' languages.	The parents each speak their own language to the child from birth.
5. Non-Native Parents	The parents share the same native language.	The dominant language is the same as that of the parents.	One of the parents always addresses the child in a language which is not his/her native language.
6. Mixed languages	The parents are bilingual.	Sectors of community may also be bilingual.	Parents code-switch and mix languages.

There are also different processes of language contact at the community level. For example, the imposition of English and French on the former British and French colonies in Africa resulted in what has been described as "diglossia" (Ferguson 1959) – a functionally differentiated distribution of languages in a community – with the colonizing languages being the High varieties and used more often in formal, public settings, with the local, indigenous languages being the Low varieties predominantly for informal, domestic contexts. Not everybody in such communities is bilingual in the colonial and local languages. In fact, people who have not had access to formal education often have not learned the colonial languages, and cannot access the resources available through those languages. Similarly, people who have learned certain languages as acts of religious and cultural identity tend to use the languages in specific religious and cultural contexts. The teaching of Arabic in the ethnically and linguistically diverse Muslim world is a case in point. In contrast, speakers of different languages who are brought together because of marriage, immigration and employment may have more opportunities to alternate between the various languages and mix them together in conversational interaction.

Different causes and processes of language contact have different consequences on the linguistic structures of the languages and language varieties involved. It is a well-known fact that languages borrow culturally specific terms from one another. English, for example, has many borrowings from Latin, French, and even Chinese. Some of these terms gradually become phonologically and morphologically integrated with the recipient languages and accepted as part of the languages. Globalization increases the chances of lexical borrowing. Technological innovation also leads to the creation of new terms, which may be spread throughout the world. Other linguistic phenomena such as codeswitching, language shift, or the creation of mixed languages may come as a result of intensive language contact in multilingual communities due to, for example, federation or immigration.

All these three broad aspects of language contact – causes, processes, and outcomes – have attracted the attention of linguists. In the next section, we focus on the theoretical and methodological perspectives on these three aspects of language contact.

2. Theoretical and methodological approaches to language contact

The study of language contact has always been highly multidisciplinary. Typically, the causes of language contact are studied within a broad, sociologically informed framework. In such a framework, language is taken as a socio-politico-economic construct and language contact as a socio-politico-economic process. Particular attention is paid to the historical context and power relations in language contact, as well as to the impact of such contact on social structures and social relationships. Early examples of sociology-of-language studies of language contact include Weinreich (1953), Haugen (1966) and Fishman (1966). More recent studies tend to focus on the ecology of language contact of specific communities and are informed by cultural anthropology. Examples include Hill and Hill (1986), Woolard (1989) and Heller (1994). Issues of linguistic hegemony, power, ideology and identity are here the focus of investigation.

The processes of language contact are usually studied from a broadly sociolinguistic perspective. Winford (2003: 23–24) provides a taxonomy of contact situations, based partly on Thomason and Kaufman (1988), in which three key processes – language maintenance, shift, and creation – are identified; cf. Table 2. These three processes are the central focus of sociolinguistic studies of language contact.

Table 2. A Taxonomy of Language Contact

a. Language maintenance

I. Borrowing situations

Degree of contact	Linguistic results	Examples
Casual	Lexical borrowing only	Modern, English borrowings from French, e.g. ballet
Moderate	Lexical and slight structural Borrowing	Latin influence on Early Modern English; Sanskrit influence on Dravidan languages
Intense	Moderate structural borrowing	German influence on Romansh

II. Convergence situations

Type of contact	Linguistic result	Examples
Contiguous geographical location	Moderate structured diffusion	Sprachbunde, e.g. the Balkans
Intra-community Multilingualism	Heavy structural diffusion	Marathi/Kannada influence on Kupwa Urdu
Intense pressure on a minority group	Heavy structural diffusion	Tibetan influence on Wutun; Turkish influence on Asia Minor Greek
Intense inter-community contact (trade, exogamy)	Heavy lexical and/or structural diffusion	The languages of Northwest New Britain; The languages of Arnhem Land, Australia

b. Language shift

Type of shift	Linguistic results (substratum)	Examples
Rapid and complete (by minority group)	Little or no substratum interference in Target Language (TL)	Urban immigrant groups shifting to English in the US
Rapid shift by larger or prestigious minority	Slight to moderate substratum interference In TL	Norman French shift to English in England
Shift by indigenous community to imported language	Moderate to heavy substratum interference	Shift to English by Irish speakers in Ireland (Hiberno-English); shift to English dialects in 17th century Barbados (intermediate "creole")

c. Language creation (new contact languages)

Type	Characteristics
Bilingual mixed languages	Akin to cases of maintenance, involving incorporation of large proportions of an external vocabulary into a maintained grammatical frame
Pidgins	Highly reduced lingua francas that involve mutual accommodation and simplification; employed in restricted functions such as trade
Creoles	Akin to cases of both maintenance and shift, with grammars shaped by varying degrees of superstrate and substrate influence, and vocabulary drawn mostly from the superstrate source.

The seminal paper by Joshua Fishman (1964) set the agenda for the sociolinguistic study of language maintenance and language shift. The principal objective here is to distinguish the factors that encourage language maintenance from those encouraging language shift, as well as to investigate the socio-cultural processes concomitant with the maintenance and shift in language use. For instance, socio-economic stability, low mobility in occupation and close-knit networks all encourage language maintenance. There is no strong reason for the language users to change their identities, aspirations or practices. In contrast, education and socio-economic changes encourage language shift, as the language users have new aspirations, wish to develop new identities and adopt new cultural practices.

It should be emphasized that language maintenance does not mean no change at all in the linguistic practices of language users. As Winford's taxonomy shows, there are a number of ways in which linguistic changes can take place within a maintenance situation. The key here is that language users are able to maintain the ownership of their languages by adapting elements from other languages to their own and to keep the domains of usage of different languages fairly separate. It should also be said that language shift is a gradual process, and can take several generations to complete. In fact, a sudden change in a community's collective language practice is rather rare and if it takes place, tends to be associated with major political changes.

It is important to remember that while a variety of factors are clearly responsible for providing the conditions necessary for language maintenance or language shift, it is the language user who makes the choice of whether to keep the old linguistic practice or to adopt a new one. Using social psychological theories and models, linguists have investigated how language users accommodate to each other in contact situations. Here, the concept of "ethnolinguistic vitality" (e.g. Giles 1977; Giles & St Clair 1979) is essential. In a language contact situation, multilingual language users constantly negotiate group boundaries. They develop a notion of ethnolinguistic vitality of specific languages on the basis of their perception of the economic, historic, social, political and cultural status of the ethnic groups that use the languages. The size and distribution of the groups and whether or not there is any institutional support for them also play a role in their perceptions. If a person perceives his or her own language as having high ethnolinguistic vitality, then that person is less likely to accept or adopt other languages. If, on the other hand, a person regards his or her own language as having low ethnolinguistic vitality, then he or she is more likely to accommodate and converge with other speakers whose language may be perceived as having higher ethnolinguistic vitality than their own. Convergence or divergence can occur at different levels. At the macro level, they can help to change the balance of power and group relations and dynamics. At the micro level, social interactions between speakers of different languages may be more or less bilingual and involve different amounts of language negotiation.

While the causes and processes of language contact tend to be studied broadly from sociolinguistic and sociological perspectives, the outcomes of language contact, which are regarded by some as the core subject matter of Contact Linguistics, tend to be studied from a more narrowly defined perspective, i.e. theoretical linguistics, focussing on the structural issues of specific contact phenomena. Winford's taxonomy in Table 2 summarises the range of linguistic outcomes of language contact. Although the diversity of the phenomena seem to invite different approaches, most of the existing linguistic studies of language contact focus on the structural constraints of lexical borrowing, diffusion and codeswitching.

Opinions differ amongst linguists as to the nature of the structural constraints on borrowing, diffusion and switching in language contact. There are two contrasting positions. One assumes bilingual language users have two discrete grammatical systems. In a language contact situation, they bring their knowledge of the two different grammars into language production. Usually one of the grammars is more dominant and constrains the ways items from the weaker, less dominant language incorporates into the strong, dominant language. Based on such assumptions, linguists look for aspects of the grammars of the languages in contact that are either compatible or incompatible. Structural constraints are developed based on congruence, equivalence, or markedness (e.g. Poplack 1980; Myers-Scotton 1993a; Muysken 2000). Borrowing, diffusion and switching can all be facilitated by compatible structures, while incompatible structures constrain or block borrowing, diffusion or switching. While accepting basic assumptions of interacting grammars, MacSwan (e.g. 1999) questions the need to posit specific structural constraints on borrowing, diffusion or switching, other than the ones already afforded by Universal Grammar. This does not mean, of course, that bilingual language users do not differentiate the languages they know and use. The central argument has to do with the roles of surface grammars of specific languages versus the principles and parameters of Universal Grammar. In contrast, some linguists reject the assumption that bilingual language users have two discrete grammars. They argue for a reconceptualisation of the bilingual user's grammatical knowledge, which should include not only the totality of all the surface grammars of specific languages they know and use but also their knowledge of how the different grammatical systems interact with each other. They believe that the attempt to identify structural constraints using abstract notions of grammar, either specific grammars or Universal Grammar, misses the point, as borrowing, diffusion and switching are linguistic strategies by the bilingual language user who use them in different ways in different situations for different purposes (e.g. Gardner-Chloros & Edwards 2003, 2007).

A considerable amount of attention in linguistic studies of contact phenomena has been given to so-called contact languages, pidgins, creoles and other bilingual mixed languages. In terms of methodology, studies of contact languages tend to adopt a much broader perspective than theoretical linguistics. They are typically, and necessarily, situated in historical and social contexts, and are based on detailed, community-based fieldwork.

Research on contact languages has theoretical implications for understanding the genesis of human languages generally as well as other linguistic phenomena such as linguistic change, language acquisition, and language attrition. Indeed, many of the structural processes of bilingual mixed languages, pidgins and creoles, such as transfer, simplification, and fossilization, find parallels in language change, acquisition and attrition.

The majority of the studies of the outcomes of language contact are motivated by theoretical concerns of grammatical models. While most linguists would make references to the bilingual language user and their community, the focus is on the linguistic structures rather than the language users themselves. It is important to remind ourselves that it is the language user who produces the linguistic structures. What effects do the various causes and processes of language contact have on the language users, especially in terms of the cognitive representation of their linguistic knowledge? How do bilingual language users put their knowledge of multiple languages to use in contact situations? Such questions seem to invite a different approach to the outcomes of language contact, focussing not on the linguistic structures but on the language user.

In one of the earliest studies of language contact by Weinreich (1953), he proposed a model of bilingual language users representing three types of relationship between the linguistic sign (or signifier) and the semantic content (signified). In Type A, the individual combines a signifier from each language with a separate unit of signified. Weinreich called them 'coordinative' (later often called 'coordinate') bilinguals. In Type B the individual identifies two signifiers but regards them as a single compound, or composite, unit of signified; hence 'compound' bilinguals. Type C relates to people who learn a new language with the help of a previously acquired one. They are called 'subordinative' (or 'subordinate') bilinguals. His examples were from English and Russian:

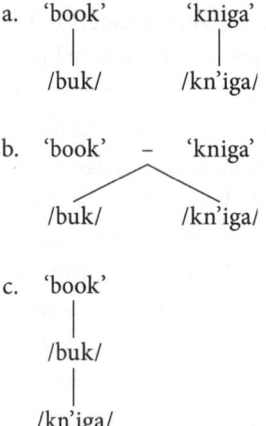

Weinreich's typology is often misinterpreted in the literature as referring to differences in the degree of proficiency in the languages. However, the relationship between language proficiency and cognitive organisation of the bilingual individual, as conceptualised in

Weinreich's model, is far from clear. Some 'subordinate' bilinguals demonstrate a very high level of proficiency in processing both languages, as evidenced in grammaticality judgements and fluency of speech, while some 'coordinative' bilinguals show difficulties in processing two languages simultaneously (i.e. in code-switching or in "foreign" words detection experiments). It must also be stressed that in Weinreich's distinctions bilingual individuals are distributed along a continuum from a subordinate or compound end to a coordinate end, and can at the same time be more subordinate or compound for certain concepts and more coordinate for others, depending on, among other things, the age and context of acquisition.

Weinreich's model provided inspiration for later psycholinguistic studies of the bilingual language user. For example, there are a number of psycholinguistic models of the bilingual lexicon, including Potter et al.'s (1984) Concept Mediation Model and Word Association Model, and Kroll and Stewart's (1984) Revised Hierarchical Model. These models take into consideration factors such as proficiency level, age and context of acquisition and have much more explanatory power than the earlier models for bilingual language use. Nevertheless, the majority of psycholinguistic studies of language contact focus on building models of the bilingual language user's linguistic knowledge. They do not directly address the question of how bilingual language users put their knowledge of multiple languages to use in actual contact situation. This question, however, is the core of research on the pragmatics of language contact.

3. The pragmatics of language contact

Back in 1965, Fishman asked the question "who speaks what language to whom and when?" as a research agenda for the sociolinguistics of bilingualism. This question also laid the foundation for the study of the pragmatics of language contact, in which language choice is central. Figure 1 below illustrates a decision-making process of the bilingual language user.

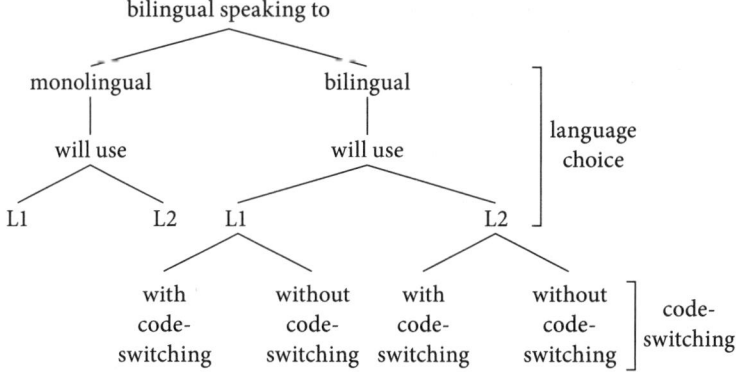

Figure 1. Decision-making in a language contact situation

From this figure one can see that the bilingual language user has a number of choices to make in a contact situation. The decision depends largely on who the addressee is; in particular, whether the addressee is also bilingual in the same language pairs. If the addressee is not bilingual, then the choice is rather limited. However, if the addressee is bilingual, the choice depends on a range of factors. Linguists have spent a considerable amount of time investigating these factors.

Fishman's domain theory (1965, 1972) was amongst the earliest models of bilingual language choice. Domain, as Fishman conceived of it, refers to a clustering of characteristic situations around a prototypical theme which structures both the language user's perception of the situation and their social behaviour, including their language choice, in the situation. To give a simplified example, husband and wife (participants) talking about domestic affairs (topic) at home (setting) would constitute a "family" domain, and the family domain would require the use of a special language or language variety which would differ from, say, that of the "work" domain. Key to the concept of domain is the notion of congruence on two levels: (i) congruence among domain components, of which participants, topic and setting are deemed to be critical; (ii) congruence of domain with specific language or language variety, i.e. there are specific norms and expectations of language choice in specific domains.

Fishman emphasised the need to establish relevant domains empirically, regardless of their number, and strongly rejected the idea of an invariant set of domains for all communities. He argued that the same domain may not be equally significant to different communities or to all members of the same community. However, he did not himself offer a taxonomy or a set of principles for delimiting domains. Nor did Fishman indicate how the model could deal with incongruent contact situations, e.g. a patient accidentally meeting her doctor in a supermarket and starting to talk about domestic issues. A parallel situation could be when there is no change at all in terms of domain components, but the speaker decides to switch from one language to another for some special communicative effects. This is what Gumperz (e.g. 1982) termed "metaphorical codeswitching".

One possible improvement of the domain analysis seems to be provided in Bell's (1984) model of "audience design". Bell proposes that language choice at all levels is a matter of audience design, that is, "people are responding primarily to other people" (p. 197). Non-audience factors such as setting and topic derive their effect on the speaker's language choice by association with the audience, particularly the addressee. For example, a setting such as the supermarket is normally associated with a more socially distant kind of addressee than a domestic setting, and a "danger of death" question (Labov 1972) mentions a topic typically associated with an intimate addressee, and so on. The audience may include addressee, auditor, over-hearers, eavesdroppers and non-participant listeners, who will have differential effects on the speaker's language choice.

While Bell's audience design theory appears to be a more economic and coherent model than domain theory in accounting for congruence situations, it still does not deal with metaphorical codeswitching or how bilingual language users make language choices in incongruent situations. Building on the work by Fishman and Gumperz and working with Swahili, English and a variety of East African languages used in Kenya, Myers-Scotton (e.g. 1993b) argues that bilingual language users have an innate theory of socially relevant markedness and indexicality. They use language choice to negotiate interpersonal relationships and they do so within a normative framework which does not restrict choices but does limit interpretations. The centrepiece of the "markedness" theory of bilingual language choice is a "negotiation principle" which directs speakers to "choose the form of your conversational contribution such that it symbolises the set of rights and obligations which you wish to be in force between speakers and addressees for the current exchange" (Scotton 1983: 116). Myers-Scotton later recast the "markedness" model in the so-called Rational Choice mode, refocusing it from external factors affecting language choice to internal aspects of speaker motivation. Citing Elster (1983), Myers-Scotton (1999) argues that bilingual language users make their language choices using cognitively based calculations to maximise benefits to themselves. "To find the best action, (i) actors consider their desires and values as well as prior beliefs; (ii) they confirm that these three elements are internally consistent; (iii) finally, they make sure that their final desires, values, and beliefs take account of available evidence" (p. 1261).

Despite its rigour and technical sophistication, the markedness model, and its more recent Rational Choice version, has been criticised for assuming too much power to rationality and neglecting the process of deliberation which clearly plays an important part in social actors' decisions. Social actors such as bilingual language users use conceptual and other tools in their deliberations. These tools are resources available to them for functioning in society. Societies differ in the range and variety of resources available to their members. In any given society, the use of some resources (e.g. specific community languages) will be commonplace, and the use of others (e.g. codeswitching) will be relatively specialised. Both the concerns and objectives that motivate social actors and the results of their deliberations will depend on the techniques and forms of thought they are able to employ. Consequently, the analysts' attention should be focused on the way social actors use the available resources in the deliberation process. The problem with the Rational Choice model is not so much that it denies the place of deliberation in the actor's decision, but rather that it treats deliberation as if it were transparently rational and therefore of little explanatory significance. But, on the contrary, the resources used by actors in their deliberations, their connections with other resources, and the ways in which these depend on social conditions are legitimate and important areas of investigation.

In considering the process of deliberation of bilingual language users, one important issue seems to be the procedural apparatus they use not only to make their language choices but also to help their interlocutors arrive at the appropriate interpretations of their choices. Using the framework provided by Conversation Analysis, Auer (e.g. 1984) seeks to investigate the procedures used by bilingual conversation participants in actual interaction. As Auer points out, "whatever language a participant chooses for the organisation of his/her turn, or for an utterance which is part of the turn, the choice exerts an influence on subsequent language choices by the same or other speaker" (p. 5). It then follows that the meaning of codeswitching in bilingual conversation, for example, must be interpreted with reference to the language choices in the preceding and following turns by the participants themselves, rather than by correlating language choice with some externally determined values. From a methodological perspective, we would require an analytic procedure that focuses on the sequential development of interaction, because the meaning of bilingual acts such as codeswitching is conveyed as part of the interactive process and cannot be discussed without referring to the conversational context. Such a procedure is provided by Conversation Analysis. Examples of Conversation Analysis of bilingual interaction can be found in Li Wei (2005b) (see also Li Wei 2002, 2005a).

4. Conclusion

Contact is an important factor in many varieties of linguistic phenomena and has been studied from a variety of disciplinary perspectives. One of the key findings of the work by linguists is the dynamic nature of language contact. Causes, processes and outcomes differ from and interact with each other, depending on the socio-historical context. Whilst the different approaches, informed by theoretical linguistics, sociology, anthropology and psychology, all contribute to our understanding of the complex relationships between various factors, their focuses differ in terms of linguistic structure versus the language user. Convergence across the different perspectives may be possible if the outcomes of language contact are seen as the language users' strategic management of their linguistic resources in context. The pragmatics of language contact is therefore both a worthwhile topic in its own right and a promising area where different research perspectives may join together.

References

Auer, P. (1984). *Bilingual conversation*. Amsterdam: Benjamins.
Bell, A. (1984). Language style as audience design. *Language in Society* 13: 145–204.
Elster, J. (1983). *Sour grapes*. Cambridge University Press.
Ferguson, C. (1959). Diglossia. *Word* 15: 325–340. Reprinted in Li Wei (ed.) (2007), *The bilingualism reader* (second edition): 33–46. Routledge.
Fishman, J. (1964). Language maintenance and language shift as fields of inquiry. *Linguistics* 9: 32–70.
—— (1965). Who speaks what language to whom and when? *La Linguistique* 2: 67–88. Reprinted with postscript in Li Wei (ed.) (2007), *The bilingualism reader* (second edition): 55–70. Routledge.
—— (1972). Domains and the relationships between micro- and macro-sociolinguistics. In J. Gumperz & D. Hymes (eds), *Directions in sociolinguistics*: 435–453. Holt Rinehart & Winston.
Fishman, J. (ed.) (1966). *Language loyalty in the United States*. Mouton.

Gardner-Chloros, P. & M. Edwards (2003). When the blueprint is a red herring: assumptions behind grammatical approaches to code-switching *Transactions of the Philological Society* 102: 103–129.
—— (2007). Compound verbs in code-switching: bilinguals making do? *International Journal of Bilingualism* 11: 73–91.
Giles, H. (ed.) (1977). *Language, ethnicity and intergroup relations*. Academic Press.
Giles, H. & R. St Clair (eds.) (1979). *Language and social psychology*. Blackwell.
Gumperz, J. (1982). *Discourse strategies*. Cambridge University Press.
Harding, E. & P. Riley (1986). *The bilingual family*. Cambridge University Press.
Haugen, E. (1966). *Language planning and conflict*. Harvard University Press.
Heller, M. (1994). *Crosswords: Language, education and ethnicity in French Ontario*. Mouton.
Hill, J. & K. Hill (1986). *Speaking Mexicano. Dynamics of syncretic language in Central Mexico*. University of Arizona Press.
Kroll, J. & E. Stewart (1984). Category interference in translation and picture naming. *Journal of Memory and Language* 33: 149–174.
Labov, W. (1972). *Sociolinguistic patterns*. Pennsylvania University Press.
Li Wei (2002). "What do you want me to say?" Con the conversation analysis approach to bilingual interaction. *Language in Society* 31: 159–180.
—— (2005a). "How can you tell?" Towards a common sense explanation of conversational code-switching. *Journal of Pragmatics* 37: 375–390.
Li Wei (ed.) (2005b). Conversational codeswitching. Special issue of *Journal of Pragmatics* 37(3).
—— (2007). Dimensions of bilingualism. In Li Wei (ed.), *The bilingualism reader* (second edition): 3–22. Routledge.
MacSwan, J. (1999). *A minimalist approach to intrasentential code-switching*. Garland.
Myers-Scotton, C. (1993a). *Duelling languages: Grammatical structure in codeswitching*. Oxford University Press.
—— (1993b). *Social motivations for codeswitching: Evidence from Africa*. Oxford University Press.
—— (1999). Explaining the role of norms and rationality in codeswitching. *Journal of Pragmatics* 32: 1259–1271.
Muysken, P. (2000). *Bilingual Speech*. Cambridge University Press.
Poplack, S. (1980). Sometimes I'll start a sentence in Spanish *y termino en español*: toward a typology of code-switching. *Linguistics* 18: 581–618. Reprinted with postscript in Li Wei (ed.) (2007), *The bilingualism reader* (second edition): 213–243. Routledge.
Potter, M.C., K.-F. So, B. Von Echardt & L.B. Feldman (1984). Lexical and conceptual representation in beginning and more proficient bilinguals. *Journal of Verbal Learning and Verbal Behaviour* 23: 23–38.
Romaine, S. (1995). [1989] *Bilingualism* (second edition). Blackwell.
Scotton, C.M. (1983). The negotiation of identities in conversation: a theory of markedness and code choice. *International Journal of the Sociology of Language* 44: 115–136.
Thomason, S. & T. Kaufman (1988). *Language contact, creolization and genetic linguistics*. University of California Press.
Weinreich, U. (1953). *Languages in contact: Findings and problems*. The Linguistic Circle of New York. (Reissued by Mouton in The Hague, 1968).
Winford, D. (2003). *An introduction to contact linguistics*. Blackwell.
Woolard, K. (1989). *Double talk: Bilingualism and the politics of ethnicity in Catalonia*. Stanford University Press.

Correlational sociolinguistics

Norbert Dittmar
Free University of Berlin

1. Introduction

In sociolinguistics, verbal means of expression are studied against the background of potential and actual social behavior. There are three aspects of this field which have attracted a lot of attention in the last few decades:

1. The correlation between the production and reception of utterances. Can verbal features of the production of utterances be systematically related to social parameters, or is it necessary to first clarify how utterances in various contexts are interpreted by the listeners before the speakers' styles can be put into explanatory contexts?
2. Are the categories of sociolinguistic analysis of the type which enable a taxonomic codification of a corpus and thereby a feature analysis, or are they dynamic categories of action which are interpretively and context-specifically defined?
3. How is the problem of the macro- and micro-level of sociolinguistic relations to be solved? Sociolinguistic styles and norms of interpretation within the framework of social behavior are inarguably of pre-eminent importance for the micro-level of sociolinguistic relations. On the macro-level, however, utterances (with or without interpretation) are not only bound to the social conditions of the speaker, but also to the prestige and market value (symbolic value) of speech varieties and of the languages of internationally competitive speech communities and states.

The subject matter of sociolinguistics is widely agreed upon: it is the description and explanation of the social meaning of verbal systems and of their variations in application (sociolinguistic styles). At present, this subject matter is studied from two different perspectives. The 'horizontal' perspective examines styles of interaction. Verbal utterances are described sequentially and context-specifically, according to type of interaction (participants), type of situation (situational framing, assumed activities), and type of communicative aims (to narrate, to advise, to assess, to discuss, etc.). Interaction involves the working out of mental maps of the aims and purposes of the interaction, the organisation of verbal means of expression, intonation and prosody, non-verbal behavior, the interpretation of the meaning of the interlocutor's utterances, appropriate reactions, prospective planning, etc.. These processes are very complex, even in short stretches of time. Therefore, the variety of discourse is the main object of systematic exploration. In other words, the exemplary qualitative description of the synchronization of verbal and non-verbal means in the process of interaction is at the centre of the discussion. The functionalization of single features and their codification in view of the formulation of correlational statements (connecting verbal and other features) would hinder the progress of research. Too many important factors would inevitably be neglected or go unnoticed.

Correlational sociolinguistics is 'vertically' oriented. Initially, the major aim of correlational sociolinguistics was to explain differences in speech varieties with the help of social constructs (by means of their correlation with verbal production features), which were abstracted from concrete interaction. The main emphasis of the research has since shifted to the question of speech variation as part of social change. A prerequisite of all studies of language change is the comparability of the phenomena which undergo change. Socially induced change is indicated by the area in which the vocabulary (lexicon) prevails and by the grammaticalization of selected means of expression, if the identity of old and new can be methodologically established. Certain semantic and grammatical features are isolated as a structural domain, where their maximal dimension is defined, and their change is described within a codified continuum. In other words, the range of variation is defined by linguistic variables. The different forms of the variables are systematically correlated with constructs of social structures; the latter appear as functionalized feature forms, whose relationship with linguistic variables is measured (there are criteria for the validity of the type and quality of the correlation figures). Underlying correlational sociolinguistics, which deals with the finality of change, is the following axiom: *Speakers have a natural basic variety which is spontaneous and not consciously controlled; verbal and non-verbal restrictions (constraints) operate on this basic variety*. Parts of the variety and norm systems can be restructured within the framework of a general social structure, adapted to new conditions, and interpreted as an achievement of assimilation to social change. While the 'horizontal' sociolinguistic perspective has its roots in speech act theory, 'vertical' sociolinguistics emerged from the tradition of dialectology. In the following sections, I will present correlational sociolinguistics (CSL) in detail and evaluate it from the viewpoint of pragmatic research.

2. Concepts of linguistic variation

Linguistic variation is regarded as the appropriate label for the topic studied by sociolinguists. The annual conferences on *New Ways of Analyzing Variation* (held since 1971) best convey the perception variation linguists (or 'variationists') have of themselves. A fully developed theory of linguistic variation exists only in the field of the surface-related description of production variation (variable rules); the concept of *variety grammar*, which was introduced by Klein (Klein & Dittmar 1979; Klein 1988), is seen by variationists as a concept closely related to their own research interests. A major attempt to theorize on the variationist paradigm was made by Poplack (1990) in her article *Variation theory and language contact: concepts, methods and data*. Basically, Poplack gives an introduction to inductive methods, but without a foundation in the theory of language. She explains how to establish a so-called mega-corpus, how to segment speech variables and operationalize non-verbal constructs, and how to choose technical instruments for description. Correlations are, in accordance with the standards of theoretical and applied statistics, quantitative measurements whose validity and reliability represent the connection between operationalized verbal and non-verbal phenomena and structures. The claim of the correlational method that it is possible to distinguish between the 'arbitrary' and the 'systematic recurrent' with an explicitly scientific method, is reflected in David Sankoff's dictum that: "Qualitative data are a metaphor for not enough data". *Quantitative data* are seen as scientifically superior data which lead to more systematic statements.

The remainder of this section summarizes the essentials of the variationist paradigm.

2.1 Tradition and innovation

Research on dialects and language contact belongs to a social dialectology that puts an emphasis on the sociology of language, which described variation and multilingualism in cities with the help of modern sociological methods. The dialectological assumption of homogeneity, i.e. the assumption that local communities are internally homogenous (viz. for each place there is exactly one local dialect) prevented a description of urban languages. Instead of seeing variation as 'two-dimensional' (the relation between 'space' and 'language'), it is now viewed as 'multi-dimensional' (a function of spacial, social, and situational parameters).

2.2 Methodology

Inductive procedure, empirical gathering of corpus data:

- sociologically stratified sample survey of speakers of different age, social status, sex, ethnic group, etc. ('random sample survey')
- representative documentation of speech behaviour for different verbal domains of expression and attitudes towards selected speech variables (the principle of *sociolinguistic validity*: those linguistic variables which are to be described must have been ascertained accordingly)
- the authentic documentation of 'natural' speech behavior in situations of communication with a different degree of formality; the central task is to overcome the 'observer's paradox': the sociolinguist has to document the speech behavior of

people in situations in which they feel absolutely unobserved, but this can only be accomplished by systematic observation (the principle of *situational validity* of speech data: the 'quality' of speech data depends on its authenticity)

2.3 Description

The description of the frequency and social function of speech variants (defined as linguistic variables), which differ in their morphological and grammatical form but not in their *referential meaning* for two or more varieties (dialects/sociolects); the frequency of occurrence of variants in the varieties are correlated with operationalized sociological indexes (interval scales of 'age', ordinal scales of 'social status' or 'networks', nominal scales of 'sex', etc.) and are recorded in quantitative 'correlation measurements'.

2.4 Explanation

Differences in the frequency of occurrences of speech variants are explained as a function of e.g. 'age', 'sex', 'social status', in the framework of structural-functionalist sociological models[1] (= the social significance of the quantitative representation of the examined variation); that is, the explanation is based on sociological constructs which are put on social groups by the 'researcher's glasses from outside' and which do not (have to) coincide with the natural social perception and awareness of the people affected. The law of statistic 'gravity' is in force: the more data is ascertained for a mean variation of social variables/quantities in a speech community, the more detailed the structural tendencies of the variation that can be recorded and the better the mechanisms of language change that can be explained (hence the significance of the term 'mega-corpus').

2.5 Theory

Only those linguistic theories endure which are empirically verified and which are legitimized by the description and explanation of large data corpuses (verbal surface structures). The 'linguistic facts' in the social reality are the touchstone of any theory in the eyes of William Labov. If the theory is economical and complete and consistently formulated from a formal point of view, this is seen as an 'addition' to or a 'dowry' of empirical description. Labov is not creative on the theory of language or grammar: to a large extent he takes the descriptive tools of generative grammar[2] or of structuralism.

---

[1]. This refers to the sociological model developed by Talcott Parsons which, in analogy with biological organisms, understands institutionalized social constructs as self-regulating mechanisms in the service of system-preservation and balance-establishment.

[2]. I.e. the model of transformational-generative grammar proposed by Chomsky (1965), in combination with the model of phonology in Chomsky & Halle (1968).

He chooses the most adequate methodology for empirical description on the basis of the composition of the empirical data; the grammar is enlarged by the quantitative evaluation of rules, so-called 'variable rules' (see also 'variety grammars'), which are founded on a generative structure model. Speech is hereby seen not as 'autonomous', but as a 'system of adaptive functions'. Two aspects are of interest for the paradigm:

a. the correlation of speech data with sociological constructs such as 'social class', 'social status',[3] etc., is theoretically justified by the possibility of empirical replication of surveys in 'real time' (= panel investigation) in accordance with explicit formal criteria; the maxim of action for correlational sociolinguistics is therefore: *synchronic description of variation in the service of systemic-linguistic description and explanation of language change* (= the explanation of the past through the present);
b. quantitative instruments are the *conditio sine qua non* of the description of variation, i.e. the so-called 'mega-corpuses' of data alone are in a position to find the 'right' solution to disputed questions on the description of speech. The process of 'interaction' is of no importance for *explanations* in the correlational variationist approach.

2.6 Application

Labov recognizes the service of linguistics to society. The linguist explains scientifically questions of variation, of norm, of the everyday usage of language, of language change, and uses findings to inform his/her schools and institutions.

3. Basic lines of argumentation: The corpus

The aim of CLS is to describe grammatical change as a socially conditioned process at a historical moment, and as a systematic occurrence (rather than a phenomenon bound to singular interaction contexts). At the same time, grammatical knowledge should not be taken as an intersection of rule-consciousness and actualization in speech, but as the production of speech in concrete speech situations. Instances of usage should be *authentic*, evaluated according to their frequency of occurrence, and differentiated by the context of speech situations. Accounts of usage are *valid* if a context style can be assigned; they are reliable if the elicitation of a given discourse type guarantees a certain occurrence for the usages accounted for.

---

3. Because of this method the paradigm is often called (quantitative) 'correlational sociolinguistics' and is methodically compared with (qualitative) 'interactional sociolinguistics'.

Examples of usage 'invented' by researchers in grammar books abstract from manner and frequency of usage in everyday life. This is why grammar books do not explain what significance a rule has and what role it plays in social life. Only wide corpus analyses, which are supposed to cover everyday and institutional language use, can secure the authenticity of rules. Instances of usage in corpuses have two functions: (1) their intra-linguistic distribution in an ensemble of linguistic segments; (2) their extra-linguistic functions in the sense of a sociolinguistic profile, involving the variable evaluation of social (as well as other) factors.

The aim of the grammatical description is to differentiate between *correct* and *incorrect* rules. 'Correct' descriptions can only be made on the basis of *mega-corpuses*. *The more data we have, the more we can find out*, is one of the principles formulated by Labov (1972).

4. Rules: How instances of usage are described

There are two categories of data that belong to a sociolinguistic description following the variationist approach: linguistic and social. A grammatical phenomenon (→ rule) is operationalized in accordance with an underlying definition in the corpus. The lexical-morphological unity, or the corresponding segment, is quantified in terms of *type* and *token*, in which the left as well as the right immediate context of the segment if specified. The bigger the corpus, and the more often the segment occurs, the more definitely or categorically the rule can be formulated. Labov expects of a mega-corpus that it forms the objective basis for claims about the general distribution of a segment or rule in the speech community.

Rules which are generally valid in a speech community and do not depend on social or pragmatic variation are termed *categorical*. A large number of the rules in a grammatical system would be labelled categorical; i.e. they are seldom broken. On the other hand, violations of *semicategorical rules* do occur, although not very often (as in expressive, emotional, emphatic situations, etc.). They occur often enough, however, to attract attention; after all, variable rules cannot be violated, as they are formal variants which are produced and perceived subconsciously. They are called *sociolinguistic indicators*, because they refer to social features of speakers (age, background, education, sex, group affiliation, etc.). The variationist methodology is closely associated with the concept of *sociolinguistic variables*; the latter can be defined as a *number of alternatives to referentially say the same thing, but to express different social meanings*. The sum of the realised variants of a linguistic variable, put into the context of all possible realizations in the corpus, is then connected to a specific sociological variable (e.g. the r-pronunciation in New York connected to status and prestige, the g-pronunciation in Berlin to city district, or the syntax of *que* in Montréal connected to education and social class). According to variationist studies available to date, the notation of rules follows the generative model; for context-specific limitations of the linguistic variable, pointed brackets are used (⟨ ⟩), as they indicate the *quantitative evaluation* of the rule constraints. A *variable rule* would in this sense specify that the liquids *l* and *r* hinder the realization of the palatal spirant in Berlinisch, while the high vowels *i* end *e* favor the application of the palatalisation rule (see Schlobinski 1987). Such a variable rule is a function of sociological parameters. The non-application of a rule can coincide with a young age group, the consistent application of a rule with a group of older speakers. The linguistic and social differentiation is effected by explicit categories which are defined independently of one another. The two sets of statements are then correlated with the help of recognized statistical procedure. The combination of the (non-) realization of a rule with a sociological category then explains the linguistic variation.

The quantification of instances of usage in the corpus of a segment follows the assumption that occurrences have an identical grammatical-linguistic meaning and are not affected by the interactive events in the course of a conversation. The sociological parameters, on the other hand, are *constructs* of social reality, which are established by scientists from an outside perspective. The two sets of statements, however, have nothing to do with interaction or behavior in everyday life and individual intentional action. They pretend to describe habitual (automated) behavior in the social context.

Dittmar (1995) labels the rules which reconstruct habitual behavior *regulative rules*. They are formulated as conditional clauses (if… then) and are typical of statements in deductive theories. In psychology or sociology, such rules are used in experiments. They follow the model of sociology as a *science*. Their model is the *rewrite-rule*:

$$A \rightarrow B/X\_\_Y$$

(if A occurs in the context of X and Y, then rewrite it as B). Recurrent linguistic behavior is described, but social behavior is not.

In contrast, in the more recent sociology dealing with interaction (ethnomethodology) a type of rule has been developed which can be described as inter-subjective *instructions* and as context-sensitive. They describe interactive meaning insofar as they include the effect which intentions have on the understanding of the hearer (interpretative result). While speech act rules in the form of *in context Z, x counts as Y* usually specify the meaning within a speaker's semantics, *interactive rules concerning behavioral instructions* are based on the communication *process* in interactions. The following would then be an *intersubjective instruction*:

> See that what's-going-on-here (c) is a quarrel, (Z), and hear in the context of the quarrel (Z) utterance (x) as an insult (Y)

We know the instruction rule from conversation analysis. Conversation analysts describe the alternation of speakers, corrections, and preferred vs. non-preferred parts in utterance pairs. While such rules record the constitution of actions in the interactive process, the regulative rules (of the *variable rule* type) describe automated 'physical' (in the sense of *Hexis* as defined by Bourdieu 1977) behavioral patterns, which are taken like a blood sample from the speaker-production as systemic manifestations, and which, in the form of linguistic indicators, express social functions (variants of one and the same underlying meaning).

Conein (1992) has rightly separated *hétérogénéité linguistique* from *hétérogénéité sociale*. Conein proves that the variables in Labov's studies show an asymmetry between the concepts of linguistic and of sociological variation. In essence, Labov's theory is based on the social perception of selected sociolinguistic indicators. Hence, he established indicators which are based on recent concepts of *social cognition* for social group affiliation. Jackendoff (1983) advocates special cognitive modules for voice recognition and the recognition of facial expressions; in his opinion, these modules contain information parallel to the systems of spatial recognition and hearer perception, whose specific task it is to deliver information to social cognition. In other words, the Labovian indicators could be interpreted as *social gestures* or *social deixis*: they supply participants in a conversation or interaction with that 'fodder' which the social cognition needs for the identification of people in social space. Hereby, the fundamental question of the place of variationist methodology and explanation in social action research (and, following from this, in sociology too) is answered on a trial basis. The results of correlational linguistic studies are part of the domain of *social orientation, social perception,* and *automated social cognition* in the domain of behavior. Gesticulatory behavior indicators, such as stereotypical and not-consciously-controlled behavior attitudes and regulations, influence interaction. Looked at in the light of verbal or non-verbal illocution, they operate on a completely different level from indicators of social behavior.

The far-reaching tendency of variationist studies to propose scientific-theoretical categorizations can be illustrated with some examples:

- In a number of sociolinguistic studies, phonological variables are said to indicate the socio-economic status of the speakers (for an overall view, see Dittmar 1976; Downes 1984; and Fasold 1990).
- Phonological segments are seen to indicate the subconscious wish of speakers to belong to a group with, in their opinion, a higher prestige, of which they are not members (e.g. hypercorrection, as documented in the case of the lower middle class in New York; see also various studies by Trudgill and others).
- Phonological variables indicate gender differences (studies by Labov, Trudgill, Eckert and others).

– Formal variants (morphological, syntactic and semantic) show the degree of formality of the speech, or the degree of relaxation of the speaker in the act of speaking, and give information about the individual and social condition of the speakers, which offers the hearer the option to adapt to the style or to react to it in an appropriate manner.

Therefore, the results of correlational sociolinguistic studies reveal social-psychological mechanisms which, in the field of social cognition, seem to be quite systematic.[4]

5. Language change: The perspective of explanations

The undisputed opinion in sociolinguistics that the variationist approach is teleogically orientated towards the recording of processes of language change is based on the correlational methodology. If the same linguistic and sociological parameters are examined at regular time intervals, then the 'measured' differences can be indicators of language change. Labov's (1972) views on the phases of language change (the problem of elimination of change, the problem of the social embedding of linguistic change, and the assessment of continual change in the speech community) can be summarized as follows.

The change has its starting point in the fluctuating, irregular language use of variants of a subgroup, which for different reasons – conscious or subconscious – sees its distinctive identity in the speech community as endangered. The altering or already altered elements of the change are called indicators, if they have spread to all members of the group-specific subculture. Those members who have played an important part in spreading the change are not aware of it; because of this, the linguistic variable affected is not stylistically stratified. The spreading of change goes beyond this group and reaches other groups in the speech community. In this way, the values of the change-initiating group are acception by other groups. The change-initiating group, and the variable which indicated the change, become the focus (the target) of social attention. When the change has reached the outer limits of its expansion, and has been adopted by the greater speech community, it then *marks* its speakers socially by the usage of the variables ('sociolinguistic marker'). At this stage, the variable already shows stylistic stratifications, but is used subconsciously. At the same time, the changing variable affects other elements of the language of the language system; Labov noticed in his 1963 study of Martha's Vineyard that the raising of the [a] in /ay/ also affected the quality of the [a] in /aw/. The hitherto depicted stages of change are of the 'subconscious' kind ('change from below').

---

4. Representative anthologies of the correlational sociolinguistic approach are Ammon, Dittmar & Mattheier (1987 and 1988); for a bibliography, see Dittmar (1995).

If the change did not have its starting in the highest status group (middle and upper class – studies show that these groups are rarely initiators of change), and if the change has not been ratified or taken on silently by this group, the change forms are *stigmatized*, i.e. they are seen as 'ungrammatical', incorrect speech.

'Stigmatization' induces the 'change from above', in which 'change from above' is synonymous with 'consciously strived for change' in contrast to 'change from below' (= subconsciously strived for change).[5] Consequently, speakers avoid variants which are, for the time being, accepted by the highest status groups, especially in formally controlled styles. The variable now increasingly marks social *and* style stratification. If the variant is conspicuously stigmatized, it can become the topic of discussion; variables which have become *thematical* in this way are called 'stereotypes'. In the course of these contrary tendencies of change, the form can disappear again or live on as a variable (e.g. without continuing the change). If the change, on the other hand, has its starting point in the higher status groups, the affected variants are as a rule not stigmatized, but are seen as 'prestigious'. The 'prestige model' is then used more in formal (controlled) than in informal styles and preferentially in the upper classes. It is also possible that a changing feature which is discretely accepted by the upper classes, loses its stigmatization and itself gains prestige. These stages make clear once again that without variability, there is no language change; but not all variations lead to a language change.

The function of sociolinguistic variables as 'fodder' for social cognition is made clear once more by this explanation. Following the *uniformitarian principle* of the Junggrammatiker, it is assumed that *today the same forces induce language change as in the past*. The comparison of two speaker samples and of two corpora makes possible the quantitative determination of the difference between the two time intervals in the production of speech. This difference proves the diffusion or the extinction of rules. The driving forces behind the difference are to be seen in the social-historically founded social evaluation of the speakers over a period of time. Changing values bring with them a restructuring in social cognition (the perception of linguistic indicators as prestigious, stigmatized, status- or education-defined, etc.). In the description of a given social value and norm system, which – on the level of speech behavior – is differentiated by different variants of language use, a Parsonian structural-functionalist influence on Labov is noticeable. At any one time, a systemic unity of values and norms differentiates linguistic variants, certain parts of which always change, while the functions are preserved.

---

5. The expressions 'change from below' and 'change from above' are sometimes wrongly equated with 'change starting in the lower social classes' and 'change starting in the upper social classes', respectively. By 'above' and 'below', however, the 'conscious level' and the 'subconscious level' are meant.

A different perspective is offered by Hopper & Closs-Traugott (1993), who looked at the "principle of grammatic inferencing" (p. 63) as constitutive for language change induced by interaction. In their view, asymmetries between language production and partially intention-following intention lead to restructuring.

6. Outlook

In his communication theory, Habermas (1981) distinguishes between everyday forms of communications (the pragmatics of speech acts) and *systemic forces* in the form of free enterprise laws, ideological maxims, etc., which are (to paraphrase his words) behind the backs of people acting in an every-day-like manner. Sankoff (1988) takes up Habermas's ideas and categorizes variation as part of the 'linguistic market' of different varieties (subconsciously acting social parameters which influence the usage of language). Sociolinguistics is not recorded from the perspective of the acting people themselves (everyday life), but from forces that act behind the speakers' backs, which function as input and motivation for language usage.

We can differentiate between automated, habitual language usage and intentional, social behavior which is formed in the process of social interaction. In pragmatics, qualitative behavior is looked at from the point of view of pragmatic parameters such as situation, presupposition, implication, changed prerequisites of knowledge, intentions of effect, cooperation, etc., while considering speaker utterance as well as hearer understanding. The often ethnographical research design aims at describing the *horizontal dimensions* of variations. The factors which change the process of interaction, and by doing so define their variation, are recorded in their coexistential shaping. Qualitative parameters such as prosody, discourse topic, roles, situational frame, etc. are looked for. Often quantifications are not carried out, as the isolation of qualitative parameters or categoric behavioral rules has up to now been only fragmentarily successful.

Correlational sociolinguistics, however, uses variable forms and segments as prototypes for the purpose of analysis. The variants of the same function inform the hearer about a characteristic of social identity. Social categorization, which can be obtained from the different linguistic forms used by the speakers, reduces hearer insecurity in the sense of social cognition. Linguistic indicators, therefore, represent a possibility of social cognition. They facilitate a categorization of the speaker in the social space, and establish an expectation of systemic social behavior. The coordinates of the sociolinguistic indicators form part of the communicative actions which are to be described qualitatively and pragmatically in terms of habitual social orientation, and help to determine, in the sense of a systemic module, the performative action. In this sense, correlational sociolinguistics contributes to the explanation of the vertical dimension of linguistic and communicative variation; it shows the systemic subliminal social forces which steer the cognitive orientation of social action in an instance of interaction.

References

Ammon, U., N. Dittmar & K.J. Mattheier (eds.) (1987–1988). *Sociolinguistics* (2 vols.). de Gruyter.
Bourdieu, P. (1977). The economics of linguistic exchanges. *Social Science Information* 16(6): 645–668.
Chomsky, N. (1965). *Aspects of the theory of syntax*. MIT Press.
Chomsky, N. & M. Halle (1968). *The sound pattern of English*. Harper & Row.
Conein, B. (1992). Hétérogénéité sociale et hétérogénéité linguistique. *Languages* 27(108): 101–113.
Dittmar, N. (1976). *Sociolinguistics*. Arnold.
——— (1995). *Studienbibliographie zur Zoziolinguistik*. Groos.
Downes, W. (1984). *Language and society*. Fontana.
Fasold, R.W. (1990). *The sociolinguistics of language*. Blackwell.
Habermas, J. (1981). *Theorie des kommunikativen Handelns* (2 vols.). Suhrkamp.
Hopper, P.J. & E. Closs-Traugott (1993). *Grammaticalization*. Cambridge University Press.
Jackendoff, R. (1983). *Semantics and cognition*. MIT Press.
Klein, W. (1988). Varietätengrammatik (Grammar of varieties). In: U. Ammon, N. Dittmar & K.J. Mattheier (eds.), vol. 2: 997–1007.
Klein, W. & N. Dittmar (1979). *Developing grammars*. Springer.
Labov, W. (1972). Some principles of linguistic methodology. *Language in Society* 1: 97–120.
Poplack, S. (1990). Variation theory and language contact. *Papers for the Workshop on Concepts, Methodology and Data*: 33–62. Strasbourg.
Sankoff, D. (1988). Sociolinguistics and syntactic variation. In F.J. Newmeyer (ed.) *Linguistics, the Cambridge survey*, vol. 4: 140–161. Cambridge University Press.
Schlobinski, P. (1987). *Stadtsprache Berlin*. de Gruyter.

Gender

Robin Tolmach Lakoff
University of California at Berkeley

1. Language and gender

We can approach the intersection of language and gender from either of two perspectives, one 'grammatical', having to do with the properties of core linguistics (phonology, morphology, and syntax), the second semantic and pragmatic. Here I will naturally concentrate on the latter, but a few words about the former may be useful, by way of contrast.

Gender can be defined as 'sexual identity'. In this sense it is often contrasted with *sex*, a word that has been replaced by *gender* in many of its traditional uses. Often *gender* is used in discussions of cultural or social understandings of the difference between males and females, leaving *sex* to cover biological distinctions. But this differentiation is by no means universal or automatic, and there are many circumstances in which either word might be used.

Traditionally, in linguistics, 'gender' refers to a system found in many languages, especially in the Indo-European languages (outside of Modern English), in which nouns are assigned to one of two or three categories: masculine, feminine, or (sometimes) neuter. The names of these categories are ancient, and appear to be based on the fact that the words for 'woman', 'girl', and so forth belong to one (therefore named 'feminine'), those meaning 'man', 'boy', and the like to a second ('masculine'), and the third category, if it exists, is therefore labeled 'neuter', meaning 'neither', by default. Adjectives and some verbal forms agree with nouns in gender. Speakers of languages that use grammatical gender must learn the gender of most nouns by rote, since aside from the few words that make obvious reference to male or female entities, there is no semantic basis for grammatical gender assignment. There has been some discussion of this point in recent literature, with claims sometimes being made that more feminine than masculine nouns in such languages have negative associations, or more masculine nouns have an aggressive component. But since the assignment of grammatical gender to specific nouns may differ greatly even among related languages, the merits of any such positions are unclear. It is true, though, that masculine gender is unmarked or neutral in these languages: for instance, if both feminine and masculine nouns are referred to, an adjective referring to both will be masculine in form. Thus in a Latin sentence like (1),

(1) Puer et puella boni sunt,
    'The boy and the girl are good,'

the adjective *boni* is masculine plural although *puella* is feminine. Even in languages without grammatical gender, like English, semantically masculine forms are conventionally unmarked:

(2)   Will everyone please take *his* seat,

although in recent years this practice has often been abandoned in favor of a more truly gender-neutral phrasing, as in:

(3)   Will everyone please take *his or her/their seat(s)*.

Example (3) suggests that even apparently purely 'grammatical' gender has a pragmatic component: the privileging of the masculine grammatical form indicates, however subtly, the privileging of the male and the masculine outside of language, representing a world in which men are 'normal' and unmarked, and of primary interest.

2.   Pragmatic aspects of gender

More to the point here, however, are the semantic and pragmatic functions of gender: the representation of human masculinity and femininity (or maleness and femaleness) in linguistic form. While grammatical gender distinctions, as noted above, are language-specific and probably do not occur in the majority of the world's languages, semantically and pragmatically based gender distinctions are universal, although different languages and cultures manifest them in somewhat different ways. For this reason such gender distinctions are diagnostic of the level of equality between women and men in any given society: the fewer and less salient pragmatically based gender differences in linguistic practice there are, the more egalitarian the society is likely to be.

Such differences manifest themselves in many ways: in lexical choices (*chairman* and *policeman* vs. *chair* and *police officer*); ways of talking about women vs. men (e.g. the sexualization of references to women; the much greater availability, in most languages, of derogatory expressions referring to women than to men); and in interactional patterns (e.g. men's tendency to dominate mixed-group conversation; women's tendency to be more deferentially polite than men). In this way, gender differences are manifested in the speech and discourse patterns of female and male speakers, and in the choice of language available in speaking of male and female subjects. Since these aspects of language are clearly pragmatically based, it is upon them that this discussion will focus.

3.   The prehistory of language and gender research

From ancient times into the present, studies of gender differences in language use are almost invariably framed as examinations of 'women's language'. This is another illustration of the principle that *masculine* is unmarked: male language is 'normal' and not subject to study; women's ways are exotic, both abnormal and inferior. There has been a little bit of research in recent years into 'men's language', but the great bulk of this tiny production really is about special kinds of men: fraternity boys, men in the armed forces, and such – while research into women's language most often is about 'women's' behavior in general. So, for instance, one of the earliest (allegedly) scientific examinations of women's language, in Otto Jespersen's magisterial tome of 1922, *Language: its nature, development, and origins*, consists of about 100 pages dedicated to 'the woman', with the rest of its approximately 500 pages implicitly about 'the man', i.e. 'the human being'.

The awareness of gender differences in language goes back at least as far as the dawn of literacy, since writers of fiction have always been concerned with the accurate representation of the speech of male and female characters, and consequently represent them differently, whether accurately or (usually) stereotypically. But Jespersen's work is, to my knowledge, the earliest attempt at scientific description, analysis, and explanation of the differences between male and female speech.

On the one hand, Jespersen makes a few valid observations: girls tend to begin to speak earlier than boys; women are more apt to be polite. But even as he is exploring these scientifically valid observations, he intersperses them with impressionistic stereotypes: women use more adjectives (while men prefer the manly verb); women talk about unimportant things. One interesting pattern is manifest in Jespersen's discussion: whenever females might seem to come out ahead in a comparison (e.g. girls begin talking sooner), he finds a way to show that that apparent superiority really is a sign of deeper inferiority: females talk earlier because they have less of importance to talk about.

Unlike Jespersen, not claiming the status of science, Virginia Woolf, in the nearly contemporaneous *A room of one's own* (1929) discusses differences between male and female writers of nonfiction. At first, she says, she is eager to read the work of men: it seems so much clearer and stronger than that of women. But then she notes, as she reads these male authors, she is increasingly distracted by an 'I' that slants across the page – the writer's egotism and certitude. One might say that Jespersen and Woolf are making a similar observation: that male speech tends to be more definite and precise than women's – but from different points of view. Woolf further discusses, or at least hints at, social reasons for this difference; Jespersen simply attributes it to the greater intelligence of the male.

Another early twentieth century area in which there were occasional investigations of gender differences is linguistic anthropology. Early anthropologists often brought back stories about (contemporary or ancient) societies in which men and women "speak different languages". The case of the Arawak (extinct long before anthropology came to exist) is perhaps the strongest: contemporary descendants claimed that

Arawak men and women literally spoke different languages and could not understand each other. Of course, this situation could not literally be the case: boys and girls were both raised principally by their mothers, so both would have understood women's language. But the existence of this myth demonstrates that, for the descendants of the Arawaks (not to say the gullible anthropologists), the notion that males and females speak differently makes sense. Other cases studied (always in 'exotic' languages) make that point more subtly. Mary Haas' paper, "Male and female speech in Koasati" (1944) demonstrated that, in that Native American language, male and female speakers used different morphological endings throughout the grammar. Numerous writers on Japanese had also discussed the gender-distinct uses of honorifics and pragmatic particles in that language. But until the 1970s, the prevailing wisdom had it that explicit gender differences might exist in exotic languages, but in English and other familiar cases (the languages of the developed world), no such differences existed. There is an unacknowledged problem, though, in studies of exotic languages: women's forms of language could only be heard from female speakers. But in many traditional societies, women do not speak to unrelated men (even anthropologists). So, since the early explorers, missionaries, and anthropologists who collected these data were overwhelmingly male, it was impossible for them to get accurate data about differences in linguistic practices between the sexes, and so mostly they ignored the question or relied on hearsay from male informants for their information. Often female anthropologists function as 'honorary males' with access to both male and female members of a group. In such cases (Mary Haas and Margaret Mead are examples), investigators can get more thorough and reliable data.

Serious work on gender-based differences in linguistic behavior had to wait until the 1970s, when four essential factors came together: the rise of the modern women's movement (creating an interest in gender issues); the possibility of women holding positions in research universities (so that there were people who wanted to study these differences, and whose work could be published and taken seriously); the incorporation of pragmatic theory into linguistics via generative semantics (creating precise ways of talking about contextualization); and the development of the cassette tape recorder (making it possible to record and transcribe natural and spontaneous speech production).

4. The history of language and gender research

4.1 The 1970s

The story of pragmatically based language and gender research can be told either topically or chronologically. But the two are not mutually exclusive: in each decade between the 1970s and now, different topics received the lion's share of attention, and different theories were ascendant. So it makes sense to examine the subject from a chronological perspective, since this will also be a topical organization.

One way to view the narrative of language and gender research is as movement and change: from word to sentence to turn to discourse; from the simplistic either/or, good/bad to the more complex, layered, ambivalent and ambiguous; in terms of the increasing complexity and inclusiveness of explanatory theories, and the integration of the methods of pragmatics and sociolinguistics. In other words, the last thirty-five years or so represent the birth and gradual maturation of a field of study.

In the early 1970s, almost everything relating to women was being reinvented, like almost everything about language a decade earlier. There was no usable prior discourse to anchor current argumentation. There were no agreed-upon methods; there was no agreed-upon frame or background that everyone in the field accepted as right, much less inevitable. The 1960s and 1970s were politically volatile in the U.S. as elsewhere, and nowhere more so than in linguistics and in gender research.

There are several reasonable stories of the creation of the field of language and gender. What follows is my own.

During the late 1960s and early 1970s, the dominant paradigm of linguistics, transformational generative grammar, was in disarray. There were two sides fighting for control of the field: the standard (and later, extended) transformational theorists, led by Noam Chomsky; and an offshoot, generative semantics. There were many points of theoretical (and stylistic) contention between the two; the one of most relevance to this discussion concerned the makeup of the deep/underlying/abstract/logical structure, the basis of the syntactic component of the grammar.

The vexing question was: what kinds of information did the basic level of syntactic structure contain? Only purely linguistic data (syntactic context, allowing the statement of cooccurrence and distribution constraints in sentences)? Or, additionally, extra-linguistic context – for instance, individual speakers' or societal beliefs, prior knowledge, desires, the real-world context in which the utterance was located? The generative semanticists took the second position, to which the other side offered a compelling (and disturbing) riposte: if you include in your syntactic grammar everything speakers know, you are building the whole world, material and immaterial, into the linguistic grammar. The grammar is supposed to be economical and thus to permit generalizations to be made. The grammar is, further, supposed to be finite (although it allows the generation of an infinite corpus). But if the grammar includes everything, it would have to be infinite.

That argument would seem to preclude any theory permitting the wholesale incorporation of extralinguistic information into the linguistic grammar. The only way to salvage this basic tenet of generative semantics would be to find a way to restrict the kinds of contextual information that could be present in syntactic underlying structures.

The generative semanticists responded that only those items of real-world context were to be part of the syntactic grammar that had direct and explicit linguistic reflexes observable at the superficial level. For example, the color of a speaker's eyes does not receive any direct linguistic encoding (there is no morphological ending that can only be used, say, by blue-eyed people) in any known language. So speaker's eye color is not one of the concepts requiring underlying-structure representation. But the relative power of participants in a conversation receives explicit encoding (in the form of politeness or directness choices, for example) in all languages. Therefore, power distinctions are to be represented in the syntactic underlying structure of all languages.

One question remained: just which aspects of the extralinguistic context of discourse needed to receive representation? That issue could only be determined empirically. The generative semanticists addressed this question in many papers. One of us (I, to be precise) raised the question: is gender one of these cases? It was a logical question, given the *Zeitgeist*: at the time, around 1971, the women's movement was achieving prominence and influence. It seemed natural – as it would not have just a few years before – to consider gender a relevant concern, and to ask whether – universally, in some languages, and specifically in English – the genders of participants and topics of discourse required grammatical representation. If so, at least one kind of extralinguistic knowledge had to be represented in underlying structures – a strong argument for generative semantics.

We knew that in 'exotic' languages such data existed. But English was, then as now, the proving ground for linguistic theories. So it was important to demonstrate that in the most un-exotic of languages and cultures, participant and/or topic gender was of deep grammatical relevance.

I was warned off by many colleagues, male and female, who told me at length that *of course* there were no salient gender distinctions in English and even if there were, who cared? There was some feeling by feminists that any differences found to exist between male and female were dangerous for the cause; and some feeling by certain male colleagues that any discussion in which the word *woman* occurred was *ipso facto* not of interest. However, I went ahead.

Since I had been trained as a transformational grammarian, my discovery procedure, as mandated by Chomsky, was introspection and intuition. At the time I am describing, sociolinguistics had not yet come into its own as a full-fledged discipline, and in any case there was an impermeable wall between incipient linguistic pragmatics and incipient sociolinguistics. So, empirical methods were not available to generative semanticists like me.

This was not necessarily a bad thing. Empirical methods are extremely useful for many kinds of work, but not for everything. Empirical methods can never do what transformational mentalism does best – envision and discuss nonexistent cases (those preceded by asterisks). Empirical methods cannot reliably ascertain what a speaker means or intends. Empirical methods are not good for differentiating between alternatives, both grammatical but context-dependent. On the other hand, intuitive approaches have well-known failings, not the least being the corruptibility of the researcher. Faced with this impasse, some researchers have argued that linguists should eschew non-empirical and perhaps even non-naturalistic methods, thus giving up on the possibility of exploring many of the most tantalizing language-related questions. Others have tried compromise (for instance, the interactional sociolinguists), with greater or lesser degrees of plausibility. It seems clear that many of the findings in the field of language and gender have been achieved by empirical means; but others, equally worthwhile, could be explored only through investigators' and/or subjects' intuitions.

Meanwhile other investigators, trained as anthropological linguists or linguistic anthropologists, were approaching the same questions on different theoretical grounds and through the use of different, generally empirical, methodologies. By the mid-1970s, conversation analysis had become an invaluable, though limited, tool; the use of questionnaires and surveys, likewise useful and likewise limited, was also prevalent.

The research led to one clear conclusion: in English, as in every other known language, gender (of speaker, hearer, and spoken-of) made a difference. The difference might be represented differently from one language and society to another, but it was always there. And it always came down to a basic reality: men held power and women did not; hence women were linguistically marginalized, derogated, and sexualized in many ways. The language we use to refer to and represent gender and sexuality mirrors the gender-based differences of the non-linguistic world. The linguistic differences we identified function as diagnostics demonstrating inequities in the positions of females and males in society at large.

Because this was the first time methods, tools, theories, and women's professional status came together, this was the first time language and gender could be studied in a scholarly way. So we were more or less on our own in devising the questions and deciding how to find the answers and what they meant. It was a very exciting period, but the novelty of it all meant that we tended to see things in what now seem overly clear and simple ways. We saw the differences between male and female choices of speech forms and reference as based purely on power: men had it, men made language, men used language to enhance their power over women, women played a passive role. Or – another, not unconnected, but equally simplistic approach – everything women did, linguistically and otherwise, was good; everything that men did was bad. Surface forms, with few exceptions, were seen as having only one meaning or function. Context, outside that of gender itself, was not a relevant focus. But over time perspectives shifted. The locus of attention moved, over the decade, from the word (*chairman*; *he/she*; *harlot*) to the sentence (e.g. the role of tag questions) to the conversational turn (interruption, topic control); but beyond this we did not progress to discourse beyond the sentence level.

An analysis of tag questions serves to illustrate some of the above points. In transformational generative grammar, tags had been the frustrating subject of recurrent analysis. They had received purely syntactic analyses: how to account for the positive/negative polarity of the auxiliary verb, the inversion of the subject noun phrase and the auxiliary, and the pronominalization of the subject noun phrase? More functionally framed questions became askable with the rise of generative semantics: how did tag questions function – as declarative utterances, questions, both, or something else? What were they as speech acts?

The full analysis of tag formations required going even further beyond core grammar. Tag question formation is one of the most complex syntactic rules in English – indeed, one of relatively few rules of syntax not found even in closely related languages. A generation of transformational syntacticians had proved, by their failure to capture the process completely and intuitively by any rule or even set of rules, that this was an exceptionally complex case. It seemed reasonable to assume (in accordance with Occam's razor) that a language would prefer to avoid such highly complex and idiosyncratic processes – unless something functionally important was gained by including them in the grammar. So it became theoretically important to explain tag question formation functionally: how did having it increase the expressive capacity of speakers of English? One might talk about the function of tags as a communicative giving with one hand (the declarative) while taking away with the other (the question). The use of a tag made an assertion requiring, as Austin had said, the speaker's belief in the truth of the utterance and confidence that the addressee would accept that truth, but at the same time relieved the speaker of the need to observe the felicity conditions on assertions by reproducing the assertion in the form of a question in the second part of the sentence. (The same analysis can be given to non-tagged declaratives with rising intonation.) But why would someone want or need to play this game?

Someone might who was in a one-down or otherwise delicate power position in a conversation. One might know something, but be unwilling or unable to represent oneself as authoritative and worthy of credence. That would be most apt to occur if a speaker had no real-world power (underling to boss, for instance), or if – as I hypothesized (1975) was true of women – that the speaker was socialized to believe that it was unfeminine and therefore socially dangerous to represent herself as powerful or authoritative. Observations of my own speech and that of my white, middle-class, professional friends and colleagues, suggested that women were more apt to use tags and rising-intonation declaratives than were men.

While later empirical studies have produced apparently mixed results, most of the putative counterexamples tend to prove my point. The demonstration that women in explicit positions of power (questioners at graduate orals, for instance) don't use tags, while male graduate students taking orals may well, merely shows that real power can (but need not) trump symbolic power or powerlessness. I came to realize that tags, like so many other constructions, were multifunctional: they could be used by those in positions of unequivocal power (e.g. district attorneys cross-examining defendants at trial), and by women, not only as a display of power-avoidance, but as a means of encouraging participation by others. Context counts.

Our understanding of the language-gender interface was created within both pragmatics and sociolinguistics, especially as conversation analysis came into widespread use as a tool for the examination of power and intimacy relationships as manifested in conversational turn-taking. The work of Pamela Fishman (1978) is one important example. Fishman recorded the conversations of heterosexual couples over a period of time, and analyzed the transcripts to demonstrate that women did the "shitwork" in such conversations: what was needed to keep them going, to keep interaction alive and therefore the relationship viable. Men, holding the power because the relationship itself was of less importance to them, could and did get away with monosyllabic grunts or less. Candace West (1979) gave evidence that men did much more interrupting than did women – and since turns are a form of power, interrupting and therefore getting more of them both illustrates male power in general and enhances the power men have in the course of a conversation. Again, while this work was extremely influential, it has proved to be insufficiently nuanced: more recent work suggests that interruption itself is complex and its determination less than clear (James and Clarke 1993); and that couples may differ in significant ways as to who holds the 'real' power, and hence who interrupts whom, and who does the shitwork (Tannen 1990). Interruption itself, and keeping conversation going itself, prove in turn to be capable of multiple interpretations, some gender-based: the fact that men are less likely to want to talk about their relationships with their female significant others may not signify their power to withhold, but merely the fact that men and women find different kinds of conversational turns and topics to be useful.

An additional methodology derived from the social sciences proved very prolific during the 1970s, if more problematized later: the questionnaire/interview. This was the basis for many of the findings that we think of as characteristic of feminist linguistics: the fact that 'gender-neutral' noun and pronoun uses favor male interpretations; the finding, of great practical importance in academia, that reviewers for academic journals were apt to judge identical manuscripts, one allegedly written by a male, the other by a female, very differently. An unavoidable problem with such studies is that they necessarily decontextualize the forms under investigation, so that it is seldom clear whether subjects are really responding with what they actually say (or think), or how they speak (or think) in the peculiar context of taking a questionnaire.

One more important area of study highly relevant to the language-gender interface, developed first during the 1970s, is that of linguistic politeness. It had always been said, impressionistically, that women were (and needed to be) more 'polite' than their male counterparts. In what ways was this true, and why? Some work suggested that male politeness and female politeness, in many cultures, were differently accomplished: while male politeness tended to be more distancing or perhaps more positive, female politeness was apt to be deferential or negative. And since politeness, like other behaviors, was likely to be evaluated from the perspective of the more powerful participant, deferential female politeness was often interpreted as mental fuzziness or illogic, rather than as conventionalized behavior exactly parallel to its male counterpart.

The study of conversational interaction led to powerful new understandings, such as the proof that old stereotypes of male and female language use were no more than that. Once actual talk could be captured on audiotape, reality began to overtake fantasy.

We came to realize that gender stereotypes, however inaccurately they portray reality, nonetheless have psychological and social power. One reason males and females use language differently is in order to effect gender polarization. If women are expected to be indirect, women will in fact tend to be indirect – thereby justifying the stereotype that women can't think clearly. But the reality is that this choice has nothing to do with how women think, and everything to do with how women are thought of – and want, for whatever reason, to be thought of. Likewise, the tendency for lexical items to acquire sexual connotations when they are applied to women (the difference, in slightly antiquated parlance, between *He's a professional* meaning 'He's a doctor or a lawyer, etc.'; and *She's a professional* meaning 'She's a prostitute') illustrates the extra-linguistic sexualization of women and their behavior.

4.2 The 1980s

On the one hand, the 1970s was an exceptionally fruitful period for the development of theory: important questions were raised and many connections between language, gender, and power were explored, and many methods for investigation were developed. On the other hand, when seen from the perspective of a generation later, many of those theories seem overly stark and simple. During the 1980s nuanced versions were created; at the same time, partly as a result of or in response to having choices, factionalization became endemic.

In looking back, it is tempting to view the 1970s as a period of heady excitement, in which feminist cooperation trumped the power games of academe. Students of the language-gender interface were more interested in establishing that there *was* such an interface, and that their findings demonstrated a political inequity based on gender: linguistic analysis allowed the disease to be diagnosed and cured. Much of the work of the 1970s was non-academic, both in style and in substance (think of Fishman's use of 'shitwork' as a technical term), a discourse connecting feminism and academic women's studies.

By the early 1980s, academe had taken over. Among the characteristics of 1980s gender-language research is theorization, and along with it, the dichotomizations so beloved of academics: essential vs. constructed, dominance vs. difference, public vs.

private. Along with these changes, and more or less as an outgrowth of them, came an increasing realization of the complexities of gender roles and the assignment of responsibility or blame for them or their consequences. Research became less concerned with showing that women's ways were good, men's bad; or that women's options were constricted by men's superior power. At least in small-group interpersonal conversation (the major discourse type studied during this period), it became apparent that some of the differences observed were attributable (at least in part) to social and psychological differences between males and females. Less attention was focused on the role of genetic or biological causation of these differences, a topic that for scientific and political reasons was to come into sharp focus in the first decade of the 21st century.

Early in the decade, Maltz and Borker (1982) published an important paper arguing, from the perspective of linguistic anthropology, that the communicative differences observed between the sexes were largely due to differences in the ways boys and girls were raised. Female and male children, for instance, played different kinds of games; boys' games encouraged the development and acceptance of hierarchical roles, while girls' games fostered individualism and equality – not good preparation for a future role in corporate structures. It was not that men disempowered and oppressed women by language, but rather that females spontaneously adopted forms of language that led to the positions they would hold in adult life. This was a comforting perspective for both men and women, researchers and readers, because it meant that the sexes did not have to see themselves as locked in hostile competition for power. Rather, in the Maltz-Borker perspective, everyone had his or her role and formed part of a cohesive and coherent society. No one need apologize or change.

This, called the 'difference' position, contrasted starkly with the 'dominance' position of the political 1970s. Difference theory seemed apolitical and lent itself ideally to 'objective' scholarship. A problem, though, was that a pure difference perspective left numerous important questions unanswered. If male and female language options were separate but equal, why in every society were women's ways downgraded; why did the forms of language considered typical of women cause their speakers to be ridiculed and not taken seriously? Why did we speak of *language*, meaning 'men's language', and why was *women's language* the marked (and inferior) version? Empirical results continued to support dominance analyses. For instance, Dale Spender's *Invisible Women: The Schooling Scandal* (1989) demonstrated through the use of recorded conversational data that the old assumption that women monopolized conversation was false. Spender's work showed, astonishingly, that in mixed-gender informal conversation, it was normal for men to hold the floor 80% of the time; when this was the case, participants and other hearers perceived it as normal. Once male contribution fell below 70%, the result was seen as abnormal, as women monopolizing the talk. Why did Spender get the results she got if men and women had equal access to the goods of conversational floor-holding?

Arguments were advanced that these differences were not the result of brutal masculine exercise of power, but explicable in a 'difference' model. True, women's natural interactive strategies meant that they interrupted less and got less conversational time. But that was because women were simply less competitive than men, and preferred enabling others (especially males) to contribute, to contributing themselves. So all of the behaviors and assumptions that 'dominance' theorists had used to argue that language was diagnostic of female subordination, said the 'difference' theorists, merely proved that women had different interests from men in engaging in discourse, and achieved their goals just as men did.

Another problem originating in the 1970s is still apparent, the dichotomization of 'male' and 'female'. Sophisticated research and argumentation, in linguistics and elsewhere, has shown that the division of humanity into 'M' and 'F' is, at best, a convenient fiction and radical overgeneralization. Rather, we all fall along a continuum, and our ways of talking do as well. At the same time, the stereotypical dichotomy M vs. F is culturally and psychologically important: we expect everyone from childhood on to organize themselves on one or the other end of the continuum: boys should be boys, and girls, girls. We often are punitive toward those who move toward the center of the continuum, so that while actual behavior is continuous, we rationalize it as dichotomous and ignore or punish non-dichotomy. While language-gender research made an invaluable contribution by exposing the dichotomy as fictional, it has sometimes been reluctant to grasp the fact that fiction is an important way that human beings construct their world.

In short, the 1980s exposed the complexity of gender and gendered behavior. Power figured, but so did choice. There was a continuum, but it existed alongside stereotyped dichotomies. During this period, another theoretical division began to play an important role in research and the politics of science: the question of whether gender roles were 'essential' or 'constructed', or both, and what that meant. This question, as we shall see, continues to be unresolved and of the greatest importance.

To what extent were the differences between males and females biologically determined at conception, by the X and Y chromosomes and their sequelae, and to what extent were observed differences the result of culture and socialization? Obviously this was a question of great importance: if these roles were inborn or 'essential', they could not be significantly changed. Neither individuals nor governments needed to alter the possibilities open to the sexes. Even if they happened to be unfair, even if one gender repressed the other, it was innate, it was natural, it was unchangeable. Sociobiology (later rechristened 'evolutionary psychology') was the scientization of this position: we are what our genes make us, and our genes are what they are because, from the beginning of the species (or the class Mammalia), that way of being has been evolutionarily desirable. Even if we could change, it would have bad consequences for our survival.

In one sense, this argument is outside the parameters of an article on language and gender. But it is relevant in a couple of ways. First, if researchers were to agree that gender differences were innate and unchangeable, worrying about communication patterns and their consequences would be futile: even if we could change those patterns, we could not effect a change thereby in biological reality; and changing language behavior would be inane if it could not create real-world change, noting gender-based differences that marked the essential inferiority of women would only re-create self-loathing and despair.

The issue is also relevant for pragmaticists who study discourse form and function. We have always had an interest in gendered language itself; but we have become increasingly concerned with the metalinguistic level: how do we, as analysts of discourse, understand the discourse of language and gender: what is spoken of, and how it is spoken of, and why at different times different things are spoken of. So if we notice that, during the 1990s, the essential/constructed debate was relatively quiescent, but that it erupted forcefully in the early part of the 21st century, how is that change to be explained?

The question has other important consequences for explanations of linguistic behavior. One topic that began to be explored in the 1980s, and has increasingly become a subject of interest is the language of groups outside the comfortable M/F dichotomy: gay men, lesbians, and transsexuals. As Judith Butler (1990), Anna Livia (2001), and many others have demonstrated, theirs is a task of (re)(de)constructing their identities continually through communicative choices (and other means). If everyone's identity is significantly developed through speaking and being spoken of and to, that is even more true of someone whose identity is liminal and continually under pressure from the dominant community. But not only gays and transsexuals find themselves continually redefining themselves in every linguistic interchange in which they participate; straight women and men do as well. We are not born male and female so much as we are made, and eventually make ourselves, one or the other or both or neither by our language and other communicative behavior.

4.3 The 1990s

By the early 1990s, the topic of language and gender had become much more complex and convoluted, as well as much more deeply factionalized and more heavily theorized and academicized. In the non-academic, political world this was a decade of great upheaval in our understanding of gender relations (cf. Lakoff 2000). Numerous prominent cases, in politics and the law, brought changes in gender roles to sharp public notice: Anita Hill's testimony to the U.S. Senate in Clarence Thomas's Supreme Court confirmation hearings; the first ladyship of Hillary Rodham Clinton; the appointment of women to major U.S. Cabinet positions (Attorney General, Secretary of State); the development of sexual harassment and sexual discrimination law. Within the academic specialty of language and gender research, there were also many significant developments.

There was increasing recognition of complexity and ambiguity. Feminism has often been criticized, with some justice, as concentrating on middle-class white women, and language and gender studies have displayed the same concentration – often unavoidably, since our subjects tend to be those we have access to and can understand: the majority of researchers are themselves white and of middle class background, and the undergraduate population of most American research universities (the source of subjects for our studies) is overwhelmingly white middle class. But work in sociolinguistics, and especially dialectology, by William Labov and especially his student Penelope Eckert (1990) was beginning to demonstrate the complex interconnections of social class and gender in dialect choice. Likewise, as the Hill/Thomas controversy focused America's interest on race issues, scholars began to take cognizance of the fact that black women's speech was quite different from that of their white counterparts (Morgan 2004). Already in Jespersen, there were suggestions that women were linguistically conservative, men innovative, or the reverse. Labov and others have shown that as usual this is a question without a simple answer. Women innovate (i.e. adopt nonstandard dialectal variants) if they are not literate; otherwise they are apt to be linguistically conservative. That in itself is connected to issues of power and control: if in a society men have power over actions, power over linguistic correctness is apt to be relegated to women. Eckert refers to language in this function as a form of *symbolic capital*, traditionally available to women as literal capital was not. Work by Eckert and Peter Trudgill (among others) illustrate the role female speakers play in language change and the standardization of particular choices.

At the start of the decade, Deborah Tannen's (1990) *You Just Don't Understand*, a popular work about differences in conversational style and content between the sexes, became a huge best-seller, remaining on the best-seller list for several years. Its success demonstrates that, at that moment in time, even people with no academic interest in linguistics were fascinated by the issues Tannen discusses. During the 1980s, women were beginning to achieve economic parity with men; as a result, the divorce rate rose sharply as for the first time women had the power to decide whether to enter and stay in heterosexual relationships. Therefore, often for the first time, it had become important for men to know how to get women to stay with them – they could no longer count on being economically or even socially indispensable. At the same time, women remained concerned with having successful relationships. So it was of great interest to both sexes to learn that they communicated differently; that it was merely a *difference* – not that one gender was smart or virtuous, the other stupid or evil – and that, with goodwill, each could learn to understand what the other meant.

During the 1990s other complexities became apparent. There was a good deal of cross-cultural work, for instance, studies of Japanese women's linguistic behavior

(Ide 1990). In the next decade, research would use changes in the patterns of Japanese honorific usage as evidence of shifting gender roles in Japan (Takekuro 2005).

Other ambiguities were recognized. In earlier work, researchers had drawn a sharp distinction between relationships of intimacy and of hierarchy or power. Traditionally speakers chose the second person pronoun T for intimate relations, V for hierarchical ones (Brown & Gilman 1960). But some linguistic choices entail hierarchy and inequality in one context, intimacy in another (Tannen 1994). On that basis, how should one interpret the tendency to first-name women much more readily than men (e.g. the fact that California's senior senator is often referred to as *Dianne* rather than *Feinstein*)? Is it a sign that women are friendlier – that is, better at intimacy – and that this is a matter of choice on Dianne's/Feinstein's part? Or does it signify that it's easier to impinge on a woman's personal space, to make her private self public, and therefore a diagnostic of continuing power imbalance? Related to this question is the whole issue of private vs. public life, and the role gender plays in determining how much interconnection there is between one and the other, and thus how women in public positions are to be spoken of and judged.

In general, throughout the decade there was increasing attention in various branches of linguistics (and other fields as diverse as law and psychotherapy) to larger and more abstract kinds of discourse units (the once-unmentionable 'structure above the sentence level') and particularly narrative. Research on the language-gender interface has tended to mirror that elsewhere in the field: thus over the 20th century, linguistics went from the sound to the word to the sentence to the turn, and finally, at the century's end, began to move toward more complex units. Gender and language work has moved in a similar trajectory, and the decade saw a lot of interesting work on women's roles in larger units (e.g. Bucholtz 2000 on television shopping networks; Hall 1995 on differences between personal ads placed in newspapers by women and men).

4.4 The 2000s: Some concluding remarks

As I write in the middle of the middle year of the first decade of the new millennium, it seems premature to make sweeping generalizations or predictions about where the language and gender field is going. One area of continuing interest, though, is that of the analysis of media reportage: why do some topics, obviously important, receive scant attention while others, obviously trivial, get immense and continuing attention? One reason is that some seemingly trivial issues reflect deep unresolved questions in a society and its members. Issues related to gender are particularly good candidates for the latter, passing what I have called (Lakoff 2000) the Undue Attention Test.

One recent example illustrates the volatility of gender discussion at present. In January, 2005, Harvard President Lawrence Summers made an off-the-cuff statement at a conference on women and technology, suggesting that the scarcity of women in prominent positions in the sciences might be due to innate biological differences between the sexes, as evidenced by an unwillingness on the part of women to undertake the eighty hour work weeks that are the norm in the sciences.

Summers' statement was hedged and tentative. But he is the president of Harvard, and even off-the-cuff statements from Harvard presidents acquire the weight of truth. An immediate firestorm erupted that did not subside for at least four months, with daily commentary in *The New York Times* for the first couple of weeks, various electronic media, and the newsmagazines – as well as heated discussion at academic gatherings, formal and otherwise. Considering that the remarks did not put in place any policy or indeed have any direct effect on reality by themselves, it seems clear that the case easily passes the Undue Attention Test.

What was extraordinary about the course of events was that mere suggestions unleashed such a flood of heated rhetoric on both sides: feminists pointed out that Summers spoke in ignorance of a great deal of data collected over many years, demonstrating that women could and did progress in scientific fields if given a fair chance; and, on the other side, a lot of counterevidence about chimpanzees and voles from the evolutionary psychologists.

But why did the issue become so heated at this time? I would suggest, because questions of gender parity and the division of roles between the sexes had itself become a heated issue politically, and the heat attached itself to Summers' comments, which would not have received this treatment even five years earlier.

Looking at cases this way, the line between real-world politics and academic rhetorical analysis becomes attenuated. Can one study the Summers case purely as an academic analysis? In choosing to remain 'objective' in this way, is a researcher forced into an essentially false analysis? Can political events be analyzed apolitically – or should they?

The questions addressed and sometimes answered by language and gender research therefore remain situated at the intersections of several complex areas: between academia and the practical world; pragmatics and sociolinguistics; reality and stereotype. The topic remains important and in need of much more work.

References

Brown, P. & S.C. Levinson (1987). *Politeness.* Cambridge University Press.
Brown, R. & A. Gilman (1960). The pronouns of power and solidarity. In T. Sebeok (ed.) *Style in Language*: 259–276. MIT Press.
Bucholtz, M. (2000). "Thanks for stopping by": Gender and virtual community in American Shop-by-Television discourse. In M. Andrews & M. Talbot (eds.) *"All the World and Her Husband: Women in Twentieth Century Consumer Culture*: 192–209. Cassell.
Butler, J. (1990). *Gender Trouble: Feminism and the Subversion of Identity.* Routledge.
Eckert, P. (1990). The whole woman: Sex and gender differences in variation. *Language Variation and Change* 1: 245–267.

Fishman, P. (1978). Interaction: The work women do. *Social Problems* 25: 397–406.

Haas, M. (1944). Men's and women's speech in Koasati. *Language* 20: 142–149.

Hall, K. (1995). Lip service on the fantasy lines. In K. Hall & M. Bucholtz (eds.) *Gender articulated: Language and the Socially Constructed Self*: 183–216. Routledge.

Ide, S. (1990). How and why do women speak more politely in Japanese. In S. Ide & N.H. McGloin (eds.) *Aspects of Japanese women's language*: 63–79. Kuroshio Shuppan.

James, D. & S. Clarke (1993). Women, men, and interruptions: A critical review. In D. Tannen (ed.) *Gender and Conversational Interaction*: 231–280. Oxford University Press.

Jespersen, O. (1922). The woman. In *Language: Its Nature, Development, and Origin*: 237–254. Allen & Unwin.

Lakoff, R. (1975). *Language and Woman's Place*. Harper & Row.

────── (2000). *The Language War*. University of California Press.

Livia, A. (2001). *Pronoun Envy: Literary Uses of Linguistic Gender*. Oxford University Press.

Maltz, D. & R. Borker (1982). A cultural approach to male-female communication. In J.J. Gumperz (ed.) *Language and Social Identity*: 196–216. Cambridge University Press.

Morgan, M. (2004). "I'm every woman": Black woman's (dis)placement in women's language study. In R. Lakoff & M. Bucholtz (eds.) *Language and Woman's Place: Text and Commentaries*: 252–259. Oxford University Press.

Spender, D. (1989). *Invisible Women: The Schooling Scandal*. Women's Press.

Takekuro, M. (2005). *Attachment Sequences of Japanese Honorific Use*. Unpublished dissertation, Linguistics Department, University of California, Berkeley.

Tannen, D. (1990). *You Just Don't Understand*. William Morrow.

────── (1994). The relativity of linguistic strategies: rethinking power and solidarity in gender and dominance. In D. Tannen (ed.) *Gender and Discourse*: 165–188. Oxford University Press.

West, C. (1979). Against our will: male interruption of females in cross-sex conversation. In J. Orasanu, M. Slater, & L. Adler (eds.) *Language, Sex, and Gender: Annals of the New York Academy of Sciences* 327: 81–100.

Woolf, V. (1929). *A Room of One's Own*. Harcourt, Brace & World.

Interactional sociolinguistics

Jef Verschueren
University of Antwerp

1. Background

Roberts et al. (2001: 56) define the topic area and methodological orientation of interactional sociolinguistics as follows:

> […] the ways in which styles of communicating index social identity and the need for a method which examines the fine-grained detail of interaction.

This definition nicely captures the two formative lines of work. On the topic side, the tradition finds its origins in the earlier sociolinguistic work of John Gumperz. In particular his ethnographic work in Northern India and in Norway led him to abandon classical sociolinguistic paradigms which assumed objectifiable correlations between socially or geographically constituted groups on the one hand, and forms of language variation on the other. Instead, his observations showed (i) that ideas or perceptions of social identity were more important than 'objective' differences either in the constitution of groups or in linguistic forms, and (ii) that the way in which linguistic forms were used to index social identities was not generalizable in the abstract but could only be investigated by close scrutiny of the functioning of linguistic repertoires or styles in real-time processes of negotiating shared understandings in face-to-face interaction, i.e. by means of an 'ethnography of communication' (Gumperz & Hymes eds. 1972). What Gumperz first called an 'interpretive', and later an 'interactional' type of sociolinguistics, found methodological inspiration in the interactional sociology of everyday encounters, as represented by the work of Garfinkel (1967) and Goffman (1967, 1981). One way of characterizing interactional sociolinguistics would be to say that it is a type of interactional sociology that concentrates on socially heterogeneous contexts with significant degrees of language variation.

Casting the net as widely as possible, interactional sociolinguistics can be said to be heir to, or to have developed in conjunction with, the ethnography of speaking, ethnomethodology, microethnography, symbolic interactionism, and cognitive anthropology (with clear Batesonean influences). Not surprisingly, it overlaps considerably with major trends in conversation analysis, discourse analysis, and anthropological linguistics. In particular, more than the core types of conversation analysis, it may be the sociolinguistic application *par excellence* of basic ethnomethodological tenets (such as the local and situated nature of the creation of meaning, the extra 'work' done by interactants in face-to-face settings on top of what is already given in 'rules', the reflexive relationship between context and verbal behavior). It is not surprising, therefore, that in principle the term covers a wider area than just those research endeavors directly associated with the label (see, e.g. Schiffrin 1993 for a more extensive discussion). The label has been well-established since John Gumperz (1982a, and ed. 1982) collected representative samples of a type of work he and a number of other linguists and anthropologists had been doing for over a decade at the intersection between sociolinguistics and anthropological linguistics, in particular with reference to problems of linguistic and cultural relativity and interethnic or intercultural communication. The tradition has earned itself a place in most sociolinguistics textbooks (e.g. Holmes 2008) and many manuals for the study of pragmatics and discourse (e.g. Cutting 2008).

2. Contributions

Interactional sociolinguistics originally pursued two related tenets. On the one hand, it traces the influence of taken-for-granted sociocultural presuppositions on the way in which interpersonal communication works. On the other hand, it investigates the processes by which aspects of social identity are communicatively produced. In this perspective, the interactive negotiation of meaning has become an important focus of attention. In particular, the interlocutors' conversational inferencing processes (i.e. "the situated or context-bound process of interpretation, by means of which participants in an exchange assess others' intentions, and on which they base their responses", Gumperz 1982a: 153) are seen as major indicators, as well as creators, of implicit sociocultural assumptions that underlie the interaction. Without reference to such assumptions, many processes of interpretation cannot be explained. In other words, aspects of speaking style assume a symbolic value with interpretive consequences that are not merely a matter of correlations between linguistic choices and independent sociolinguistic variables.

As the tradition matured, a third tenet developed, viz. the search for a convincing balance between the micro-analysis of small moments of human interaction and the wider social structures which confine (and define) their occurrence. Such a balance is achieved, for instance, in Rampton's (1995) analysis of the creative ways in which British-born adolescents with different ethnic backgrounds but institutionally similar positions, play with differences in their communicative repertoires, defying – to a certain extent – the wider context of social inequality which they are perfectly aware of. Similar analyses of what Rampton calls 'crossing' and 'stylization', with significant implications for broad societal issues, have been carried out in the institutional setting of urban multi-ethnic schools (Rampton 2006; Jaspers 2005, 2006, 2008). And awareness of the need to look at identity work at the local level of face-to-face interaction not just in terms of the free agency of individuals but in the wider context of social constraints, including class stratification, is now quite widely accepted (see also Rampton 2003, Heller ed. 2007).

Favorite topics are, quite in line with these theoretical objectives, encounters in socially defined settings, whether institutional or not, and whether intercultural or not. These range from court proceedings (Gumperz 1982b; Atkinson 1992; Drew 1992; Jacquemet 1996), job interviews (Akinnaso & Seabrook Ajirotutu 1982; Button 1992; Roberts & Sayers 1987), doctor-patient interaction (Heath 1992; Ehernberger Hamilton 1994; Peräkylä 1995; Heritage & Maynard eds. 2006), service encounters and multi-ethnic workplaces (Erickson & Schultz 1982; Jupp et al. 1982; Roberts, Davies & Jupp 1992), educational settings (Roberts et al. 2001; Cook-Gumperz 2006), to conversations between strangers (Heller 1982), male-female interaction (Tannen ed. 1993), and informal intercultural encounters, often involving code-switching (Hinnenkamp 1991), to name just a few. Unlikely as this may seem, thoughts have also been voiced about the usefulness of insights from interactional sociolinguistics for computational natural language processing (Ballim 2003). Of particular interest is a book-length study (Young 1994), which traces the development of Chinese communicative ideologies and practices from Confucius, through the famous 'eight-legged essay' to the board rooms and streets of Hong Kong, and documents how they affect Sino-American communication.

Methodologically, the tradition borrows most of its procedures from ethnomethodology and, for the more technical aspects, linguistic field elicitation methods and conversation analysis. The approach is thoroughly empirical, rigorously centered around observable phenomena such as patterns of intonation, rhythm, stress, choices of code and register, certain lexical and syntactic options, formulaic expressions, as well as openings, closings, and sequencing strategies. The assumption is that especially such choices, on which interpretations are based even though they largely result from highly automatic forms of processing, signal and produce habitual – though still quite flexible – frames of interpretation.

The major contribution, in a pragmatic perspective, is the reorientation which interactional sociolinguistics has forced researchers to undergo in relation to the notion of 'context' (a reorientation equally supported by related lines of interactional research such as microethnography; see e.g. McDermott et al. 1978). One of the key notions in Gumperz's approach is 'contextualization'. The empirical work is centered around prosody which, when analyzed from the perspective of contextualization, can be shown to play an important role both in interpretation and in the maintenance of conversational coherence (see Couper-Kuhlen & Selting eds. 1994), and around other often metalinguistic features. These features, which would be called 'metapragmatic' in

Silverstein's terminology, are described as 'contextualization cues' in the interactional sociolinguistic tradition:

> A basic assumption is that this channelling of interpretation is effected by conversational implicatures based on conventionalized co-occurrence expectations between content and surface style. That is, constellations of surface features of message form are the means by which speakers signal and listeners interpret what the activity is, how semantic content is to be understood and *how* each sentence relates to what precedes or follows. These features are referred to as *contextualization cues*. For the most part they are habitually used and perceived but rarely consciously noted and almost never talked about directly. Therefore they must be studied in the process and in context rather than in the abstract.
>
> Roughly speaking, a contextualization cue is any feature of linguistic form that contributes to the signalling of contextual presuppositions. (Gumperz 1982a: 131)

The meanings of the features in question are thus highly implicit. Silverstein (1992) would call them 'pure indexicals'; in contrast to lexicalized indexicals, they do not have meanings of their own. Moreover, there is no fixed relationship between linguistic choices and a language-external context. Rather, as has been clarified in numerous recent studies triggered by the interactional sociolinguistics tradition (two outstanding examples of which are Duranti & Goodwin eds. 1992 and Auer & di Luzio eds. 1992), context is itself interactively constructed in the course of verbal communication. It is the interactive negotiation of meaning that determines the signaling value of any given feature, the choices from a potentially infinite range of extra-linguistic contextual elements which together make up a relevant context, as well as the relationships between these two.

Especially the applications of interactional sociolinguistics in the area of intercultural communication did not go unnoticed, nor unchallenged. Since meaning inferencing based on highly implicit contextualization cues tends to escape conscious processing and is strongly habit-based, types of miscommunication may arise when people interact who have been socialized in different communicative styles, which, in turn, may contribute to the emergence or maintenance of prejudice. This approach has proved its usefulness in intercultural training, by raising awareness of the fact that attributing specific intentions or attitudes to one's interlocutor may be misguided by one's own habits of interpretation. A challenge was formulated by Singh et al. (1996), who argued that the interactional sociolinguistic approach paid too little attention to wider patterns of dominance, and that the emphasis on flexibility was in fact aimed at assimilation of the powerless. While this critique was itself not free of misplaced attributions of intentionality, it certainly served as a good warning to balance attention for linguistic detail and technicalities with a focus on political contexts and implications, a balance which is actively sought by many researchers within the interactional sociolinguistic tradition.

3. Program

In an interview in which he was asked about his own current research goals, John Gumperz said:

> A main aim of my current work on discourse and conversation is to show how indexical signs, including prosody, code- and style-switching, and formulaic expressions, interact with symbolic (i.e. grammatical and lexical) signs, sequential ordering of exchanges, cultural and other relevant background knowledge to constitute social action. (Gumperz in Prevignano & di Luzio 2003: 9)

Put in such terms, the true target of interactional sociolinguistics amounts to no less than the construction of an adequate theory of social action involving language use. In the process, a complete pragmatic theory of how levels of explicit and implicit meaning interact to generate socially significant meanings, would be needed. Significant contributing steps have been taken in the study of relationships between interactional and 'grammatical' phenomena (e.g. Ford 1993, Couper-Kuhlen & Selting eds. 1994, Ochs, Schegloff & Thompson eds. 1996). Perhaps major new challenges are to be found in attempts at integrating interactional sociolinguistics with studies of multimodal interaction (see, e.g. Jewitt 2009). Above all, however, a central integration into this ambitious program of a full awareness of variability as a mode of being – the real trigger for the emergence of interactional sociolinguistics in the first place – may require more work of the 'crossing' and 'stylization' type, as well as new ways of looking at forms of multilingualism as language systems in their own right.

References

Akinnaso, F.N. & C. Seabrook Ajirotutu (1982). Performance and ethnic style in job interviews. In J.J. Gumperz (ed.): 119–144.
Atkinson, J.M. (1992). Displaying neutrality. In P. Drew & J. Heritage (eds.): 199–211.
Auer, P. & A. di Luzio (eds.) (1992). *The contextualization of language.* John Benjamins.
Ballim, A. (2003). A commentary on a discussion with John J. Gumperz. In S.L. Eerdmans et al. (eds.): 79–84.
Button, G. (1992). Answers as interactional products. In P. Drew & J. Heritage (eds.): 212–231.
Cook-Gumperz, J. (2006). *The social construction of literacy* (2nd edition). Cambridge University Press.
Couper-Kuhlen, E. & M. Selting (eds.) (1994). *Prosody in conversation: Interactional studies.* Cambridge University Press.
Cutting, J. (2008). *Pragmatics and discourse: A resource book for students* (2nd edition). Routledge.
Drew, P. (1992). Contested evidence in courtroom cross-examination. In P. Drew & J. Heritage (eds.): 470–520.
Drew, P. & J. Heritage (eds.) (1992). *Talk at work.* Cambridge University Press.
Duranti, A. & C. Goodwin (eds.) (1992). *Rethinking context.* Cambridge University Press.

Eerdmans, S.L., C.L. Prevignano & P.J. Thibault (eds.) (2003). *Language and interaction: Discussions with John J. Gumperz*. Amsterdam: John Benjamins.

Ehernberger Hamilton, H. (1994). *Conversations with an Alzheimer's patient: An interactional sociolinguistic study*. Cambridge University Press.

Erickson, F. & J. Schultz (1982). *The counsellor as gatekeeper: Social interaction in interviews*. Academic Press.

Ford, C.E. (1993). *Grammar in interaction: Adverbial clauses in American English conversations*. Cambridge University Press.

Garfinkel, H. (1967). *Studies in ethnomethodology*. Prentice-Hall.

Goffman, E. (1967). *Interaction ritual: Essays on face-to-face behavior*. Penguin.

────── (1981). *Forms of talk*. University of Pennsylvania Press.

Gumperz, J.J. (1982a). *Discourse strategies*. Cambridge University Press.

────── (1982b). Fact and inference in courtroom testimony. In J.J. Gumperz (ed.): 163–195.

Gumperz, J.J. (ed.) (1982). *Language and social identity*. Cambridge University Press.

Gumperz, J.J. & D. Hymes (eds.) (1972). *Directions in sociolinguistics: The ethnography of communication*. Holt, Reinhart and Winston.

Heller, M. (1982). Bonjour, hello? Negotiation of language choice in Montreal. In J.J. Gumperz (ed.): 121–130.

Heath, C. (1992). The delivery and reception of diagnosis in the general-practice consultation. In P. Drew & J. Heritage (eds.): 235–267.

Heller, M. (ed.) (2007). *Bilingualism: A social approach*. Palgrave Macmillan.

Heritage, J. & D.W. Maynard (eds.) (2006). *Communication in medical care: Interaction between primary care physicians and patients*. Cambridge University Press.

Hinnenkamp, V. (1991). Talking a person into interethnic distinction. In J. Blommaert & J. Verschueren (eds.) *The pragmatics of intercultural and international communication*: 91–110. John Benjamins.

Holmes, J. (2008). *An introduction to sociolinguistics* (3rd edition). Pearson Education Limited.

Jacquemet, M. (1996). *Credibility in court: Communicative practices in the Camorra trials*. Cambridge University Press.

Jaspers, J. (2005). Linguistic sabotage in a context of monolingualism and standardization. *Language and Communication* 25(3): 279–297.

────── (2006). Stylizing Standard Dutch by Moroccan boys in Antwerp. *Linguistics and Education* 17(2), 131–156.

────── (2008). Problematizing ethnolects: Naming linguistic practices in an Antwerep secondary school. *International Journal of Bilingualism* 12(1/2): 85–103.

Jewitt, C. (2009). Different approaches to multimodality. In C. Jewitt (ed.) *The Routledge handbook of multimodal analysis*: 28–39. Routledge

Jupp, T.C., C. Roberts & J. Cook-Gumperz (1982). Language and disadvantage. In J. J. Gumperz (ed.): 232–256.

McDermott, R., K. Gospodinoff & J. Aron (1978). Criteria for an ethnographically adequate description of concerted activities and their contexts. *Semiotica* 24(3/4), 245–276.

Ochs, E., E.A. Schegloff & S.A. Thompson (eds.) (1996). *Interaction and grammar*. Cambridge University Press.

Peräkylä, A. (1995). *AIDS counselling: Institutional interaction and clinical practice*. Cambridge University Press.

Previgna NO, C.L. & A. DI Luzio (2003). A discussion with John Gumperz. In S.L. Eerdmans et al. (eds.): 7–29.

Rampton, B. (1995). *Crossing: Language and ethnicity among adolescents*. Longman.
—— (2003). Hegemony, social class and stylisation. *Pragmatics* 13(1): 49–84.
—— (2006). *Language in late modernity: Interaction in an urban school*. Cambridge University Press.
Roberts, C., M. Byram, A. Barro, S. Jordan & B. Street (2001). *Language learners as ethnographers*. Multilingual Matters.
Roberts, C., E. Davies & T.C. Jupp (1992). *Language and discrimination*. Longman.
Roberts, C. & P. Sayers (1987). Keeping the gate. In K. Knapp, W. Enninger & A. Knapp-Potthoff (eds.) *Analyzing intercultural communication*: 111–135. Mouton de Gruyter.
Schiffrin, D. (1993). *Discourse analysis*. Oxford University Press.
Silverstein, M. (1992). The indeterminacy of contextualization: When is enough enough? In P. Auer & A. di Luzio (eds.): 55–76.
Singh, R., J. Lele & G. Martohardjono (1996). Communication in a multilingual society: Some missed opportunities. In R. Singh (ed.) *Towards a critical sociolinguistics*: 237–254. John Benjamins.
Tannen, D. (ed.) (1993). *Gender and conversational interaction*. Oxford University Press.
Young, L.W.L. (1994). *Crosstalk and culture in Sino-American communication*. Cambridge University Press.

Language dominance and minorization

Donna Patrick
Carleton University

1. Introduction

An important subject in sociolinguistic research is language dominance and its relation to minority languages, as found in local, regional, national, and global contexts. Language dominance can be best understood in terms of the notion of 'linguistic hierarchy' and the social, political, and ideological dimensions of attributing power and prestige to particular language varieties and their speakers (Grillo 1989; Gal 1989; Woolard & Schieffelin 1994; Silverstein 1998). Minorization can be understood as a social process occurring at local, regional, national, and supranational levels that constructs minority groups with less political, economic, and social power than some dominant group. Dominant or minority status is thus attributed not on the basis of numbers of speakers, but rather on the basis of the social positioning of particular social groups within a hierarchical social structure.

Social categorization plays a key role in the construction of minority groups. This process of categorization involves an intersection of social categories marking difference, including class, race, ethnicity, and gender, and the formation and maintenance of these categories through interactional and other social processes. Categories are thus constructed through a complex interplay between social structure and human agency, in which language use plays a constitutive role. This process can be conceived as part of social structuration (Giddens 1984) – that is, an interactive process whereby social actors construct, maintain, and modify social structures, which in turn limit and constrain social action. The construction and definition of social categories of difference is a key part of the construction of dominant and minority social groups and subsequent dimensions of social inequality (Heller 2007a).

Both minority and dominant social groups are formed and maintained through language and other markers of social identity, which serve to construct boundaries that define, include, and exclude members of particular groups (Barth 1969; Meinhof & Galasinski 2005). Social boundaries are, however, not fixed; and subjectivities – the constitution of subjects or 'selfhood' – and the complex identities of speakers can lead to a range of allegiances and even contradictory stances with respect to minority and dominant group status.

Dominant language varieties include official and national forms of language and globally dominant languages that are legitimized within and across states and institutions (through the media, schools, the courts, government, and international organizations) and through their association with particular forms of political, economic, and social power. Minority languages and language varieties become salient in relation to dominant languages within particular geographical regions and institutional spheres. In such regions and spheres, there can be overt exclusion of and discrimination against minority language varieties and their speakers. Such processes often lead to political and social struggles for inclusion, which can take the form of citizenship, recognition, and social justice.

In what follows, I shall be examining the rise of language dominance and its 'naturalization' through processes such as nation-building and colonization, industrialization, language standardization, the rise of public education and other social institutions, and the emergence of transnational economies and globalized communicative relations. (Although the question of what actually counts as a language or language variety is a matter of continuing debate among linguists, philosophers, anthropologists, and others (as discussed in e.g. Silverstein 1998), I shall leave this question aside in the discussion that follows.)

The process of 'naturalization', whereby language dominance comes to be taken for granted, arises through the production of related hegemonic ideologies, including the notion that a 'national' language (e.g. English) unifies citizens into 'one nation'; and that one variety of this language (e.g. standard English) is 'better' for official and textual purposes because it is more suited to scientific thought, modernization, international communication, or other purposes. Thus, in national contexts, language dominance often coincides with the promotion of monolingualism and monoculturalism. In transnational contexts, the dominance of a 'global' language – most notably English, but also French, Spanish, and Hindi-Urdu, among other languages – has also favoured monolingualism among speakers from the dominant language metropoles. However, for speakers of other national languages, who wish to engage in transnational communication, multilingualism has become the norm.

I shall also be discussing processes of minorization and the linguistic debates as well as political, economic, ideological, and social struggles that speakers of minority languages become involved in. Processes of language domination and minorization, in which both national and global languages play a part, are rooted in the expansion of empires and nation-building associated with the colonial and post-colonial eras. These processes are thus relevant not only to the history of colonization, annexation, modernization, and social stratification (see e.g. Errington 2001 on the development of sociolinguistic hierarchies in a colonial context), but also to the development of modern nation-states and global economies, including the increased circulation of commodities, ideas, and people across the globe (see e.g. Heller 2003, 2007b; Collins, Slembrouck & Baynham 2009).

Finally, I shall be discussing the category of ethnicity. In particular, I shall be discussing how this category cuts across social class, producing groups that, historically, have had limited social or economic power within nation-states; and how configurations of these groups have shifted, expanded, and been further limited through neo-liberal regimes governing mobility, regulation, and capitalist production in the new economic order. Linguistic minorities have often been constructed as homogeneous entities and marginalized as culturally and linguistically 'different' from, less educated than, or more 'traditional' (i.e. less modern) than the ruling, dominant group. Nevertheless, they have been provided with a range of 'social spaces' – or opportunities within nation-states – to confront these inequities and to mobilize for recognition, rights, and representation in the national arena. In doing so, these groups have often drawn on international discourses, originating from such organizations as the United Nations and the United Nations Educational, Scientific and Cultural Organization (UNESCO); and supranational bodies such as the European Union (EU) have played a major role in providing the discursive and legal forums in which minority groups can act. It is important to note, however, that this spread of universal language rights discourses through globalization is not in itself unproblematic. Among the new difficulties that it creates is that in recognizing the rights of any one 'group', one puts aside not only the heterogeneity and overlapping allegiances of the speakers of that 'group', but also the legitimacy of other possible 'groups'.

Although I shall be treating dominant and minority languages as separate entities, it is important to remember that each is constructed only in relation to the other. Existing alongside dominant groups within and across nation-states are minority Indigenous, immigrant, and other ethnic groups, which have found themselves in particular political, social, and economic relations with the dominant group, whether through colonization, annexation, enslavement, migration, or globalization. I shall be looking more closely at some of these minorities as they exist within nation-states and across national borders. Of particular interest will be how these minority groups have been constructed by dominant modes of discourse with particular material effects; and how, in some cases, the groups themselves have rallied around issues of language, culture, and ethnicity to voice their desire for increased recognition and social justice.

2. Linguistic hierarchy and nation-building

Linguistic hierarchy involves the ranking of languages with respect to their prestige and their association with forms of social, economic, and political power. This relationship between language and various forms of authority and power is maintained by ideologies (that is, belief systems) regarding the inherent inferiority or superiority of a given language. Hierarchy accordingly involves (i) the ranking of different languages, with one language being viewed as more 'logical', 'cultured', 'useful', 'modern', or 'civilized' than another (see e.g. Higonnet 1980: 50; Grillo 1989: 31ff.; and Jaffe 1999 for the rationales behind French language 'superiority'); and (ii) the ranking of the language varieties of a single 'language', with standardized, 'pure', non-dialectal forms (historically legitimized by standardized practices under a centralized state and political authority) being seen as superior to dialectal forms (Blommaert 1999: 431; see also Milroy & Milroy 1991; Crowley 1989; Silverstein 1996; Bex & Watts 1999 on the ideological bases of standard English). In the next sections, I shall describe some of the processes and ideologies of language dominance in nationalist state discourses. As I shall show, these have material and social consequences for the speakers of minority languages or marginalized language varieties, which have been excluded from various state and institutional domains. I shall then turn to the dynamic effects of neoliberal globalization on minorized social groups – processes which contribute to transformations in social identification and the movement of peoples and their languages across borders.

2.1 Language and nationalism

Linguistic dominance is the result of interconnected historical, political, economic, and social processes. In Europe, the development of dominant state languages can be traced to the Middle Ages (Balibar 1991: 87). Originally associated with monarchical power and used for legal and other administrative purposes, such languages came to be associated with the aristocracy and then with the development of modern nation-states (ibid.; see also Grillo 1989: 27–30). The concept of nationhood, as Grillo (1989: 30) notes, includes the construction of 'citizens' as subjects of the nation, who are loyal to this nation rather than to a monarch. Furthermore, as discussed in Anderson (1991: 43–45), the rise of print-capitalism has also been crucial for the creation of a national consciousness and the promotion of particular forms of dominant languages for the purpose of unifying nations. Crucial to nation-building have been the following processes: the formation of state institutions, such as courts, and the implementation of a legal system, schools, and other state-run organizations; industrialization and shifts from subsistence and agrarian to market economies; and social processes that construct local and ethnic identities. Language and social hierarchy figure in all of these processes, as does the hegemonic view of one language as functioning to unify the nation and of one variety of this language as superior to all others.

The belief that a single language contributes to the efficient functioning of the state has its source in the Enlightenment and in the ideology, deriving largely from the Romantic philosophy of Herder (1744–1803), of 'one nation, one culture, one language', which links nationhood to a language and a *Volk*, or 'people' (Bauman & Briggs 2003; Gal 2006). Although such beliefs seem only indirectly linked to the actual development of various Western European nation-states (Hobsbawm 1990: 59), the 'organic', 'homogenizing', essentialist view of language, ethnicity, and nationhood that they reflect persists in popular notions of nationality (national 'character') and nationalisms, as found both in nations established in the 19th century and in independent post-colonial states established after the Second World War (Heller 2007b). The notion that a particular group is united by its language and 'cultural character' is prevalent in contemporary as well as historical public discourse (see e.g. Blommaert & Verschueren 1992; Blommaert 1999: 428; Jaffe 1999; Bauman & Briggs 2003; Gal 2006). This notion continues to play a significant role in nation-building processes especially; and the socially constructed notions 'minority language' and 'dominant language' figure prominently in the media, government debates and policies, and elsewhere on the national landscape.

A second ideological ingredient in nation-building and language dominance likewise emerged from ideas associated with the Enlightenment and with the French Revolution. In 1794, the Abbé Grégoire, a priest, revolutionary, and proponent of liberal causes, presented a report to the National Convention in which he argued for the universalization of French for the benefit of the Bretons, Occitanians, Basques, and Alsatians in their social transformation within revolutionary France (Grillo 1989: 24; Dorian 1998: 6). The spread of French was seen to have practical benefits as well, since heterogeneity was a 'hindrance to centralization' and to the efficient running of the state (Grillo 1989: 34). Today, such arguments are heard in debates over the virtues of monolingualism in the running of democratic nations and states (see e.g. Silverstein 1996 and Woolard 1989b on monoglot 'standard' ideologies in America; Gal 2006).

2.2 Official languages

In the process of nation-building, governments often need to choose 'national' and 'official' languages of the state. National languages refer to those that have usually been ideologically constructed to unify nations by creating political, socio-cultural, and geographic integrity. As noted above, English in England, French in France, and other languages in Western nations have been standardized and legitimized and become dominant over the course of the nation-building process. In post-colonial states, national languages have often been chosen for political reasons, because of their associations with independence and national identity. Thus Paraguay, for example, has as a national language not only Spanish but also the Indigenous language Guarani, which is spoken by the vast majority of the population and which has a strong symbolic function in Paraguayan identity (even though Spanish, as a global language, is dominant with respect to Guarani). Tanzania is another country in which a non-European national language – namely, Swahili – was chosen for political, ideological, and practical purposes. Swahili was seen as egalitarian (in not belonging to any one ethnic group), non-colonial (in being an African rather than a European language), and practical (in having widespread use as a lingua franca; in already being taught in primary schools; and in being perceived, as a Bantu language, as easy for other Bantu-language speakers to acquire). Furthermore, the language was strongly linked to Tanganyika's independence movement and thus served to unify post-colonial Tanzania (Blommaert 1999: 89–92). Despite the efforts to implement full 'Swahilization' in independent Tanzania – that is, to have Swahili adopted as the sole official language and the language of upper-level education – English has remained the language of secondary and higher education and continues to have official functions in government and the economic sphere (Blommaert 1999: 93). Thus, as in other post-colonial countries such as Paraguay, India, the Philippines, and Papua New Guinea, the language of the former colonizer retains its official role alongside a non-European language. Moreover, even though non-European languages have been accorded 'national' status in these and other countries, it is still the case that they often have less power than the languages associated with European expansion, global economies, and the circulation of goods and information. And in many other post-colonial countries, the power and ideological positioning of European languages have meant that the former colonial language has become the 'official' language of the newly independent state.

Official languages, which are often the same as national languages, are those that have been given 'official' status and that have functions associated with legitimate power, as related to the government and the civil service, the media, education, the judiciary, industry, and trade. The granting of official status to one (or sometimes more than one) language is usually an important part of nation-building, defining the character of a nation and the individuals who count as legitimate speakers and players at national and international levels. In countries such as the United Kingdom and the United States, however, there is no official language – although English does have a de facto 'national' status in both countries and although there is considerable support in the U. S. for constitutional recognition of English as the 'official' language. (As Crawford 2000: 28 notes, twenty-two states already have official language laws, most of them passed in the 1980s and 1990s; see also May 2001: 204–224 and Silverstein 1996 for discussion.) As it happens, there has been no analogous movement in the U. K. – arguably because the British public has not felt threatened by large numbers of minority-language speakers, as some segments of the American public have by the rapidly increasing Hispanic minority and other immigrant groups. Nor has there been the same level of debate as in the U. S. regarding bilingual education and the use of minority languages in schools (Crawford 2000: 84ff.; Schmidt 2000; Shannon 1999; see also Herriman & Burnaby 1996 for an overview of language policies in the U. K., the U. S., and other English-speaking countries; and Collins 1999 on the late 20th-century debates regarding the use of African American Vernacular English (AAVE) in American schools).

2.3 Other dominant language ideologies

There are other ideologies associated with historical processes of Western European contact and domination, in the web of empires and modernization, that have favoured the spread of a more prestigious language (associated with a dominant power group) over less prestigious languages (associated with conquered groups or those with lower socio-economic status). Dorian (1998) makes the point that this shift from low- to high-prestige languages is the norm, and that these processes of language dominance are supported by a number of Western dominant-language ideologies. One such ideology has been referred to as the 'ideology of contempt' for non-standard or subordinate languages. This ideology, which has been claimed by Grillo (1989: 173–174) to be 'an integral feature of the system of linguistic stratification in Europe', was reflected in the belief that the minority population was barbarous or savage, and so was their language; or that the language itself was barbarous, and so were the people who spoke it (Grillo 1989: 174).

A second ideology supporting the dominance of certain languages over others has involved the claim that some languages but not others are linked to 'progress' and that progress is inevitable. This ideology draws support from a social-Darwinian belief in the 'linguistic survival of the fittest' (Dorian 1998: 10): in other words, that those languages that can adapt and spread are 'naturally' built to survive. This notion has been associated especially with English, both during its colonial history and in contemporary modernization and globalization enterprises.

A third ideology, that of 'efficiency', is associated with the claim made by many language planners, among others, that efficiency in running a state (and state institutions such as courts, government bureaucracies, schools, and the like) is 'hampered by "too many" languages' (Blommaert 1996: 210). Also associated with this ideology is the claim that local (minority) languages need to be 'modernized' and 'improved upon' if they are to function on a par with 'dominant languages'. What underlies this claim, as Blommaert (1996: 211) notes, is the assumption that global (i.e. European) languages are superior, more complex, and more sophisticated, and can function as global languages 'as they are' – that is, without requiring any 'modernization'. Moreover, the transnational currency and status of these former colonial languages as 'global languages' further justify and strengthen their dominance over local, minority languages.

A fourth ideology is related to the claim that the number of languages with national or official status should be kept to a minimum, in order to preserve a state's integrity. Having a large number of languages within a state is seen as increasing the potential for ethnic and regional divisions and as incompatible with the notion of a 'nation' (Blommaert 1996: 211–212).

A fifth and final ideology is the common (though primarily Anglophone) one related to the claim that bilingualism and multilingualism are 'onerous' to individuals and detrimental to cognitive ability (Dorian 1998: 11–12). This ideology, in particular, has supported educational models promoting monolingualism, and as such has had serious consequences for minority-language students (see Heller & Martin-Jones 2001 for a discussion of the social consequences of such models). Together, these dominant-language ideologies have played a major role in the construction of minority-language groups and in the process of minorization. This process has, in turn, led to the ideological and material struggles that have engaged minority-language groups. I shall describe the nature of these struggles in the next section, in the context of the shifting socio-economic conditions of minority language groups in the twentieth and twenty-first centuries.

3. Minorization

One characteristic of modern nation-states has been their need to manage and control minority-language groups within their geopolitical borders. This has often been accomplished through processes of marginalization or undervaluing of non-dominant languages, and usually by implementing assimilatory policies. Linguistic minorities, therefore, have often been absorbed into a nation and experienced a shift towards its dominant (national) language (see e.g. Dorian 1981, 1989 on Gaelic-speaking minorities in the U. K.; Gal 1979 on Hungarians in Austria; Mar-Molinero 2000 on Galician and other minorities in Spain). In the latter part of the twentieth century, many of these groups, which lacked state recognition in the past, have been affected by supranational minority language discourses and policies. These include policies from supranational bodies such as the European Union (Mar-Molinero & Stevenson 2005) and the United Nations (Duchêne 2008) and various NGOs taking up the cause of minority language rights and language endangerment (Muelhmann & Duchêne 2007; Patrick 2007a).

Various 'annexed' minorities have had different kinds of outcomes. Some have been subject to their own nationalist movements, which take the promotion and maintenance of linguistic difference as primordial goals (e.g. Handler 1988; Levine 1990; Oakes & Warren 2007 on French in Quebec; Woolard 1989a and Mar-Molinero 2000 on Catalan in Spain). Colonialist processes have also produced minorities within both colonized territories and post-colonial states (Errington 2001). In many nation-states, Indigenous (or 'autochthonous') language minorities, oppressed under colonial and neo-colonial regimes, have become politicized, engaging in struggles for increased recognition (May 2001: 273ff.; see also Wardaugh 1987: 155ff. on African multilingualism; Patrick 2007b). The slave trade, which fuelled colonial power, caused the forced migration of peoples who have now been subject to centuries of minorization in different nation-states. Former colonizing countries themselves have felt the effects of the colonial enterprise in the late twentieth century, in the form of immigration from former colonies and subsequent race-related tensions (see e.g. Hewitt 1986; Rampton 1995). Other modern nation-states have felt similar effects, especially given the increasing numbers of economic refugees and immigrants whose relocation and reterritorialization reflects the increasing globalization of industry and markets and has had profound effects on communicative practice (see e.g. Broeder & Extra 1999 on immigration statistics in Western Europe; Heller 1999 on the changing demographics of the French-speaking minority in Canada; Rampton 2006; Collins, Slembrouck & Baynham 2009).

Closely related to relocation and reterritorialization has been the emergence of a hierarchy of global languages. This hierarchy reflects the fact that certain languages – such as English, but other dominant languages as well – have gained far greater international currency than others; and, equally important, that only certain prestigious, 'international' varieties of these languages travel beyond local and regional contexts and are valued in global markets, with the vast majority of languages being assigned little or no value in the transnational domain (Heller 2003; Blommaert 2005). In other words, globalization has, paradoxically, 'minorized' the majority of the world's population in international contexts.

Together, the processes of globalization and minorization have created diverse populations of speakers within and across nation-states – including groups that have undergone varying degrees of minorization and been subject to differential treatment by the state, supranational networks and organizations, and dominant language groups. In what follows, I shall examine some of the processes involved in minority language struggles historically and then turn to more recent analyses of global economic transformations and of the shift to neoliberal regimes, both of which have affected language movements and minorization in significant ways.

For linguistic minorities, language has been a salient marker of difference, which intersects with ethnicity, religion, and social class. Crucially, however, the boundaries between groups, like the language practices that construct them, are fluid ones. This has resulted in some uncertainty or ambiguity for individual members and groups regarding who is and who is not included and the negotiation of relationships with other minorities and with the dominant group or groups. These instances of fluidity and ambiguity exist for national and Indigenous minorities, annexed or subjugated under particular state structures, as well as for migrant groups, whose trajectories reflect the history and laws of the group's adoptive nation and the connections between people and the places that members of the group have left behind.

The categorization of a group of speakers as a 'minority' and their ability to mobilize as a group depend on specific social, economic, and historical conditions. While some linguistic minorities have displayed little resistance to assimilation towards the dominant group, others have demonstrated intense language loyalty – as fostered by, for example, a common religion, cultural affiliations, or independent economic practices. Such loyalties and commonalities have functioned to unify these groups, which have mobilized to win greater power within nation-states and in global networks and markets (Heller 1999a).

Canada provides one such example of specific socio-historical conditions providing political spaces for minority language movements. By examining colonial history, we can trace the growth of movements for increased political autonomy in Quebec and in Indigenous (or 'First Nations') territories, and see how language has become a key aspect of these movements. The role of language can be seen in the policies that Britain put in place after its 1759 conquest of New France but before the American War of Independence, which would significantly shape the cultural, linguistic, and political life of Canada. In particular, the *Royal Proclamation of 1763* and the *Quebec Act* of 1774, issued by the British King George III, sought not only to provide the legal means to insure the survival of the Aboriginal and French-speaking minorities but also to manage these minorities; these policies had significant consequences as the nation developed (Heller 1999b: 147).

Following the *Royal Proclamation*, many Indigenous groups signed treaties to turn their lands over to the Crown in exchange for reserve land and aid from the Canadian state. This set the scene for Indigenous assertion of territorial rights and for Indigenous land claims and the eventual recognition of Indigenous rights in the Canadian Constitution. Linked to this constitutional recognition have been claims for language rights to support these languages institutionally (Patrick 2007b). The 1774 *Quebec Act* took a different tack as regards the French-speaking inhabitants of the former colony of New France, offering to protect their Roman Catholic religion and their French language in order to ensure their loyalty to Canada rather than to the Americans to the south, who were about to break their ties with Great Britain. These historical conditions can be seen to have set the stage for the later assertion of language rights among both of these two national minority groups. It is important to recognize, however, that the assertion of Indigenous and French language rights in Canada is a struggle that is far from over, and one that has been complicated by the fact that the minority group members in question are not always bounded geographically, do not always speak the same language varieties, and have much larger political issues at stake than the recognition of language rights alone.

What is also important to recognize about the Canadian context is that it highlights how minority languages are tied to particular economic activities and to struggles over particular rights and institutional practices within state structures. Among these rights and practices are those related to the language of instruction in schools, the language used in courts, and the representation of minority groups in the media, museums, and other cultural institutions. Significantly, the promotion of these rights and practices is being transformed through access to late twentieth-century international discourses (stemming from the UN and various NGOs); through the rise of neoliberalism, which has led to greater individualism and to the emergence of discourses of economic development; and through global economic shifts of capital, labour, and markets. These shifts especially have resulted in new forms of commodified language and culture; a 'rescaling' of these commodities in a geographic sense, forming a continuum of scales from local to global; and increased and differentiated forms of mobility, involving both peoples and the linguistic and cultural commodities that they produce (Heller 2003; Blommaert 2005; da Silva & Heller 2009; Collins et al. 2009; Glick Schiller & Çaglar 2009).

In sum, the terms on which minority language groups have mobilized have shifted as the neoliberal economic order and discourses associated with this shift have come into play. The discourses in question include those relating to increased competitiveness, economic accountability and sustainability, and ecological niche economic development, in the form of tourism and heritage industries, to name just a few. Under these historical conditions, no single factor can predict the strength of language loyalty or the perseverance of a minority language within any state structure or region. However, what we can observe is that groups, and marginalized ones in particular, have often rallied around issues of language and culture to gain upward mobility, greater institutional and economic control over their communities, and greater social justice. Although the conditions for collective mobilization have been changing with the rise of neoliberalism and globalization, many of the goals of minority social groups and language speakers, such as improvement of their socioeconomic circumstances and participation in institutional structures, remain. And for many minority groups, access to international rights discourses has kept alive their movements for rights-based claims for recognition and support.

3.1 International declarations of minority language rights

Since the post-WWII period, minority language groups have used international declarations and reports on language rights as resources to lay claim to minority and Indigenous group status. The first such document was the United Nations' *Universal Declaration of Human Rights*, issued in 1948. One result of the creation of this document was the convening of a UNESCO group to study the use of vernacular languages in education. The final report of this group, entitled *The Use of Vernacular Languages in Education* (1953), recommended that 'the use of the mother tongue be extended to as late a stage in education as possible [and that] pupils [...] begin their schooling through the medium of the mother tongue' (UNESCO 1953: 48). More recent documents on related issues include the *European Charter for Regional or Minority Languages* (Council of Europe 1992), the *Declaration on the Rights of Persons Belonging to National or Ethnic, Religious or Linguistic Minorities* (United Nations 1992), the 1996 *Universal Declaration of Linguistic Rights*, the 2005 *Convention on the Protection and Promotion of the Diversity of Cultural Expressions*, and the UN *Declaration on the Rights of Indigenous Peoples* (2007) (see de Varennes 2001 and Skutnabb-Kangas 2001 for discussion of some of these). In addition, a number of international NGOs have arisen to promote linguistic diversity and raise concerns about language endangerment (see Muehlmann & Duchêne 2007). Such organizations and the documents produced by them might not have a direct impact on minority language rights and educational policies. Nevertheless, they can have an important legitimizing function, thus helping to mobilize support for minority language rights and eventually to bring about greater recognition of these rights (see e.g. Patrick & Shearwood 1999 for discussion of the possible influence of such discourses on Inuktitut language education policy in Canada).

Yet in assessing the importance of such discourses, it is worth noting that declarations of rights alone do not address the linguistic and social inequities that persist in different minority contexts. One recent contribution to such inequity is the increasing movement of Indigenous and minority groups to urban centres and beyond territorial boundaries. If rights are granted within particular territories, those who find themselves beyond these territories risk further marginalization. A second contribution to inequity is related to the unifying and homogenizing ideologies that shape minority language groups appealing to rights discourses. Given the heterogeneity of minority language groups, it is inevitable that certain language varieties, and not others, will benefit from discourses of 'authenticity' and be considered for standardization and promoted as 'bounded' (i.e. codified) minority 'languages'.

Minorization processes, as we have seen, are subject to particular socio-historical and economic conditions, which shape the political spaces available to minority-language groups and their access to the resources needed to support their languages. In addition, government language planning efforts mean that certain language varieties will be promoted and legitimized while others will not. A number of factors can affect these decisions, including the dominant and 'national' language ideologies discussed above (see Tollefson 1991, 2002 on language planning in relation to dominant and minority languages). Furthermore, while macro-level processes – related, for example, to language rights and language planning – affect the status of minority languages, micro-level processes, including face-to-face interactions, are also crucial to the production and reproduction of linguistic minorities. Sociolinguistic practices involving language choice, the marking of social identities and difference through language use, and the implications of these practices in hierarchical 'orders of indexicality' or structures of meaning, movement across scales, and mobility (Silverstein 2003; Blommaert 2005) shape the social and cultural conditions for language loyalty, language change, or language shift. Thus, the cultural and social values attached to micro-level practices among linguistic minorities are central to the acquisition and use of a dominant language among the members of a minority-language group and to the viability of the minority language for this group (see Silverstein 1998 for an overview of the anthropological literature on this topic; see also e.g. Woolard 1989a; Kulick 1992; Patrick 2001, 2003).

What this suggests, then, is that the recognition of the 'rights' of a given language does not address such questions as which language or language variety, which speakers, and which rights are being favoured over others. Nor does it confront the fact that legal discourses on rights related to language and culture remain controversial (see Cowan et al. 2001 for a critical discussion of cultural rights in international contexts), given their tendency to essentialize and idealize language boundaries and ethnic identities and to idealize language itself, instead of viewing it as a variable social and political construct. Here, empirical and contextual analysis, which takes local circumstances into account, can provide some insight into how minority groups have adopted the discourse of language rights, what consequences this has had, and how changing social and economic conditions have shifted the terms of the debate about language rights.

4. Conclusion

In this article, I have described how language dominance and minorization are processes shaped by particular historical, social, economic, and political conditions. Whether situated within nation-states, supranational bodies, or global economies, a dominant group, on the one hand, and a minority group or groups, on the other, sustain each other through processes of interaction and minorization. I have also shown how the production and maintenance of a minority language, which involves the construction of fluid boundaries for a dynamic minority group, can be examined from an historical perspective in association with other nation-building and global processes. Specific historical and social conditions both produce the social groups that become minorized and create the social spaces within which these groups can mobilize their linguistic and cultural resources to gain greater recognition and power. Minorization, as a process, results in the differential treatment of particular groups with respect to social institutions, the labour market, public policy, and their representation in the media and other discourses. While some minority groups may, by adopting nationalist discourses of inclusion and exclusion, ironically reproduce the systems of oppression that led to their collectivization in the first place, others seek to negotiate more inclusive spaces, but with the goals of increased autonomy intact. This tension shapes much of the contemporary process of minorization and collective efforts to create more equitable institutions, policies, and practices and to achieve a greater share of the economic wealth produced in national and global markets.

References

Anderson, B. (1991). *Imagined communities: Reflections on the origin and spread of nationalism.* Verso.
Barth, F. (1969). *Ethnic groups and boundaries.* Little, Brown.
Bauman, R & C.L. Briggs (2003). *Voices of modernity: Language ideologies and the politics of inequality.* Cambridge University Press.

Bex, T. & R.J. Watts (eds.) (1999). *Standard English: The widening debate*. Routledge.
Balibar, E. (1991). The nation form: History and ideology. In E. Balibar & E. Wallerstein (eds.) *Race, nation, class: Ambiguous identities*: 86–106. Verso.
Blommaert, J. (1996). Language planning as a discourse on language and society: The linguistic ideology of a scholarly tradition. *Language Problems and Language Planning* 20(3): 199–222.
—— (1999). *State ideology and language in Tanzania*. Rüdiger Köppe Verlag.
—— (2005). *Discourse*. Cambridge University Press.
Blommaert, J. & J. Verschueren (1992). The role of language in European nationalist ideologies. *Pragmatics* 2(3): 355–375.
Broeder, P. & G. Extra (1999). *Language, ethnicity & education*. Multilingual Matters.
Collins, J. (1999). The Ebonics controversy in context: Literacies, subjectivities, and language ideologies in the United States. In J. Blommaert (ed.) *Language ideological debates*: 201–234. Mouton de Gruyter.
Collins, J., S. Slembrouck & M. Baynham (ed.) (2009). *Globalization and language in contact: Scale, migration, and communicative practices*. Continuum.
Cowan, J.K., M-B. Dembour & R.A. Wilson (eds.) (2001). *Culture and rights: Anthropological perspectives*. Cambridge University Press.
Crawford, J. (2000). *At war with diversity: US language policy in an age of anxiety*. Multilingual Matters.
Crowley, T. (1989). *Standard English and the politics of language*. University of Illinois Press.
da Silva, E. & M. Heller (2009). From protector to producer: The role of the State in the discursive shift form minority rights to economic development. *Language Policy* 8: 95–116.
de Varennes, F. (2001). The existing rights of minorities in international law. In M. Kontra, R. Phillipson, T. Skutnabb-Kangas & T. Varady (eds.) *Language: A right and a resource*: 117–146. Central European University Press.
Dorian, N. (1981). *Language death: The life cycle of a Scottish Gaelic dialect*. University of Philadelphia Press.
—— (1989). *Investigating obsolescence*. Cambridge University Press.
—— (1998). Western language ideologies and small-language prospects. In L. Grenoble & L. Whaley (eds.) *Endangered languages*: 3–21. Cambridge University Press.
Duchene, A. (2008). *Ideologies across nations: The construction of linguistic minorities at the United Nations*. Mouton de Gruyter.
Errington, J. (2001). Colonial linguistics. *Annual Review of Anthropology* 30: 19–39.
Gal, S. (1979). *Language shift: Social determinants of language change in bilingual Austria*. Academic Press.
—— (1989). Language and political economy. *Annual Review of Anthropology* 18: 45–67.
—— (2006). Migration, minorities and multilingualism: Language ideologies in Europe. In C. Mar-Molinero & P. Stevenson (eds.). *Language ideologies, policies and practices: Language and the future of Europe*: 13–27. Palgrave Macmillan.
Giddens, A. (1984). *The constitution of society: Outline of a theory of structuration*. Polity Press.
Glick Schiller, N. & A. Caglar (2009). Towards a comparative theory of locality in migration studies: Migrant incorporation and city scale, *Journal of Ethnic and Migration Studies* 35(2): 177–202.
Grillo, R.D. (1989). *Dominant languages*. Cambridge University Press.
Handler, R. (1988). *Nationalism and the politics of culture in Quebec*. University of Wisconsin Press.
Heller, M. (1999a). *Linguistic minorities and modernity: A sociolinguistic ethnography*. Longman.

—— (1999b). Heated language in a cold climate. In J. Blommaert (ed.) *Language ideological debates*: 143–170. Mouton de Gruyter.
—— (2003). Globalization, the new economy, and the commodification of language and identity. *Journal of Sociolinguistics* 7(4): 473–492.
—— (2007a). Distributed knowledge, distributed power: A sociolinguistics of structuration. *Text & Talk* 27(5/6): 633–653.
Heller, M. (ed.) (2007b). *Bilingualism: A social approach*. Palgrave Macmillan.
Heller, M. & M. Martin-Jones (eds.) (2001). *Voices of authority: Education and linguistic difference*. Ablex.
Herriman, M. & B. Burnaby (1996). *Language policies in English-dominant countries: Six case studies*. Multilingual Matters.
Hewitt, R. (1986). *White talk, black talk: Inter-racial friendship and communication amongst adolescents*. Cambridge University Press.
Higonnet, P.L.-R. (1980). The politics of linguistic terrorism and grammatical hegemony during the French Revolution. *Social History* 51: 41–69.
Hobsbawm, E.J. (1990). *Nations and nationalism since 1780: Programme, myth, reality*. Cambridge University Press.
Jaffe, A. (1999). *Ideologies in action*. Mouton de Gruyter.
Kulick, D. (1992). *Language shift and cultural reproduction: Socialization, self and syncretism in a Papua New Guinean village*. Cambridge University Press.
Levine, M. (1990). *The reconquest of Montreal: Language policy and social change in a bilingual city*. Temple University Press.
Mar-Molinero, C. (2000). *The politics of language in the Spanish-speaking world: From colonisation to globalisation*. Routledge.
Mar-Molinero, C. & P. Stevenson (eds.) (2005). *Language ideologies, policies and practices: Language and the future of Europe*. Palgrave Macmillan.
May, S. (2001). *Language and minority rights: Ethnicity, nationalism and the politics of language*. Longman.
Meinhof, U.H. & D. Galasinski (2005). *The language of belonging*. Palgrave Macmillan.
Milroy, J. & L. Milroy (1991). *Authority in language*. Routledge.
Muehlmann, S. & A. Duchene (2007). Beyond the nation-state: International agencies as new sites of discourse on bilingualism. In M. Heller (ed.): 96–110.
Oakes, L. & J. Warren (2007). *Language, citizenship and identity in Quebec*. Palgrave Macmillan.
Patrick, D. (2001). Languages of state and social categorization. In M. Heller & M. Martin-Jones (eds.): 297–314.
—— (2003). *Language, politics and social interaction in an Inuit community*. Mouton de Gruyter.
—— (2007a). Language endangerment, language rights and indigeneity. In M. Heller (ed.): 111–134.
—— (2007b). Indigenous language endangerment and the unfinished business of nation states. In A. Duchêne & M. Heller (eds.) *Discourses of endangerment*: 35–56. Continuum.
Patrick, D. & P. Shearwood (1999). The roots of Inuktitut-language bilingual education. *Canadian Journal of Native Studies* 19(2): 249–262.
Rampton, B. (1995). *Crossing: Language and ethnicity among adolescents*. Longman.
—— (2006). *Language in late modernity: Interaction in an urban school*. Cambridge University Press.
Schmidt, R. Sr. (2000). *Language policy and identity politics in the United States*. Temple University Press.

Shannon, S.M. (1999). The debate on bilingual education in the U. S.: Language ideology as reflected in the practice of bilingual teachers. In J. Blommaert (ed.) *Language ideological debates*: 171–199. Mouton de Gruyter.

Silverstein, M. (1996). Monoglot 'standard' in America: Standardization and metaphors of linguistic hegemony. In D. Brenneis & R. Macaulay (eds.) *The Matrix of language: Contemporary linguistic anthropology*: 284–306. Westview Press.

—— (1998). Contemporary transformations of local linguistic communities. *Annual Review of Anthropology* 27: 401–426.

—— (2003). Indexical order and the dialectics of sociolinguistic life. *Language and Communication* 23: 193–229.

Skutnabb-Kangas, T. (2001). Linguistic diversity, human rights and the 'free' market. In M. Kontra, R. Phillipson, T. Skutnabb-Kangas & T. Varady (eds.) *Language: A right and a resource*: 187–222. Central European University Press.

Tollefson, J.W. (1991). *Planning language, planning inequality: Language policy in the community*. Longman.

—— (2002). *Language policies in education: Critical issues*. Erlbaum.

Wardhaugh, R. (1987). *Languages in competition*. Blackwell.

Woolard, K. (1989a). *Double talk: Bilingualism and the politics of ethnicity in Catalonia*. Stanford University Press.

—— (1989b). Sentences in the language prison: The rhetorical structuring of an American language policy debate. *American Ethnologist* 16(2): 268–278.

Woolard, K. & B. Schieffelin (1994). Language ideology. *Annual Review of Anthropology* 23: 55–82.

Language ideologies – Evolving perspectives

Paul V. Kroskrity
University of California at Los Angeles

1. Introduction

This entry briefly explores 'language ideologies' as beliefs, feelings, and conceptions about language structure and use which often index the political economic interests of individual speakers, ethnic and other interest groups, and nation states. These conceptions, whether explicitly articulated or embodied in communicative practice, represent incomplete, or 'partially successful', attempts to rationalize language usage; such rationalizations are typically multiple, context-bound, and necessarily constructed from the sociocultural experience of the speaker. This is a comparatively recent trend largely centered in, but hardly limited to, North American linguistic anthropological research. Though much of the work in this tradition is contemporaneous with the development among discourse analysts of Critical Discourse Analysis (e.g. the work of Norman Fairclough, Ruth Wodak, and Teun van Dijk) which represents a shared concern with power and social inequality (Blommaert & Bulcaen 2000), it is nevertheless a discrete movement with its own distinctive history, theoretical relevances, and substantive foci.

2. The historical emergence of language ideologies

This theoretical notion of 'language ideologies', which I use as a default plural concept (for reasons which will explicated later), is meant to circumscribe a body of research which simultaneously problematizes speakers' consciousness of their language and discourse as well as their positionality (in political economic systems) in shaping beliefs, proclamations, and evaluations of linguistic forms and discursive practices (Kroskrity 2000). Work in this largely linguistic anthropological tradition can be traced to the publication of Michael Silverstein's (1979) 'Language Structure and Linguistic Ideology'. In this article, Silverstein finds in the work of Benjamin Lee Whorf (e.g. 1956) an intellectual forerunner for the project of understanding the shaping role of linguistic ideologies on linguistic structures (e.g. Silverstein 1979, 2000). This pioneering article argued for the recognition of a more central, mediating role for linguistic ideology as an influential part, or 'level', of language. Silverstein argued that speakers' awareness of language and their rationalizations of its structure and use were often critical factors in shaping the evolution of a language's structure. In a later formulation of this position, he summarized, "The total linguistic fact, the datum for a science of language, is irreducibly dialectic in nature. It is an unstable mutual interaction of meaningful sign forms, contextualized to situations of interested human use and mediated by the fact of cultural ideology" (Silverstein 1985: 220). Demonstrating the role of ideology in shaping and influencing such linguistic structures as gendered pronouns and pronominal alternation and change in English as well as Javanese speech levels, he clearly revealed the role of such 'partially successful' folk analyses in contributing to significant analogic change (Silverstein 1979, 1985). This change alters, regularizes, and rationalizes such linguistic changes as the rejection of generic 'he' (in the second half of the 20th C.) and the shift to 'you', thus eliminating 'thou' from non-Quaker English speech (since the beginning of the 18th C.).

It should be emphasized that this recognition of a more central role for linguistic ideology represented a dramatic reversal of scholarly assumptions within both anthropology and linguistics. Within anthropology, the foundational figure of Franz Boas was more concerned with the description and analysis of languages as categorization systems and with historical linguistics rather than with the understanding of culturally contexted speech. In his view, the linguistic consciousness of natives produced nothing of analytic value but only "the misleading and disturbing factors of secondary explanations" (Boas 1911: 69). He clearly favored a 'direct method' which privileged the linguist's expertise and bypassed what could be termed the 'linguistic false consciousness' of culturally deluded natives who could not adequately interpret the linguistic facts. Thus though Boas is properly credited with viewing language as an indispensable part of the totalizing analysis of anthropology, his preoccupation with linguistic structure as the locus of the cultural mind of natives lead him to dismiss any local notions about language as unworthy of attention.

In linguistics of the early and mid 20th century, a similar marginalization or proscription of linguistic ideology also dominated the field. Modern linguistics, since Saussure has tended to exhibit what Vološinov (1973) has described as its 'abstract objectivist' emphasis – "they are interested only in the inner logic of the system of signs itself, taken [...] independently of the meaning that gives signs their content" (p. 58). For him, such an emphasis ignores the position that meaningful signs are inherently ideological. Since American structuralist linguistics under scholars like Leonard Bloomfield (1933) largely ignored meaning, this neglect of ideology was paradigmatically propagated. Though Bloomfield occasionally addressed such 'secondary responses' of speakers in a variety of publications, (e.g. 1933: 22, 1944) in each case he ultimately concluded that speakers' linguistic ideologies – even those cast as prescriptive norms – had a negligible effect on their actual speech.

As Bloomfield's taxonomic structuralism was replaced by Chomsky's transformational-generative version and its various successors in the second half of the 20th Century, the pattern of dismissing speakers' linguistic ideologies was maintained.

Though such theoretical orientations admitted the grammatical 'intuitions' of speakers, their linguistic ideologies, were not viewed as a part of language or as evidence of human agency in linguistic change. Rather than being viewed as partially aware or as potentially agentive, speakers – in Chomskyan models, were merely hosts for language.

Given this marginalization and dismissal in both anthropological and linguistic treatments of linguistic ideologies, Silverstein's (1979) article represents a dramatic reversal of traditional linguistic theorizing, one which rescued linguistic awareness from ongoing scholarly neglect. But a single emphasis on native consciousness of linguistic structures would not suffice in explaining the genesis of the linguistic anthropological approach to language ideologies. Another neglected topic which was inadequately explored was the non-referential functions of language. Most models, including Chomsky's linguistic models and those of ethnoscience within anthropology, reduced linguistic meaning to denotation, or 'reference', and predication. This kind of meaning emphasizes the work of language in providing 'words for things'. But semiotic models of communication based on the theories of C.S. Peirce (1931–58) recognized a broad variety of sign-focused 'pragmatic' relations between language users, the signs themselves, and the connections between these signs and the world. One of the key theoretical advantages, for researchers, of these semiotic-functional models is their recognition that many 'meanings' that linguistic forms have for their speakers emerge from 'indexical' connections between the linguistic signs and the contextual factors of their use. This theoretical orientation, especially as formulated by Jakobson (1957, 1960) and later translated into a functional idiom by Hymes (1964), created the foundation for 'an ethnography of communication' – for the long overdue examination of language use to settings, topics, institutions, and other aspects of speakers and their relevant sociocultural worlds.

This inclusion of speakers along with their languages began a period in linguistic anthropology of greater integration with the concerns of sociocultural anthropology and general social theory. The pioneering figures of ethnography of communication and interactional sociolinguistics created important precedents for developing interests in language ideologies. Dell Hymes (1974: 33), for example, called for the inclusion of a speech community's local theories of speech and John Gumperz (e.g. Gumperz & Blom 1972: 431) often considered local theories of dialect differences and discourse practices and how linguistic forms derived their 'social meaning' through interactional use.

This movement continued in the late 1970's and into the 1980's as linguistic anthropologists were becoming increasingly influenced by the same concerns that were sweeping sociocultural anthropology. These include an emphasis on practice theory and the agency of social actors as well as a syncretic attempt to wed Marxist materialism with a Weberian idealism (Ortner 1984: 147) in an attempt to achieve analytical balance in the representation of human agency within the structure of social systems (Giddens 1979). As Marxist and other political economic perspectives became staples for then contemporary sociocultural theory, they also inspired some of the earliest work in the linguistic anthropological tradition of language ideologies to integrate these concerns with the legitimated interests in speakers' awareness of the linguistic system. These works include Susan Gal's (1979) *Language Shift* and 'Language and Political Economy' (1989), Jane Hill's (1985) 'The Grammar of Consciousness and the Consciousness of Grammar' and Jane and Kenneth Hill's *Speaking Mexicano* (1986), Judith Irvine's (1989) 'When Talk Isn't Cheap: Language and Political Economy', and Kathryn Woolard's (1985) 'Language Variation and Cultural Hegemony'. These works adumbrated many key concerns which have since flourished through the remainder of the twentieth century and into the current century, producing a number of anthologies devoted to language ideological work (e.g. Schieffelin, Woolard & Kroskrity 1998; Blommaert 1999; Kroskrity 2000; Gal & Woolard 2001). More recently, with the increase in researchers who are informed by a language ideological approach, anthologies have appeared which focus on specific regions including the Pacific and Native America (Makihara & Schieffelin 2007; Kroskrity & Field 2009).

3. Some key concepts

To further explore the significance and utility of this notion which has moved from a marginalized topic to an issue of central concern, it is useful to regard language ideologies as a cluster concept, consisting of a number of convergent dimensions. Four partially overlapping layers of significance may be analytically distinguished in an attempt to identify and exemplify language ideologies – both as beliefs about language and as a concept designed to assist in the study of those beliefs.

One, *language ideologies represent the perception of language and discourse that is constructed in the interest of a specific social or cultural group.* A member's notions of what is 'true', 'morally good', or 'aesthetically pleasing' about language and discourse are grounded in social experience and often demonstrably tied to political-economic interests. These notions often underlie attempts to use language as the site at which to promote, protect, and legitimate those interests. Nationalist programs of language standardization, for example, may appeal to a modern metric of communicative efficiency, but such language development efforts are pervasively underlain by political-economic considerations since the imposition of a state-supported hegemonic standard will always benefit some social groups over others (see Woolard 1985, 1989; Errington 1998, 2000; Silverstein 1996; Collins 1996). What this proposition refutes is the myth of the sociopolitically disinterested language user or the possibility of unpositioned knowledge, even of one's own language. Though interests are rendered more visible when they are embodied by overtly contending groups – as in the struggle for airtime on Zambian radio (Spitulnik 1998), the disputes of Warao shamans (Briggs 1998), the political debates in Corsica about the institutional status or cultural role of the Corsican language (Jaffe 1999b), or the confrontations of feminists with the traditional grammarian defenders of the generic 'he' (Silverstein 1985), one can also extend this emphasis on grounded social experience to seemingly homogeneous cultural groups by recognizing that cultural conceptions "are partial, contestable, and interest-laden" (Woolard & Schieffelin 1994: 58). Even shared cultural language practices, such as Arizona Tewa kiva speech (Kroskrity 1998), can represent the constructions of particular elites who obtain the required complicity (Bourdieu 1991: 113) of other social groups and classes. Viewed in this manner, the distinction between **neutral ideological analysis** (focusing on 'culturally shared' beliefs and practices) and **critical ideological analysis** that emphasizes the political use of language as a particular group's instrument of symbolic domination may seem more gradient than dichotomous.

But even though so-called neutral ideologies contribute to our understanding of members' models of language and discourse, an emphasis on the dimension of interest, taken in the political-economic sense, can stimulate a more penetrating sociocultural analysis by rethinking supposedly irreducible cultural explanations. In studies of the indigenous languages of the Pueblo Southwest, for example, a scholarly tradition of explaining such practices as indigenous purism by attributing 'linguistic conservatism' as an essential feature of Pueblo culture had obscured the relevant association between such purism and the discourse of kiva speech that is controlled or regimented by a ceremonial elite (Kroskrity 1998).

Rosina Lippi-Green's (1997) *English with an Accent: Language, Ideology, and Discrimination* explicitly emphasizes language ideologies in her examination of contemporary educational and other institutionalized policies and practices, by demonstrating the class-based interests behind what she calls, following Milroy & Milroy (1999), the **standard language ideology**. She defines it as "a bias toward an abstracted, idealized, homogenous spoken language which is imposed and maintained by dominant bloc institutions and which names as its model the written language, but which is drawn primarily from the speech of the upper, middle class" (Lippi-Green 1997: 64). This language ideology promotes 'the language subordination process' which amounts to a program of linguistic mystification undertaken by dominant institutions designed to simultaneously valorize the standard language and other aspects of 'mainstream culture' while devaluing the nonstandard and its associated cultural forms. So called 'double negatives' (as in 'He does not have no money') may seem repulsive embodiments of ignorance to those of us trained to the norms of the standard and yet its supposed deficiency is not traceable to any logical flaw which obscures its 'meaning' but rather comes from its association with a class of speakers who use it. For Lippi-Green, in accord with a language ideological stance, the proclaimed superiority of Standard English rests not on its structural properties or its communicative efficiency but rather on its association with the political-economic influence of affluent social classes who benefit from a social stratification which consolidates and continues their privileged position.

Two, *language ideologies are profitably conceived as multiple* because of the plurality of meaningful social divisions (class, gender, clan, elites, generations, and so on) within sociocultural groups that have the potential to produce divergent perspectives expressed as indices of group membership. Language ideologies are thus grounded in social experience which is never uniformly distributed throughout polities of any scale. Thus, in Hill's (1998) study of Mexicano linguistic ideologies when older Mexicano speakers in the Malinche Volcano area of Central Mexico say the Mexicano equivalent of 'Today there is no respect', this nostalgic view is more likely to be voiced by men. Although both genders recognize the increased 'respect' once signaled by a tradition of using Nahuatl honorific registers and other polite forms, 'successful' men are more likely to express this sense of linguistic deprivation of earned deference. Mexicano women, on the other hand, are more likely to express ambivalence; having seen their own lot in life improve during this same period of declining verbal 'respect', some women are less enthusiastic in supporting a symbolic return to practices of former times (Hill 1998: 78–79).

Another very revealing application of multiplicity is the exploration of internal diversity as a driving force in linguistic change. Errington's (1998, 2000) research on the complementary if not contradictory language ideologies underlying the development of standard Indonesian. Errington examines the conflicted efforts of the New Order to domesticate exogenous modernity and modernize domestic traditions. Though often viewed as a success story in terms of 'the national language problem', standardized Indonesian does not readily conform to a number of facile claims by scholars and policy makers who share an instrumentalist ideology of language development in nationalism. Gellner (1983), for example, sees development of a national standard language as a key element in making the transformation to nationalism. According to Gellner, state-level polities typically emerge from a religiously based society anchored in local communities controlled by literate elites who derive their authority from knowledge of a sacred script. Here Gellner portrays standardized Indonesian as an 'ethnically uninflected, culturally neutral language' that is both universally available to its citizens and itself subject to development by the state.

But Errington provides several key examples suggesting that the 'instrumentalist' ideals of creating a linguistically homogeneous tool for economic development are clearly not resulting in a culturally neutral national language. Though the New Order attempts to efface the derivativeness of national high culture and national language by erasure of its ethnic and class sources, the language itself provides a key example of an apparent contradiction. Recent lexical change displays a proliferation of both archaic or archaicized terms traceable to Old Javanese and Sanskrit, as well as the incorporation of almost one thousand terms from English. This dual development of the lexicon can hardly be defended as 'communicatively efficient' or as contributing to some neutral language widely available to all as an emblem of national identity. Rather, it represents continuity with a supposedly abandoned linguistic past in which exemplary elites rule through a language over which they have specialized control. And since knowledge of the local prestige charismatic languages (Javanese and Sanskrit) and the prestige international language, English, is socially distributed, this standardizing project joins other nationalist projects in both creating and legitimating a state endorsed social inequality (Alonso 1994).

Another trend in this emphasis on multiplicity is to focus on contestation, clashes or disjunctures in which divergent ideological perspectives on language and discourse are juxtaposed, resulting in a wide variety of outcomes (e.g. Briggs 1996). In one such example from Alexandra Jaffe's research on language politics in Corsica (1999a, b), she examines the ideological debate regarding the translation of French literature into Corsican – a language which has undergone language shift and has lost many functions to the state's official, written language – French. The contestation which emerges is between instrumentalists who see such translations as acts of promotion or enhancement for the symbolic value of Corsican and romanticists who adopt a more classic language and identity perspective. For them, such translations are a perversion of language and identity relationships because the act of translation suggests a common or colonized identity rather than an expression of a uniquely Corsican identity. In Jaffe's analysis, as in others which use this strategy, contestation and disjuncture disclose critical differences in ideological perspectives that can more fully reveal their distinctive properties as well as their scope and force.

Three, *members may display varying degrees of awareness of local language ideologies.* While the Silverstein (1979) definition quoted above suggests that language ideologies may often be explicitly articulated by members, researchers also recognize ideologies of practice that must be read from actual usage. Sociological theorists, such as Giddens (1984: 7), who are concerned with human agency and the linkage of micro and macro allow for varying degrees of members' consciousness of their own rule-guided activities, ranging from discursive to practical consciousness. I have suggested (Kroskrity 1998) a correlational relationship between high levels of discursive consciousness and active, salient contestation of ideologies and, by contrast, the correlation of practical consciousness with relatively unchallenged, highly naturalized, and definitively dominant ideologies. Rampton (1995: 307), following Bakhtin, has emphasized the connections of language ideologies to consciousness, and context.

The types of sites in which language ideologies are produced and commented upon constitute another source of variation in awareness. Silverstein (1998: 136) developed the notion of *ideological sites* "as institutional sites of social practice as both object and modality of ideological expression". One type of especially authorizing sites are religious ceremonies such as those performed in Pueblo kivas (Kroskrity 1998). Sites may also be secular, institutionalized, interactional rituals that are culturally familiar loci for the expression and/or explication of ideologies that indexically ground them in identities and relationships. Susan Philips (2000) clarifies the relationship between different types of sites and ideological awareness. She develops the notion of *multi-sitedness* to recognize how language ideologies may be indexically tied, in complex and overlapping ways, to more than a single site – either a *site of ideological production* or a *site of metapragmatic commentary*. This distinction becomes especially important in the case of Tongan *lea kovi* 'bad language' (Philips 2000). Since 'bad language' is a profaning topic, there are few opportunities for its explicit ideological elaboration in its prototypical family contexts of use in which members display 'mutual respect' by strictly adhering to a variety of proscriptions on their discourse (including one against 'bad language'). Though *lea kovi* is not explicitly discussed in this domestic 'site of use', its elaboration does occur in the courts, where such notions must be clearly discussed as part of the legal process.

The legal setting thus becomes a site of 'metapragmatic commentary' on *lea kovi*, in which Tongan magistrates explicitly rationalize why a cultural proscription on intra-familial interaction should be generalized to larger Tongan society. Thus a language ideology which would normally be tacit, embodied in interaction which conforms to the cultural norm but very rarely brought up to the level of discursive consciousness is fully explicated in the one social context in which, by law, it must be verbally elaborated. By further refining the concept of ideological sites, Philips permits us to see ideological awareness as related to the number and nature of sites in which members deploy and explicate their language ideologies. Sites of ideological production are not necessarily sites of metapragmatic commentary and it is only the latter which both requires and demonstrates the discursive consciousness of speakers. In cases where the government monopolizes state resources, sites of ideological production and explication are one and the same. Under the influence of *Ujamaa*, the socialist ideology of the Tanzanian state, explicit state language ideologies promoted Swahili and encouraged bilingual writers to develop new genres of Swahili literature (Blommaert 1999b) designed to develop indigenous forms and reject foreign literature. Having a monopoly on publishing, the state could use state controlled media to explicate the state endorsed language ideologies and then publish only those works which exemplified those ideologies.

Awareness is also a product of the kind of linguistic or discursive phenomena that speakers, either generically or in a more culturally specific manner, can identify and distinguish (Silverstein 1981). Nouns, our 'words for things', display an unavoidable referentiality that makes them more available for folk awareness and possible folk theorizing than, say, a rule for marking 'same subject' as part of verb morphology. In my own analysis (Kroskrity 1993, 1998) of the contact history of the Arizona Tewa, a consistent pattern of indigenous purism can be established as both a local language ideology of the group and an established fact of language contact. I have traced the efficacy of this purist project to the pervasive influence of *te'e hiili*, or 'kiva speech' – the prestigious code associated with a theocratic elite. But this program of purism is selectively imposed on linguistic phemonena that are more word-like while grammatical diffusion from Apachean and Hopi seems to have evaded Tewa folk scrutiny (Kroskrity 1998). Clearly we still have much to learn about folk awareness and cultural and historical variation in the popular salience of aspects of linguistic and discursive structures. The importance of attending to awareness as a dimension of ideology is both the reversal of a longstanding scholarly tradition of delegitimating common people's views of language – a tradition extending back at least as far as Locke and Herder (Bauman & Briggs 2000) – and the recognition that when speakers rationalize their language they take a first step toward changing it (Silverstein 1979). As Coupland and Jaworski (2004: 37) have powerfully stated: "The concept of language ideology is the final rejection of an innocent, behavioural account of language and the focus of the strongest claim that sociolinguistics must engage with metalinguistic processes in the most general sense."

Four, ***members' language ideologies mediate between social structures and forms of talk*** (Woolard & Schieffelin 1994). Language users' ideologies bridge their sociocultural experience and their linguistic and discursive resources by constituting those linguistic and discursive forms as indexically tied to features of their sociocultural experience. These users, in constructing language ideologies, display the influence of their consciousness in their selection of features of both linguistic and social systems that they do distinguish and in the linkages between systems they construct. The mediating role of language ideologies is further explored and analyzed in research by Irvine & Gal (2000). Using a semiotically inspired orientation, they develop three especially useful analytical tools for revealing productive patterns in language ideological understanding of linguistic variability over populations, places, and times. Irvine & Gal regard these language ideological processes as universal and "deeply involved in both the shaping of linguistic differentiation and the creating of linguistic description" (p. 79).

The three productive semiotically based features underlying much language ideological reasoning are ***iconization, fractal recursivity,*** and ***erasure***. Irvine and Gal (2000) illustrate these processes in each of three sections devoted to detailed examinations of specific historical situations in Africa and Europe. Iconization, for example, emerges as a highly productive feature of folk linguistic ideologies as well as those imported by European linguists attempting to interpret the exotic languages of Africa and the Balkan frontier. Here iconization is a feature of the representation of languages and aspects of them as pictorial guides to the nature of groups. It becomes a useful tool for understanding how Western European linguists misinterpreted the South African Khoisan clicks as degraded animal sounds rather than phonological units and viewed the linguistic and ethnic diversity of the Balkans as a pathological sociolinguistic chaos that could only be opposed to Western Europe's transparent alignment of ethnic nation, standardized national language, and state. Irvine & Gal also see iconization as a typical feature of folk linguistic models in their account of how click sounds enter the Nguni languages through their expressions of politeness or formality – what linguists usually refer to as 'respect' or 'avoidance' registers – from neighboring Khoisan languages. By first viewing the clicks as sounds produced by foreign and subordinate others, Nguni language speakers can 'recursively' incorporate such iconic linkages for use as a linguistic marker of a Nguni language register, or speech level, designed to show respect and deference under various culturally prescribed situations.

Erasure of differentiation is a selective disattention to often unruly forms of variation that do not fit the models of speakers and/or linguists. In their study of nineteenth-century European linguistic treatment of Senegalese languages, Irvine & Gal (2000) document the erasure of multilingualism and linguistic variation required to produce linguistic maps analogous to those of Europe. Erasure permits us to measure the difference between comprehensive analytical models, which attempt to understand a broad spectrum of linguistic differentiation and variation, and a more dominating or even hegemonic model in which analytical distinctions are glossed over in favor of attending to more selective yet locally acknowledged views. Erasure, like iconization and recursivity, is a sensitizing concept, inspired by semiotic models of communication, for tracking and ultimately locating the perspectivally based processes of linguistic and discursive differentiation that inevitably represent the products of ideological influence on positioned social actors. All three processes provide useful means of describing and comparing the productive features of language ideologies employed by both nation-states, the social groups within them, and even individuals within those groups.

4. Recent developments

While many of the conceptual features mentioned above (e.g. multiplicity, awareness) continue to make a language ideologies approach an attractive alternative to those which are either preoccupied with a singular hegemonic language ideology or which deny language users appropriate agency, several research trends became well-established during the past decade which are especially promising as resources for future research. One trend is the 'historiography of language ideologies' (Blommaert 1999: 1) – an emphasis on the diachronic view of language ideological change. Though the concept of a historiography of language ideologies, especially as captured in the imagery of 'language ideological debates' suggests a congruence with well established analytical conventions for emphasizing multiplicity by focusing on overt contestation, it was actually intended by Blommaert and the authors included in his volume by the same name to identify a relatively neglected area of scholarly concern: "the historical production and reproduction of language ideologies" (Blommaert 1999a: 1). Among other pertinent questions on this topic, he has asked, "How do language ideologies come about? What makes the difference between a successful language ideology – one which becomes dominant – and other, less successful ones?".

Rather than focus on synchronically punctual debates, Blommaert invokes a more metaphorical notion of debates which locates conflict and contestation against a larger expanse of historical time. He argues persuasively that not only are language phenomena intrinsically historical but that the notions of power typically invoked in language ideological analysis are also necessarily historical (as in a Gramscian (1971) model of hegemony). Thus in her treatment of the press as a medium and channel of ideological production regarding the use of Catalan and other symbols of stateless national identity during the Barcelona Olympics of 1992, DiGiacomo (1999) not only emphasizes the historical moment in which symbols of Catalonian nationhood are contrastively displayed against competing Spanish symbols. She also invokes a larger historical stage which includes the long antiregionalist oppression of the Franco regime and the extensive tradition of valuing Catalan as a political symbol of autonomy (cf. Woolard 1989). Also taking the long view, Collins (1999) situates the Ebonics controversy in the historical context of evolving U.S. national language ideologies surrounding the increasing valorization of Standard English and stigmatization of minority languages and non-standard varieties. As such, these studies and this emphasis on a historiography of language ideologies provide a more inclusive arena of analysis – one which has advanced language ideological research by providing an appropriate theoretical frame for further capturing the dynamic character of language viewed against the historical flow of evolving sociocultural symbols and transforming power relations. A special issue of the *Journal of Linguistic Anthropology* appeared in which articles by Blommaert (2004), Woolard (2004), and Inoue (2004), among others, provided important historical studies of language ideologies in Zaire, Spain, and Japan respectively. More recently, Morgan (2009) has emphasized the coercive power of language ideologies regarding literacy imposed on Assiniboine and Gros Ventre speaking peoples on the Fort Belknap Reservation (Montana). Educational goals of achieving English literacy were indexically linked to modern identities as "civilized" people while colonial control was exercised through such literate forms as treaties, ration tickets, and enrollment records. Morgan traces the division in Native American support for indigenous literacy to ideological positions that have historically emerged from the multiple-indexing of English literacy as both an instrument of power and prestige, on the one hand, and as a symbol of colonial subordination on the other.

This historical emphasis takes a reflexive turn in the important book by Bauman and Briggs (2004) *Voices of Modernity: Language Ideologies and the Politics of Inequality*. Building upon earlier treatments of Herder and Locke (Bauman & Briggs 2000), the authors extend their analysis to what might be termed the "professional language ideologies" (Kroskrity 2000) of such important figures in folklore and anthropology as the Brothers Grimm, Henry Schoolcraft, and Franz Boas, noting the ideological bases of their attempts at producing purified, "authentic" textual representations of folk discourses.

A second trend which has been very productive in recent research is the exploration of the role of language ideologies in the production of social identities of various kinds, including ethnic, gender, indigenous, and national identities (Shankar 2008; McIntosh 2005; Queen 2005; Hoffman 2008; Makihara 2007; Bunte 2009; Kroskrity 2009a; LeMaster 2006). Language, especially shared language, has long served as the key to naturalizing the boundaries of social groups. Though much has changed since Herder and other European language philosophers valorized and naturalized the primordial unity of language, nation, and state, contemporary theorists of nationalism, such as Anderson (1991) still rely heavily on shared language products and activities as a crucial means of achieving 'the imagined community' of national identity. Language ideological research counters or complements this focus on shared linguistic forms not only by reminding us that when language is used in the making of national or ethnic identities, the unity achieved is underlain by patterns of linguistic stratification which typically subordinates those groups who do not command the standard (e.g. Lippi-Green 1997; Errington 2000). Other concerns are the role of various language ideologies as crucial elements in the production of identities that are interactionally produced through such microlevel processes as code-switching. Local language ideologies of purism and compartmentalization interact with code-switching practices of the Arizona Tewa to maintain a linguistic repertoire of maximally distinctive languages by discouraging mixing and promoting the iconization of each language in the repertoire with a corresponding identity (as Tewa, Hopi, 'American'). Forms of "elder purism" in case studies of Shoshoni-speaking communities in the U.S. (Loether 2009) and the Indigenous Kaska of the Canadian Yukon (Meek 2007) suggest that even in the absence of formal standardization, language ideologies may emerge that valorize the speech of elders and de-authenticate the speech of younger speakers. But for many groups, local ideologies valorize hybridity as expressed through code-switching. For example, in the Puerto Rican community of El Barrio in New York City's East Harlem (Zentella 1997) speaking both Spanish and English in the form of intra-sentential code-switching is a valued expression of their status as bilingual 'Nuyoricans'. Hybridity can also take the form of language ideological change and augmentation as indigenous language ideologies come in contact with those associated with their nation-states and with the standardized, official languages of those states. In Rapa Nui an especially puristic variety of the language has emerged which is both modeled on Spanish-based linguistic purism yet designed to provide an alternative linguistic symbol of an authentic indigenous identity (Makihara 2007). This form is limited to the political displays of identity by leaders while a norm of speaking a more creolized speech is present in everyday discourse. For some U.S. indigenous groups, such as the Western

Mono of Central California or the San Juan Paiute of Northern Arizona, their multilingual, multicultural, and multiethnic adaptations did not encourage an indigenous iconization (Irvine & Gal 2000) of group identity to a single heritage language until after their experience of having English imposed on them by institutions representing the nation-state (Kroskrity 2009a; Bunte 2009). Only after seeing the powerful example of English as the icon of national identity, did these communities reideologize specific heritage languages as "their" exclusive tribal language via the operation of fractal recursivity (Irvine & Gal 2000) – or the nested replication of language and identity relationships.

Language ideologies are also especially relevant in the analysis of subordinated, 'converted', and appropriated identities. As the children of Zentella's study grow up and become more exposed to the language ideologies promoted by educational and other dominant bloc institutions, many children learn to see deficiency in their language skills and view the linguistic feat of their code-switching as nothing more than a crutch-like compensation for their imperfect command of either language. Researchers have also found such ideological construction of subordinated and converted identities in research sites involving colonialism and missionary activity (Errington 2000; Keane 2007) – forces that figure prominently in the changing language ideologies of the Pacific region (Makihara & Schieffelin 2007). Another powerful instance of an identity imposed via language ideologies and language practices, Bambi Schieffelin's (2000, 2007) studies of the missionary introduction of Kaluli literacy products and processes examines the disjuncture between indigenous language ideologies of a cultural group in Papua New Guinea and the 'modernizing' and Christianizing ideologies embodied in a missionary-introduced literacy program. In her careful analysis Schieffelin effectively demonstrates how these primers "(re)presented and (re)constituted social identities" (2000: 296). For example, by referring to the Kaluli themselves as *ka:na:ka:* (a derogatory term for Pacific Island native from Tok Pisin) and systematically depicting Kaluli practices as backward and inferior, these texts influenced the Kaluli to construct themselves from the pejorative perspective of outsiders. Studies of 'crossing' (e.g. Rampton 1995) and 'styling' (e.g. Bucholtz 1999; Cutler 1999) also powerfully demonstrate the language ideological construction of linguistic otherness which motivates such acts of identity appropriation, creation, and hybridization. Often the process of language ideological construction of one's own identity is embedded in the construction of oppositional others. In Stasch's (2007) study of how members of a Papuan community construct Indonesian, he represents the ambivalent view of that community with its demonization of some aspects of Indonesian society and its admiration of others. In contrast many indigenous groups of the American Southwest have constructed hegemonic English as deficient – lacking in spiritual value, imaginative thinking, and sensitivity to the natural world while valorizing the superiority of their heritage languages along these dimensions (Gomez de Garcia, Axelrod & Lachler 2009). By exploring the power of language ideologies to create and destroy identities, researchers will continue to foster an awareness of the important yet often neglected functions of language in social life.

5. Perspectives for future research

In the past decade several language ideological trends have emerged that indicate productive directions for future research. Several of these can be briefly identified here. One of these is the language ideological deconstruction of linguistic racism (e.g. Bucholtz & Trechter 2001; Meek 2006; Barrett 2006; Reyes & Lo 2009). Within this literature, Jane Hill (2008) has expanded upon earlier work (Hill 1999) by using language ideological emphases on awareness to account for contrasts between stark linguistic racism (e.g. use of racial epithets) and "covert" forms of linguistic racism displayed in everyday usage by non-Hispanics of "mock Spanish". Though a speaker's use of this register is often associated with his or her attempt to be jocular or to convey a colloquial stance and not with attempts to be intentionally "racist," Hill nevertheless reveals a consistent pattern of pejoration that is indexically tied to negative stereotypes of Mexican-Americans and other Hispanics as lazy, immoral, drunken or otherwise negative. In her argument, American English speakers' linguistic ideologies of personalism and referentialism dilute and deflect attention away from the verbal harm done to others as a consequence of their propagation of defamatory images of Chicano "others." This indirection coupled with the alternative ideological emphasis combines to explain why such "covert racist" practices flies below the radar of awareness for many speakers who would find overt racist speech reprehensible.

Another trend that is quite apparent is the application of language ideological approaches to situations of language shift and to those attempts at reversing this process which are typically called language renewal and linguistic revitalization (Cavanaugh 2004, 2006; Nevins, 2004; Messing 2007; LeMaster 2006; Meek 2007; Smith-Hefner 2009; Kroskrity 2009a). Because language ideological approaches can treat the interaction of multiple ideologies and not merely attend to the beliefs and practices of dominant groups, they are particularly useful in the analysis of dynamic situations involving cultural contact, socioeconomic change, evolving gender relations, and even the hegemonic influence of states on linguistic and cultural minorities. Language ideologies, of course, have long been recognized as critical forces that figure in the promotion of language shift or persistence (Dorian 1998; Dauenhauer & Dauenhauer 1998) but studies produced within the past decade have featured a more detailed ethnographic probing of on-the-ground language ideologies (e.g. Cavanaugh 2009; Meek 2007) rather than invoking language ideologies as generalized beliefs. Not surprisingly, researchers have found language ideologies to be bound up not only in processes of heritage language attrition and death but also in the very activities of language renewal and revitalization (Nevins 2004; Kroskrity & Field 2009) even including the rhetoric and imagery used by outside activists/experts in the language endangerment literature and in language renewal efforts. Both Jane Hill and Deborah Cameron (Hill 2002; Cameron 2007) have critiqued such tropes as the "universal ownership" of the intellectual "treasure" of the world's dying languages and the biological imagery of the loss of linguistic diversity and the threat of their extinction as justifications for outside intervention and as appeals to members of dominant groups designed to deflect attention away from the socioeconomic factors that are often associated with language endangerment. Focusing on activism and language renewal within communities whose heritage languages are threatened, many authors have turned to "language ideologies" as a crucial means of understanding the interaction of indigenous and state-imposed ideologies (Bunte 2009; Kroskrity 2009a; Loether 2009) as well as the existence of multiple ideologies within heritage language communities themselves thus providing ground-level views of such communities as the Kiowa, Maliseet, Mayan (Guatemala), and Scottish Gaelic communities (Neely & Palmer 2009; Perley 2009; Reynolds 2009; McEwan-Fujita 2010).

The final trend that I would like to mention here concerns what might be called "professional language ideologies" wherein the language ideologies of specific professions – including academic ones (Kroskrity 2000) are revealed and analyzed as performing important roles not only in the displays of professional competence but also insofar as they contribute to and otherwise create the very institutions in which various professions typically perform. The legal profession has already justifiably received considerable attention in the past (Mertz 1998; Philips 1998) but this work has further expanded into more comprehensive studies of the practices of law schools in their training of lawyers (Mertz 2007) and into new domains of law including interrogations of the ideological assumptions regarding the assumed transparency of language in U.S. Law (Haviland 2003) and the examination of Native American tribal law (Richland 2008). In addition to Law, other studies have emerged that use language ideologies as a means of unpacking important processes involved in translation (Schieffelin 2007; Collins & Slembrouck 2006) in missionary and social service contexts, in mass media production (Spitulnik 2002; Moore & Tlen 2007), in educational and psychotherapeutic practice (Jaffe 2003; Razfar 2005; Smith 2005), and in the production of verbal art including the bilingual (English, Navajo) performances of contemporary Navajo poets (Webster 2006, 2009; Kroskrity 2009b).

In sum, language ideologies, as a theoretical orientation, is continuing to prove useful as both conceptual resource and methodological inspiration thereby encouraging and expanding ethnographic encounters with diverse discursive forms. Because it has proven valuable in linking multiplicity, inequality, positionality, and awareness, research in this tradition is likely to expand in response to the challenge of understanding increasingly complex linguistic and discursive phenomena within the contexts of globalization, decolonization, and the overall transformation of contemporary language and speech communities.

References

Alonso, A.M. (1994). The Politics of Space, Time, and Substance: State Formation. *Annual Review of Anthropology* 23: 379–405.
Anderson, B. (1991 [1983]). *Imagined Communities: Reflections on the Origins and Spread of Nationalism*. Verso.
Barrett, R. (2006). Language Ideology and Racial Inequality: Competing functions of Spanish in an Anglo-owned Mexican Restaurant. *Language in Society* 35: 163–204.
Bauman, R. & C.L. Briggs (2000). Language Philosophy as Language Ideology: John Locke and Johann Gottfried Herder. In P. Kroskrity (ed.): 139–204. School of American Research.
—— (2004). *Voices of Modernity: Language Ideologies and the Politics of Inequality*. Cambridge University Press.
Blom, J.-P. & J.J. Gumperz (1972). Social Meaning in Linguisic Structures: Code-switching in Norway. In J.J. Gumperz & D. Hymes (eds.) *Directions in Sociolinguistics*: 407–434. Holt, Rinehart & Winston.
Blommaert, J. (1999a). The Debate is Open. In J. Blommaert (ed.): 1–38. Mouton de Gruyter.
—— (1999b). *State Ideology and Language in Tanzania*. Rudiger Köppe Verlag.
—— (2004). Grassroots Historiography and the Problem of Voice: Tshibumba's *Histoire du Zaire*. *Journal of Linguistic Anthropology* 14: 6–23.
Blommaert, J. (ed.) (1999). *Language Ideological Debates*. Mouton de Gruyter.
Blommaert, J. & C. Bulcaen (2000). Critical Discourse Analysis. *Annual Review of Anthropology* 29: 447–466.
Bloomfield, L. (1933). *Language*. Henry Holt.
—— (1944). Secondary and Tertiary Responses to Language. *Language* 20: 44–55.
Boas, F. (1911). Introduction. In F. Boas (ed.) *Handbook of North American Indian Languages*: 1–83. Bulletin of the Bureau of American Ethnology, vol. 40.
Bourdieu, P. (1991). *Language and Symbolic Power*. Harvard University Press.
Briggs, C.L. (1996). Conflict, Language Ideologies, and Privileged Arenas of Discursive Authority in Warao Dispute Mediation. In C.L. Briggs (ed.) *Disorderly Discourse: Narrative, Conflict, and Inequality*: 204–242. Oxford University Press.
—— (1998). "You're a Liar — You're Just Like a Woman!": Constructing Dominant Ideologies of Language in Warao Men's Gossip. In B.B. Schieffelin et al. (eds.): 229–55.
Bucholtz, M. (1999). You da man: Narrating the Racial Other in the Linguistic Production of White Masculinity. *Journal of Sociolinguistics* 3(4): 443–460.
Bucholtz, M. & S. Trechter (2001) (eds.). *Discourses of Whiteness*. Special Issue of *Journal of Linguistic Anthropology* 11(1).
Bunte, P.A. (2009). "You Keep Not Listening with Your Ears": Ideology, Language Socialization, and Paiute Identity. In P. Kroskrity & M. Field (eds.): 172–189.
Cameron, D. (2007). Language Endangerment and Verbal Hygiene. In A. Duchene & M. Heller (eds.) *Discourses of Endangerment*: 268–285. Continuum.
Cavanaugh, J.R. (2004). Remembering and Forgetting: Ideologies of Language Loss in Northern Italian Town. *Journal of Linguistic Anthropology* 14: 24–38.

—— (2006). Little Women and Vital Champions: Gendered Language Shift in a Northern Italian Town. *Journal of Linguistic Anthropology* 16: 194–210.

—— (2009). *Living Memory: the Social Aesthetics of Language in a Northern Italian Town*. Wiley-Blackwell.

Collins, J. (1996). Socialization to Text: Structure and Contradiction in Schooled Literacy. In M. Silverstein & G. Urban (eds.) *Natural Histories of Discourse*: 203–228. University of Chicago Press.

—— (1999). The Ebonics Controversy in Context: Literacies, Subjectivities, and Language Ideologies in the United States. In J. Blommaert (ed.): 201–234. Mouton de Gruyter.

Collins, J. & S. Slembrouck (2006). "You Don't Know What They Translate": Institutional Procedure, and Literacy Practice in Neighborhood Clinics in Urban Flanders. *Journal of Linguistic Anthropology* 16: 249–268.

Coupland, N. & A, Jaworski (2004). Sociolinguistic Perspectives on Metalanguage: Reflexivity, Evaluation, and Ideology. In A. Jaworski, N. Coupland & D. Galasinski (eds.) *Metalanguage: Social and Ideological Perspectives*: 15–51. Mouton de Gruyter.

Cutler, C.A. (1999). Yorkville Crossing: White Teens, Hip Hop, and African American English. *Journal of Sociolinguistics* 3(4): 428–442.

Dauenhauer, N.M & R. Dauenhauer (1998). Technical, emotional, and ideological issues in reversing language shift. In L.Grenoble & L.Whaley (eds.) *Endangered Languages*: 57–98. Cambridge University Press.

Dorian, N. (1998). Western Language Ideologies and small language prospects. In L. Grenoble & L. Whaley (eds.) *Endangered Languages*: 3–21. Cambridge University Press.

Digiacomo, S.M. (1999). Language Ideological Debates in an Olympic City: Barcelona 1992–1996. In J. Blommaert (ed.): 105–142. Mouton de Gruyter.

Errington, J. (1998). Indonesian('s) Development: On the state of a language of state. In B.B. Schieffelin et al. (eds.): 271–284.

—— (2000). Indonesian('s) Authority. In P.V. Kroskrity (ed.): 205–227.

Gal, S. (1979). *Language Shift: Social Determinants of Language Change in Bilingual Austria*. Academic Press.

—— (1989). Language and Political Economy. *Annual Review of Anthropology* 18: 345–367.

Gal, S. & K. Woolard (2001). *Languages and Publics: the Making of Authority*. St. Jerome Publishing.

Gellner, E. (1983). *On Nations and Nationalism*. Cornell University Press.

Giddens, A. (1984). *The Constitution of Society*. University of California Press.

Gomez de Garcia, J., M. Axelrod & J. Lachler (2009). "English is the Dead Language". In P. Kroskrity & M. Field (eds.): 99–122.

Gramsci, A. (1971). *Selections from the Prison Notebooks*. International Press.

Haviland, J. (2003). Ideologies of Language: Some Reflections on Language and U.S. Law. *American Anthropologist* 105: 764–774.

Hill, J.H. (1985). The Grammar of Consciousness and the Consciousness of Grammar. *American Ethnologist* 12: 725–737.

—— (1998). "Today There Is No Respect": Nostalgia, "Respect", and Oppositional Discourse in Mexicano (Nahuatl) Language Ideology. In B.B. Schieffelin et al. (eds.): 103–122.

—— (1999). Language, Race, and the White Public Space. *American Anthropologist* 100: 680–689.

—— (2002). "Expert Rhetorics" in Advocacy for Endangered Languages: Who Is Listening and What Do They Hear? *Journal of Linguistic Anthropology* 12: 119–133.

——(2008). *The Language of Everyday White Racism*. Wiley-Blackwell.

Hill, J.H. & K.C. Hill (1986). *Speaking Mexicano: Dynamics of Syncretic Language in Central Mexico*. University of Arizona Press.
Hoffman, K.E. (2008). *We Share Walls: Language, Land, and Gender in Berber Morocco*. Blackwell.
Hymes, D.H. (1964). Introduction: Toward Ethnographies of Communication. In J.J. Gumperz & D.H. Hymes (eds.) *The Ethnography of Communication*: 1–34. American Anthropologist 66(6), Part 2.
―― (1974). *Foundations in Sociolinguistics: An Ethnographic Approach*. University of Pennsylvania Press.
Inoue, M. (2004). What Does Language Remember?: Indexical Inversion and the Naturalized History of Japan. *Journal of Linguistic Anthropology* 14: 39–56.
Irvine, J.T. (1989). When Talk Isn't Cheap: Language and Political Economy. *American Ethnologist* 16: 248–267.
Irvine, J.T. & S. Gal (2000). Language Ideology and Linguistic Differentiation. In P.V. Kroskrity (ed.): 35–83.
Jaffe, A. (1999a). *Ideologies in Action: Language Politics in Corsica*. Mouton de Gruyter.
―― (1999b). Locating Power: Corsican Translators and Their Critics. In J. Blommaert (ed.): 1–38.
―― (2003). Misrecognition Unmasked?: "Polynomic" Language, Expert Statuses and Orthographic Practices in Corsican Schools. *Pragmatics* 13: 515–537.
Jakobson, R. (1957). *The Framework of Language*. University of Michigan Press.
―― (1960). Concluding Statement: Linguistics and Poetics. In T. Sebeok (ed.) *Style in Language*: 350–373. MIT Press.
Keane, W. (2007). *Christian Moderns: Freedom and Fetish in the Mission Encounter*. University of California Press.
Kroskrity, P.V. (1993). *Language, History, and Identity: Ethnolinguistic Studies of the Arizona Tewa*. University of Arizona Press.
―― (1998). Arizona Tewa Kiva Speech as a Manifestation of a Dominant Language Ideology. In B.B. Schieffelin et al. (eds.): 103–123.
―― (2000). Regimenting Languages. In P. Kroskrity (ed.): 1–34. School of American Research.
―― (2009a). Embodying the Reversal of Language Shift: Agency, Incorporation, and Language Ideological Change in the Western Mono Community of Central California. In P. V. Kroskrity & M. Field, (eds).: 190–210.
―― (2009b). Narrative Reproductions: Ideologies of Storytelling, Authoritative Words, and Generic Regimentation. *Journal of Linguistic Anthropology* 19: 40–56.
―― (ed.) (2000). *Regimes of Language: Ideologies, Polities, and Identities*. School of American Research.
Kroskrity, P.V. & M.C. Field (eds.) (2009). *Native American Language Ideologies: Beliefs, Practices, and Struggles in Indian Country*. University of Arizona Press.
Lemaster, B. (2006). Language Contraction, Revitalization, and Irish Women. *Journal of Linguistic Anthropology* 16: 211–228.
Lippi-Green, R. (1997). *English with an Accent: Language, Ideology, and Discrimination in the United States*. Routledge.
Loether, C. (2009). Language Revitalization and the Manipulation of Language Ideologies: A Case Study. In P.V. Kroskrity & M.C. Field (eds.): 238–255.
McEwan-Fujita, E. (2010). Ideology, Affect, and Socialization in Language Shift and Revitalization: the Experiences of Adults Learning Gaelic in the Western Isles of Scotland. *Language in Society* 39: 27–64.

McIntosh, J. (2005). Baptismal Essentialisms: Giriama Code Choice and the Reification of Ethnoreligious Boundaries. *Journal of Linguistic Anthropology* 15: 151–170.

Makihara, M. (2007). Linguistic Purism in Rapa Nui Political Discourse. In M. Makihara & B. Schieffelin (eds.): 46–69.

Makihara, M. & B. Schieffelin. (eds.) (2007). *Consequences of Contact: Language Ideologies and the Sociocultural Transformation of Pacific Societies*. Oxford University Press.

Meek, B.A. (2006). And the Injun Goes "How!": Representations of American Indian English in White Public Space. *Language in Society* 35: 93–128.

—— (2007). Respecting the Language of Elders: Ideological Shift and Linguistic Discontinuity in a Northern Athapascan Community. *Journal of Linguistic Anthropology* 17: 23–43.

Mertz, E. (1998). Language Ideology and Praxis in U.S. Law School Classrooms. In B. Schieffelin et al. (eds):149–62.

—— (2007). *The Language of Law School: Learning "To Talk Like a Lawyer"*. Oxford University Press.

Messing, J. (2007). Multiple Ideologies and Competing Discourses: Language Shift in Tlaxcala, Mexico. *Language in Society* 36: 555–577.

Milroy, J. & L. Milroy (1999). *Authority in Language: Investigating Language Prescription and Standardisation*. Routledge.

Moore, P. & D. Tlen (2007). Indigenous Linguistics and Land Claims: The Semiotic Projection of Athabaskan Directionals in Elizah Smith's Radio Work. *Journal of Linguistic Anthropology* 17: 266–286.

Morgan, M.J. (2009). *The Bearer of This Letter: Language Ideologies, Literacy Practices, and the Fort Belknap Indian Community*. University of Nebraska Press.

Neely, A. & G. Palmer Jr. (2009). Which Way is the Kiowa Way? Orthography Choices, Ideologies, and Language Renewal. In P.V. Kroskrity & M.C. Field (eds.): 271–297.

Nevins, E. (2004). Learning to Listen: Confronting Two Meanings of Language Loss in the Contemporary White Mountain Apache Speech Community. *Journal of Linguistic Anthropology* 14: 269–288.

Ortner, S.B. (1984). Theory in Anthropology Since the Sixties. *Comparative Studies in Society and History* 26: 126–166.

Peirce, C.S. (1931–58). *Collected Papers of Charles Sanders Peirce*. Harvard University Press.

Perley, B. (2009). Contingencies of Emergence: Planning Maliseet Language Ideologies. In P.V. Kroskrity & M.C. Field (eds.): 255–270.

Philips, S. (1998). *Ideology in the Language of Judges*. Oxford University Press.

—— (2000). Constructing a Tongan Nation-state through Language Ideology in the Courtroom. In P.V. Kroskrity (ed.): 229–257.

Queen, R. (2005). "How Many Lesbians Does It Take …": Jokes, Teasing, and the Negotiation of Stereotypes About Lesbians. *Journal of Linguistic Anthropology* 15: 239–257.

Rampton, B. (1995). *Crossing: Language and Ethnicity Among Adolescants*. Longman.

Razfar, A. (2005). Language Ideologies in Practice: Repair and Classroom Discourse. *Linguistics and Education* 16: 404–424.

Reyes, A. & A. Lo (2009). *Beyond Yellow English*. Oxford University Press.

Reynolds, J.F. (2009). Shaming the Shift Generation: Intersecting Ideologies of Family and Linguistic Revitalization in Guatemala. In P.V. Kroskrity & M.C. Field (eds.): 213–237.

Richland, J.B. (2008). *Arguing With Tradition: the Language of Law in Hopi Tribal Court*. University of Chicago Press.

Schieffelin, B.B. (2000). Introducing Kaluli Literacy: A Chronology of Influences. In P.V. Kroskrity (ed.): 293–327.

—— (2007). Found in Translating: Reflexive Language across Time and Texts in a Bosavi, Papua New Guinea. In M. Makihara & B. Schieffelin (eds.): 140–165.
Schieffelin, B.B., K.A. Woolard & P.V. Kroskrity (eds.) (1998). *Language Ideologies, Practice and Theory*. Oxford University Press.
Shankar, S. (2008). Speaking Like a Model Minority: "FOB" Styles, Gender, and Racial Meanings Among Desi Teens in Silicon Valley. *Journal of Linguistic Anthropology* 18: 268–289.
Silverstein, M. (1979). Language Structure and Linguistic Ideology. In P. Clyne, W. Hanks & C. Hofbauer (eds.) *The Elements*: 193–248. Chicago Linguistics Society.
—— (1981). The Limits of Awareness. Working Papers in Sociolinguistics, no. 84. Southwest Educational Development Library. [Reprinted in A. Duranti (ed.) *Linguistic Anthropology: A Reader*: 382–402. Blackwell].
—— (1985). Language and the Culture of Gender. In E. Mertz & R. Parmentier (eds.) *Semiotic Mediation*: 219–259. Academic Press.
—— (1996). Monoglot "Standard" in America: Standardization and Metaphors of Linguistic Hegemony. In D. Brenneis & R.S. Macaulay (eds.) *The Matrix of Language*: 284–306. Westview.
—— (1998). The Uses and Utility of Ideology: A Commentary. In B.B. Schieffelin et al. (eds.): 123–145.
—— (2000). Whorfianism and the Linguistic Imagination of Nationality. P.V. Kroskrity (ed.): 85–138.
Smith, B. (2005). Ideologies of the Speaking Self in the Psychotherapeutic Theory and Practice of Carl Rogers. *Journal of Linguistic Anthropology* 15: 258–272.
Smith-Hefner, N.J. (2009). Language Shift, Gender, and Ideologies of Modernity in Central Java, Indonesia. *Journal of Linguistic Anthropology* 19: 57–77.
Spitulnik, D. (1998). Mediating Unity and Diversity: the Production of Language Ideologies in Zambian Broadcasting. In B.B. Schieffelin et al. (eds.): 163–188.
—— (2002). Alternative Small Media and Communicative Spaces. In .G. Hyden, M. Leslie, & F.F. Ogundimu (eds.) *Media and Democarcy in Africa*: 177–205. Transaction.
Stasch, R. (2007). Demon Language: The Otherness of Indonesian in a Papuan Community. In M. Makihara & B. Schieffelin (eds.): 96–124.
Webster, A. (2006). From *Hoyee* to *Hajinei*: On Some Implications of Feelingful Iconcity and Orthography in Navajo Poetry. *Pragmatics* 16: 535–549.
—— (2009). The Poetics and Politics of Navajo Ideophony in Contemporary Navajo Poetry. *Language and Communication* 29: 133–151.
Whorf, B.L. (1956). *Language, Thought, and Reality*. MIT Press.
Woolard, K.A. (1985). Language Variation and Cultural Hegemony: Toward an Integration of Sociolinguistics and Social Theory. *American Ethnologist* 2: 738–748.
—— (1989). *Double Talk: Bilingualism and the Politics of Ethnicity in Catalonia*. Stanford University Press.
—— (1998). Language Ideology as a Field of Inquiry. In B.B. Schieffelin et al. (eds.): 3–47.
—— (2004). Is the Past a Foreign Country?: Time, Language Origins, and the Nation in Early Modern Spain. *Journal of Linguistic Anthropology* 14: 57–80.
Woolard, K.A. & B.B. Schieffelin (1994). Language Ideology. *Annual Review of Anthropology* 23: 55–82.
Zentella, A.C. (1997). *Growing Up Bilingual: Puerto Rican Children in New York*. Blackwell.

Language rights

Tove Skutnabb-Kangas
Roskilde University

1. Introduction: Language rights, linguistic human rights, and (linguistic) assimilation or integration

As many researchers have noted since the 1960s, schools can in a couple of generations kill languages which had survived for centuries, even millennia, when their speakers were not exposed to formal education of the present-day type. Schools can today participate in committing linguistic genocide through their choice of the medium of formal education – and they do.

This entry clarifies some of the basic concepts and dichotomies involved when discussing language rights and the subcategory linguistic human rights, both in general and, especially, in education. These are seen in relation to the integration of societies. All the rights that people or collectivities have in relation to languages (their own or others) are *linguistic rights* or *language rights* (LRs). These two terms are mostly used as synonyms. Some researchers regard linguistic rights as a somewhat broader concept than language rights; in this case they are often discussing rights not only to various languages but also to varieties *within* the 'language' label, e.g. regional, gender-based or class-based varieties. Intralinguistic rights are according to this approach seen as a part of linguistic but not language rights. Others feel that both labels include all the rights, regardless of whether we are talking about languages or varieties. Language rights have been discussed for centuries, and the first multilateral treaties about language rights are from the 1880s (see May 2001; Skutnabb-Kangas & Phillipson 1994; Skutnabb-Kangas 1997; Thornberry 1997; de Varennes 1996 for overviews).

Our present *human rights* (HRs) are from the period after the Second World War but there were many human rights treaties signed as early as under the League of Nations after the First World War.

The concept of *linguistic human rights* (LHRs) combines language rights with human rights and is a fairly recent phenomenon.[1] So far, it is not clear what should

---

1. Even if LHRs have been discussed in some articles earlier, the first full-length book with LHRs in the title seems to be Skutnabb-Kangas & Phillipson 1994. Now there are many more; a Google search with the phrase "linguistic human rights" (February 2010), showed 1,470,000 entries; In May 2005 there were 4,880 and in December 2006 33,600 entries.

and what should not be considered LHRs; there are lively ongoing debates about the topic. Therefore, concept clarification is in order.

LHRs should be those (and only those) LRs, which, first, are necessary to satisfy people's basic needs (including the need to live a dignified life), and which, secondly, therefore are so basic, so fundamental that no state (or individual or group) is supposed to violate them. There are many LRs which are not LHRs. It would, for instance, be good if everybody could, even in civil court cases, have a judge and witnesses who speak (or sign) this person's language, regardless of how few users the language has. Today, it is mostly only in criminal cases that one has any linguistic *human* rights, namely the right to be informed of the charge against oneself in a language that one understands (i.e. not necessarily the mother tongue). In all other court contexts, people may or may not have a *language* right, depending on the country and language; in the best cases, interpreters paid for by the state are used. Some basic rights prohibit discrimination on the basis of language (*negative rights*); others ensure equal treatment to languages, individuals or language groups (*positive rights*). Most binding LHRs are today still negative rights only.

Many of the fears that prevent states from guaranteeing LHRs originate from claims that granting LHRs and thus maintaining linguistic diversity will prevent the integration of a state through a common language. A special type of language policy goal, namely linguistic assimilation of minorities, is said to further this integration. For instance, the Turkish Constitutions have since Mustafa Kemal's (Atatürk's) times stressed "the indivisible integrity of the state with its territory and nation":

> Language is one of the essential characteristics of a nation. Those who belong to the Turkish nation ought, above all and absolutely, to speak Turkish. [...] Those people who speak another language could, in a difficult situation, collaborate and take action against us with other people who speak other languages. (Kemal 1931)

The U.S.A. president Theodore Roosevelt expressed in 1919 similar sentiments in a letter:

> In the first place, we should insist that if the immigrant who comes here in good faith becomes an American and assimilates himself to us, he shall be treated on an exact equality with everyone else, for it is an outrage to discriminate against any such man because of creed, or birthplace, or origin. But this is predicated upon the person's becoming in every facet an American, and nothing but an American [...] There can be no divided allegiance here. Any man who says he is an American, but something else also, isn't an American at all. We have room for but one flag, the American flag [...] We have room for but one language here, and that is the English language [...] and we have room for but one sole loyalty and that is a loyalty to the American people. (http://urbanlegends.about.com/library/bl_roosevelt_on_immigrants.htm; accessed 24 February 2007)

Turkey still sees any official use of Kurdish as a threat to this unity (see Skutnabb-Kangas & Fernandes 2008). The attempts in the U.S.A. to make English the only official language and to ban the use of other languages from schools as much as possible speak to the same (unfounded) fears.

The concepts of integration and assimilation need to be defined to see whether a language policy denying LHRs really leads to integration.[2] *Assimilation* can initially be defined as (a) disappearance of distinctive features, i.e. objectively the loss of specific elements of material and non-material culture and subjectively the loss of the feeling of belonging to a particular ethnic group; and (b) simultaneously, objectively, adoption of traits belonging to another culture, which replace those of the former culture, accompanied by the subjective feeling of belonging to the second culture. *Integration*, in contrast, is formation of a series of common features in an ethnically heterogeneous group.

Assimilation is *subtractive*, whereas integration is *additive*. We can illustrate the concepts with the education of indigenous and minority children. In subtractive teaching, minority children are taught through the medium of a dominant language, which replaces their mother tongue. They learn the dominant language at the cost of the mother tongue. In additive teaching, minority children are taught through the medium of the mother tongue, with good teaching of the dominant language as a second language. Additive teaching can make them high level bilingual or multilingual. They learn other languages in addition to their own language and may learn them all well.

The concepts of subtractive and additive can now be used for another definition of assimilation and integration: *Assimilation* is enforced subtractive 'learning' of another (dominant) culture by a (dominated) group. Assimilation means being transferred to another group. *Integration* is characterized by voluntary mutual additive 'learning' of other cultures. Integration means a choice of inclusive group membership(s).

In terms of both these definitions, it is clear that most state attitudes towards indigenous peoples and minorities are still in a phase where assimilation/integration are only discussed in terms of what happens and is envisaged in relation to the indigenous peoples/minorities, whereas very little takes place in relation to the dominant population which is not asked or envisaged to change. If real integration of societies, rather than assimilation, is the goal in both education and language policy in general, what kind of LHRs are needed for real change?

In discussions of LRs and HRs, several pairs of dichotomies and/or continua are used. Many of them are presented below, also to determine which language rights are necessary so that indigenous peoples and minorities do not need to assimilate but can participate in mutual integration of societies. Granting such LRs is seen as part of necessary conflict avoidance.

---

2. The definitions of integration and assimilation are from Skutnabb-Kangas (2000: 123–134).

2. Basic concepts, continua and dichotomies

2.1 Who or what can have rights?

Languages themselves may have rights to be used, developed and maintained. Alternatively, or in addition, people or collectivities of people (*individuals, groups, peoples, organizations,* or *states*) may have rights to use, develop and maintain languages or they may have duties to enable the use, development or maintenance of them. Two of the most important European LRs documents, from the Council of Europe, can be seen as examples of these two types of right. The *European Charter for Regional or Minority Languages* (hereafter the *European Charter*)[3], grants rights to languages, not speakers[4] of the languages concerned. The *Framework Convention for the Protection of National Minorities* (hereafter the *Framework Convention*)[5], on the other hand, grants rights to (national) minorities, i.e. groups.

Once a state has both signed (promised to start the process which enables it to ratify them) and ratified one of these human rights instruments (changed their laws and regulations and put processes in place that enable them to fulfill the obligations that they have promised to undertake), these are binding for the state. States usually have a duty to report at specified intervals how they have acted to guarantee the rights, and there is also normally some kind of a monitoring body that scrutinizes the reports and gives feedback and guidance to the states.

2.2 Individual versus collective rights

2.2.1 *Individual rights*

An *individual* from a certain group or with specific characteristics in a specific country may, for instance, have the right to use her or his mother tongue in various contexts, e.g. in dealing with authorities, local, regional or state-wide, orally, in writing or signing it, or all of these. However, the authorities do not necessarily need to reply in the same language. The *mother tongue* is often for legal purposes defined in a strict way, as the first language that a person learned, and still speaks, and with which s/he identifies. A definition often used in situations where forced assimilation of indigenous peoples has made the older generation speak the dominant language to their children, is sometimes

---

3. See http://conventions.coe.int/treaty/en/Treaties/Html/148.htm.

4. *Speaker* is here used as a generic term to be understood as 'speaker or signer', i.e. it includes users of Sign languages. No state has ratified the *European Charter* for any Sign language, though. (For a discussion of the (false) arguments used to exclude Sign languages, see Skutnabb-Kangas 2002.)

5. See http://conventions.coe.int/treaty/en/Treaties/Html/157.htm.

less strict: a mother tongue, with LRs connected to it, is defined as a language which is, or has been, the first language of the individual her/himself, or of (one of) the parents or grandparents. In most cases both a degree of competence and/or use of the language are required, together with identification; in a few cases identification with the language may be enough.

Individuals may also have rights in relation to *other languages* than their mother tongues/first languages. Mostly these rights relate to a dominant/official/national language in the country. Some people have also started to demand that access to an international language, in most cases English, should be seen as a language right.

2.2.2 Collective rights

Since many human rights instruments, especially the first ones to emerge after the Second World War, are concerned with rights of individuals (like the United Nations *Universal Declaration of Human Rights*, or the UN *Convention on the Rights of the Child* (CRC, 1989)[6], *collective rights* of various groups have re-emerged later. A few of these are language-related. The human rights regime of the League of Nations between the two 'World' Wars contained many collective rights; in principle, most minority rights should be collective rights (see Thornberry & Gibbons 1997). In the United Nations regime after 1945, it was claimed that no collective rights were necessary since every person was protected as an individual, by individual rights. Collectivities like 'minorities' were by many negotiators (e.g. the U.S.A. human rights negotiator Eleanor Roosevelt) seen as 'a European problem', meaning they were not seen as *universal*. Somewhat simplified, Western countries have largely opposed collective rights and African countries have supported many of them, while Asian countries have stood so divided that this issue has been one of the major hurdles preventing an acceptance of regional Asian human rights instruments. The *European Charter* and the *Framework Convention* are regional, not universal instruments. So are the Council of Europe's 1950 *Convention on Human Rights and Fundamental Freedoms* and the corresponding African and American instruments, *The African Charter on Human and Peoples' Rights*[7] from 1981 and the *American Convention on Human Rights*[8] from 1969.

Some important language-related instruments try to combine individual and collective rights, by using 'persons belonging to a minority' or a similar phrase. This is what, for instance, Article 27 of the UN *International Covenant on Civil and Political*

---

6. Most of the human rights instruments can be found at the website of the Office of the United Nations Human Rights Commissioner, http://www2.ohchr.org/english/law/.

7. See http://www.achpr.org/.

8. See http://www.wcl.american.edu/pub/humright/digest/index.html.

Rights, ICCPR, uses. Article 27 is still the most far-reaching Article in (binding) human rights law granting linguistic rights:

> In those states in which ethnic, religious or linguistic minorities exist, persons belonging to such minorities shall not be denied the right, in community with other members of their group, to enjoy their own culture, to profess and practise their own religion, or to use their own language.

Many international *organizations* and most *states* have a language policy that spells out the official languages of the organization or state and, by implication, the LRs of the people, groups, and states dealing with, and working within, that entity. The United Nations have six official languages, the Council of Europe only two. The European Union has several times increased the number of its official languages. After its latest expansion, in January 2007, the Union now has 23 official languages; all official documents have to be made available in all of these. Many organizations also have working languages; their number may be more restricted. A number of states have only one official (or state) language; most have two or more (English is *an* official language in more than 70 states; see Skutnabb-Kangas 2000). South Africa has 11 official languages, India 24. In addition, many states specify one or several national, additional, link, or national heritage languages in their constitutions; in most cases, speakers of these have fewer rights than speakers of the official languages have (see de Varennes 1996).

2.2.3 *What is a minority?*

The concept *minority* is extremely important when considering LHRs. There are no legally accepted universal definitions of what a minority is, even if the issue has been discussed extensively (e.g. Andrýsek 1989; Capotorti 1979). Most definitions are fairly similar, though, and resemble the definition below (from Skutnabb-Kangas & Phillipson 1994: 107, Note 2).

> A group which is smaller in number than the rest of the population of a State, whose members have ethnic, religious or linguistic features different from those of the rest of the population, and are guided, if only implicitly, by the will to safeguard their culture, traditions, religion or language.
>
> Any group coming within the terms of this definition shall be treated as an ethnic, religious or linguistic minority.
>
> To belong to a minority shall be a matter of individual choice.

If a group claims that they are a national minority and an individual claims that she belongs to this national minority, the State may claim that such a national linguistic minority does not exist. Then there is a conflict. The State may refuse to grant the minority person and/or group rights, which it has accorded or might accord to national minorities. In many definitions of a minority, minority rights thus become conditional on the acceptance by the State of the existence of a minority in the first place. According to the definition of a minority above, minority status does *not* depend on the acceptance of the State, but is either 'objectively' ('coming within the terms of this definition') or subjectively ('a matter of individual choice') verifiable, or both. This interpretation was confirmed by the UN Human Rights Committee in 1994. Article 27 (cf. above) was reinterpreted by the Committee in a General Comment (UN Doc. CCPR/C/21/Rev.1/Add.5, 1994).

Until the reinterpretation, the Article was mostly interpreted as

- excluding (im)migrants (who were not earlier seen as minorities);
- excluding groups (even if they are citizens) which were not recognised as minorities by the State;
- only conferring some protection against discrimination (= negative rights) but not a positive right to maintain or even use one's language;
- not imposing any obligations on the States.

The UN Human Rights Committee saw the Article as

- protecting all individuals on the State's territory or under its jurisdiction (i.e. also immigrants and refugees), irrespective of whether they belong to the minorities specified in the Article or not;
- stating that the existence of a minority does not depend on a decision by the State but requires to be established by objective criteria;
- recognizing the existence of a 'right';
- imposing positive obligations on the States.

For Deaf people this means that various countries minimally have to see the Deaf as a (linguistic) minority, protected by Article 27. Likewise, the reinterpretation means that minorities, including the Deaf, are supposed to have positive language rights, not only the negative right of protection against discrimination. The states where Deaf live, i.e. all states in the world, thus do have positive obligations towards the Deaf as a linguistic minority. In addition, the Deaf can of course also be seen as a group with a 'disability', if they so choose[9], but whether they choose this or not has no consequences for their minority status: they *are* national linguistic minorities.

Numbers matter: a group has to have a certain size in order to have language-related rights. It often depends on how many individuals there are in the unit under consideration (in the country, area, region, municipality, etc.) whether individuals

---

9. See http://www.wfdeaf.org for the World Federation of the Deaf; the site also gives access to the 2006 *UN Convention on the Rights of Persons with Disabilities*.

(speakers or signers) belonging to that group have any LRs. Two of the most important European LRs documents use group size as a criterion, but do not in any way define it. The *European Charter*, and the *Framework Convention* use formulations such as "in substantial numbers" or "pupils who so wish in a number considered sufficient" or "if the number of users of a regional or minority language justifies it". It is obviously necessary to limit the size, to adjust to various contexts and also for economic reasons, but it is also possible for reluctant states to use the lack of what states claim are "sufficient" numbers as a legitimation for a lack of political will.

For proper integration of indigenous peoples and minorities in society at large, both individual and collective rights are thus necessary. One or the other type alone is not sufficient. It is not a question of either/or, but both/and.

2.3 Negative versus positive rights

Negative rights have been defined by Max van der Stoel, the former OSCE High Commissioner on National Minorities, as "the right to non-discrimination in the enjoyment of human rights" whereas positive rights have to do with "the right to the maintenance and development of identity through the freedom to practise or use those special and unique aspects of their minority life – typically culture, religion, and language" (1999: 8). Negative rights must

> ensure that minorities receive all of the other protections without regard to their ethnic, national, or religious status; they thus enjoy a number of linguistic rights that all persons in the state enjoy, such as freedom of expression and the right in criminal proceedings to be informed of the charge against them in a language they understand, if necessary through an interpreter provided free of charge. (van der Stoel 1999: 8)

Positive rights are those

> encompassing affirmative obligations beyond non-discrimination [...] include a number of rights pertinent to minorities simply by virtue of their minority status, such as the right to use their language. This pillar is necessary because a pure non-discrimination norm could have the effect of forcing people belonging to minorities to adhere to a majority language, effectively denying them their rights to identity. (van der Stoel 1999: 8–9)

An example of really good positive rights would be if the following demands were to be met:

> All language communities are entitled to have at their disposal all the human and material resources necessary to ensure that their language is present to the extent they desire at all levels of education within their territory: properly trained teachers, appropriate teaching methods, text books, finance, buildings and equipment, traditional and innovative technology.

The quote comes from Article 25 of the 1996 Draft of the *Universal Declaration of Linguistic Rights*; a document initiated by the International PEN Club and the Catalonian UNESCO Committee[10]. But such demands are completely unrealistic and cannot be considered part of LHRs. At this moment, only a few dozen language communities in the world have these kinds of positive rights.

Many political scientists seem to think that it is only (large) national minorities that should have their languages promoted by the state, i.e. have positive rights, whereas small national minorities and small indigenous peoples and, especially, immigrant minorities, cannot expect more than toleration-oriented negative rights. However, toleration and non-discrimination, understood in liberal terms of the state not interfering on behalf of a group's special characteristics (as in the case of religion where the state does not need to have a 'state religion'), does not work in relation to language. A state has to choose some language(s) as the language(s) of administration, courts, education, possibly the media, etc., and this necessarily privileges some language(s) (see Rubio-Marín 2003). The claim here is that, for proper integration, positive promotion-oriented rights are necessary. Negative toleration-oriented rights are not sufficient and may lead to forced assimilation.

2.4 Personal versus territorial rights

If an individual can use the right to all mother tongue medium services anywhere in her or his country, a *principle of personality* applies. Usually, only members of large groups with excellent protection have this kind of right. In most cases, it is restricted to the dominant language speakers in a country. Often such speakers are not even aware of how precious these rights are, and how unusual it is to possess such rights for any of the world's linguistic minorities (or even some linguistic majorities: e.g. in several African countries, the old colonial languages still have more rights than the indigenous African languages have).

If, on the other hand, LRs are connected to a specific region, a *principle of territoriality* is applied. This is the case in Switzerland. If you live, e.g. in a 'German' or 'Italian' canton in Switzerland, you have a right to services in that language only, regardless of what your mother tongue is. Speakers of French or Romansch can use their respective languages only in certain other cantons (where German-speakers do not have the right to use German, or Italian speakers Italian). In practice, this means that if Italian-speaking Swiss parents want their children to be educated through the medium of Italian, they have to move to the only canton (Tessin) where this is a right. Finland combines both these principles in its language laws (McRae 1983, 1997).

---

10. See http://www.linguistic-declaration.org/; see also Skutnabb-Kangas, 2000: 541–548 for a presentation and critical assessment of the Draft.

For proper integration, both territorial and personal rights are necessary. Territorial rights only serve those minorities well who have a traditional territory and live within its borders. Personal rights (you have a right in your personal capacity, regardless of where you live) are more important for the Deaf, the Roma, immigrant minorities and other non-territorial minorities. They are also vital for dispersed people in diaspora outside a group's territory. Oslo, the capital of Norway, has the largest Saami population in Norway but is not part of the Saami administrative area. Therefore most Saami children in Oslo do not get mother tongue medium education whereas they would in the northern parts of Norway which are part of the 'Saami territory'. In Finland, more than half of the Saami children live outside the 'Saami territory' (Aikio-Puoskari 2005; Aikio-Puoskari & Pentikäinen 2001).

2.5 Rights in 'hard law' versus 'soft law'

Strictly speaking, only traditional 'hard-law' rights, *binding rights*, coded in laws or regulations of various kinds (often called Conventions, Covenants, Charters or Treaties) and binding on the state which has ratified them, count as rights. They often include a monitoring body and a complaint procedure. In most cases, binding rights also include a *duty-holder* who has to see to it that the rights can be enjoyed by the *beneficiaries*. A state or a regional authority can, for instance, have the duty to organize education through the medium of a certain language for certain individuals or groups (beneficiaries) in a specific place. In addition to these 'rights proper', there are many 'soft law' rights, *non-binding* Recommendations, Declarations, and other intentions and wishes about LRs. This includes various Supreme Court decisions. These can in time, for instance through (more) litigation, start to function as precedents that courts need to be familiar with and that they often follow. Eventually they can be included in more binding rights. There are also other ways of moving towards more binding rules. An example is UNESCO's *Universal Declaration on Cultural Diversity*[11] from 2001, which was later developed into a *Convention on the Protection and Promotion of the Diversity of Cultural Expressions 2005*.[12]

For proper integration, both traditional 'hard law' rights and 'soft law' rights are necessary. Most hard law instruments reflect the phases directly after the Second World War, or the main decolonisation phase. They do not reflect present postcolonial challenges.

---

11. See http://www.cesmap.it/ifrao/unescode.htm.

12. http://portal.unesco.org/en/ev.php-URL_ID=31038&URL_DO=DO_TOPIC&URL_SECTION=201.html

2.6 Expressive versus instrumental rights

Two kinds of interest in language rights have been distinguished. One is "the expressive interest in language as a marker of identity," the other an "instrumental interest in language as a means of communication" (Rubio-Marín 2003: 56; these correspond fairly closely to what Skutnabb-Kangas & Phillipson (e.g. 1994) have called 'necessary' and 'enrichment-oriented' rights). The *expressive* (or non-instrumental) language rights "aim at ensuring a person's capacity to enjoy a secure linguistic environment in her/his mother tongue and a linguistic group's fair chance of cultural self-reproduction" (Rubio-Marín 2003: 56). It is only these rights that Rubio-Marín (2003: 56) calls "language rights in a strict sense"; in other words, these could be seen as the most important LHRs. The *instrumental* language rights "aim at ensuring that language is not an obstacle to the effective enjoyment of rights with a linguistic dimension, to the meaningful participation in public institutions and democratic process, and to the enjoyment of social and economic opportunities that require linguistic skills" (Rubio-Marín 2003: 56).

Both types of right are needed for integration of a society.

2.7 LHR hierarchies

Various groups can be placed in a hierarchical order relative to how good their human rights protection is. The descending order is as follows:

1. Linguistic majorities/dominant language speakers, versus minority/dominated language speakers.
2. Linguistic minorities. Within minorities, the following hierarchy often applies:
    2.1
    a. National (autochthonous) minorities
    b. Indigenous peoples
    c. Immigrant minorities
    d. Refugee minorities
    2.2 Speakers of oral languages versus users of Sign languages

Speakers of oral languages have many more rights than users of Sign languages (even if users of Sign languages have some rights as a 'disability' group). One example has already been mentioned: no state has ratified the *European Charter* for any Sign languages, only for spoken languages, even if the definitions of "regional or minority languages" for the purposes of the Charter would have allowed it. This is fatal for the Deaf, even if there might be a specific Charter on its way for them; the *European Charter* might in its Educational Article 8 grant a group at least some educational rights if the group is included by the state; inclusion in the *European Charter* would also have meant an official acceptance of the Deaf as a *linguistic* minority group.

All LHRs are extremely important for indigenous peoples and minorities. The next section concentrates on educational LHRs. These are central for the reproduction of a minority as a minority, and to avoid forced assimilation and linguistic genocide. However, these rights, including especially the unconditional right to mother tongue medium education, are still mainly absent today as binding rights.

3. LHRs in education

3.1 Are there any binding LHRs in education?

Language is one of the most important of those human characteristics on the basis of which people are not supposed to be discriminated against. Others are gender, 'race' and religion. Still, language is treated in a less generous manner in human rights instruments than are other important human characteristics (see Skutnabb-Kangas 1997, 2000 and Skutnabb-Kangas & Dunbar 2010 for an overview of these rights). Language often disappears in the educational paragraphs of binding HRs instruments.

For instance, the paragraph on education (26) in the *Universal Declaration of Human Rights* (1948) does not refer to language at all. The main thrust of the paragraph is to ensure free universal education. Even this right is violated in dozens of countries, as the former United Nations Special Rapporteur on The Right to Education, human rights lawyer Katarina Tomaševski, states in many of her reports.[13] There are also references to the "full development of the human personality" and the right of parents to "choose the kind of education that shall be given to their children," but this does not include the right to choose the language in which this education is given, as the famous Belgian Linguistic Case has shown[14] (but see Magga et al. 2004).

If language is present in binding educational clauses of human rights instruments, the clauses have more opt-outs, modifications, alternatives, etc. than other Articles of such instruments have. One example is the UN *Declaration on the Rights of Persons Belonging to National or Ethnic, Religious and Linguistic Minorities*, 1992, where the general identity-oriented clauses 1.1 and 1.2 have many obligating measures whereas the education clause (4.3) is full of opt-outs, modifications and 'claw-backs' (emphases added in the two quotes below: 'obligating' and positive measures in *italics*, 'opt-outs' in **bold**):

> 1.1. States *shall protect* the existence and the national or ethnic, cultural, religious and linguistic identity of minorities within their respective territories, and *shall encourage* conditions for the *promotion* of that identity.
> 1.2. States *shall adopt* **appropriate** legislative *and other* measures *to achieve those ends*.

---

13. See http://www.right-to-education.org/; see also http://www.katarinatomasevski.com/ for her last report, *The State of the Right to Education Worldwide. Free or Fee: 2006 Global Report*.
14. Cf. *Case Relating to Certain Aspects of the Laws on the Use of Languages in Education in Belgium*, 23 July 1968, European Court of Human Rights, Series A, Vol. 6.

> 4.3. States **should** take **appropriate** measures so that, **wherever possible**, persons belonging to minorities have **adequate** opportunities to learn their mother tongue **or** to have instruction in their mother tongue.

The *Framework Convention* and the *European Charter* also have many of these modifications, alternatives, and opt-outs. The Framework Convention's education Article reads as follows (emphases added):

> In areas inhabited by persons belonging to national minorities traditionally or in substantial numbers, **if there is sufficient demand**, the parties shall **endeavour** to ensure, **as far as possible** and **within the framework of their education systems**, that persons belonging to those minorities have **adequate** opportunities for being taught in the minority language **or** for receiving instruction in this language.

Even when compromises are needed when writing binding formulations that are sensitive to local conditions, it is clear that the 'claw-backs' in the *European Charter* and the *Framework Convention* permit reluctant states to meet the requirements in a minimalist way. They can legitimate this by claiming that a provision was not "possible" or "appropriate," or that numbers were not "sufficient" or did not "justify" a provision, or that it "allowed" the minority to organize teaching of their language as a subject, at their own cost. The Articles covering medium of education are so heavily qualified that the minority is completely at the mercy of the state. Other regions of the world have even fewer general HRs instruments than Europe pertaining specifically to minority languages or speakers of minority languages, even if a few specific named languages may have extensive rights. A very important recent instrument is the *United Nations Declaration on the Rights of Indigenous Peoples*, especially its Articles 13 and 14, but even these contain modifications and clawbacks.[15]

Some soft law documents make recommendations which are much more in line with research recommendations. The *Hague Recommendations Regarding the Education Rights of National Minorities*[16] (1996) recommend mother tongue medium education for minorities at all levels, also in secondary education, with obligatory teaching of an official language as a second language, preferably taught by bilingual teachers (Articles 11–13). The Explanatory Note (p. 5) has the following to say about submersion education:

> [S]ubmersion-type approaches whereby the curriculum is taught exclusively through the medium of the State language and minority children are entirely integrated into classes with children of the majority are not in line with international standards.

---

15. UNDRIP, 61/295, 2007, http://www.un.org/esa/socdev/unpfii/en/drip.html

16. From the OSCE's High Commissioner on National Minorities; OSCE stands for 'Organisation for Security and Cooperation in Europe' and it has 55 member states. See http://www.osce.org/hcnm/.

This means that most indigenous and minority education – which is submersion – is not in line with international human rights standards. If we combine the Hague Recommendations with the UN Human Rights Committee's General Comment on Article 27 (see 2.2.3 above), states become firm duty-holders, and the Hague rights above should also apply to immigrant minorities.

The human rights system should protect people in the globalization process, rather than giving the corporate market forces free range. Human rights, especially economic and social rights, are, according to Tomaševski (1996: 104), supposed to act as *correctives to the free market*. "The purpose of international human rights law is [...] to overrule the law of supply and demand and remove price tags from people and from necessities for their survival" (Tomaševski 1996: 104). These necessities for survival thus include not only basic food and housing (which would come under economic and social rights), but also basics for the sustenance of a dignified life, including basic civil, political *and cultural* rights. It should, therefore, be in accordance with the spirit of human rights to grant people full linguistic human rights.

Without binding educational linguistic human rights, most minorities have to accept subtractive education through the medium of a dominant/majority language. The transmission of languages from the parent generation to children is *the* most vital factor for the maintenance of languages. But when more and more children get access to formal education, much of the more formal language learning that earlier took place in the community will take place in schools. If an alien language is used in schools, i.e. if children do not have the right to learn and use their language in schools as the main medium of education, the language is not going to survive (cf. Milloy 1999). Children educated through the medium of an alien language are not likely to pass their own language on to their children and grandchildren (Janulf 1998). Assimilationist, subtractive education of indigenous and minority children can therefore be considered genocidal. However, linguistic genocide is still a very controversial issue.

3.2 Linguistic genocide

When people hear the term 'genocide' about languages and education, they often claim that the term is too strong – it should only be used of physical killing. There have been many attempts to censor discussions about linguistic genocide, to accuse researchers that use it of being emotional and not scientific, and to blame the messenger rather than examining the message. Most indigenous (and minority) education does in fact fulfil the criteria set out in The UN *International Convention on the Prevention and Punishment of the Crime of Genocide*[17] ('the Genocide Convention'). The Convention

---

17. E793, 1948; 78 U.N.T.S. 277, entered into force Jan. 12, 1951; for the full text, see http://www1.umn.edu/humanrts/instree/x1cppcg.htm.

has five definitions of genocide. Three of them are about physical or biological killing, but the remaining two fit most of today's (and earlier) indigenous and minority education (emphasis added):

> Article II(e): "forcibly transferring children of the group to another group," and
> Article II(b): "causing serious bodily *or mental* harm to members of the group."

Educational systems and mass media are (the most) important direct agents in linguistic (and cultural) genocide. Behind them are the world's economic, techno-military, social and political systems. Skutnabb-Kangas and Dunbar (2010) is a thorough educational, sociological and legal treatment of linguistic genocide in education. A few examples from various studies follow; all of them show either the forcible transfer of children from a linguistic group to another linguistic group, or serious mental harm caused to children through submersion education.

Pirjo Janulf (1998) showed in a longitudinal study that of those Finnish immigrant minority members in Sweden who had had Swedish-medium education, not one spoke any Finnish to their own children. Even if they themselves might not have forgotten their Finnish completely, their children were certainly forcibly transferred into the majority group linguistically.

Edward Williams's (1998) study from Zambia and Malawi, with 1,500 students in grades 1–7 showed that large numbers of Zambian pupils (who had all their education in English) "have very weak or zero reading competence in two languages" (Williams 1998: 62). The Malawi children (taught in local languages during the first 4 years, with English as a subject) had slightly better test results in the English language than the Zambian students. Williams's conclusion is: "there is a clear risk that the policy of using English as a vehicular language may contribute to stunting, rather than promoting, academic and cognitive growth" (Williams 1998: 63–64). This fits the UN genocide definition of "causing serious mental harm".

Anne Lowell and Brian Devlin's (1999) article describing the "Miscommunication between Aboriginal Students and their Non-Aboriginal Teachers in a Bilingual School," clearly demonstrated that "even by late primary school, children often did not comprehend classroom instructions in English" (Lowell & Devlin 1999: 137). Communication breakdowns occurred frequently between children and their non-Aboriginal teachers (1999: 138), with the result that "the extent of miscommunication severely inhibited the children's education when English was the language of instruction and interaction" (1999: 137). Their conclusions and recommendations include the following: "the use of a language of instruction in which the children do not have sufficient competence is the greatest barrier to successful classroom learning for Aboriginal Children" (1999: 156).

Katherine Zozula and Simon Ford's (1985) report "Keewatin Perspective on Bilingual Education" analyses Canadian Inuit "students who are neither fluent nor literate in either language" and presents statistics showing that the students "end up at only Grade 4 level of achievement after 9 years of [English-medium] schooling."[18] The Canadian Royal Commission on Aboriginal Peoples Report (1996) notes that "submersion strategies which neither respect the child's first language nor help them gain fluency in the second language may result in impaired fluency in both languages". The Canadian Nunavut Language Policy Conference in March 1998 stated: "in some individuals, neither language is firmly anchored". Mick Mallon and Alexina Kublu (1998) claim that "a significant number of young people are not fully fluent in their languages", and many students "remain apathetic, often with minimal skills in both languages". A Canadian report, *Kitikmeot struggles to prevent the death of Inuktitut* (1998) shows that "teenagers cannot converse fluently with their grandparents".

Many studies on Deaf students (e.g. Branson & Miller 2002; Jokinen 2000; Ladd 2003; Lane 1992) show that assimilationist submersion education where Deaf students are taught orally only and Sign languages have no place in the curriculum, often causes mental harm, including serious prevention or delay of cognitive growth potential.

In sum, subtractive teaching prevents students from attaining profound literacy and from gaining the knowledge and skills that would correspond to their innate capacities and would be needed for socio-economic mobility and democratic participation. It wastes resources and perpetuates poverty. According to Nobel Prize laureate Amartya Sen (e.g. Sen 1985), poverty is not only about economic conditions and growth; expansion of human capabilities is a more basic locus of poverty and more basic objective of development. Dominant-language medium education for indigenous children often curtails the development of the children's capabilities (Misra & Mohanty 2000a, 2000b; Mohanty 2000). Thus it perpetuates poverty, it may cause serious mental harm, and it transfers children to another linguistic group through enforced language shift. Indigenous and minority students (and their parents and communities) need LHRs as one of the necessary (but not sufficient) measures to stop linguistic genocide.

In studying causes for the disappearance of languages, two explanatory paradigms can be found: language death, and language murder or linguistic genocide paradigms. The first one assumes that languages just die naturally, like everything in nature – they arise, blossom, wither and disappear. This is the '(natural) death' paradigm. The other paradigm asserts that languages do *not* just disappear naturally; languages do *not* 'commit suicide'. In most cases, speakers do *not* leave their languages voluntarily, for instrumental reasons, and for their own good. Rather, languages are 'murdered'. Most disappearing languages are victims of linguistic genocide. This latter paradigm is taken to be the likely one in this entry on Language rights. One of the differences

---

18. This and the following Canadian studies are quoted in Martin (2000a, 2000b; no page-references given).

between the two positions from an analytical point of view is that nothing can be done about languages disappearing if one accepts that the disappearance is natural and inevitable.[19] In the 'death' paradigm, there is no agent causing the disappearance of languages. The only ones that can be blamed are the speakers themselves, and they are claimed to have profited from language shift. In the genocide paradigm one can analyse agency, the forces behind the disappearance of languages, and one may be able to do something about it.

Obviously the *structural and ideological* direct and indirect agents behind the killing of languages are the same social, economic and political techno-military forces that promote corporate globalization. But some of the most important *direct* agents confronted by most people are the educational systems and the media. These are both indirectly and directly homogenizing societies linguistically and culturally; and ideologically: they are, through their consent-manufacturing capacities (Herman & Chomsky 1988), making people accept the homogenizing processes as somehow necessary and even natural (see McMurtry's 2002 sophisticated analysis of this; see also McMurtry 1999). The United Nation's 2004 Human Development Report[20] links cultural liberty to language rights and human development and argues that there is

> no more powerful means of 'encouraging' individuals to assimilate to a dominant culture than having the economic, social and political returns stacked against their mother tongue. Such assimilation is not freely chosen if the choice is between one's mother tongue and one's future.

4. To conclude

Educational LHRs include both the right to have the basic education mainly through the medium of the mother tongue, *and* the right to learn the official/dominant language well. These two are not contradictory; quite the opposite. In additive learning situations, high levels of majority language skills are added to high levels of mother tongue skills. Arlene Stairs's (1994) study shows that "in schools which support initial learning of Inuttitut, and whose Grade 3 and Grade 4 pupils are strong writers in Inuttitut, the results in written English are also the highest". The Alaska Yu'piq teacher Nancy Sharp (1994) offers this comparison: when Yu'piq children are taught through the medium of English, they are treated by 'White' teachers as handicapped, and they do not achieve;

---

19. This reasoning represents a misunderstood and misguided interpretation of the Darwinian "survival of the fittest" (see Harmon 2002 for a refutation).

20. Cf. http://hdr.undp.org/reports/.

when they are taught through the medium of Yu'piq, they are "excellent writers, smart happy students". All serious research shows that mother-tongue-based bilingual education achieves the best results in the education of minorities. Thomas & Collier (2002: 7), for instance, in their study with some 210,000 students state: "the strongest predictor of L2 student achievement is the amount of formal L1 schooling. The more L1 grade-level schooling, the higher L2 achievement." Many edited books (e.g. Skutnabb-Kangas 1995; Garcia et al. 2006; Mohanty et al. 2009; Heugh & Skutnabb-Kangas 2010) show in detail how additive teaching that leads towards high levels of multilingualism and respects educational and other LHRs can be organized.

Some politicians have started acknowledging that full LHRs in education, including mother tongue medium education for indigenous and minority children, can lead to profound literacy, creativity, high levels of multilingualism for the student, and a maintenance of the languages. But the counterargument usually is that maintenance of all or most of the world's languages cannot be possible, or economically viable. A good example here is Papua New Guinea, a fairly small country, with a population of around 6 million. It has the highest number of languages in the world: over 850. According to David Klaus (2003) from the World Bank, as of 2002, 470 languages were used as the media of education in preschool and the first two grades. Some of the results are as follows: Children become literate more quickly and easily. They learn English more quickly and easily than their siblings did under the old English-medium system. Children, including girls, stay in school. Grade 6 exams in the 3 provinces that started mother tongue medium teaching in 1993 were much higher than in provinces which still teach through the medium of English from Day One.

In many parts of the world indigenous peoples are now demanding and starting to get mother tongue medium education.[21] That is, it seems perfectly possible to organize education so that it does not participate in committing linguistic genocide.

There is a growing scholarly literature on linguistic human rights, with a convergence between the concerns of lawyers (e.g. de Varennes 1996), sociolinguists (Skutnabb-Kangas & Phillipson 1994; Hamel 1997), media researchers (Hamelink 1998), economists (Grin & Vaillancourt 2000), political scientists (McRae 1997; MacMillan 1998), educational sociologists (May 1999), anthropologists (Maffi et al. 1999) and others; Kontra et al. (1999) is an example of multidisciplinary efforts. The entire field is explored in depth, and related to overall language policy and to language ecology in Skutnabb-Kangas (2000) and Phillipson (2000, 2009).

The final question then is: To what extent has research in applied linguistics and in pragmatics contributed to possible solutions, to language planning that supports

---

21. There are promising large-scale projects in, for instance, Orissa, India (see Mohanty et al. 2009; Heugh & Skutnabb-Kangas 2010, for articles on them; see also http://www.nmrc-jnu.org/).

the maintenance of linguistic diversity and works for LHRs as a necessary prerequisite for not only preventing linguistic genocide but also for supporting the diversity of knowledges, ideas, identities and ways of conceptualising the world that are encoded in the various languages and are needed for solving today's catastrophic problems of our own making. Raising consciousness is a necessary but not sufficient start – action is urgently needed.

References

Aikio-Puoskari, U. (2005). *The Education of the Sámi in the Comprehensive Schooling of Three Nordic Countries: Norway, Finland and Sweden*. The Resource Centre for the Rights of Indigenous Peoples (http://www.galdu.org).

Aikio-Puoskari, U. & M. Pentikäinen (2001). *The language rights of the indigenous Saami in Finland under domestic and international law*. Juridica Lapponica 26. University of Lapland.

Andrýsek, O. (1989). *Report on the Definition of Minorities*. SIM Special No 8. Netherlands Institute of Human Rights, Studie- en Informatiecentrum Mensenrechten (SIM).

Branson, J. & D. Miller (2002). *Damned for Their Difference. The Cultural Construction of Deaf People as Disabled*. Gallaudet University Press.

Capotorti, F. (1979). *Study of the Rights of Persons Belonging to Ethnic, Religious and Linguistic Minorities*. United Nations.

García, O., T. Skutnabb-Kangas & M. Torres-Guzmán (eds.) (2006). *Imagining Multilingual Schools. Languages in Education and Glocalization*. Multilingual Matters.

Grin, F. & F. Vaillancourt (2000). On the financing of language policies and distributive justice. In R. Phillipson (ed.) *Rights to Language. Equity, Power, and Education*: 102–110. Lawrence Erlbaum.

Hamel, R.E. (ed.) (1997). Linguistic human rights from a sociolinguistic perspective. *International Journal of the Sociology of Language* 127.

Hamelink, C.J. (ed.) (1998). Special Issue on Human Rights. *Gazette. The International Journal for Communication Studies* 60(1).

Harmon, D. (2002). *In Light of Our Differences: How Diversity in Nature and Culture Makes Us Human*. The Smithsonian Institute Press.

Herman, E.S. & N. Chomsky (1988). *Manufacturing Consent: the Political Economy of the Mass Media*. Pantheon.

Heugh, K. & T. Skutnabb-Kangas (eds.) (2010). *Multilingual education works: from the Periphery to the Centre*. Orient BlackSwan.

Janulf, P. (1998). *Kommer finskan i Sverige att fortleva? En studie av språkkunskaper och språkanvändning hos andragenerationens sverigefinnar i Botkyrka och hos finlandssvenskar i Åbo*. ['Will Finnish survive in Sweden? A study of language skills and language use among second generation Sweden Finns in Botkyrka, Sweden, and Finland Swedes in Åbo, Finland']. Almqvist & Wiksell.

Jokinen, M. (2000). The linguistic human rights of Sign language users. In R. Phillipson (ed.) *Rights to Language. Equity, Power and Education*. 203–213. Lawrence Erlbaum.

Kemal, M. (Atatürk) (1931). Quoted in *Cumhuriyet*, February 14, 1931. In S. Meiselas (1997) *Kurdistan. In the Shadow of History*, 145. Random House.

Klaus, D. (2003). The use of indigenous languages in early basic education in Papua New Guinea: A model for elsewhere? *Language and Education* 17(2): 105–111.
Kontra, M., R. Phillipson, T. Skutnabb-Kangas & T. Várady (eds.) (1999). *Language: A Right and a Resource. Approaches to Linguistic Human Rights*. Central European University Press.
Ladd, P. (2003). *Understanding Deaf Culture. In Search of Deafhood*. Multilingual Matters.
Lane, H. (1992). *The Mask of Benevolence: Disabling the Deaf Community*. Alfred Knopf.
Lowell, A. & B. Devlin (1999). Miscommunication between Aboriginal students and their non-Aboriginal teachers in a bilingual school. In S. May (ed.) *Indigenous Community-based Education*. 137–159. Multilingual Matters.
MacMillan, C.M. (1998). *The practice of language rights in Canada*. Toronto University Press.
Maffi, L., T. Skutnabb-Kangas & J. Andrianarivo (1999). Language diversity. In D. Posey (ed.) *Cultural and Spiritual Values of Biodiversity. A Complementary Contribution to the Global Biodiversity Assessment*. 19–57. Intermediate Technology Publications, for and on behalf of the/United Nations Environmental Programme.
Maffi, L. (ed.) (2001). *On Biocultural Diversity. Linking Language, Knowledge and the Environment*. The Smithsonian Institute Press.
Magga, O.H., I. Nicolaisen, M. Trask, R. Dunbar & T. Skutnabb-Kangas (2004). *Indigenous Children's Education and Indigenous Languages. Expert paper written for the United Nations Permanent Forum on Indigenous Issues*. United Nations.
Martin, I. (2000a). Aajjiqatigiingniq. Language of instruction research paper. A report to the government of Nunavut. Unpublished manuscript. Department of Education, Iqaluit, Nunavut, Canada.
────── (2000b). Sources and issues: A backgrounder to the discussion paper on language of instruction in Nunavut schools. Unpublished manuscript. Department of Education, Iqaluit, Nunavut, Canada.
May, S. (2001). *Language and minority rights: ethnicity, nationalism, and the politics of language*. Longman.
────── (ed.) (1999). *Indigenous community-based education*. Multilingual Matters.
McMurtry, J. (1999). *The Cancer Stage of Capitalism*. Pluto Press.
────── (2002). *Value Wars. The Global Market Versus the Life Economy*. Pluto Press.
McRae, K.D. (1983). *Conflict and compromise in multilingual societies, Switzerland*. Wilfrid Laurier University Press.
────── (1997). *Conflict and compromise in multilingual societies, Finland*. Wilfrid Laurier University Press.
Milloy, J.S. (1999). *A National Crime. The Canadian Government and the Residential School System, 1879 to 1986*. The University of Manitoba Press.
Misra, G. & A.K. Mohanty (2000a). Consequences of Poverty and Disadvantage: A Review of Indian Studies. In A.K. Mohanty & G. Misra (eds.) *Psychology of Poverty and Disadvantage*. 121–148. Concept Publishing.
────── (2000b). Poverty and Disadvantage: Issues in Retrospect. In A.K. Mohanty & G. Misra (eds.) *Psychology of Poverty and Disadvantage*. 261–284. Concept Publishing.
Mohanty, A.K. (2000). Perpetuating Inequality: The Disadvantage of language, Minority Mother Tongues and Related Issues. In A.K. Mohanty & G. Misra (eds.) *Psychology of Poverty and Disadvantage*. 104–117. Concept Publishing.
Mohanty, A.K., M. Panda, R. Phillipson & T. Skutnabb-Kangas (eds.) (2009). *Multilingual Education for Social Justice: Globalising the Local*. Orient BlackSwan. (http://www.multilingual-matters.com/display.asp?isb=9781847691897)

Phillipson, R. (2009). *Linguistic imperialism continued*. Routledge/Taylor & Francis.
Phillipson, R. (ed.) (2000). *Rights to Language. Equity, Power and Education*. Lawrence Erlbaum.
Rubio-Marín, R. (2003). Language rights: Exploring the competing rationales. In W. Kymlicka & A. Patten (eds.) *Language Rights and Political Theory*. 52–79. Oxford University Press.
Sen, A. (1985). *Commodities and Capabilities*. North Holland.
Skutnabb-Kangas, T. (1997). Human rights and language policy in education. In R. Wodak & D. Corson (eds.) *The Encyclopedia of Language and Education*. vol. *Language Policy and Political Issues in Education*. 55–65. Kluwer.
——— (2000). *Linguistic Genocide in Education – or Worldwide Diversity and Human Rights?* Lawrence Erlbaum Associates.
——— (2002). Irelands, Scotland, education and linguistic human rights: some international comparisons. In J.M. Kirk & D.P. Ó Baoill (eds.) *Language Planning and Education: Linguistic Issues in Northern Ireland, the Republic of Ireland, and Scotland*. 221–266. Belfast Studies in Language, Culture and Politics 6. Cló Ollscoil na Banríona.
——— (ed.) (1995). *Multilingualism for All*. Swets & Zeitlinger.
Skutnabb-Kangas, T. & R. Dunbar (2010). *Indigenous Children's Education as Linguistic Genocide and a Crime Against Humanity? A Global View*. Guovdageaidnu/ Kautokeino: Gáldu, Resource Centre for the Rights of Indigenous Peoples. www.galdu.org.
Skutnabb-Kangas, T. & R. Phillipson (1994). Linguistic human rights, past and present. In T. Skutnabb-Kangas & R. Phillipson (eds.) *Linguistic human rights. Overcoming Linguistic Discrimination*. 71–110. Mouton de Gruyter.
Skutnabb-Kangas, T. & D. Fernandes (2008). Kurds in Turkey and in (Iraqi) Kurdistan: A comparison of Kurdish educational language policy in two situations of occupation. *Genocide Studies and Prevention* 3(1): 43–73.
Stoel, M. van der (1999). *Report on the Linguistic Rights of Persons Belonging to National Minorities in the OSCE Area. + Annex. Replies from OSCE participating states*. OSCE High Commissioner on National Minorities.
Thomas, W.P. & V.P. Collier (2002). *A National Study of School Effectiveness for Language Minority Students' Long Term Academic Achievement*. George Mason University, Center for Research on Education, Diversity & Excellence (CREDE). (http://www.crede.ucsc.edu/research/llaa/1.1_final.html.)
Thornberry, P. (1997). Minority Rights. In Academy of European Law (ed.) *Collected Courses of the Academy of European Law*. vol. VI, book 2: 307–390. Kluwer Law International.
Thornberry, P. & D. Gibbons (1997). Education and Minority Rights: A Short Survey of International Standards. *International Journal on Minority and Group Rights* 4(2): 115–152.
Tomaševski, K. (1996). International prospects for the future of the welfare state. *Reconceptualizing the Welfare State*. 100–117. The Danish Centre for Human Rights.
Varennes, F. de (1996). *Language, Minorities and Human Rights*. Martinus Nijhoff.
Williams, E. (1998). *Investigating Bilingual Literacy: Evidence from Malawi and Zambia*, Education Research No. 24. Department For International Development.

Marxist linguistics

Niels Helsloot[†]

1. Introduction

Philosophically, Marxism is a branch of Hegelianism. According to the 'dialectics' of Hegel, history would develop towards its point of self-fulfillment in a process in which contradictory principles ('thesis' and 'antithesis') merge into a synthesis – which again evokes its own contradiction. Marxism shares the optimism about historical progress inherent in this view. While Hegel, however, saw this development – idealistically – as a coming to itself of the Spirit (Geist), Marx considered the process – materialistically – as taking place in the everyday social circumstances of people, especially in the struggle that settles their economic relationships. Whereas the dynamic principle that Hegelianism introduced in its view of history remained rather abstract, Marxism relates this principle to concrete historical relationships between people (in Marx's times, to class relationships). Therefore, Marxism is in a position to criticize idealism as being too academic; in case of social oppression and exploitation, it is not mental change, but material change which is called for. The urge to emancipate the oppressed leads to a political drive opposite to that of Hegelianism, which is expressed in the adage of historical materialism: the economic base determines the ideological superstructures (and not the other way around). The direction of this determinism has been the moving force of Marxist sciences, but the very adoption of determinism proved to be its central weakness as well. This is especially clear in Marxist attempts to develop a theory of language.

In early Marxism, language is usually related to the ideological superstructure (cf. Marx & Engels 1974, a selection of linguistically relevant passages from the *Marx/Engels-Werke*; and e.g. Erckenbrecht 1973; Houdebine 1977; Höppe 1982). It is a conceptual device which reflects material circumstances and needs (the economic base). Categorizations, concepts and names are considered as expressions of specific social relationships. Thus, language is not an object of study in its own right. Generally, if language use is being studied at all, it is interpreted along the lines of social theory (i.e. as being biased by class interests) without any linguistic reservations about the necessity of this theory. This approach leads to observations of the way many concepts are ideologically charged. For instance, the German terms *Arbeitgeber* (employer, lit. 'labour-giver') and *Arbeitnehmer* (employee, lit. 'labour-taker') contain a reversal of the real give-and-take relationship, in which the employee *gives* his labour, and the employer *takes* it.

Such criticism of concepts (however illuminating it may be) can be practised with different results from any point of view. If it is to be more than an arbitrary illustration of one's own view of 'the real relationships', it is to be demonstrated that the underlying social theory is more 'scientifically valid' than others. Marxism has indeed claimed the scientificity of its historical materialist approach; yet, an assumption of outstanding scientific truth is contradictory to the 'relationalism' implied by its historicism and social determinism. If values, interpretations, categorizations, truths, etc. are stakes of social struggle, it is more consistent to study language as being a material force itself. In that case, however, it is not possible to fix a direction of social development that is historically necessary in isolation of concrete developments in the domain of language (with the risk of a relapse into idealism).

2. Marr vs. Stalin

In the thirties, in the Soviet Union, the effort to combine the conception of language as a superstructure with an idea of linguistic struggle led to an official Marxist linguistics in the work of Nikolaj Marr (1864–1934). Marr (1974) questions the presupposition of an Indo-European state of harmony in comparative linguistics, which just takes notice of dominant languages. Instead of one proto-language having decayed into a multitude of national languages, Marr starts from a multitude of conflicting dialects tending to unite in history. In his view, original tribal and class differences are still present in contemporary national languages (Thomas 1957; Marcellesi & Gardin 1974: 33–87; Marcellesi 1977).

Marrism was dominant in Marxist linguistics until, in a notorious intervention in linguistics, Stalin (1951) rejected it by de-historicizing and de-socializing language. Language is no superstructure, since it does not change with every economic change; it is a means of communication serving each member of a people equally well. Thus, 'the language' is declared politically neutral, like science. Stalin's attempt to unite nationalities under one Russian language required that minority languages ('dialects') were no longer seen as language. Such a unitary language policy allows for one sort of linguistics, the linguistics of dominant languages. As nearly all linguistics has been exactly that, from the fifties, Stalinism gave rise to formalizing and rationalizing forms of linguistics without any outspoken political involvement characterizing it as being Marxist.

Meanwhile, in Western 'capitalist' countries, attempts to develop Marxist forms of linguistics had to pay attention to the material effects of phenomena that, on the one hand, used to be disregarded as merely 'superstructural' derivatives of the economic base and, on the other hand, were banished from the domain of social struggle altogether. As the controversy between Stalin and Marr indicates, denying language (and ideology) a material effectivity of its own tends to lead to a fixation and hypostatization of either fundamental linguistic heterogeneity or fundamental linguistic unity. When in the sixties and seventies Stalin's hold over Marxist linguistics fades, this tension comes to light.

3. Recent trends

In attempts to develop a sociolinguistics, on the one hand, one stresses the unevennesses between the social opportunities offered by different linguistic codes (i.e. sociolects within 'one language': Bernstein 1971; cf. Atkinson 1985); on the other hand, one takes a more egalitarian stance (in line with Labov 1970; cf. Dittmar 1973) based on Chomsky's cognitivistic assumption of a universally human linguistic competence. Starting from this same assumption, Habermas (1981) puts the individualistic theories of pragmaticists like Austin, Searle and Grice in a social perspective motivated by a – utopian and humanistic – ideal of equal communication. This ideal is diametrically opposed to 'poststructuralist' theories that treat the communicative human subject itself as a discursive, linguistically and socially contradictory outcome of social and historical struggle (esp. Althusser 1971). Instead of orienting themselves towards a utopian community, such theories directly deal with the differences and power relationships considered constitutive of any society (cf. Foucault 1970; Derrida 1990).

Until now, this tension between rationalism and 'relationalism' has not been solved. The dominance of cognitivist egalitarianism, which since the fifties makes itself felt in both 'communist' and 'capitalist' countries, and the arrogant declaration of an end of ideology after the decline of the Soviet Union impede a re-evaluation of this tension. It may be part of a social and historical struggle to find out whether Marxism will ever be able to regain any respectability in linguistics. If it is to exist, a Marxist linguistics is in need of (1) a non-deterministic reconceptualization of the interplay between base and superstructure, (2) a view of language and ideology as material, non-neutral stakes of differences and struggle, and (3) a historical and social theory of science, in which the scientist is nothing less cultural than the subject of research.

It is impossible here to give an overview doing justice to the various contributions that have been made to the development of a Marxist linguistics (e.g. Schaff 1962; Baudrillard 1972; Coward & Ellis 1977; Bourdieu 1982; Mey 1985; Fairclough 1989). Instead, the delicate position of Marxist linguistics between one-sided forms of 'apolitical' egalitarian rationalism and one-sided forms of 'idealistic' isolation of differential ideological-linguistic superstructures will be illustrated by examining three Marxist theorists of language which came into vogue in the seventies (though two of them are much older): Antonio Gramsci (1891–1937), Valentin Vološinov (1895–1936), and Michel Pêcheux (1938–1983). Because of their delayed discovery in a period of dominant rationalism and declining Marxism, their importance for a well-balanced linguistics is largely underestimated. Together they give a positive impression of the possibility of breaking away from the 'Stalinist' presupposition of linguistic unity without relapsing into a conception of essential differences à la Marr.

4. Gramsci

The Italian linguist and politician Gramsci is particularly concerned with the effects of language as a source of social coherence. Because in everyday life the use of language from different sections of the population coexists and intermingles in incoherent ways, he sees an organizing task for intellectuals, which especially bears on language (Lo Piparo 1979; Bochmann 1988; Helsloot 1989). In the theatrical productions of Pirandello, Gramsci (1985: 2, 136–146) finds one way to change popular taste through language. Gramsci (1985: 268) is interested in the amount of applause Pirandello manages to get, as a criterion for his 'getting in tune with the public'. Although Pirandello's portrayal of man is too individualistic in Gramsci's eyes, it is of critical cultural and moral importance; it is linked up with lived historical-cultural experiences. Confused though it is, his subjectivism forms part of popular culture. Thus, his work contributes to a change – a deprovincialization and modernization – of the audience's taste. With respect to linguistic production, both theatrical and otherwise, Gramsci is particularly concerned with two things, (1) whether it contributes to the development of the people, as an organic part of a coherent cultural and social movement, and (2) supposing that its content does contribute, whether it would fit the everyday thinking of the people. His criticism of Pirandello illustrates how his conception of language may lead to a political stand that does not wave historical dividedness (individualism) aside too easily, but nevertheless remains directed towards the practical augmentation of social coherence. Nothing automatically has the same meaning for everyone; all of our knowledge is connected to language, and is therefore 'subjective'. But in spite of this conclusion, knowledge is not relative. A historical struggle is taking place in which the attainment of objectivity – i.e. of agreement in subjective judgments – is continuously at stake (Gramsci 1971: 440–448). According to Gramsci, intellectuals should contribute by aiming at mass adherence.

5. Vološinov

Vološinov is a member of the Leningrad circle of Bakhtin, with whom he is often identified (cf. Todorov 1984; Clark & Holquist 1984; Morson & Emerson 1990). Like Gramsci, he is convinced of the social character of language. Yet, he counterbalances Gramsci in that, in his eyes, the ideal of objectivity is no more than a description of the way in which power is actually established. The knowledge and values to which social groups in power adhere are claimed to be objective because this allows the members of these groups to suggest an eternal truth that underpins and legitimizes their position of power. Linguists, however, should recognize what lies hidden behind such objective truths. As truths are only apparently formulated with one voice, such a recognition literally means identifying different voices in apparent monologues. Every linguistic utterance consists of reformulations of what has been said by others, and thus consists of various kinds of dialogues. This fusion of voices can clearly be demonstrated by analyses of their manifestations by syntactic means like direct discourse ('direct speech'), indirect discourse, and free indirect discourse (*erlebte Rede*) (1986: 107–159). Vološinov relates the use of such constructions to historical social circumstances. He describes a development from authoritarian towards rationalist forms of dogmatism as having taken place from the Middle Ages until the 17th and 18th century. At these times, when the possibility of difference of opinion would hardly have been recognized, direct discourse prevailed. At the end of the 18th and the beginning of the 19th century, realist and critical forms of individualism arose. In this process, a shift occured towards indirect discourse, which cleared the way for the author's replication and comment. According to Vološinov, this transition from dogmatism towards individualism and relativism started with the occurrence of free indirect discourse in La Fontaine. In his fables, this hybrid of direct and indirect discourse provided a new way to include the words of others. The change involved a shift in speakers' experience of autonomy and individuality: the linguistic construction of personhood was at stake. From then on, voices flow together, as it were. Vološinov argues that this infects current language and ideology with a disturbing lack of balance and certainty. Language is no longer a monument or a document of a responsible social position, but expresses contingent subjective qualities, which do no more than tie together words of others. Thus, it implies an acceptance of the kind of subjectivism Gramsci rejects in Pirandello. However, whereas Gramsci regards individualization as a hindrance that should be overcome in order to enable solidarity, Vološinov considers the differences between individuals less problematic; the multitude of social perspectives turns every fixation of meaning or identity into something transient. One is never won over for ever.

6. Pêcheux

In the seventies, the 'poststructuralist' linguist Pêcheux offered a radical continuation of the way in which both Gramsci and Vološinov – in the 1920s and 1930s – had turned down overevaluations of the subjective. In opposition to them, however, he initially considers the domain of linguistics as being more or less autonomous. He attempts to formulate a method of discourse analysis that is regulated 'automatically', and therefore doesn't need subjective intervention (cf. Hak & Helsloot 1994). This forces him to try to come to terms with the ideological presuppositions of the linguistic theories needed to get such an undertaking off the ground (cf. Maldidier 1990; Pêcheux 1982). Gradually, it becomes clear that the automatic nature of his analysis does not allow for an escape from ideology and language any more than other approaches, be they apparently objective (like rationalism) or explicitly subjective. Pêcheux is particularly concerned with the spontaneous ideology of intellectuals, and less with the conditions under which intellectual products get spread among the people, which was important for Gramsci. Like Vološinov, he stresses the importance of dividedness; but whereas Vološinov regards polyphony as a feature of language itself, Pêcheux tends to agree with Gramsci in seeing both the aim at unity and the aim at polyphony as political strategies. Both the insertion of a voice in what is said by others and the disconnection of different voices affect social relationships. Pêcheux increasingly values the possibility of disconnecting sentences and making other voices sound through as a way to force open the dominant ideology instead of supporting it. The acceptance of difference and contradiction, which he describes and advocates, comes close to the polyphony Vološinov presented as real. According to Pêcheux, however, texts do not just show disconnection but also insertion; in an historical perspective, both tendencies emerge. He argues that, being a scientist, one should take part in history by bringing about 'events'. In this respect, he comes close to Gramsci's populism, albeit that 'the people' is almost restricted to the university population, and that his dreams are modest: 'a little theoretical event, and not a university happening'. The practical lack of belief in political control of broad social movements – the incapacity to carry on a 'war of position' in theory with clear perspectives in the longer run – has to do with a persistent undecidability between two kinds of writing distinguished by Pêcheux, and with the split subject position resulting from this undecidability: He neither argues against a Chomskyan closure of linguistic rationality once and for all, nor does he opt for Derrida's deconstructivist unfixity once and for all. He opposes a tendency towards arbitrary decision; like Vološinov, he assumes that dividedness can be found already within unity, and that it is more fruitful, therefore, to pick up the alien voices within apparent monologue (or the ungrammaticality within unified grammar).

7. Marxist linguistics today

Gramsci accepts neither the unity of language nor linguistic dividedness as given. Both possibilities are results that are to be attained in a social process. This gives him reason to aim at social unity in an absolutely straight line. Although this implies a sympathy (ahead of his time) to a 'Stalinist' aim at unity, he starts from the 'Marrist' assumption that what is given in language are differences and contradictions. Vološinov attaches more value to this dividedness. This allows for replacing the idea of one class struggle for a multitude of divergent social struggles (emancipating people on the basis of differences in class, nationality, race, sexuality, age, life style, etc.). Like Marr's protolinguistic class differences, this polyphony is regarded as a given characteristic of language. It is true that language is ideological by definition, and that the construction of unity belongs to its formal possibilities as well; but, to Vološinov, this is reason enough to aim at recognition of the actual dividedness in an absolutely straight line. Just like Gramsci (and in opposition to Marr), Pêcheux does not accept unity or dividedness as given; and, just like Vološinov (and in opposition to Stalin), he tries to show the diversity within totalizing forms of unity. The hope in his earlier work for an escape from ideology by 'objective' formalization and mechanization of the linguistic procedure is disclaimed by Gramsci and Vološinov, who gave up such scientism a long time before, either because it theoretically presupposes the unity that is still to be established socially, or because it abstracts from dividedness.

A Marxist linguistics might be possible by joining together insights like these. It is still important to aim at such a connection, because without it linguistics, however pragmatic, cannot do justice to the everyday, historical, social, and cultural status of language and linguistics.

References

Althusser, L. (1971). Ideology and ideological state apparatuses. In L. Althusser, *Lenin and philosophy, and other essays*: 127–186. Monthly Review Press.
Atkinson, P. (1971). *Language, structure and reproduction*. Methuen.
Baudrillard, J. (1972). *Pour une critique de l'économie politique du signe*. Gallimard.
Bernstein, B. (1971). *Class, codes and control*, vol. 1. Routledge & Kegan Paul.
Bochmann, K. (ed.) (1988). Schwerpunkt: Antonio Gramsci. *Beitraege zur Romanischen Philologie* 27: 205–268.
Bourdieu, P. (1982). *Ce que parler veut dire*. Fayard.
Clark, K. & M. Holquist (1984). *Mikhail Bakhtin*. Harvard University Press.
Coward, R. & J. Ellis (1977). *Language and materialism*. Routledge & Kegan Paul.
Derrida, J. (1990). *Limited Inc*. Galilée.
Dittmar, N. (1973). *Soziolinguistik*. Athenaion.
Erckenbrecht, U. (1973). *Marx' materialistische Sprachtheorie*. Scriptor.
Fairclough, N. (1989). *Language and power*. Longman.
Foucault, M. (1970). *The order of things*. Tavistock.
Gramsci, A. (1971). *Selections from the prison notebooks*. International.
—— (1985). *Selections from the cultural writings*. Lawrence & Wishart.
Habermas, J. (1981). *Theorie des kommunikativen Handelns*. Suhrkamp.
Hak, T. & N. Helsloot (eds.) (1994). *Michel Pêcheux, Automatic discourse analysis*. Rodopi.
Helsloot, N. (1989). Linguists of all countries …! On Gramsci's premise of coherence. *Journal of Pragmatics* 13: 547–566.

Höppe, W. (1982). *Karl Marx, Friedrich Engels: Sprache und gesellschaftlicher Gesamtkomplex*. Bouvier.
Houdebine, J.-L. (1977). *Langage et marxisme*. Klincksieck.
Labov, W. (1970). The logic of nonstandard English. In J.E. Alatis (ed.) *Report of the 20th annual round table meeting on linguistics and language studies*: 1–43. Georgetown University Press.
Lo Piparo, F. (1979). *Lingua, intellettuali, egemonia in Gramsci*. Laterza.
Maldidier, D. (ed.) (1990). *L'inquiétude du discours*. Éditions des Cendres.
Marcellesi, J-B. (ed.) (1977). Langage et classes sociales. *Langages* 46.
Marcellesi, J-B. & B. Gardin (1974). *Introduction à la sociolinguistique*. Larousse.
Marr, N.J. (1974). [1927] Die japhetitische Theorie. In T. Borbé, *Kritik der marxistischen Sprachtheorie N.Ja. Marr's*. Scriptor.
Marx, K. & F. Engels (1974). *Über Sprache, Stil und Übersetzung*. Dietz.
Mey, J.L. (1985). *Whose language?* John Benjamins.
Morson, G.S. & C. Emerson (1990). *Mikhail Bakhtin, Creation of a prosaics*. Stanford University Press.
Pêcheux, M. (1982). *Language, semantics and ideology*. Macmillan.
Schaff, A. (1962). *Introduction to semantics*. Pergamon.
Stalin, J. (1951). On Marxism in Linguistics. In *The Soviet Linguistic Controversy*: 70–76. King's Crown Press.
Thomas, L.L. (1957). *The linguistic theories of N. Ja. Marr*. University of California Press.
Todorov, T. (1984). *Mikhail Bakhtin, The dialogical principle*. Manchester University Press.
Vološinov, V.N. (1986). *Marxism and the philosophy of language*. Harvard University Press.
[*See also*: Critical linguistics and critical discourse analysis]

'Other' representation

Nikolas Coupland
Cardiff University

Representations in general, and most obviously representations through language, are a clear-cut instance of the semiotic mediation of social life, and hence an important focus for pragmatics. The concept of 'the other' is less obviously central to pragmatics, although it is increasingly used to explain how texts and practices position individuals and groups, especially as ways of deprecating or socially excluding them. In this chapter I shall first comment on the process of representation itself, then trace how the concept of 'the other' has developed historically and in more recent usage. The main body of the chapter will outline several of the most important discourse processes through which social distancing and 'othering' are achieved.

It will be important to recognise that casting a person or a group as 'other' is not inherently and necessarily to marginalise or disparage them. In fact, one of the challenges for future studies is to demarcate how a wide range of social 'effects' can be achieved through patterns and contexts of representation. In the selected examples, I will emphasise the more negative and punitive effects of 'other representation', simply because this is where most of the evidence from existing research lies. All the same, I am able to present only a small, illustrative selection of enormously diverse representational processes analysed in substantial literatures. I include instances from the context of interethnic relations, which is the focus of most sociolinguistic and pragmatic research. I also include some issues and examples from the intergenerational domain, where 'othering' discourses are also prevalent and where systematic research is needed.

This means that, through space constraints, I cannot deal adequately with 'othering' in the domain of gender, except one brief instance. (For a substantial theoretical treatment of this issue, see Lacan's claim that "women are symbolically fixed in relation to masculinity as the lacking Other" – Elliott 1996: 185; Lacan 1966). Nor, for that matter, can I explore George Herbert Mead's famous observation that society as a whole stands for the 'generalised other' – the sum-total of other people's perceptions of the individual which conspire to form that person's internalised 'me', as opposed to her/his creative, agentive 'I' (Mead 1934). Yet another 'casualty' is intergroup theory in social psychology, although it can claim to be a rich and coherent, but resolutely non-pragmatic, alternative view of the role of language in intergroup relations. (I make a few comments about this tradition of work at the end of the chapter.) These are only some of many other productive perspectives relevant to this chapter's concerns.

1. On representation

Representations are the totality of semiotic means by which items and categories, individuals and social groups, along with their attributes and values, are identified, thematised, focused, shaped and made intelligible. In this sense, representing a class of items or people is more than "merely referring to" them. It is the generalised set of processes by which collectivities, including human identities and attributes, are symbolically forged, confirmed or challenged.

Representations are ideological, if (by design or inadvertently, overtly or covertly) they express social or cultural values and priorities (Kress & van Leeuwen 1996). Newly coined representations (including visual images, such as refashioned product or company logos, linguistic labels for new musical or dress styles, or textual accounts such as a new pamphlet summarising a political party's pre-election manifesto) can construct new categories, or attach new values to old categories. Using familiar, existing representations (such as using our workplace's headed notepaper, or simply building common words and descriptions of categories and processes into our everyday talk) solidifies and further naturalises our represented worlds. And this is also true of the linguistic labels we use to represent social groups – whether they are 'standard', widely ratified terms (e.g. 'Welsh people', 'Black people', 'The Irish', 'Travellers') or pejorative, racist ones used in deprecation (e.g. 'Taffies', 'Niggers', 'Micks', 'Gypsies').

From some theoretical standpoints, social collectivities exist primarily or even exclusively in the semiotic acts that represent them, for example through print media. (This anti-realist position is debated by, for example, Anderson 1983; Gal & Woolard 1995; and Rampton (this volume). For an alternative, realist perspective and critique of this, see Carter & Sealey 2000, and adjacent papers.) Whether or not this is an overreaching claim, representing is a fundamental symbolic activity, a symbolic packaging of our social worlds which has important implications for social organisation and social relations. The study of linguistic representations develops Whorf's perspective on cultural and linguistic relativity (e.g. Whorf 1997; see also Gumperz & Levinson 1996; Lee 1992), seeing language as a means of fixing world views which are unlikely to be consistent across social groups. On the other hand, linguistic representations tend to be durable once established within a group's usage. Sacks suggested that "a large amount of the knowledge that Members hold about how a society works [is]… 'protected against induction'. And what that means is that it isn't automatically modified if events occur which it doesn't characterize" (Sacks 1995: 196). Since communication requires linguistic or some other form of representation, and since all realities must be represented, it follows that communicators do not have the option of refashioning representations on each instance of their use.

When we think of human social groups (our own groups and groups of 'others'), it is also obvious that linguistic representations lie at the heart of both social integration and cohesion, and social division and exclusion. A form of social integration will be experienced when people share representations and find them unexceptional, although representations shared within a group may easily work to the disadvantage of other groups. Social divisions will become salient when representations are contested, although contesting a representation may provide an avenue for reappraising and reformatting social relations.

Representation is simultaneously a cognitive and a linguistic/discursive process. Moscovici (1984) shows how particular social representations are 'objectified' by particular groups – and most significantly by powerful groups – leading to a naturalisation of their perspectives. Objectified representations encode the values and assumptions that are taken to define 'common sense' (Gwyn 1996). As Gwyn explains, "when we classify, or name something ('test-tube babies'; 'retirement pregnancies'; 'designer babies') we always compare it to a conceptual prototype (e.g. 'normal babies', 'the correct age to have babies', etc.), always ask ourselves whether the the object compared is normal or abnormal in relation to that prototype" (Gwyn 1996: 69). This is what Moscovici calls the process of social 'anchoring' through representation. It is a fixing or consolidation of 'normal' perspectives and assumptions. The linguistic representation 'babies' arguably anchors that class of beings in a social matrix where motherhood and babyhood are mutually implicated, and where, within this association, motherhood entails conception through sexual intercourse, child-bearing and birth from pregnancy. By contrast, the representation 'test-tube babies' marks a deviation from normative birthing practices. It bestows a non-normative, marked and perhaps even 'alien' quality upon that group of neonates.

In an equally loaded theoretical sense, representations can be seen as one of three dimensions of social practice (Fairclough 2000; Chouliaraki & Fairclough 1999). Social practices, by this view, involve production (or work or achievement), identification (every practice locates particular 'positions' for people) and representation. Fairclough (2000: 168) writes that "people never simply act; their representations of their actions and domains of action are an inherent part of action; action is reflexive". The self-monitored or reflexive quality of linguistic and textual representations has been emphasised for some time within linguistic anthropology (e.g. R. Bauman 1996; Lucy 1993). As we shall see below, people may not simply construct or use representations of their own and other social groups. Speakers' and writers' representations will often be designed in the knowledge of their anticipated effects in particular ideological climates. Decisions about how we represent ourselves will be taken in relation to how others may represent themselves, and how each party may represent the other. There is therefore an important *relational* dimension to representing, where self representation and other representation can be mutually influencing processes.

2. On 'the other'

Riggins (1997: 3) points out that the term 'other' has an extensive history in philosophy, traceable to Plato "who used it to represent the relationship between an observer (the Self) and an observed (the Other)". In this formulation, 'the other' and 'otherness' are rather neutral notions, as is the everyday distinction between 'oneself' and 'another person'. Taken this way, the term 'other' suggests a sociologically rather uninteresting, physical boundary – perhaps defined at the outer surfaces of one's skin or clothes. Contemporary usage of the term 'other' in cultural studies and social theory, and in disciplines including pragmatics which now borrow from these sources, is more interesting and often more socio-political, although it is also highly variable. Riggins initially takes 'the other' "to refer to all people the Self perceives as mildly or radically different" (1997: 3), which is still an unduly bland definition. The dominant sense of the term 'other', in a cultural context, is in identifying a group – or an individual held to typify that group – that is considered not only different or distant but also alien or deviant, relative to the norms and expectations of the speaker's own group – in line with the preliminary sketch of the 'test-tube babies' example, above. 'Other' is normally, therefore, an *intergroup* perception (Giles & Coupland 1991). It raises issues about group boundaries; it is often a perception that accompanies group-based discrimination and intergroup conflict.

From a pragmatic perspective, representing a person or a group as 'other' is also an active, constitutive process. 'Othering' is the process of representing an individual or a social group *to render them* distant, alien or deviant. Often, as previously indicated, to 'altercast' someone this way is to relegate them to a socially disadvantaged position. It is the construction of an outgroup ('outgrouping'), a process of social exclusion or marginalisation. But alternatively, we can conceive of distancing as conferring mystery, magical qualities and even reverence, as a process of 'totemising' or 'fetishising'. The 'othered' group (which may be a group invoked to define an individual) will often be a minority group. But again it need not be, since majority groups will often be cast as 'other' to minorities. Still, we could say that a group (or a group member) is commonly minoritised in the process of 'othering', and this process will usually be carried forward through patterns of linguistic/textual representation.

Although 'the other' is therefore a politically important concept, it remains an extremely generalised one, subsuming a wide range of motivations and outcomes. There may be some regularities in how language is used to relegate a group to the status of 'other' – homogenisation, pejoration, marginalisation, silencing, and so on – and these are the ones I focus on below. But discourses of social exclusion are likely to be different when the issue is exclusion across racial/ethic lines, as opposed to socio-economic classes, gender, age, sexuality or other social dimensions. Each site and time-period of intergroup conflict will have its own distinctive themes and tendencies, its own patterns and strategies of prejudicial representation, its own modes of resistance and rebuttal. Each will be a culturally and temporally specific formation.

To take one example, ageism and anti-ageist resistance have surfaced rather recently as publicly acknowledged ideologies and social practices in the UK. Racism and sexism have been far more strongly profiled than ageism, although of course we should be wary of implying that these are in any way simply parallel issues within the moral domain of 'equal opportunities'. Ageist representations can certainly have a socio-structural basis, featuring in social policy debates about social priorities and scarce resources. Newspaper features on the 'looming elderly health disaster', for example, represent old people as an economic burden on a 'society' which, by implication, excludes them. The more general representation of ageing as a health and social policy 'problem' frames old people as objects rather than autonomous agents (Coupland, Coupland & Giles 1991). It takes only a subtle realignment of macro-economic strategy to construe old people, alternatively, as a 'burgeoning resource' (by virtue of the often-quoted 'greying' of western society), as a relatively 'untapped' market sector and as an opportunity to draw more tax revenue. Both perspectives imply that the non-working elderly are a drain on resources. But then, there are discrediting representations of old people in work, as illegitimately 'taking jobs from unemployed young people' and 'clinging on to positions of power and influence after their time'. (The complementary age-perspective is that groups of *young* people are also subject to ageist representation and minoritisation – see Williams & Coupland 1998 on 'Generation X' in the USA.)

As this discussion suggests, the forms taken by societal ageism respond to wider social contexts and frames of representation. But they also differ between traditional and (late-) modern societies (Coupland & Coupland 1999; see also Cole 1986; Green 1993). The 'othering' of the very old, in a general sense, has been a detectable feature of European and North American societies over many centuries – see Woodward's (1991) comments about the 'unwatchability' of deep old age, and popular revulsion at the aged body and physiognomy. However, phobic representations are now more common and more intense, as traditional social structures (e.g. the family, and 'natural' career progression with seniority) have loosened. Structural ideologies are still relevant, but ageist practice is shifting into more personal domains, for example in expressions of 'fear of own ageing' and the general ideology of 'anti-ageing' strategies and initiatives (Coupland & Coupland 1999). If social scientists and social actors feel themselves less committed to the politics of anti-ageism than, say, anti-sexism, it may well be because we have internalised one powerful ageist principle – the 'legitimate' and 'natural' phobic construal of 'what we will inevitably become' – that is, old.

We should therefore be wary of investing too heavily in a unitary concept of 'othering' as a social or discursive process. 'The other' is a reductive concept, in two senses. Quite obviously, the *social process* of 'othering' is itself reductive. It captures how representations can simplify and homogenise people and groups (see below).

But *conceptually*, as a candidate generalisation about group-relevant representations, alignments and effects, it can only hint at a hugely differentiated set of ideological stances, practices and consequences. At this stage 'the other' is probably a useful analytic concept, opening up an important empirical and theoretical field. Later research may benefit from moving beyond this engaging but rather limiting construal of intergroup discourses. (This is one reason why I persist in enclosing the term 'other' within inverted commas in this chapter, although it is also useful to be able to distinguish this semi-technical usage from non-technical usage.)

In fact, contemporary theorising of 'the other' stems most directly from one influential but idiosyncratic source – Simmel's concept of 'the stranger', developed in the earliest years of the 20th century (Simmel 1950; Rogers 1999). Simmel wrote about individuals present in a social system who are nevertheless socially distant from that system and who do not endorse local norms:

> The stranger is ... not ... the wanderer who comes today and goes tomorrow, but rather is the person who comes today and stays tomorrow. (Simmel 1950: 402; Rogers 1999: 61)

Not surprisingly, Simmel's 'strangers' could easily be interpreted to be migrants, and Robert Park, a student of Simmel's, went on to study the first-generation American children of European in-migrant parents. Park characterised the in-migrant as 'a marginal man', 'a cultural hybrid, a man living and sharing intimately in the cultural life and traditions of two different peoples; never quite willing to break, even if he were permitted to do so, with his past and traditions, and not quite accepted, because of racial prejudice, in the new society in which he now sought to find a place' (Park 1924: 890; Rogers 1999: 64).

Indeed, most pragmatic research on 'the other' takes racial and ethnic issues as its focus. For example, the Riggins (1997) collection includes chapters on the representation of refugees, indigenous Mexican populations, Travelling People, Muslims, Jews and Black Canadians. An important stimulus to this work is Edward Said's thesis on 'Orientalism', which he defines as 'the corporate institution for dealing with the Orient – dealing with it by making statements about it, authorizing views on it, describing it, by teaching it, settling it, ruling over it: in short, Orientalism as a Western style for dominating, restructuring, and having authority over the Orient' (Said 1978: 3; see the commentary in Karim 1997: 154).

It is worth noting that Simmel's 'stranger' was by no means a uniformly disadvantaged individual, and by implication that 'the other' need not be a repressed other. Simmel saw definite strengths in the stranger position, including improved perspective, objectivity and a certain form of freedom (from normative constraint) and openness to innovation. Several of these perspectives have been developed under the rubric of intercultural communication research in the United States (e.g. Gudykunst & Kim 1997).

There is no inevitable association between social distance and minoritisation, and the perception or construction of social distance can equally be associated with admiration, mystique and even envy (Riggins 1997: 18). Nevertheless, as noted earlier, the tradition that dominates in pragmatic research on 'the other' is showing how linguistic/textual representations contribute to social exclusion and minoritisation, and unpacking the complexities and nuances of these discourses.

Pragmatics has contributed the crucial observation that representations of 'the other' can not be read at the surface of language – that discourses of social exclusion have their effects implicitly. It provides the interpretive apparatus to unpack such representations and possibly to challenge them. Except perhaps in the grossest instances of, for example, racist slurs (Essed 1997, see below) the 'othering' effect of talk or text will result from a complex interplay of textual and social contextual factors. Most obviously, it will depend on the social position from which a speaker's outgroup reference or description is made, on the social relations between speakers, and on the ideological set or frame taken to be obtaining. Forms of address and reference which are discriminatory, offensive, alienating or patronising in a social situation with a salient intergroup dimension may be adjudged innocent among ingroup members or when intergroup salience is low. Because communication, as noted earlier, will often be framed reflexively, speakers are likely to mitigate and even disguise their discriminatory stances, especially in public discourses in liberal democracies. As Sacks showed (1995, 1999), social categorisation is never neutral. We invoke group-level categories for specific rhetorical and social purposes.

Finally in this section, we should recall the theoretical link between self identification and 'other' representation. Our representations of *ourselves*, even *to* ourselves, require a form of social comparison. In psycho-analytic terms (Elliott 1996), self-identification involves borrowing aspects of identity from others, or adopting traits and values associates with fictional and even mythical figures, perhaps to cope with threatening circumstances. Riggins (1997: 4) says that the experience of self-estrangement can be captured through a concept of the 'internal other'. 'The other' is therefore viewed as capable of penetrating the self in various ways, and in some ways this renders the concept of 'otherhood' even more tantalisingly abstract and elusive. At the same time it opens up new avenues for linguistic/pragmatic research, exploring the creative means by which individuals and groups fashion identities for themselves. One coherent set of possibilities is subsumed under the term 'crossing' (see below) where speakers invoke apparently outgroup speech norms and rework them, investing them with new cultural significances. Support for this flexible view of 'the other' is provided by the concept of hybridity, developed in post-colonial theory (Ashcroft, Griffiths & Tiffin 1998). Hybridity is the creation or existence of mixed or multiple forms or identities. The concept challenges the orthodox view of cultural groups as sealed systems, and people as unique exemplars of cultural types. Hybridity is mainly associated with the theoretical work of Bhabha (e.g.1994), and his perspective that people sustain complex, mixed subjectivities and occupy ambiguous cultural spaces.

3. Discourse strategies in representations of 'the other'

In this section I organise examples of 'othering' representational processes under various headings. The categories should not be seen as fully distinct. Since the social meanings attributed through these discourse strategies are achieved contextually, and often implicitly, any list will overstate the boundedness of its elements. But the following categories at least identify different recurrent themes in 'other representation'.

3.1 Homogenisation

'Treating people as individuals' is a cornerstone of the ethics of liberal democracies. It is directly linked to political processes such as individual suffrage and the protection of human rights which are held to be invested in individuals. Correspondingly, denying individuals their individuality is illiberal, but also a productive means of outgrouping and minoritisation. Following Said, Karim (1997: 155) explains how Muslims are homogenised in European/Northern discourses: It has been a general tendency to portray Muslims, whether they be religious figures, caliphs, sultans, community leaders, presidents, prime ministers, dictators or terrorists, behaving in accordance with dominant scripts that prescribe how they should act; their individual characters have been reduced to fit into the core stereotypes of Muslims.

Social stereotyping (Hewstone & Giles 1999) entails a selective focusing on salient cultural traits and investing them with iconic status – skin colour, physiognomic or postural features, religious 'fanaticism', but also details of speech style are obvious if clichéd signifiers in interethnic 'othering'. The corollary of this focusing is a levelling or neutralisation of the features which, for ingroup members, mark inter-individual or inter-sub-group differences (social or professional status markers, personal idiosyncrasies, and so on).

Karim points to the homogenising effect even of ethnic group labels, for example the terms 'Muslim fundamentalist' and 'Islamic radical' in European newspaper reports. In isolation, and in their local texts, these representations may be of individuals. But in their proliferation they become short-hand cultural referents, identifying apparently predictable cultural types. Interestingly too, there is implicit syntactic inversion, where the representation of 'a fundamentalist' who is attributively 'Muslim' is more likely to be read as 'a Muslim', and indeed an example of a deindividuated class of 'all Muslims', who are attributively 'fundamentalist'. In such usage, Muslims are constructed as deviant from the European norm of 'uncommitted and non-threatening Christians'. Linguistic/pragmatic homogenisation expresses the political orientation that Blommaert & Verschueren (1998) call 'homogeneism' – *'the idea that the ideal society should be as uniform or homogeneous as possible'* (p. 117, emphasis in the original). Blommaert and Verschueren comment that 'homogeneism abnormalises the presence of foreigners while normalising the autochthonous population's negative reactions to their presence'. Lippi-Green (1997: 64) critiques the sociolinguistic correlate of this process – allegiance to 'an idealized nation-state that has one perfect, homogeneous language'.

The linguistic 'theying' of ethnic outgroups (where the term 'outgroup' is itself outgrouping) is often a more indirect process than the simple use of category labels or even the pronoun 'they' itself. 'We' versus 'they' is too obvious an opposition for many public contexts of talk, so it has to be implied rather than stated on-record (cf. Wodak 1997). It is in fact part of liberal-democratic discourse to ridicule this overtly 'othering' usage and to claim an awareness and moral superiority over those who engage in it. For example, the representation of Black people or Asians as 'all looking alike' was pilloried in British television sitcoms of the 1960s and 1970s.

In the context of ageing similarly, the prescription that carers of old people should 'treat them as individuals' and 'not talk down to them' is endemic in training regimens for UK nurses and home care assistants (Atkinson & Coupland 1988). Even so, the age instance is interesting, as I suggested earlier, because of the relatively restricted consciousness of age-political issues among the general populace. Homogenising representations of the elderly are still common in the UK, as for example in the imagery of road signs warning drivers that they are approaching a residential home for old people – portraying two bent figures, one with a walking stick, being helped across a road. The imagery of decrement, frailty and incompetence is still generally acceptable as an icon of late life in the UK, even in travel brochures, insurance pamphlets and television ads. In a recent analysis of older patient/family member/doctor triads in UK geriatric medical interactions (Coupland & Coupland 1998, 1999, 2000), we found occasional outgrouping linguistic representations such as the following:

Extract 1

Doctor E: (professor), male, in his sixties
Patient 115: female, aged 75, accompanied by her daughter
(The doctor has finished taking the patient's medical history.)
Doctor: no (.) right okay fine (.) right would you like to pop onto the couch (.) we'll pull the curtain around you and we'll come and have a little look at you
Daughter: it'll be alright don't worry (.)
(to doctor, outside the patient's hearing) if I wasn't here she wouldn't speak at all (laughs slightly)

Doctor:	(laughs slightly) yes (.) they do get a bit nervous don't they? (.) strange places
Daughter:	[yeah they ((get a bit))
	(20 seconds pause, as the doctor goes through case notes)
Daughter:	she's a *worr*ier
Doctor:	pardon?
Daughter:	she is a worrier
Doctor:	yes (.) gets a bit *anx*ious does she?
	(15 seconds pause)
Daughter:	she's not quite sure whether she's got an*gi*na or what ((this could be))
Doctor:	[yes well we'll sort all that out (.) yes now (3.0) yes it's difficult when you know (.) when one's not quite certain what *is* wrong (.) then people get much more *anx*ious about (.) er
Daughter:	I think they do get a bit nervous don't they (.) confused actually
Doctor:	[yes yes]
Daughter:	(Some seconds later) and this is what I tried to explain but (.) when they get to their age they think well why are they *do*ing it=
Doctor:	=yes

The doctor and the patient jointly fashion a representation of the patient as behaving in an age-prototypical way and generalise rather freely about old people as a homogeneous and deficient group. In the utterance *they do get a bit nervous don't they?*, and later in the extract, *they* clearly refers to 'old people' (cf. *when they get to their age*). Old people are represented as conforming to a predictable pattern of behaviour, which is then held to provide an adequate account of the patient's circumstances in this case. The instance is significant because the Outpatients clinic where this interaction was recorded is overtly committed to a firmly anti-ageist ideological stance, as we have documented elsewhere.

3.2 Pejoration

The instances just considered show degrees of pejoration linked to homogenisation. That is, such representations project not only categorial uniformity but qualities such as barbarism and instability or incompetence and nervousness. There are almost limitless dimensions in which 'others' can be minoritised, with traits and qualities differentially salient for different social groups. The evaluative loading of group labels and attributions is context specific, so it is impossible to read degrees of prejorativeness from linguistic forms. Take, for example, the following written response provided by a twelve-year-old boy in a 1939 survey of racial attitudes in Britain, as part of the Mass-Observation project:

> Niggers, or rather negroes ['blackies' crossed out] are the inhabitants of Africa and numerous small islands in the Pacific.
>
> The negroes ['blackies' crossed out] we find in America are not true inhabitants of that country, they were imported from Africa as Slaves...
>
> A black person's teeth are usually white, so are the whites of his eyes.
>
> Negroes ['niggers' crossed out] are keen spiritualists as their songs show us...
>
> A nigger has often [usually crossed out] a very good voice. (Kushner 1995: 7)

The crossings out show that the child was sensitive to the fact that the term 'blackies' was offensive, although he tolerates two instances of the term 'nigger'. In the historical and ideological context in which the text was produced, there is an attempt to represent attributes presumed to be positive (white teeth and good voices) and to acknowledge a repressive social history (slavery). Even so, the text is shocking to contemporary eyes, not least for the study to have sought and collated texts of this type and for even a child to feel able to make such global representations of a minoritised racial group.

In the most blatant and violating cases, however, pejoration includes verbal as well as physical abuse and 'racist slurs' (e.g. Essed 1991, 1997). In the 1997 chapter, Essed documents reports by black women in the USA and the Netherlands, many of whom had direct experience as the targets of racist verbal abuse, face-to-face. A black student in the USA, for example, reported an argument with a white housemate who at one point said 'I am sick of you stupid N____rs. You look like apes anyway.' (Essed 1997: 138, repeated as transcribed). 'Slurs' of this sort have their pragmatic effect by forcing an addressed individual into a social group designation, then pejorating that group, by adding explicitly negative attributes or by invoking generally tabooed group labels (and both of these processes in the cited instance).

Direct, confrontational, outgrouping representations are rarely reported in the academic literature, which is itself subject to normative control (cf. Potter & Wetherell 1987). There is, however, a growing literature on 'hate speech', particularly examining the controversy of whether hateful, injurious utterances should be classed as 'actual' violence and subject to legal process (Cover 1986; Matsuda, Lawrence, Delgado & Crenshaw 1993). Butler (1997) provides a detailed critical and philosophical review of the issue.

3.3 Suppression and silencing

Social exclusion can also be achieved through zero representation or restricted representation. Silence has many functions (Jaworski 1993, 1997), including potentially signalling solidarity and intimacy. But in some contexts, especially those public domains of discourse like the mass media where social collectivities can expect their identities and concerns to be represented, limited representation can be a strategy of 'othering'. An instance argued in the literature is that old people are 'invisible' in many genres of print journalism – Kubey 1980. More subtly, when groups *are* represented, they may be minoritised through selective representation. Their ingroup names may be suppressed, for example identifying travelling people by labels such as 'Gypsies', 'tinkers', or 'vagrants' (Helleiner & Szuchewycz 1997).

Another possibility is suppressing the diversity of a group's actual roles and perspectives, through stereotyping. For example, representations of women in the middle years of the twentieth century tended to be restricted to domestic roles in product advertising (Talbot 2000). In such cases, dominant groups' representations articulate just those dimensions of a minoritised group's experience that suit their own agendas and priorities. The claim Talbot makes is that male ideology has historically found it convenient to picture women, even 'liberated women', as finding fulfilment in routine housework. She also argues that even much more recent and apparently 'liberal' and even feminist representations of women are selective and ideological. Talbot comments on the British Telecom advertising campaign, "It's good to talk", which represents the importance and value of women's apparently more sociable and expansive communicative style on the telephone. The overt theme is that men should use the telephone more as women do, because women appreciate the value of social and relational talk. This positive representation of women's practice is, however, subordinated to the goal of selling more talk-time and obviously suits the company's financial interests. In this way, even feminist sociolinguistics is corralled into commercial promotion.

Similar to this last instance are strategies where representations of cultural groups subtly reconfigure their statuses. Galasinski and Jaworski (forthcoming) consider the voicing of local 'others' in British newspaper travel reports. They argue that local populations in tourist destinations are represented as elements of scenic environments (e.g. *Many of the locals are stunningly beautiful, their ancestors being multicultural before the word was invented*), or as passing curiosities, for the diversion of tourists. Their 'cultural' function is portrayed as being to support and enrich the tourist experience, almost as colonial slaves, facilitators of 'the tourist gaze' (Urry 1990).

3.4 Displaying 'liberalism'

Representation can be 'innocent', at least in the sense that speakers may not be aware of the cultural loadings of their language. But it follows from earlier remarks about the potential reflexivity of social representations that speakers will often monitor the impact of their own representations of 'others', and design them accordingly. In particular, speakers may anticipate being categorised as illiberal (racist, ageist, sexist, etc.). Depending on the ideological set obtaining in any one context of talk, they may in consequence lose varying degrees of esteem (e.g. as 'being racist', or perhaps as 'being ignorant' [of norms for public discourse], or as merely 'being incautious'). Outgrouping representations may therefore be 'mitigated' (in speakers' own judgement) by speakers working to display 'liberal' (e.g. 'non-racist') orientations. That is, minoritising, outgroup representations may be tagged with more favourable self-identifying representations.

The classical instance is the denial of racism (Van Dijk 1999; see also Van Dijk 1993, 1997). Van Dijk reports that it is precisely the most blatantly racist discourse that tends to have disclaimers, of the form "I'm not a racist but…". Therefore to an extent at least, denials seem to be *intended* to mitigate the racist content of talk. In another sense, however, we could see them as facilitating racist talk. They attend to the threat that voicing racist views may carry to the speaker's face or good standing. They allow a speaker to (try to) protect his/her own face without avoiding making the racist representation or attribution. They certainly show speakers' awareness of the non-normative nature of their talk, and of possible inferences that will be drawn from what they say. One example is: "It sounds prejudiced, but I think if students use only English…" (Van Dijk 1999: 544). This speaker is acknowledging that the argumentative line that it is better for non-first-language-English speakers to use English *can be* 'prejudiced'. But the speaker also implies that this *is not* the case on this occasion, and presumably that s/he is a sufficiently sophisticated social actor to be aware of, and purportedly to have circumvented, 'prejudiced' behaviour.

I am not aware of comparable discourses in the domain of ageing (such as 'I'm not ageist, but isn't talking to old people dull') and this again suggests that ageism and anti-ageism have not gained much overt recognition as yet as ideological stances, at least in my own cultural context. Ageist discourse is prevalent, but discourses of ageism (and anti-ageism) are not.

3.5   Subverting tolerance

Displays of apparent liberalism pay lip service to that ideology. Alternatively, there are diverse means of undermining it, in such a way as to legitimise racist, ageist or other punitive ideologies. People following this line will again show awareness of liberal ideologies (they are not 'ignorant racists', etc.) but do discursive work to show that liberalism is over-idealistic or naïve or dull or outmoded. The label 'political correctness' ('PC' – see Cameron 1995) was coined to counter and to subvert liberalism (e.g. liberal feminism and environmentalism). In that usage, the sense of the word 'correct' is 'unwarrantly correct' or 'hypercorrect', and that is just the sense that sociolinguists, for example, have for a long time adduced in their discussions of 'standard' language varieties (e.g. Milroy & Milroy 1985). The term 'PC' and anti-PC ideology cleverly invoke the critical apparatus of liberalism to subvert it. There are close parallels to what Wodak (e.g. 1997) terms 'victim-victimizer reversal' as part of racist practice.

Humour is a widely used strategy in anti-PC discourse because it can imply that PC itself is humourless. Humour is multi-facetted, however, because it obfuscates on-record versus off-record stances. So it allows its users to claim, if challenged, that they are 'only kidding'. Many commonplace pejorating representations of racial, age and other groups involve humour, although the distribution of this sort of humour across text and discourse genres is strictly policed. The vast commercial enterprise of producing, selling and mailing greetings cards in western societies invests heavily in group stereotyping, and in age-stereotyping as a large part of this. A dominant genre of UK birthday cards involves humorous age taunts, such as 'Still naughty at forty' or 'Still nifty at fifty'. In fact there is a regular pattern associating age-talk among adults with humour or sarcasm, even in people's accounts of their own age (Coupland & Coupland 1989). One is open to the charge of 'taking age too seriously' if one does not operate within these norms. Racist humour has at some times been permissible, and even normative, in stand-up comedy, but outlawed in the greetings cards industry.

Parodic representations of minority groups' language styles are found widely (see, for example, the Rampton 1999 collection of studies). Hill (1993, 1995) analyses linguistic and ideological issues attaching to the use of 'Junk' or 'Mock Spanish'. Similarly, Ronkin and Karn (1999) report on a tradition of racist representation of Ebonics (Black English) on the Internet, as a carrier of anti-Ebonics ideology. Mock Ebonics combines vulgar and pejorative characteristics of black speakers with stylised representations of black speech, substituting *bitch* for 'girl', *shit* for 'stuff', *nig* or *nigger* for 'man', and so on. Some writers have set up computer software to generate these parodic texts automatically. The proliferation of websites carrying this material suggests there is a substantial body of producers and consumers of it. These texts do more than recycle racial and linguistic stereotypes. They imply (especially in the computer-programmed forms) that black English is derived from standard English by a set of simple if risible rules. In the name of 'humour', they undermine the case for Ebonics to be treated as a legitimate, independent language suitable for public discourse, as endorsed, for example, in the 1996 Oakland (California, USA) resolution (Rickford 1999).

4. Beyond minoritisation

I have illustrated several of the recurrent pragmatic means by which 'others' are minoritised in and through acts of representation. The main research challenge so far has been to reveal the discourse strategies of social exclusion, and much more work remains to be done to increase critical awareness of these processes (Fairclough 1992). This is essentially the case for a pragmatic sociolinguistics featuring as part of education for citizenship.

Even so, it is important to stress that representational processes can function to *resist* as well as to voice social exclusion. We see some particular acts of resistance in the academic texts already cited as sources. Essed's missing typographical characters (as in 'stupid N____rs', above) reflects her commitment to silencing racist terminology, or at least to avoiding making it more available than it already is. Others (including Ronkin and Karn, above, and to a small extent this chapter) have decided to reproduce racist and similar forms, assuming academic readers will approach the data with the same ideology of resistance that characterises sociolinguistic and pragmatic research itself. There is no simple solution to this issue.

Minoritised groups have in many cases chosen to resist by seeking to *reclaim* the pejorative language that has been used to or about them. Rather than silencing such language, the strategy is one of recontextualisation – rehabilitating representations within the targeted group and thereby 'drawing their sting'. Just as 'queer' has become the most neutral available term for representing lesbian and gay-male groups and perspectives in academic discourse (Thorne & J. Coupland 1998), so 'nigger' has been invested with a sense of ingroup solidarity, e.g. in contemporary rap music lyrics (Essed 1997: 137). The current convention for written representations (e.g. in compact disk inserts) is however 'nigga' rather than 'nigger', perhaps symbolising the divide between ingrouping and outgrouping usages. In the age context there are signs of political opinion being mobilised against patronising representations such as 'senior citizen', 'old timer' and 'golden ager'. I have been taken to task in an academic context for referring to 'the elderly' rather than 'old people'. Sensitivity to the lexis of group representation indicates ideological contestation and potential for change, although labelling remains only a small part of the process of representing a social group.

The final segment of this overview should, I believe, attend to the concept of *groupness*. I have suggested that the concept of 'the other' is inherently reductive, and there is a substantial risk that studies which focus on 'other representation' may overstate the finiteness of groups themselves. As mentioned above, people's representations are often themselves pragmatically reductive – as we have seen, they often homogenise as well as pejorate targeted groups. But academic study is itself representational, and very obviously so in the social sciences where social groups are a primary concern. The question then is: how confident can we be that our own representations are not unduly fixing and essentialising social collectivities? – where 'unduly' means 'with greater fixity than group members have as part of their own group experience'.

Several sources in social and cultural theory are positing that individuals' social and cultural experiences, in late or high modernity (e.g. Giddens 1991) are regularly 'hybrid' (see above). Giddens theorises late modernity as an environment where traditional boundaries of many sorts are loosened and made available for more creative reworking. He writes about the compression and disembedding of time and space, through vastly more sophisticated telecommunication links, rapid international travel and the reflexivity promoted through of the mass media. It follows that self-identity, which Giddens insists is an ongoing 'project' rather than a fixed set of allegiances or priorities, will be malleable and relativised.

One related, resonant quotation (cited in Rampton, this volume) is that social life has been 'dissipated into a series of randomly emerging, shifting and evanescent islands of order' (Z. Bauman 1992: 189). The reality posited in this quote and in Giddens' and others' accounts of social identity seems quite incompatible with a model that drives any analysis of majority groups and their relations with, and representations of, groups of 'others'. Relativised and shifting social identities are certainly incompatible with the concepts of ingroup and outgroup, which are central to *intergroup theory* in social psychology (Tajfel 1981; Tajfel & Turner 1979; see also Giles & Coupland 1991). Tajfel's perspective has provided the basis for a rich programme of research on language intergroup relations, including theoretical refinement of processes of social stereotyping (Hewstone & Giles 1997), empirical studies of attitudes to language variation (Ryan & Giles 1982), and the theorising of ethnolinguistic identity (Giles & Johnson 1987). As I mentioned at the outset, it is not possible to review this approach here, other than to note that its emphases are more cognitive than pragmatic, more experimental than discourse analytic, and that it subsumes a vast amount of cumulative, theory-driven empirical research on intergroup relations. Its main thrust is, however, that our social worlds are indeed structured, pervasively, through group-relevant perceptions, and that these mediate our social relations and communication practices.

Can these perspectives be reconciled? I suspect they can not, but that it would be unwise to force them into simple opposition with each other, as if one is 'more correct' or 'less naïve' than the other. There is certainly a 'modern' (as opposed to 'late-' or 'high-modern') quality to 'othering' and to intergroup theory alike. After all, many of the patterns of representation we considered above express intergroup dissonance of the sort forged during the mid-years of western Industrialisation. At that time, for example, Afro-Carribean people were recruited in great numbers to fill newly created roles in UK service industries, and cities in the UK first confronted racial diversity. As I noted above, early conceptualisations of 'the other' were linked to demographic trends in immigration. (Blommaert & Verschueren's detailed analysis (1998) of the discourses of 'migrant policies' in Belgium is a significant recent contribution to this line of research.) It would certainly be wrong to dismiss the documented evidence of discursive 'othering', and evidence that intergroup boundaries in general are often perceived to be hard and impermeable, under the weight of a new form of social theorising about identity in late modernity.

It is certainly plausible to argue that increasing globalisation and, in some domains, multi-ethnicisation, has already encouraged more fluidity of group definition, and less adversarial and more complex group relations and representations. We might expect this trend to accelerate. But it is probably true that late modernity has, so far, been better theorised than it has been empirically demonstrated. In terms of theory, the risk of over-relativising social identities is perhaps as significant as the risk of essentialising them.

I am suggesting, then, that the relative 'correctness' of the hybridity and intergroup models is largely an empirical matter. To look at it slightly differently, it makes sense to see 'othering' and 'outgrouping' as one broad ideological tendency working against another – hybridity and the relative dissipation of social identification. However much late-modern social life might predispose us to adopt reflexive and contingent definitions of ourselves and others (Giddens 1994), there will be a tendency to fix social identities, in the service of ideologies. There really are no grounds to believe that the practice of group-level ideological representation will weaken or cease. As intergroup theory claims, social representation is too fundamental a facet of our socio-cognitive functioning for that to be a feasibility.

The hybridity model is based partly on high-abstraction theoretical generalisations about late modern social conditions, and partly (as in the case of Said's influential analyses) on personal reactions to hegemonic, 'othering' discourses. We need research which can assess the degree of openness/closure of social identification, in preference to research that pre-defines its frameworks either in intergroup or in hybridity terms. Rampton's (1995) analyses of sociolinguistic 'crossing' – the (sometimes stylised) use of language varieties other than those traditionally conceived as one's own, e.g. by young black, Asian and white kids in UK cities – is the most compelling data-linked treatment to date. It is highly suggestive of sociolinguistic hybridity at work, as is new international research influenced by this approach (Rampton 1999). The speech events Rampton analyses are culturally inventive and often playful in social identity terms. They are certainly ambiguous, but seem to work towards breaking down clear definitions between 'self' and 'other'. Young Asians using stylised Asian English (Rampton 1995: 67ff.) offer possibly parodic versions of their ethnic selves which, while they conform to some stereotyped expectations of Asian speech, also undermine the racist ideology often associated with these representations. We might construe this as a sort of 'self-othering', although any self-deprecation entailed in it is short-lived, and locally contextualised. Just how many social situations and groups demonstrate representational crossing, and whether, on the basis of new studies, there are recurrent and substantial indications of 'othering' being yesterday's cultural model, remains to be seen.

References

Anderson, B. (1983). *Imagined Communities: Reflections on the Origin and Spread of Nationalism.* Verso.

Ashcroft, B., G. Griffiths & H. Tiffin (1998). Key Concepts in Post-Colonial Studies. Routledge.

Atkinson, K. & N. Coupland (1988). Accommodation as ideology. *Language and Communication* 8(3/4): 321–328.

Bauman, R. (1996). Transformations of the word in the production of Mexican festival drama. In M. Silverstein & G. Urban (eds.) *Natural Histories of Discourse*: 301–327. University of Chicago Press.

Bauman, Z. (1992). *Intimations of Post-Modernity*. Routledge.

Bhabha, H. (1994). *The Location of Culture*. Routledge.

Blommaert, J. & J. Verschueren (1998). *Debating Diversity: Analysing the Discourse of Tolerance*. Routledge.

Butler, J. (1997). *Excitable Speech: A Politics of the Performative*. Routledge.

Cameron, D. (1995). *Verbal Hygiene*. Routledge.

Carter, B. & A. Sealey (2000). Language, structure and agency: A social realism perspective. *Journal of Sociolinguistics* 4(1): 3–20.

Chouliaraki, L. & N. Fairclough (1999). *Discourse in Late Modernity: Renewing Critical Discourse Analysis*. Edinburgh University Press.

Cole, T.R. (1986). The 'enlightened' view of ageing: Victorian morality in a new key. In T.R. Cole & S.A. Gadow (eds.) *What Does It Mean to Grow Old?*: 117–130. Duke University Press.

Coupland, N. & J. Coupland (1998). Reshaping lives: Constitutive identity work in geriatric medical consultations. *Text* 18(2): 159–189.

—— (1999). Ageing, ageism and anti-ageism: Moral stance in geriatric medical discourse. In H. Hamilton (ed.) *Language and Communication in Old Age: Multidisciplinary Perspectives*. 177–208. Garland Publishing Inc.

—— (2000). Relational framing and pronominal address in geriatric medical discourse. In S. Sarangi & M. Coulthard (eds.) *Discourse and Social Life*: 207–229. Longman.

Coupland, N., J. Coupland & H. Giles (1991). *Language, Society and the Elderly: Discourse, Identity and Ageing*. Blackwell.

Coupland, N. & A. Jaworski (eds.). *Sociolinguistics: A Reader and Coursebook*. Macmillan.

Cover, R.M. (1986). Violence and the word, 96. *Yale Law Journal* 1595, 1601 n I.

Elliott, A. (1996). Psychoanalysis and social theory. In B.S. Turner (ed.) *The Blackwell Companion to Social Theory*: 177–193. Blackwell.

Essed, P. (1991). *Understanding Everyday Racism: An Interdisciplinary Theory*. Sage.

—— (1997). Racial intimidation: Sociopolitical implications of the use of racist slurs. In S.H. Riggins (ed.): 131–152.

Fairclough, N. (1992). *Critical Language Awareness*. Longman.

—— (2000). Discourse, social theory and social research: The discourse of welfare reform. *Journal of Sociolinguistics* 4(2): 163–195.

Gal, S. & C. Woolard (1995). Constructing languages and publics: Authority and representation. *Pragmatics* 5(2):129–138.

Galasinski, D. & A. Jaworski (forthcoming). Meeting the local other: Representations of local people in British press travel sections.

Giddens, A. (1991). *Modernity and Self-Identity*. Polity.

—— (1994). Living in a post-traditional society. In U. Beck, A. Giddens & S. Lash, *Reflexive Modernization: Politics, Tradition and Aesthetics in the Modern Social Order*: 56–109. Polity Press.

Giles, H. & N. Coupland (1991). *Language: Contexts and Consequences*. Open University Press.

Giles, H. & P. Johnson (1987). Ethnolinguistic identity theory: A social psychological approach to language maintenance. *International Journal of the Sociology of Language* 68: 66–99.

Green, B.S. (1993). *Gerontology and the Construction of Old Age: A Study in Discourse Analysis*. Aldine De Gruyter.

Gudykunst, W.B. & Y.Y. Kim (1997). *Communicating with strangers: An Approach to Intercultural Communication*. McGraw-Hill.

Gumperz, J.J. & S.C. Levinson (eds.) (1996). *Rethinking Linguistic Relativity*. Cambridge University Press.

Gwyn, R. (1996). *The Voicing of Illness*. Unpublished PhD Diss., Cardiff University.

Helleiner, J. & B. Szuchewycz (1997). Discourses of exclusion: The Irish press and the Travelling people. In S.H. Riggins (ed.): 109–30.

Hewstone, M. & H. Giles (1997). Social groups and social stereotypes. In N. Coupland & A. Jaworski (eds.): 270–283.

Hill, J. (1993). Hasta la vista, baby: Anglo Spanish in the American Southwest. *Critique of Anthropology* 13: 145–176.

—— (1995). Junk Spanish, covert racism and the (leaky) boundary between public and private spheres. *Pragmatics* 5(2): 197–212.

Jaworski, A. (1993). *The Power of Silence: Social and Pragmatic Perspectives*. Sage.

Jaworski, A. (ed.) (1997). *Silence: Interdisciplinary Perspectives*. Mouton de Gruyter.

Jaworski, A. & N. Coupland (eds.). *The Discourse Reader*. Routledge.

Karim, K.H. (1997). The historical resilience of primary stereotypes: Core images of the Muslim other. In S.H. Riggins (ed.): 153–183.

Kress, G. & T. Van Leeuwen (1996). *Reading Images*. Routledge.

Kubey, R.W. (1980). Television and aging: Past, present and future. *The Gerontologist* 20: 16–35.

Kushner, T. (1995). *Observing the 'Other': Mass-observation and Race*. Mass-Observation Archive Occasional Paper 2, University of Sussex.

Lacan, J. (1966). *Ecrits*. Seuil.

Lee, D. (1992). *Competing Discourses: Perspectives and Ideology in Language*. Longman.

Lippi-Green, R. (1997). *English with an Accent: Language, Ideology and Discrimination in the United States*. Routledge.

Lucy, J.A. (1993). Reflexive language and the human disciplines. In J.A. Lucy (ed.) *Reflexive Language: Reported Speech and Metapragmatics*: 9–32. Cambridge University Press.

Matsuda, M.J., C.T. Lawrence, R. Delgado & K.W. Crenshaw (eds.) (1993). *Words that Wound: Critical Race Theory, Assaultive Speech and the First Amendment*. Westview Press.

Mead, G.H. (1934). *Mind, Self and Society*. Chicago University Press.

Milroy, J & L. Milroy (1985). *Authority in Language: Investigating Language Prescription and Standardisation*. Routledge.

Moscovici, S. (1984). The phenomenon of social representations. In R. Farr & S. Moscovici (eds.) *Social Representations*. Cambridge University Press.

Park, R.E. (1924). The concept of social distance. *Journal of Applied Sociology* 8: 339–344.

Potter, J. & M. Wetherell (1987). *Discourse and Social Psychology*. Sage.

Rampton, B. (1995). *Crossing: Language and Ethnicity among Adolescents*. Longman.

Rampton, B. (ed.) (1999). *Styling the Other*. Special issue of *Journal of Sociolinguistics* 3(4).

Rickford, J. (1999). The Ebonics controversy in my back yard: A sociolinguist's experiences and reflections. *Journal of Sociolinguistics* 3(2): 267–275.

Riggins, S.H. (1997). The rhetoric of othering. In S.H. Riggins (ed.): 1–30.

Riggins, S.H. (ed.) (1997). *The Language and Politics of Exclusion: Others in Discourse.* Sage.

Rogers, E.M. (1999). Georg Simmel's concept of the stranger and intercultural communication research. *Communication Theory* 9(1): 58–74.

Ronkin, M. & H.E. Karn (1999). Mock Ebonics: Linguistic racism in parodies of Ebonics on the Internet. *Journal of Sociolinguistics* 3(3): 360–380.

Ryan, E. & H. Giles (eds.) (1982). *Attitudes to Language Variation.* Edward Arnold.

Sacks, H. (1995). *Lectures on Conversation.* Blackwell.

────── (1999). Everyone has to lie. In A. Jaworski & N. Coupland (eds.): 252–262.

Said, E. (1978). *Orientalism.* Routledge and Kegan Paul.

Simmel, G. (1950). *The Sociology of Georg Simmel.* Free Press.

Tajfel, H. (1981). Social sterotypes and social groups. In J.C. Turner & H.Giles (eds.) *Intergroup Behaviour*: 144–165. Blackwell.

Tajfel, H. & J. Turner (1979). An integrative theory of intergroup conflict. In W.C. Austin & S. Worchel (eds.) *The Social Psychology of Intergroup Relations*: 33–53. Brooks/Cole.

Talbot, M. (2000). 'It's good to talk': The undermining of feminism in a British Telecom advertisement. *Journal of Sociolinguistics* 4(1): 108–119.

Thorne, A. & J. Coupland (1998). Articulations of same-sex desire: Lesbian and gay male dating advertisements. *Journal of Sociolinguistics* 2(2): 233–258.

Urry, J. (1990). *The Tourist Gaze.* Sage.

Van Dijk, T. (1993). *Elite Discourse and Racism.* Sage.

────── (1997). Political discourse and racism: Describing others in Western parliaments. In S.H. Riggins (ed.): 33–64.

────── (1999). Discourse and the denial of racism. In A. Jaworski & N. Coupland (eds.) *The Discourse Reader*: 541–558.

Whorf, B.L. (1997). The relation of habitual thought and behavior to language. In N. Coupland & A. Jaworski (eds.): 443–463.

Williams, A. & J. Coupland (1998). Talking about Generation X: Defining them as they define themselves. *Journal of Language and Social Psychology* 16(3): 251–277.

Wodak, R., Ruth *Das Ausland* and anti-Semitic discourse: The discursive construction of the other. In S.H. Riggins (ed.): 65–87.

Woodward, K. (1991). *Aging and its Discontents: Freud and Other Fictions.* Indiana University Press.

Social institutions

Richard J. Watts
University of Bern

1. Introduction

As the attributive adjective 'social' implies, terms such as 'social class', 'social network', 'social role', 'social institution', 'social process', etc., are interpreted as being part of that domain of knowledge which concerns itself with human society, viz. sociology. However, since the study of human society automatically involves the researcher with other domains of knowledge, the interdisciplinary link with those domains is also documented by attributing the adjective 'social' or adding the prefix 'socio-', so that we get 'sociolinguistics', 'social psychology', 'social anthropology', 'sociopragmatics', etc.

Fundamental to the study of human society is a concern with human language. Interaction between human beings need not always involve human language, but if it does not, it is always predicated on it.

This paper focuses on the study of social institutions from the angle of pragmatics, not so much because this is necessarily the best or the only way to study them, but rather because researchers have indicated the need for a close pragmatic analysis of verbal interaction in institutional settings without going very far towards carrying it out (e.g. Sarangi & Slembrouck 1996; Fairclough 1992, 1993; Fowler et al. 1979; Redish 1983; Wilson 1990).

A thorough micro-analysis of socio-communicative verbal interaction within institutional settings must involve various approaches to the study of the generation and negotiation of meaning, i.e. it must involve various types of linguistic pragmatics. However, if we seriously consider theories of sociology such as social constructivism and social reproduction, a micro-analysis of verbal interaction will ultimately lead to a reshuffling of what constitutes a social institution. Taking the argument to its logical conclusion we might then say that all verbal interaction is inherently institutional.

For reasons of space, this paper will first outline only one of the clearest statements within the framework of social constructivism of what characterizes a social institution, viz. that provided by Berger and Luckmann (1991), then broadening the scope of sociological enquiry by bringing in ideas of social reproduction and symbolic resources posited by Bourdieu and his associates to show how a micro-level analysis of institutional discourse of the kind that Sarangi and Slembrouck (1996) aim at reveals discourse features which are also to be found in the discourse of individual families. One research goal that thus emerges for pragmaticists and discourse analysts is to consider these forms of discourse as also being fundamentally institutional.

2. The social constructivist approach to 'social institutions'

The underlying tenet in Berger and Luckmann's theory of social constructivism is that the individual's basic apprehension of reality, while remaining rooted in her/his bodily interaction with the environment, is nevertheless one which is shared with others. Indeed, through face-to-face interaction with others in the conscious here-and-now, the prototypical case of social interaction, reality becomes social and intersubjective. The individual's construction of reality and knowledge is thus grounded in individual physical experience, but is in essence social and interactive.

The significance of human language in this process cannot be over-stressed. Berger and Luckmann suggest that language has "an inherent quality of reciprocity that distinguishes it from any other sign system" in that conversational partners can synchronize their language with "the ongoing subjective intentions of the conversants" (1991: 52). Partners in face-to-face verbal interaction have what Berger and Luckmann call "a continuous, synchronized, reciprocal access to […] two subjectivities, an intersubjective closeness in the face-to-face situation that no other sign system can duplicate" (1991: 52). Their first important hypothesis is that conceptualizations of reality are derived from the socio-communicative interaction of the individual with others and that the most fundamental form of reality, from which all others are derived, is that of 'everyday life'. Berger and Luckmann suggest that everyday life is above all life "with and by means of the language" which the individual shares with others. In other words, human language is the primary medium through which everyday life is constructed and managed. Their second important hypothesis is that all socio-communicative interaction takes place within social institutions which are created in the course of time through interaction and are also perpetuated and adapted by it.

Berger and Luckmann maintain that during the individual's socialization via the dialogic medium of language in everyday life, s/he objectifies interpersonal, interactional experiences into a conceptualization of 'reality' which is, therefore, essentially a social construct. In doing so the individual structures a system of social roles, social ethics and social constraints to which values are assigned and reaffirms these values by accepting (or rejecting) those aspects of 'social reality.'

They call this process 'institutionalization', which they define as follows:

> Institutionalization occurs whenever there is a reciprocal typification of habitualized actions by types of actors. Put differently, any such typification is an institution.
> (1991: 72)

The term 'typification of habitualized actions' implies reciprocity, face-to-faceness, the ego and the alter. It is a fundamentally interactive, dialogic concept and thereby open to pragmatic analysis. In order for a typification process to constitute an institution, it must be repeated frequently; it must acquire its own historicity:

> Institutions [...] imply historicity and control. Reciprocal typifications of actions are built up in the course of a shared history. They cannot be created instantaneously. Institutions have a history, of which they are the products. (1991: 94)

Thus, at one and the same time, institutions are cultural products and essential constitutive factors that help us to define a culture. To challenge the 'reality' of an institution is to threaten an important element of the culture itself. The important phrase here is "reciprocal typifications of [habitualized] actions [...] built up in the course of a shared history", since it is through the identification of such reciprocal typifications of actions that we can identify an institution.

Berger and Luckmann also maintain that the individual acquires a social self, an ego, within social institutions, a social self which is experienced "as distinct from and even confronting the self in its totality". Within that social self the individual learns to function in institutionally specific ways and thus contributes towards perpetuating the institution, i.e. towards giving it a history.

Two points can be derived from this discussion. On the one hand, social institutions can only develop through social, i.e. essentially verbal, interaction, thus entailing that a pragmatic micro-level analysis of that interaction can reveal the ways in which the social self is developed. On the other hand, reciprocal typifications of habitualized actions through which more ephemeral institutions such as individual families are created will have a restricted historicity and will be restricted in their scope. In other words, there is absolutely no reason why individual families, gangs, groups of friends, school classes, etc. should not also be considered types of institution. I will illustrate this in Section 5.

3. Social reproduction and the notion of symbolic resource

Bourdieu carries the constructivist concept of institution into the realms of economics by positing that the socialization of an individual involves his/her participation in the processes of social production and distribution. Bourdieu actually suggests that the basis of all social production lies in the field of 'material' capital, i.e. that the production and distribution of social and symbolic capital derive from more tangible forms of capital (Bourdieu 1977).

However, one can accept the notion of 'symbolic capital' just as easily if one takes it to be a metaphor. Linguistic capital is a form of symbolic and cultural capital, which acquires various values through the access that it gives to the individual to increase his/her material capital. But it also has the function of disguising the ways in which material wealth can be acquired, and in doing so, legitimating and contributing to that wealth (cf. Heller 1994).

Institutions thus function towards the production and reproduction of sets of social values, including forms of language, thereby creating the social resources which the individual will need to accumulate material wealth. Looked at from this viewpoint, social institutions act as gatekeepers controlling entry to marketplaces in which valued and valuable symbolic resources can be traded, and they act as a means by which forms of cultural knowledge may be objectified.[1] Individuals must also learn how to act like a member of the social institution concerned, i.e. in Bourdieu's terms s/he must adopt, and act in accordance with, a habitus.[2]

Bourdieu also recognizes the pivotal role that language plays in social production and reproduction and consistently implies that it is through the use of language in interaction that the value of language as a symbolic resource is assessed. In a report on academic discourse published by Bourdieu and his associates in France in 1965 we read the following: "Language is the most active and elusive part of the cultural heritage which each individual owes to his (sic!) background". (Bourdieu & Passeron 1994: 8) A little later in the text the relationship between language, social heritage and symbolic value is made even more specific: "[…] what we inherit from our social origins is not only a language, but — inseparably — a relationship to language and specifically to the value of language". (1994: 21)

Once again, we can assume that a pragmatic micro-level analysis of verbal interaction should be able to reveal the ways in which the symbolic value of language is assessed and the ways in which the social institution objectifies the forms of cultural knowledge that individuals will need to acquire in the linguistic marketplace and to reproduce the habitus appropriate to the institution. The pragmatic analysis of verbal interaction should, amongst other things, be in a position to reveal the kinds of social process through which social institutions are reproduced.

4. The discourse of social control: The reproduction of social institutions

Sarangi and Slembrouck (1996) go some way towards showing how the discourse of social institutions, which they choose to restrict to the discourse of bureaucracy, may be looked at from a micro-level perspective. They focus quite explicitly on ways in which the social roles of client and bureaucrat are pre-established before the client's interaction with a member of a bureaucratic institution and how those social roles are reproduced

---

1. Cf. also Berger and Luckmann (1991) on processes of objectivisation.
2. Note here the link with Berger and Luckmann's notion of the "reciprocal typification of habitualized actions."

through the interaction itself. They capitalize directly on Bourdieu's notions of habitus and the unequal distribution of cultural capital in concluding that "the occurrence of kinds of discursive behaviour is a result of the actual distribution of symbolic resources over groups of the population" (1996: 183). I would add that the principal reason for recognizing (or not recognizing) the appropriate forms of discourse strategy in a communicative interaction with a representative of a social institution is the different ways in which client and institutional representative interpret typified actions.

Sarangi and Slembrouck also stress the importance of looking more closely at the ways in which information is exchanged in institutional encounters, and they favor a socio-pragmatic approach to the analysis of those encounters. They give a wealth of examples of successful and less successful interactions involving the kinds of information exchange through which the roles of client and bureaucrat are reproduced socially. These include letters, application forms, written memoranda, interviews, telephone calls, etc. Despite their insistence on a micro-level analysis, however, what is missing from their approach is an analysis which is linked to the notions of emergent and latent social networks as these are developed in Watts (1991, 1992, 1994).

The concept of emergent network has been developed from that of social network in sociology and social anthropology (cf. Barnes 1954; Bott 1957; Rosser & Harris 1965; Clyde 1969; Boissevain 1974; Milroy 1980). A social network is understood to be a set of interconnected functional relationships between the members of a community, i.e. as one type of sociological 'given'. In this sense it also reflects the reciprocal typification of actions which constitutes a social institution and is always latently present during any ongoing verbal interaction, particularly in those types of verbal interaction which are most likely to be considered institutional.

The emergent network, on the other hand, must be understood dynamically. Coparticipants in social interaction establish functional interpersonal links during the course of the interaction regardless of whether or not they are members of the same latent social network (or in this case institution) prior to the activity. In verbal interaction the most obvious type of interpersonal link is an on-record speaking directed at a coparticipant, and the social network is said to emerge from and by virtue of such interaction. Verbal interactions are structured sequentially in accordance with shifts of discourse topic or shifts in the focus of an already active topic, and these shifts will signal the beginnings and endings of emergent networks. Hence emergent networks will have a relatively brief temporal extension and are also different from latent social networks in that their gradual development from the moment they are initiated to the moment at which they close can be observed.

In Sarangi and Slembrouck's work any verbal interaction between a client and the member of an institution may involve challenges on the part of clients to the authority of the institutional member or requests for more information or explanations concerning institutional procedures. Such discourse strategies on the part of the client belong to the emergent network being developed at that point in time and are almost always interpreted by the institutional member as being external to the set of habitual actions which both client and member would count as being typical of the institution. In addition, they can be seen as skewing the values of the cultural resources under negotiation in the verbal interaction. The reproduction of the latent social network represented by the institution is thereby questioned, if not directly challenged. This may be one of the reasons for the system of hierarchical network layers beyond the institutional member who comes into immediate or mediate contact with the client and also for the complex of discourse strategies which can be invoked to counter such requests and challenges.

What is really needed in the analysis of institutional discourse is a close micro-level analysis of such crucial emergent networks in verbal interactions between clients and institutional members against the background of a macro-theory of social reproduction in which explicit links are made between latent social networks and on-line emergent networks. Watts (1996) examined points at which family discourse becomes conflictual from the methodological perspective of relevance theory, i.e. through one approach to pragmatic analysis which is rarely if ever applied to real sociolinguistic data. Section 5 reviews this analysis, showing that family discourse may also be considered as a form of institutional discourse.

5. Family discourse as a form of institutional discourse

Consider the following stretch of family discourse:

(1) 1 R: W-why then is the Civil Service able to [1.5] :er: pension you off, or not
2   Pension you off as the case may be, at age sixty? [0.9] :er: retirement age is
3   not reduced, or is not being reduced from sixty-five to sixty. [1.7]Why that
4   discrepancy?
5 D: [1.0] the majority of people who [.] work in the Civil Service have done their
6   full time, forty years or thereabouts [0.9] and they get a half-rate pension. But
7   you see, I've/ ???? ???? [I've done a [—
8 R: [mm   [
9 B: [But even on a half-rate pension David,
10   [you couldn't really live without the retirement pension.
11 A: [mm
12 D: Very likely not.[[1.7] When I left the Ottoman Bank it was in the days be/
13 B: [no
14   [0.9] The current legislation is that if you [.] leave the job,[you take your pension
15 A: [mm
16   rights with you. But that's only fairly recent legislation. [[1.5] When I left the bank,
17 B: [??? years

18		I lost all- all the pension I had earned. [Gone
19	B:	[??? years.
20	D:	Yes.
21	B:	mm
22	D:	Lost.
23	B:	mmhmm
24	R:	Good Lord!
25	A:	mm
26	R:	[1.2] You mean at that time there was no [0.8] provision for you to::[[1.0]
27	D:	[No. No.
28		take that pension with you and put it into another pension fund?
29	D:	No. No. [2.3] So that went straight down the drain.
30	R:	[2.7] <whistles>
31	D:	[1.6] So if- if I'm forced to retire at age sixty, I [.] have got to look [.] for something,
32		some other means of making a living. [0.8] <laughs>
33	A:	mmhmm
34	R:	[3.0] hm well. [1.9] yeah
35	D:	[1.0] So I'll have to start up my own business again.
36	R:	[5.1] Well what/[0.8] to/do- do they expect people [1.0] to do between sixty and
37		sixty-five? Simply to go on the dole?
38	D:	No. A certain majority of them can re/[1.0] who've done their forty years, can
39		retire at half pay and reckon that's enough.
40	B:	[2.0] Yes but half pay :er: :er: of a- about nine thousand a year [1.6] is only
41		four and a half thousand. Well if you've been living on- on nine thousand, how can
42		[they expect you to —
43	D:	[<They have a>- they also/ Yeah. They also get a lump sum [2.9] depen/ again when/
44		[1.0] depending on the number of years you've served.
45	B:	So you get a little lump sum as well.
46	A:	mmhmm
47	R:	But a- again it will be a pity that <that sum won't be enough>
48	D:	Yeah. Yeah it- it depends on the years I've served. [0.7] Which means
49		not all that much.
50	A:	mm mm [1.7] mm
51	R:	[1.0] :er: did you know about this be- beforehand, or- or is that something
52		that's come with the —
53	A:	mmhmm
54	D:	When I joined you could then go on to sixty-five. [[0.8] This is only covering
55	A:	[mm
56		the last[[0.7] sort of three or four years. Which is/ you've almost certainly
57	B:	[mmhmm

58		got to retire at age sixty.
59	A:	mm
60	R:	[2.3] So you've known that for some time?
61	D:	Yeah [2.4] So I've been thinking of ways and means of how I can earn a crust
62		of bread at age sixty.
63	R:	[7.5] It's crazy.
64	B:	And what ideas have you got? I mean I [—
65	D:	[I told you. I told you what ideas I'd got.
66	B:	They don't seem feasible to me.
67	D:	Alright. Well they don't. We'll have to wait and see.
68	B:	[1.7] Well it's- it's- it's- it's/ To my mind saying "Well we'll have to wait and see?
69		is- is rather- is rather negative and leaving it rather late. [1.0] I mean—
70	D:	[4.2] Well. brrahahahaa [4.5] Well got any ideas?
71	R:	[1.7] ??? ???
72	B:	<Well it's just a>/ I mean- [2.9] I don't know. I mean/[0.7] what- what can- what
73		can you do? [0.6] You're not likely to get anybody to employ you. [[0.6] And
74	D:	[True.
75		And it's very very difficult to set up a business on your own without a fair
76		amount of capital behind you. Look how many one-man businesses go down
77		the drain.
78	D:	Yes. I should know that in my job.
79	B:	Of course you do [[0.8] So [0.6] what are you optimistic about?[and saying
80	R:	[I see. [
81	A:	[mm
82	D:	[I've never been-
83	B:	"Oh we'll wait and see"? Because[—
84	D:	[I've never been a pessimist.
85	B:	ai yai yai I know that. [[1.7] You've got to be practical.
86	A:	[mm [0.9] mmhmm
87	R:	[10.6] Yes, okay. But it's not a nice thing to be practical about is it? [1.2] If you
88		[2.2] have worked on the assumption that whe- when you take a job, retirement
89		is age sixty-five. And you [1.3] tune yourself in as it were to that thought. [0.8]
90		And then suddenly legislation comes in that in fact you retire <at sixty having>
91		[—
92	D:	[There might be a possibility for me to continue in the Civil Service for up to
93		[1.0] <clears throat> [1.5] twenty years service.
94	A:	[3.5] mmhmm
95	R:	mm
96	D:	So if I joined in nineteen seventy, they might allow me to go on till nineteen ninety
97		[1.0] and not force me to retire at sixty. [2.0] But that sill leaves a gap. [3.1] Or

	98		would leave a gap.
	98	B:	[0.8] And::- and it still wouldn't give you much more in the way of [1.0] pension
	99		would it?
	100	D:	No. An extra- an extra two and a half years.
	101	R:	It would simply give you a little time to think about things.
	102	D:	Yeah.
	103	A:	[0.7] mm
	104	R:	[2.2] hmm

I will focus on certain sections of the overall extract which I consider significant in light of the discussion in Section 4. The extract is taken from an after-dinner conversation in 1985 between my mother (B), my stepfather (D), my wife (A) and myself (R). During the conversation the topic of retirement was touched upon. We all knew that this was likely to be a potentially conflictual topic for the following reasons. D used to work in a bank in London until he married my mother in 1961. At that time the pension he had earned at the bank was lost completely on his leaving. They opened up a restaurant and guesthouse in Cornwall, which they then sold to open up a clothes shop and to buy an old millhouse. The business did not run too well, and D was forced to sell it and to retrain as a civil servant in the Department of Health and Social Security, for whom, at the time of the recording, he had worked for 15 years. Since he is ten years younger than my mother, both were very worried at the prospect of an enforced retirement at age 60 on a very low pension. My mother had just returned from her first trip to Australia, where she had visited her cousins, and she had come back full of praise for the country. At the point when the extract begins the topic of pensions had been raised and D had mentioned that he would have to retire at age 60.

The conflict in the interaction had been latent from the beginning and was inherent in the deep feelings of anxiety shared by D and B about how they would live after D's retirement. In lines 1–4 R asks for information on the discrepancy between the statutory retirement age of 65 and the Civil Service's new imposed limit of 60, and at this point the latent conflict comes to the surface. It is opened explicitly by B in lines 9–10:

(2) B: But even on a half-rate pension, David, you couldn't really live without the retirement pension.

The contradiction expressed by the marker *but* is not with anything D has so far uttered. A relevance theoretical ananlysis would reveal that *but* has not only content meaning in expressing a contradiction but also procedural meaning in directing the addressee to a mutually shared set of assumptions rather than to anything expressed directly. That set of assumptions is not shared totally by R and A, and they do not therefore share in the typification of habitualized actions which constitutes the institution 'family' for B and D. R's request for an explanation thus lies beyond the set of typified habitualized actions characterizing the familial relationship between B and D and, as a member of the wider family group, his explanation challenges the institution.

However, from line 12 to line 39 D continues his explanation until B again enters in line 40 to contradict him. Ostensively, B's utterance in (3) is a response to D's assertion that a majority of civil servants who have worked for forty years can live on half pay during retirement:

(3) B: Yes but half pay of about nine thousand a year is only four and a half thousand.

On the other hand, two earlier assertions by D in lines 31–32 and line 35 (given as [4] and [5]) have prompted the contradiction:

(4) D: So if I'm forced to retire at age sixty, I have got to look for something, for some other means of making a living.

(5) D: So I'll have to start up my own business again.

Evidence that it is this that B is concerned about as a way of escaping from the impasse of not having enough to live on is provided later in the interaction when she challenges him directly in line 64 about his ideas for making a living ("And what ideas have you got?") in response to D's assertion in lines 61–62 "So I've been thinking of ways and means of how I can earn a crust of bread at age sixty". The open conflict between D and B is enacted after this point, and it reaches a stalemate in a very awkward, long 10.6 second pause in line 87.

Conflictual situations such as these reveal open challenges to the pre-established social network to which B and D belong, and this is even more the case for peripheral family members like R and A. A relevance theoretic approach to the data can help to highlight points of open challenge in conflictual parts of the overall interaction, and it is through an analysis of such sections against the background of pre-established reciprocal typifications of habitualized actions that family members can reassess the values of the social reproduction of their own family institutions.

The 10.6 second pause in line 87 is excessively long by the normal standards of inter-turn pause length, amounting to an embarrassing silence. It is broken by R's utterance to B in line 87:

(6) R: Yes. OK. But it's not a nice thing to have to be practical about, is it?

R's discourse strategy here is very risky, since the utterance can be taken as a direct criticism of B's immediately prior admonishment to D in line 85 to be practical. If it is not countered in turn by B (and it is not), it will effectively rob her of discourse status. Since it also gives rise to at least one explicature which adds to the contextual effects for all the participants and does so at very little processing effort, it is likely to be high on a scale of relevance to all the family members. This is particularly the case when R goes on to support the position in lines 87–90 by spelling out what it is that is not a nice thing:

    (7)   R: If you have worked on the assumption that when you take a job, retirement is at age sixty-five, and you tune yourself in as it were to that thought and then suddenly legislation comes in that in fact you retire at sixty …

R does not finish his turn in (7) since he is intervened by D. The intervention does not appear to constitute an interruption, i.e. it is not face threatening, since R has made the point he wished to make. D, however, realizes that B has lost discourse status through R's counter-position, and his intervention in lines 92–98 is an attempt to bring in a further piece of information which has not yet been given and thereby gain discourse status himself:

    (8)   D: There might be a possibility for me to continue in the Civil Service for up to twenty years service. So if I joined in nineteen seventy, they might allow me to go on till nineteen ninety and not force me to retire at sixty. But that still leaves a gap. Or would leave a gap.

It is immediately countered by B in line 98–99:

    (9)   B: And it still wouldn't give you much in the way of pension, would it?

The conflict is beginning to emerge once again, so that after D has conceded in line 102 that it would give him an extra two and a half years, R again attempts to neutralize the situation in line 101 with the following statement:

    (10)   R: It would simply give you a little time to think about things.

The attempt to resolve conflict in this interaction is thus fraught with the danger of a third party like R, who is peripheral to the 'family institution' composed of B and D, losing discourse status, and throughout the rest of the interaction this tense and rather brittle truce is held.

6. Conclusion

A close micro-level analysis of family discourse like the one briefly presented in Section 5 is able to reveal points at which the typification of habitualized actions is challenged, thus revealing the institutional status of the family itself. In effect the challenge is to the social values attached to the institution, but this can only be revealed if the latent social network, involving pre-established social connections, knowledge about the historicity of the institution, awareness of what habitualized actions have been typified as characterizing the family, etc. have been revealed. In other words, the micro- and the macro-levels of analysis must always complement each other.

Social institutions are interesting precisely because of the shared typifications of habitualized actions which constitute their history and ensure their further survival through processes of social reproduction. Individual families can be shown to possess most of the features of a social institution in that any challenge to those structures of typification represents a challenge to the value of the symbolic resources contained within the family and the power that the family has to exercise social control over its members. However, much more close pragmatic analysis of institutional discourse, interconnected with the theory of emergent and latent social networks, is necessary before we can develop a greater sense of how social institutions, on whatever level of social structure they exist, function and how their functioning may be made more transparent, less anonymous and more humane.

References

Barnes, J. (1954). Class and committees in a Norwegian island parish. *Human Relations* 7.
Berger, P.L. & T. Luckmann (1991). *The Social Construction of Reality: a Treatise in the Sociology of Knowledge*. Penguin.
Boissevain, J. (1974). *Friends of Friends: Networks, Manipulators and Coalitions*. Blackwell.
Bott, E. (1957). *Family and Social Network*. Tavistock Press.
Bourdieu, P. (1977). L'économie des échanges linguistiques. *Langue française* 34: 17–34.
Bourdieu, P. & J.-C. Passeron (1994). Introduction: Language and relationship to language in the teaching situation. In P. Bourdieu, J.-C. Passeron and M. de Saint Martin (eds.) *Academic Discourse*: 1–34. Polity Press.
Clyde, M. (ed.) (1969). *Social Networks in Urban Situations*. Manchester University Press.
Fairclough, N. (1992). *Discourse and Social Change*. Longman.
——— (1993). Critical discourse analysis and the marketisation of public discourse. *Discourse and Society* 4: 133–168.
Fowler, R., R. Hodge, G. Kress & T. Trew (1979). *Language and Control*. Routledge.
Heller, M. (1994). *Crosswords: Language, Education and Ethnicity in French Ontario*. Mouton de Gruyter.
Milroy, L. (1980). *Language and Social Networks*. Blackwell.
Redish, J.C. (1983). The language of bureaucracy. In R.E. Bailey and R.M. Fosheim (eds.) *Literacy for Life: The Demand for Reading and Writing*: 154–174. The Modern Language Association of America.
Rosser, C. & C. Harris (1965). *The Family and Social Change: A Study of Family and Kinship in a South Wales Town*. Routledge and Kegan Paul.
Sarangi, S. & S. Slembrouck (1996). *Language, Bureaucracy and Social Control*. Longman.
Sperber, D. & D. Wilson (1986). *Relevance: Communication and Cognition*. Blackwell.
Watts, R.J. (1991). *Power in Family Discourse*. Mouton de Gruyter.
——— (1992). Acquiring status in conversation: 'Male' and 'female' discourse strategies. *Journal of Pragmatics* 16: 467–503.

———— (1994). Male vs. female discourse strategies: Tabling conversational topics. In G. Brünner & G. Graefen (eds.) *Texte und Diskurse: Methoden und Forschungsergebnisse der Funktionalen Pragmatik:* 218–237. Westdeutscher Verlag.

———— (1996). Resolving conflict in family discourse. Paper held at the 5th. International Pragmatics Conference, July 1996. Mimeo.

———— (1997). Relevance theory and verbal interruptions: Assessing discourse status. *Multilingua* 16. In press.

Wilson, J. (1990). *Politically Speaking.* Blackwell.

Speech community

Ben Rampton
King's College

'Speech community' has been a troubled term, caught in a number of methodological, epistemic and political cross-currents, and in this paper I will try to trace some of its most important shifts in meaning since the 1960s.

Some of this movement has occurred within the arena of sociolinguistics itself. The meaning of an analytic concept is always likely to be influenced by the particular methodological preferences of the scholars who use it, and in the course of the paper, I will address a number of different schools and sub-paradigms, pointing to some substantial differences in the inflections that they give to the concept. But at the same time, sociolinguistics has always been more than just a technical activity, and 'speech community' has been especially hard to tie down as a analytic term isolated from the much larger debates that affect our understanding of community as a concept in everyday language and in social science more generally. Within this larger field, a number of shifts have recently become salient. Rather than our actions being seen as a mere reflection of our belonging to 'big' communities that pre-exist us, there is now more emphasis on the part that here-and-now social action plays in the production of 'small' but new communities, and rather than just concentrating on behaviour at the core, there is a burst of interest in interaction with 'strangers' inside, outside and at the boundaries. Comparably, scholarship itself doesn't simply report on communities – it also helps to create them, destroy and prevent their inception. To give a clearer idea of these more general changes in perspective and focus, I will try to embed the discussion of sub-disciplinary schools and themes in a larger epistemic frame. More specifically, I will suggest that during the 1960s and 70s (and often much later), treatments of 'speech community' were dominated by a preoccupation with the encounter between 'tradition' and 'modernity', while we can make better sense of more recent developments if we refer to the discourses of late/post-modernity.

From the start of sociolinguistic discussion of speech community, the aim has been to show that social organisation and language use are profoundly interwoven, and so when our sense of speech community alters, there are often consequences for the kinds of language practice that we attend to. In line with this, I also try to describe important changes in linguistic focus, covering shifts of interest running, for example, from competence to reflexivity, from practice and representation to artful performance, and from regularity to spectacle.

My discussion is divided into the following sections: (1) Community *speech* and speech *community*: Pragmatic vs. distributional perspectives; (2) Speech community at the interface of 'tradition and modernity'; (3) Late modern discourse, language and community; (4) Communities of practice; (5) Community as a semiotic sign; (6) Language ideologies and the production of community; (7) From the 'linguistics of community' to a 'linguistics of contact'; (8) Community and discourse in the Information Age; (9) Conclusion.

1. Community speech and speech community: Pragmatic vs. distributional perspectives

Sociolinguistic discussion of 'speech community' in the 1960s and 70s was animated by opposition to at least two tendencies:

- first, a neglect of the social and cultural in linguistics: for example, Chomsky's assertion that serious linguistic study was only possible if it assumed an 'ideal speaker–hearer in a homogeneous speech community', or, less radically, the logo-centric reduction of community to language which Hymes saw as an effect of Bloomfield's definition (Hymes 1972a: 54, 1974: 47; Bloomfield 1933: Ch. 3; Lyons 1970: 326)
- second, normative mono-dialectalism, particularly in education: "the erroneous and deadening fiction that there is always *only one* (and always the same one) correct variety [in the speech community]" (Fishman 1972b: 321; Hymes 1972b; Labov 1969; Halliday 1978).

But developing an alternative to these views could lead in two directions. On the one hand, a primarily 'pragmatic' analysis could focus on the way in which speech itself is permeated by the socio-cultural, documenting "the rules of use without which the rules of grammar would be useless" and examining the practical misunderstandings that can arise if one neglects norms of appropriacy and assumes speech community co-membership solely on the basis of linguistic structure (Hymes 1972b: 287ff, 278). On the other hand, a 'distributional' approach could try to demonstrate that the heterogeneity of the speech community is actually structured, that there is pattern rather than randomness in the obvious across-context and inter-speaker differences displayed among members of a language group, and that far from being broken and disorderly, the grammar of non-standard speakers has integrity and system (Labov 1982).

These two perspectives figure side-by-side in programmatic discussions of 'speech community' during this period (e.g. Gumperz 1962, 1968; Hymes 1972a; Labov 1972a; Fishman 1972a; Halliday 1978), but their empirical elaboration pulls them apart (Kerswill 1994: 26), and while 'speech community' becomes a redundant concept in pragmatic analysis, it remains pivotal in the distributional. The reasons for this bifurcation are as follows.

In the pragmatic approach, membership of a particular speech community is postulated *in the background* as the origin of the social norms that determine the appropriacy of speech, producing social meaning above and beyond referential intelligibility (Hymes 1972a; Gumperz 1968: 381). With the emphasis on the complexity of communicative action, on acts and events in their ecology, there is a need for quite substantial immersion in the fieldwork setting and for analysis which treats language as just one among a great many resources for the creation of meaning (Bauman & Sherzer 1974: 89). The practicalities of data elicitation and analysis generally require fairly deep involvement with a relatively small number of informants, and the outcome is likely to be the detailed portrait of an internally differentiated but fairly coherent group, outlining the cultural integrity of distinctive speech practices, as well, sometimes, as the ways in which they are transmitted intergenerationally. Anthropology and ethnography provide the most obvious home and method for this approach. The tendency has been for studies to focus on groups who are unfamiliar to the educated western reader, and like ethnographic case-studies more generally, the findings seek much of their power and validity through their comparability and translatability to settings that the reader actually does know (LeCompte & Goetz 1982). Claims about the extent to which the particular group being studied is representative of a larger population tend to be weak (Irvine 1987: 18), and the demands of fieldwork and analysis in this approach generally inhibit any empirical specification of limits to the demographic spread of a particular practice. From the outset, ethnographically oriented definitions of speech community have declared their own tentativeness and dependance "on the level of abstraction we wish to achieve" (Gumperz 1962: 31, 1968: 381; Hymes 1972a: 54), and rather than serving as a descriptive tool, the notion of 'speech community' functions more as an ontological marker, "a necessary primary term in that it postulates the basis of description as a social, rather than a linguistic entity" (Hymes 1972a: 54). In line with both this and the injunction that the "essential thing is that the object of description be an integral social unit" (Hymes 1972a: 55), studies within this tradition move rapidly beyond any technical notion to more intuitive everyday uses of 'community' to describe the settings where their fieldwork is located (cf. the papers in e.g. Cazden, John & Hymes (eds.) 1972; Heath 1983; Section 2 below).

All this is in striking contrast to the distributional approach. In the distributional approach, speech community is an empirical territory spanned by the patterned variability of a linguistic structure – "Any description of language must take the speech community as its object if it is to do justice to the elegance and regularity of linguistic structure" (Labov 1989: 52). As in the pragmatic perspective, social norms are thought to have a profound influence on the shape and interpretation of speech, but rather than taking this as a cue to explore the relation of language to normative expectations across many dimensions of socio-cultural organisation, analysis homes in on the shared evaluative rating (of the speech) of different social subgroups, which is seen as the central principle structuring linguistic variability and as a key element constituting speech community itself (Labov 1972a: 120–121; Trudgill & Giles 1978; Bell 1984). The multi-layered complexity of communicative action is subordinated to an interest in the social and historical spread, change and maintenance of specific linguistic variables, and speech events are standardised to facilitate economical elicitation of comparative data from quite large numbers of speakers, who are often a systematic sample from larger populations (Labov 1981; Trudgill 1974; Kerswill 1994: 23; Hudson 1996: 28). The outcome of this survey is a map of the speech community which can point to its outer boundaries, which claims to be able to identify inauthentic members (Labov 1980), and which may well include the reader him/herself, this latter attribute contributing much to the reproach to armchair theorists that animated early variationists (Labov 1972a: Ch. 8). At the same time, however, it may only be a handful of linguistic variables that provide the empirical basis for this map (J. Milroy 1992: 61), and this means that it is very vulnerable to revision by researchers looking at more or others (Kerswill 1994: 26–27). As it becomes clear that different variables actually have different social distributions, with people in different regions sharing some linguistic features but not others, the meaning of speech community becomes increasingly item-specific and therefore technical, amounting to not much more than (some aspect of) the sociolinguistic patterning encompassed within the spread of a particular variable and/or its evaluation. Thus defined, the ground covered within 'speech community' might either massively expand, encompassing the "community of all speakers of English" on some variables (Labov 1989: 2, cited in Hudson 1996: 30), or alternatively, where the focus is on the innovation of a new linguistic item, it could shrink down to a total population of just two (J. Milroy 1992: 221; cf. Kerswill 1994: 159–160 on nested speech communities). This technical specialisation edges 'speech community' back towards the logo-centricity criticised in Chomsky and Bloomfield: the linguistic definition comes first and social attributes are only adduced afterwards, the identification of important social dimensions relying more on the importation of social theories from elsewhere, or on the researcher's own commonsense about society, than on inductive cultural description (Gumperz 1982: 26; Williams 1992: 73; Labov 1972: 120; J. Milroy 1992: 61,201).

It would be a mistake to try to allocate sociolinguists unambiguously to either of these two approaches to speech community. Labov has obviously done important work within the ethnographic/pragmatic approach (1972b), Bernstein engaged in the systematic distributional analysis of rules of use (1973), and the Milroys developed a relatively ethnographic focus on close groups within variationism (L. Milroy 1980; J. Milroy 1992: 207). Even so, the logics of pragmatic and distributional enquiry lead in different directions, and this tends to undermine attempts to achieve a unified summative sociolinguistic definition of 'speech community' (Hudson 1996: 24–30; Wardhaugh 1986: Ch. 5; Duranti 1997: 79–83).

In the formative period of contemporary sociolinguistics, then, there were major methodological fissures underlying the treatment of speech community. Seen at a more abstract level, however, the research I have discussed shared a common orientation to the problematic interface between 'tradition' and 'modernity', and below, I shall try to show that this distinguishes it from more recent work.

2. 'Speech community' at the interface of 'tradition and modernity'

The interface between 'tradition' and 'modernity' has been enormously formative for the social sciences. According to Giddens (1990a: 15–16):

Sociology has its origins in the coming of modernity – in the dissolution of the traditional world and the consolidation of the modern. Exactly what 'traditional' and 'modern' should be taken to mean is a matter of chronic debate. But this much is plain. With the arrival of industrialism, the transfer of millions of people from rural communities to cities, the progressive development of mass democracy, and other quite fundamental institutional changes, the new world was savagely wrenched away from the old. What began as a series of transformations substantially internal to Europe and North America has increasingly traversed the globe. The lurching juggernaut of change which the West launched is still careering erratically over the surface of the earth. Sociology was born of the attempt to track its path, but until well into the twentieth century was itself rather too strongly stamped by the context of its own origins.

In definitions of speech community in the 60s and 70s, the encounter between 'tradition' and 'modernity' was often mentioned, and as I have already suggested, one of the central missions of sociolinguistics was to make *modern* institutions, especially schools, more hospitable to the diverse and often supposedly *non*-modern populations that they served. In the process, debates about the relationship between children and schools generated a large variety of binary dichotomies, many of which resonated with arguments about the philosophical underpinnings of liberal modernity[1]. The dichotomies ranged across:

---

1. The liberal tradition is complex and contested, but among other things, it can be characterised in terms of

a. a strong sense of reason as impartiality, with the reasoner standing "apart from his own emotions, desires and interests... abstracting... away from the concrete situation" (Frazer & Lacey 1993: 48);

b. a belief that public and private realms should be clearly separated, with state activity limited to the public sphere and human diversity and difference regarded as private (ibid 47);

- modes of expression: vernacular vs. standard, oral vs. literate, concrete vs. abstract, implicit vs. explicit, narrative vs. argument, metaphorical vs. rational, contextualised vs. decontextualised, particularistic vs. universalistic, grounded in high vs. low shared knowledge;
- types of social organisation: home vs. school, close vs. open networks, homogeneous vs. heterogeneous, solidarity- vs. status-based, and
- social categories: migrant vs. host, minority vs. majority, female vs. male, working vs. middle class.

Sociolinguists often devoted considerable energy to contesting these polarities and the collocational chains that they tended to form (e.g. vernacular + oral + narrative + particularistic + close networks + working class + traditional vs. standard + literate + argument + universalistic + open networks + middle class + modern). Efforts were made to complicate, uncouple and refute these associations, and/or to negate or reverse their valuation as better vs. worse (Hymes 1980: 129–30; Bauman & Sherzer 1989: xvii; Labov 1969; Heath 1982; Street 1984), and when tradition and modernity figured in their discussions of 'speech community', Gumperz, Hymes, Fishman and others were highly sensitive to the risks of prejudging what 'simple' and 'complex' societies actually were. Hymes excepted (1972a: 54), programmatic definitions proposed 'speech community' as a neutral *superordinate* concept, capable of embracing all types of society, from small face-to-face bands to modern nations, and the intention was that the differences between societies could be analysed with lower level concepts like network, role repertoire, and compartmentalisation (Gumperz 1962, 1968; Fishman 1972a).

In this way, sociolinguists made deliberate efforts to prevent 'speech community' from being primarily associated with the 'tradition' side of the 'tradition-modernity' dichotomy, and indeed they also resisted the more ordinary associations of 'community' with notions of mutuality, fellowship, or locally based interactive

---

c. an a-historical and 'disembodied' view of the individual, seen as having a "moral primacy… against the claims of any social collectivity" (Gray 1986: x) and grounded in the "presocial or transcendent features of human beings" (Frazer & Lacey 1993: 45);
d. an insistence that the legitimacy of the state be based on consent and on a public and universal conception of law committed to rationality (ibid 49–50);
e. a conviction that social reality is knowable, and that social policy and technology might be used to ameliorate poverty, unhappiness and other ills (ibid 50).

Within sociolinguistics, these values have been at issue in the debates about concrete vs. abstract etc. modes of expression, in disputes about the extent to which school and other institutions should recognise different home cultures, in the argument with Chomsky, in the hypostasisation of system and coherence, and lastly, in the commitment to social intervention. (For fuller discussions of liberal modernity relevant to sociolinguistics, cf. Scollon & Scollon 1995: Ch. 6; Collins 1998, Heller 1999).

Gemeinschaft (Tonnies 1963; Yeo & Yeo 1988). Nevertheless, it was difficult to stop 'speech community' from becoming the conceptual frame within which modernity's 'others' were studied, especially when it coalesced with more everyday uses of community.

In research focusing only on the efficient functioning of modern bureaucratic institutions, community is an unnecessary term, since "formal organisational criteria can be counted upon to identify and separate the personnel within which relationships, behaviour and attitude are to be studied" (Arensberg 1961: 247) – it is sufficient to talk of 'middle managers', 'research officers', 'clients', 'patients', 'pupils' etc. But where (a) the focus turns to people and groups who don't conform to the expectations of modern institutions and where (b) there is a drive to conceptualise their performance in terms of difference rather than deficit – i.e. not just as 'awkward patients', 'dim pupils' – it is difficult to find any term other than community to encompass the diversity of the alternative organisational forms within which their non-standard abilities are held to be well-adapted and develop. In the end, this makes it very hard to hold to the neutral definition of speech community that the early theorists intended, and for a number of reasons (including the fact that it was actually subordinate groups that sociolinguists tended to study), speech community often came to be associated with the *marked* elements in the binary dichotomies I mentioned above (vernacular, oral modes of expression; close, solidary, home-based networks; minority and working class groups).[2]

At the same time, sociolinguistics participated in a current of romanticism that ran deep in the social sciences (Duranti 1988: 225), and along with its "announcement of the universal democracy of acquisition", its "celebration of everyday oral language" and its suspicion of "official socialisers" (Bernstein 1996: Chs. 3 & 7),[3] sociolinguistics also often treated community belonging as the condition for *any* valid language use.

---

2. This can be seen in Labov's shift from a differentiated item-by-item view of points where white and black people belonged to similar and different speech communities (1972a: 118) to a view where for practical/educational purposes, differences are totemised in the representation of the African American speech community as a disadvantaged social group (Labov 1982; cf. Morgan 1994: 328-9, 337-9).

3. In an account of sociolinguistics and other social sciences, Bernstein discusses the influence of ideas about 'competence', which he characterises as follows:

The social logic of the concept competence may reveal:

1. an announcement of the universal democracy of acquisition. All are inherently competent. There is no deficit.
2. the individual as *active* and *creative* in the construction of a *valid* world of meaning and practice. There can only be *differences* between such worlds, meanings and practices
3. a celebration of everyday, oral language use and a suspicion of specialised languages

Both pragmatic and distributional approaches emphasised shared norms and consensus – supposedly key community characteristics – as the condition in which people developed their communicative competence. The existence of internal differentiation was obviously an article of faith, but the assumption was that this was describably structured (Section 1; Bauman & Sherzer 1974: 8,89). System-in-grammar and coherence-in-discourse were to be described in ways that *accommodated* diversity within the community, and in the process, these properties retained their position as (a) the most highly prized attributes that analysis could recover, (b) as principal arguments in public advocacy of non-standard varieties, and (c) more generally, as cornerstone modernist values themselves (see note 1). M. L. Pratt calls this cluster of assumptions about system, coherence and socialisation to consensual norms the 'linguistics of community' (1987; also LePage 1980; Barrett 1997: 190; Rampton 1997a), and argues that "when social division and hierarchy [were] studied, the linguist's choice [was] often to imagine separate speech communities with their own boundaries, sovereignty, fraternity and authenticity,… giv[ing] rise to a linguistics that seeks to capture identity, but not the relationality of social differentiation", looking within but not across "lines of social differentiation, of class, race, gender, age" (1987: 56, 59, 61). Conflict and misunderstanding were certainly recognised, but they were often thought to occur in the gap between integrated cultural and linguistic systems, this gap being seen as the place for practical interventions that could try to help the proponents of different systems to understand each other and adjust, not as itself a locus for the description of practices and relationships where people managed without regard for the linguist's ontology. Code-mixing and switching were also analysed, but again, rather than intergroup improvisations, the central interest was in systematic patterns attributed to participation *within* relatively stable bilingual ingroups (Woolard 1988: 69–70; Rampton 1995a: Ch. 11).

Overall, then, an imprint of the encounter between 'tradition' and 'modernity' can be seen in the way that treatments of 'speech community' in the 1960s, 70s and 80s participated in a particular project. This was a broadly romantic project that set itself against the grain of popular opinion and that sought to rehabilitate subordinate and marginal groups – modernity's others – by attributing system and coherence to their conduct, system and coherence being rational properties that modernity rated much more highly than, say, sanctity or splendour. In the following sections, I shall try to show that it is increasingly hard to sustain this trajectory as we move into

---

4. official socialisers are suspect, for acquisition is a tacit, invisible act, not subject to public regulation or, perhaps, not primarily acquired through such regulation
5. a critique of hierarchical relations, where domination is replaced by facilitation and imposition by accommodation (1996: 150)

late/post-modernity, where modernity itself becomes an object of inspection rather than just a vantage point. Disputes about deficit, difference and domination – the inter-group politics nourished by a view of communities as separate socio-cultural blocs – lose much of their purchase when the clarity, permanence and omni-relevance of specific community memberships are questioned, and when community belonging is treated as a product created in the here-and-now, not just as an inherited condition. Similarly, system and coherence lose their compelling force when their status as culturally specific values becomes clearer and when analysis moves into the gap *between* relatively stable groupings, where regularities and conventions are much less certain.

It is worth beginning the account of this shift by outlining some key ideas in the discourses of late modernity.

3. Late modern discourse, language and community

Periodising the pre-modern, the modern and the late or post-modern is notoriously difficult, and it would be a serious mistake to assume that a 'modernity-postmodernity' interface now makes 'tradition vs. modernity' irrelevant, that all of the concepts and methods formulated within it are now redundant, or, at a time of US imperial ascendancy, that nation-states have ceased to matter (Billig 1995: Ch. 7; Morley & Robins 1995: 37). Broadly speaking, however, there are at least two strands of thought on the significance of late/post-modernity (Frazer & Lacey 1992). One line argues for the emergence of a *new perspective*, abandoning the liberal project of rationality together with the hope that social science can understand and harness the laws of social life.[4] The other proposes that western societies are actually *in a new era*, profoundly affected by new information technologies, by a decline in traditional political institutions and by the rise of new social movements. How are these developments related to sociolinguistics and to speech community?

Contesting the possibility of an objectively knowable reality and of a rational/scientific 'voice from nowhere', one of the most important elements within the 'new perspective' approach to late modernity has been social constructionism, the view that instead of being the product of forces that actors neither control nor comprehend, human reality is extensively reproduced and *created anew* in the socially and historically specific activities of everyday life (Giddens 1976, 1984). There is a strong case that

---

4. The liberal values of individuality, freedom and equality are themselves regarded as biased in the interests of powerful groups, and 'grand theories' which make claims to 'truth' are either treated sceptically or seen as repressive instruments of power.

this actually has rather deep roots in sociolinguistics (Sapir [1931] 1949: 104; Bauman & Sherzer 1974: 8, 1989: xvii–xix; Halliday 1978: 169–70), though it is only relatively recently that "agent- and practice-centred perspectives" have become mainstream orthodoxy, and comprehension of the "dynamic interplay between the social, conventional, ready-made in social life and the individual, creative, and emergent qualities of human existence" remains a "key problem demand[ing] a great deal more work" (Bauman & Sherzer 1989: xix; also e.g. Bernstein 1975: 151–2). But at the very least, social constructionism makes "[t]he assumption that speech communities, defined as functionally integrated social systems with shared norms of evaluation, can actually be isolated ... subject to serious question" (Gumperz 1982: 26).

The response has been to take the analysis of speech community in two directions (both of them already flagged up in earlier discussions):

a. to a close-up analysis of face-to-face interaction in relatively consolidated social relationships (cf. Hymes 1972a: 54, Fishman 1972a: 23), and
b. to an investigation of 'community' as itself a semiotic sign and ideological product (cf. e.g. Gumperz 1962: 34 & Fishman 1972a: 23).

These two enterprises are broadly compatible: social constructionism is typical in both; they are often informed by more and less explicit ideas about a political economy of language, with notions of e.g. markets and symbolic capital becoming something of a new common-sense (cf. Bourdieu 1977, 1991; Eckert & McGonnell-Ginet 1992: 469, 474, 479; Lave & Wenger 1991: 70; Duranti 1997: Chs. 2 & 3; Hanks 1996; Irvine 1989; Gal 1989; Urcioli 1996); and generally speaking, they both move some way beyond the romanticism critiqued in Bernstein's account of the 'social logic of competence' (see above & note 3).

There is probably a difference, however, in their implications for the conceptual vocabulary of sociolinguistics. Borrowing from LePage and Tabouret-Keller (1980, 1985),[5] it is obvious that both take 'focussing' rather than 'diffusion' as their central object – the first group of studies looks at interaction in focussed settings where feedback draws conduct into close conformity with dominant expectations, and the second looks at how a sense of community itself gets constructed (focussing processes themselves). But in the second perspective there is a constitutive and therefore more insistent sense of 'otherness' and of life *without* 'community'. This opens the door, first to recognition of the inherent bias towards focussed situations in a number of major sociolinguistic concepts

---

5. Le Page and Tabouret-Keller have used their research in creole communities to develop one of the earliest and most thorough critical alternatives to modernist assumptions in contemporary sociolinguistics.

themselves, and second, to attempts to develop conceptual tools better suited to analysis of movement in diffuse, indeterminate and border territories.

I shall address approaches to community that have a constitutive sense of 'otherness' in Section 6, moving on to the reassessment of basic concepts in Section 7. It is necessary to begin, though, with the concern with close-up interaction analysis, focusing in particular on the notion of 'communities of practice'.

4. Communities of practice

The move to 'communities of practice' as a key unit of analysis tunes with late modern uncertainty about grand theoretical totalisations (Z. Bauman 1992a: 65). It synchronises with the development of micro-ethnography as an alternative to traditional ethnography, itself increasingly problematised (Trueba & Wright 1981; Clifford 1983) and there is a rejection both of the abstraction and idealisations of atomistic cognitive individualism in psychology (Lave & Wenger 1991), and of a tendency to treat speakers in sociolinguistics as if they are "assembled out of independent modules: [e.g.] part European American, part female, part middle-aged, part feminist, part intellectual" (Eckert & McGonnell-Ginet 1992: 471). Instead, the focus is on mind as "embodied, situated and social" (New London Group 1996: 82), and on the constitution and inter-articulation of multiple memberships and identies in social practice.

There is in fact still a great deal in common with the ethnographic/pragmatic approach outlined in Section 1, though the shift from 'speech' to 'practice' is significant, speech being de-privileged by an intensified empirical gaze which treats situated activity as a multi-modal semiotic process involving visual, gestural, and proxemic channels as well as the physical environment, material artefacts and other objects (McDermott, Gospodinoff & Aron 1978; Goodwin 1980; Hanks 1996: Ch. 11). A range of social relationships of varying duration are conceptualised as communities of practice (e.g. unions, trades, boards of directors, marriages, bowling teams, classrooms – Lave & Wenger 1991: 98; Eckert & McGonnell-Ginet 1992), though there are firmer limits than before on the level of abstraction to which the analyst can take the term 'community' and an orientation to the lived texture of situated experience prohibits its extension to cover to all forms of social organisation, as intended in the formulations of 'speech community' by Gumperz and Fishman (Section 2). 'Community' as a concept is also much less likely to slip towards the folk/vernacular side of the tradition-modernity divide, and in fact notions from the discourse of 'situated learning' and 'communities of practice' are not only used to analyse workplace interaction but also have currency in 'fast capitalist' management theory (Gee et al. 1996: 65 et passim).

Arguments as to whether intergroup relationships are best described in terms of deficit, difference or domination are shifted into a much more fine-grained and complex account of imposition, collusion and struggle in communicative practice, as people invoke, avoid or reconfigure the cultural and symbolic capital attendant on identities with different degrees of purchase and accessibility in specific situations, and there is scope for Goffmanesque analysis of frame play and manipulation, defection and disloyalty included (Goffman 1959, 1974; Lave & Wenger 1991: 64; McDermott & Tylbor 1983). And so rather than being seen as identities separated and largely determined by biological or cultural inheritance, 'ethnics' and 'mainstreamers', men and women, are much more likely to be viewed as co-participants in discourses of power that position them differently within partly shared environments where constraints and possibilities are unequally distributed.

But even though the ongoing production of community involves the partial coordination of heterogeneous strategies and resources, as well as an unending process of improvisation within micro-contexts that are continuously shifting (Hanks 1991: 16, 20), there is a temptation to prioritise relations *within* groups rather than *between* or *across*. If one reduces the magnification and steps back from the microscopic flow, 'community' puts principal emphasis on the repetitive affirmation of relatively durable social ties in practical activity, rather than their collapse, rupture or irrelevance. Although there is nothing that makes them mutually exclusive (see below), more attention tends to be given to movement inside the horizons of a particular institutional activity system (Lave & Wenger 1991: 98), to its evolving reproduction, to the local use of resources, and to the socialisation, 'prime' and 'eventide' of its *members*, than to commodity exchange between communities, their plans for territorial expansion, their treatment of intruders, and the construction, policing or invasion of their boundaries.

The relationship *between* communities of practice is certainly identified as an important issue, and there is extensive recognition that particular communities of practice are affected by larger social and historical processes (Eckert & McConnell-Ginet 1992: 464, 473, 487; Lave & Wenger 1991: 70, 92, 122). McDermott (1988) addresses the sometimes desperate struggle for self-expression of people whose loyalties lie with subordinate communities not recognised within the communities of practice where they find themselves, and Goodwin provides a critically reflexive analysis of how "theories, artifacts and bodies of expertise" become "the insignia" of a professional community of practice in courtroom and mass-mediated communication (1994: 606). Eckert and McConnell-Ginet insist that the sociolinguistic description of situated practice should hold itself accountable to social theory (1992: 485), and at time when there is a feeling that social totality has been "dissipated into a series of randomly emerging, shifting and evanescent islands of order" (Z. Bauman 1992: 189), research on communities of practice may be particularly well-pitched. Even so, attention to stereotypes, to outgroup imagery, to the profile that particular communities might have when they are seen from outside or far off, is vulnerable to one of the central preoccupations of the theory of situated practice. The theory of practice is grounded in a major critique of abstract models, rules and representations, which are regarded as being historically overprivileged in social science and blind to their own embedding in tacit, locally and historically situated activity (Bourdieu 1977: Ch. 1; Lave & Wenger 1991: 20; Lave 1993: 22ff; Hanks 1996: 240; New London Group 1996: 84). As an inexorable fact of all thought and action, situatedness does indeed demand analysis, but on its own, it is not sufficient as a perspective on e.g. a fear of outsiders, a longing for elsewhere, or the anxiety of being guideless 'abroad' in unknown terrain. If one wants to understand experiences such as these, then models and representations also call for serious and sustained analytic attention. Putting it a little differently, 'community' can't only be seen as co-participation in locally embedded practice – analysis also has to extend to the way in which 'community' serves as a symbol and sign itself.

5. 'Community' as a semiotic sign

There are no absolute reasons why community-as-symbol shouldn't be combined with community-as-coparticipation-in-activity, but there has actually been quite a lot of variation in the extent to which work on the former – on 'community' as a relational sign – has taken culturally contexted communicative action into account.

Hudson's (1980, 1996) discussion of 'speech community' draws heavily on LePage and Tabouret-Keller (1985) and it has been often cited, but it represents one of the least socially embedded approaches. It originates in a grammarian's commitment to developing a non-Chomskyan, non-modular view of linguistic competence and structure (Hudson 1996: xiv, 3), and it is part of an attempt build social information into grammar with the aid of a model of culture drawn from cognitive anthropology (cf. Foley 1997: 18ff & Hudson 1996: 71). Language is seen as being "in the individual" (1984: 31–42, 1996: 29),[6] and community, group and other social entities are regarded as mental categories linked to specific linguistic items (1996: 48–49). Overall, Hudson's approach is more closely tuned to the variationist/distributional tradition than the ethnographic/pragmatic one; there is relatively little concern with discourse data or with processes involved in the (co-)construction of socio-cognitive typifications; and the view is that "[h]owever important power may be in life and society at large … in most languages, most of the time, power is irrelevant to speech" (1996: 240).

---

6. The rejection of structural-functionalist ideas about normative social systems emerges through an argument with Labov's notion of 'community grammar' as a collective phenomenon (Hudson 1980: 183ff, 1996: 29–30; cf. also LePage 1980).

'Community' as a mental representation is much more closely integrated with pragmatics and discourse processing by Clark (1996a: Ch. 4, 1996b), who argues that multiple attributions of community membership in terms of nationality, education, occupation, hobby etc. play a major part in establishing common ground between participants in interaction (1996b: 332–334) and are vital to processes as basic as the interpretation of word meaning – "it is essential to specify for every convention the communities in which it holds" (1996b: 337, 338–340). The enunciation of this perspective might be framed in relatively idealised terms, but it is easily transferred to empirical description of the strategic projection of group identities in e.g. urban situations where "new ethnic identities rely on linguistic symbols to establish speech conventions that are significantly different", and that "can act as powerful instruments of persuasion in everyday communicative situations for participants who share [the] values [of the group that is thereby indexed]" (Gumperz & Cook-Gumperz 1982: 6).

When attention turns to the strategic use of socially distinct speech features and to the way that they "can serve as the rallying point for interest group sharing" (ibid p. 7), community-as-representation is treated not only as a antecedent resource required in the coordination of meaning, but also as a productive device in the structuring of subsequent interaction. In the logic of social constructionism, the interplay between practice and representation in fact carries further, with inherited perceptions of 'community' being themselves challenged, ratified or reshaped in interaction and new forms of solidarity emerging in the process, temporarily at least (Hewitt 1986; Rampton 1995a; Eckert & McConnell-Ginet 1992: 462,464).

The integration of community-as-sign and community-of-practice is well illustrated in cases such as these, and indeed the social affiliations that develop are subject to varying degrees of institutionalisation, conscious planning and design (see e.g. Swales 1990: Ch. 2). Following on from that, however, it needs to be emphasised that community as a sign (or symbol) often has an effect that extends well beyond the face-to-face arena. The ways in which ideas of language and community have contributed both to the construction of wider communicative spaces, and to the conventions regulating participation in them, is a major interest in studies of language ideology.

6. Language ideologies and the production of community

Language ideologies are at work in interpersonal encounters, and can certainly be studied within a communities-of-practice perspective (Volosinov 1973: II, Ch. 3; Rampton 1995a: Ch. 12). In linguistic anthropology, though, there is growing feeling that the tools of face-to-face analysis are limited when it comes to "the ways in which linguistic practices contribute to the reproduction and legitimation of hierarchy in larger social institutions such as the state, or about the ways in which speech communities are linked to broader political economic structures… Similarly, within this framework it has been difficult to analyze adequately the processes of mass-mediated communication that often connect disparate communities and that are increasingly of interest in social theory" (Gal & Woolard 1995: 134–135; Gal & Irvine 1995: 987; Gal 1995: 416; Hannerz 1992a, 1992b).

Anderson's work on the role that mass-produced print genres played in the 'imagining' and production of nation-states as communities is an important reference point (1983), and the aims here are to see how a spread of people gets constituted as a 'community' in the first place, and how "linguistic units come to be linked with social units", languages with peoples (Gal & Irvine 1995: 970). This differs from the community of practice view in emphasising boundaries of exclusion and the production of 'Others' contrastively defining 'Us'. It also often focusses on relatively macro-scopic historical contexts, rather than on here-and-now situated interactional processes in the co-construction and inter-articulation of identities *within* communities. In addition, the critical investigation of 'totalising' overgeneralisation in the representation of social groups moves beyond the communities-of-practice attempt to develop modes of analysis that are less freighted with the assumptions of modernity, to an account of the production of key features of modernity itself (Urla 1993a, 1993b; Gal & Irvine 1995; Appadurai 1988).

Within this approach, analysis addresses several forms of 'Them' and 'Us'. Among the stereotyped Thems/Others formulated in rhetorical practice and evoked, for example, through linguistic code selection, some may be constructed as targets of fear, contempt and/or charity (Hinnenkamp 1987; Potter & Wetherall 1992; Billig 1995; Blommaert & Verschueren 1998), while others may be produced as objects of desire, fashion accoutrements and/or marketised life-style options, with 'authenticity' becoming as much an issue of commodity branding as a matter of ethnic roots (Lury 1996; Hill 1993, 1995; K. Hall 1995: 201–3; Urcioli 1996; Hoechsmann 1997). As well as 'them', 'them for us' or 'them for you', discourse and language choice can also construct 'us for you', as revealed in studies of conversationalisation in advertising and official communications (Fairclough 1992; New London Group 1996: 70), and one of the principal effects of this recognition of the semiotic constructedness of communities (and 'cultures' [plural]) is to throw earlier distinctions between 'vernacular' and 'official' into disarray, challenging

> notions of culture…which have tended to be predicated on such hierarchies and polarities as high and low,…elite and popular…. Where popular culture is often the product of urban, commercial and state interests, where folk culture is often a response to the competitive cultural policies of today's nation-states, and where traditional culture is often the result of conscious deliberation or elaboration, these terms clearly need rethinking. (Appadurai & Breckenridge 1988).

The analytic lens moves perhaps closest to 'Us' when it turns to cultural production of the bourgeois 'public sphere'. Here, discursive participation has been ideologically styled as disinterested, rational, egalitarian and decontextualised through the anonymity of print, but in practice, contributions to it normally aid and are abetted by domination and a range of exclusions (e.g. by class and gender) (cf. Scollon & Scollon 1995: Ch. 6; Gal & Woolard (eds.) 1995). At the same time, the norms regulating public discourse are subject to change and resistance, and there can also be efforts to maintain or create alternative public arenas (Fairclough 1992; Urla 1995; Collins 1998; Gilroy 1987). In fact, this analysis of the bourgeois public sphere, an important component in liberal modernity, is particularly significant in the way that it feeds off and into critical reflection on the assumptions, values and practices of the academic 'community' in general and linguistics in particular. Disciplinary knowledge has played an important public role in the political construction of both modernity and its others, and recognition of this adds impetus to the reassessment of inherited concepts and methods within linguistics.

7. From the 'linguistics of community' to a 'linguistics of contact'

The role that language scholarship and its 'philological incendiaries' (Anderson 1983: 81) played in the development of the 19th century European nation-state has been long and widely recognised, as has the important role that it has played in the expansion and organisation of empires (cf. Fishman 1972b: 230; Robins 1979: Chs. 6 & 7; Hymes 1980; Anderson 1983; Pratt 1987; Gal & Irvine 1995; Said 1978; Bolinger 1975: 507; Collins 1998: 5, 60; Blommaert (ed.) 1999). Within these processes of language and identity construction, epistemology and politics have often been mutually endorsing. The idea of autonomous languages free from agency and individual intervention meshed with the 19th century differentiation of peoples in terms of spiritual essences (Gal & Irvine 1995; Taylor 1990), while much more recently, the post-war British and American commodification and export of English has been aided by models which treat language (a) as an isolable structural entity that is much more aligned with the universals of mind than anchored in the specifics of culture, but that is nevertheless (b) guaranteed authentic only in and by 'native speakers' (cf. Phillipson 1992; Pennycook 1994; Rampton 1995a: Ch. 13, 1995c).

This recognition that "theory making is itself a social practice in the 'real world'" (Cameron 1994: 19; Hymes [1973] 1980) has initiated a wide-ranging review of concepts and methods which is still far from complete. But following Pratt (1987), as well as the paradigm-shifting work of LePage and Tabouret-Keller (1985), a substantial part of this reorientation can be described as a move from the 'linguistics of community' to a 'linguistics of contact'.

Linguistics can itself be said to have emerged through the experience of contact with other groups and languages (Hymes 1980: 55; Volosinov 1973: Part II, Ch. 2; Williams 1977; Robins 1979), but disorderly hybridity and mixing have been overwhelmingly repressed, either regularised and idealised out (as in Chomskyan approaches), or analysed in ways that discover system and rationality beneath the surface (sociolinguistics). Randomness and disorder have however become much more important in recent social theory, where instead of trying to define the core features of any social group or institution, there is major interest in the flows of people, knowledge, texts and objects across social and geographical space, in the boundaries of inclusion and exclusion, and in fragmentation, indeterminacy and ambivalence. Groups that were hitherto conceived of as minorities inside the nation-state are conceptually relocated within transnational diaspora (Safran 1991; Clifford 1994), and according to Hall (1992: 310):

> everywhere, cultural identities are emerging which are not fixed, but poised, *in transition* between different positions; which draw on different cultural traditions at the same time; and which are the product of those complicated cross-overs and cultural mixes which are increasingly common in a globalised world… [People with experience of living in two places] are not and will never be *unified* in the old sense, because they are irrevocably the product of several interlocking histories and cultures, belong at one and the same time to several 'homes' (and to no one particular 'home'). People belonging to such *cultures of hybridity* have had to renounce the dream or ambition of rediscovering any kind of 'lost' cultural purity, or ethnic absolutism. They are irrevocably *translated*…. (cf. also Leung et al. 1997: 551)

The experience of being in transition between places, institutions and groups is a major new focus (Hannerz 1990; Clifford 1992), and looking at life within the 'ingroup', there is now recognition of the 'stranger' who "calls the bluff of the opposition between friends and enemies as the compleat mappa mundi [map of the world], as the difference which consumes all difference and hence leaves nothing outside itself… [Strangers] unmask the brittle artificiality of division" (Z. Bauman 1990: 145, 148; Rampton 1995b: 488–9). This shift in the agenda of social theory opens uncharted (and partly unchartable) horizons, but there are already implications for our conceptualisation of communication.

With the experience of anomalous social difference now treated as a central rather than subsidiary characteristic of contemporary life, there are grounds for questioning the significance of 'negotiation' as a central pragmatic principle. In Barth's view,

> '[n]egotiation' suggests a degree of conflict of interests but within a framework of shared understandings. The disorder entailed in the religious, social, ethnic, class and cultural pluralism of Sohar goes far beyond what can be retrieved as ambiguities of interest, relevance, and identity resolved through negotiation. (1992: 27; cf. also Pratt 1986, 1987)

Instead, rather than being treated as common ground to which interactants can fall back in moments of difficulty, the identification of any common ground available as a starting point itself needs to be seen as a major task (Barrett 1996: 188–191; Gee 1999: 15ff.). Similarly, the traditional priority given to 'competence' looks over-optimistic and increasingly inadequate, and instead, ignorance itself becomes a substantive issue for theory and ethnographic description, not just a technical problem contracted out to the applied linguistics of language teaching (Rampton 1997a: 330; Zentella 1997).[7] The salience of non-shared knowledge increases the significance of "knowing one's own ignorance, knowing that others know something else, knowing whom to believe, developing a notion of the potentially knowable" (Hannerz 1992a: 45; Rampton 1997c) and indeed, as well as not being able to take cooperation and mutual understanding for granted, winning and holding attention is itself seen as a challenge. All these factors draw into focus the different ways in which people reflect meta-linguistically, meta-pragmatically and meta-culturally on the shape of their own discourse and its reception by others (Briggs & Bauman 1990; Lucy 1993; Urcioli 1996; Hannerz 1992a: 44, 1992b: 43), and among other things, "[l]inguistic features are seen as reflecting and expressing broader cultural images of people and activities… [S]peakers have, and act in relation to, ideologically constructed representations of linguistic practice" (Gal & Irvine 1995: 973).

This reflexivity and 'loss of innocence' in speech requires us to look beyond (tacit) practice to (artful) 'performance', construed as speech where there is "heightened awareness of both the act of expression and the performer" (Bauman 1986: 3; Bauman & Briggs 1990). In Bakhtin's terms, we need to look beyond "direct unmediated discourse directed exclusively toward its referential object, as an expression of the speaker's ultimate semantic authority" to 'double-voicing', where someone else's discourse and the presence of various influences "enter into the project that th[e speaker's] discourse has set itself" (1984: 187). Methodologically, this shift beyond style to stylisation and the 'arts of the contact zone' (Pratt 1991) makes the premium that linguistics has traditionally placed on the unconscious and the repetitive seem rather 'Fordist',[8] and if Zygmunt Bauman is right that in late modernity, "[s]ignificance and numbers have parted ways" and that "[s]tatistically insignificant phenomena may prove to be

---

7. Among other things, efforts to understand what happens in unfamiliar and uncertain situations could benefit from a reconciliation of interpretive sociolinguistics and second language acquisition research, even though there are some substantial methodological obstacles (Rampton 1997a, 1997c).

8. Gee et al. characterise Fordism as follows: "[w]orkers, hired from the head down had only to follow directions and mechanically carry out a rather meaningless piece of a process they did not need to understand as a whole, and certainly did not control" (1996: 26).

decisive" (1992a: 192), then regularity, consistency and system lose their primacy and our focus needs to extend to the unusual and spectacular.

For a spectacular practice or event to be significant, of course, it can't be just done once and forgotten. As a spectacle, its salience derives by definition from the fact that it breaches routine expectations, but some record or memory of it must be retained and circulated over time and space. To study this, it is no longer adequate just to concentrate on the producer's communicative competence, on their durable, underlying but situation-sensitive disposition, even though this certainly still has an important role to play. Instead, analysis needs to address the *multiple* people and processes involved in: the design or selection of textual 'projectiles' which have some hope of travelling across contexts; in the alteration and revaluation of texts in 'transportation'; in their embedding in new contexts. Broadly compatible 'hit-or-miss' conceptions of speech itself can be found in LePage and Tabouret-Keller's notion of 'projection' across inner worlds (1985: 181), and more recently, a similar cluster of concerns has developed in linguistic anthropology, where for example, 'entextualisation' is seen as a process to be studied "in formal and functional terms by exploring the means available to participants in performance situations to render stretches of discourse discontinuous with their discursive surround, thus making them into coherent, effective and memorable texts" (Bauman & Briggs 1990: 73–74; see also Silverstein & Urban (eds.) 1996; Spitulnik 1997).

Most of the phenomena and processes that the 'linguistics of contact' draws attention to have been going on since human societies began, and a lot of the recent growth of sociolinguistic interest in them could be attributed to the influence of post-modernism-as-an-epistemic-perspective (Section 3). Even so, this shift of interest from 'production-within' to 'projection-across', from the 'use-' to the 'exchange-value' of language practice, takes on a particular relevance in debates about post-modernity-as-a-new-historical-era, where new electronic media are seen as leading to the accelerated collapse of traditional space and time distances, to the loss of difference between public, private, home, work and abroad, and to the invasion of local life-worlds by global interests (Giddens 1990b; Castells 1996: 336, 360–361). There is a view that the relationships between discourse and community are being dramatically reconfigured in this new age, and it is worth briefly sketching out some of the main issues.

8. Community and discourse in the Information Age

Discussion of the impact of new information and communication technologies (ICTs) is complicated by a number of factors: by the range and interconnectedness of the media involved, by the complexity of the ways in which they're integrated into our everyday lives at work, leisure and home, by the diversity of interactional and textual genres they are bound up with, and by the tendency for technological innovation to generate debates which swing dramatically between utopian and nightmare visions of the future (Bausinger 1984; Fisher 1985; Sefton-Green (ed.) 1998). If research on literacy is anything to go by (Basso 1974; Street 1984; Barton 1994), then there is a vast amount of descriptive and analytic work to be done coming to grips with the fluid and dynamic relationship between the electronic worlds of words and images and the activities of embodied, breathing, people.

Even so, Castells suggests two broad directions in the development of ICTs which are particularly relevant for any discussion of their effects on discourse and community:

> *The multimedia world will be populated by two essentially distinct populations: the interacting and the interacted,* meaning those who are able to select their multi-directional circuits of communication, and those who are provided with a restricted number of prepackaged choices. And who is what will be largely determined by class, race, gender and country. The unifying power of mass television... is now replaced by a socially stratified differentiation, leading to the coexistence of a customised mass media culture and an interactive electronic communication network of self-selected communes. (1996: 371; original emphases)

Within one of these strands, it looks as though language and text play an enhanced role in the construction of communities, while in the other, their significance diminishes.

Research on computer mediated communication (CMC) and on 'virtual communities' focuses on the relatively privileged, literate groups that Castells refers to, and at least until the technology develops, communication in electronic networks will continue to rely overwhelmingly on written text, unsupported by the semiotics of gaze, voice, body and three-dimensional physical space (Jones (ed.) 1995; Herring (ed.) 1996; Yates 1996b; Reich (nd)). Admittedly, the scope for rapid interaction between senders and receivers leads to the development of registers that are typical of neither writing nor speech (Yates 1996a; Werry 1996) and up to a point, verbal and graphological resources have been developed to replace other semiotic channels – 'emoticons' like '(:-)' can be used to represent facial expressions, and 'MUDs' and 'MOOs' are "synchronous chat environments in which participants textually construct their identities, physical appearance and the physical setting" (Herring 1996a: 8). Even so, the absence (and/or entextualisation) of sign systems based on the body permits a number of new angles on community.

In some of the most optimistic visions, CMC permits the revitalisation of the public sphere, an arena of one-(and many-)to-many dialogue where participation is freed from the constraints on access that operate in broadcasting and print media, and where disembodiment permits interaction uninhibited by the 'trappings' of race, ethnic, class and gender difference. Beyond that, compared with face-to-face interaction and writing technologies based on paper, the entextualisation of physical markers (as in MUDs, MOOs, but also just in e.g. names) is itself often said to provide individuals with far greater opportunities to design different identities for themselves, and to ratify and elaborate these identities in ongoing interactive social lives. Conversely, others argue much more pessimistically that CMC entices people into fantasy worlds isolated from the responsibilities of everyday life.

There are no doubt some situations where these are all fair descriptions, but the realities are usually much more complex. Far from permitting the elaboration of a common public discourse, the concerns of 'virtual communities' are often highly specialised, and their proliferation may itself fragment the public sphere (Fernback & Thompson (nd)). CMC access to virtual communities is constrained by money, education, time and often gender, and established social identities announce themselves in the grammatical, semantic and pragmatic texture of discourse, not just in accent and physical appearance. And while the idealisation of CMC as a democratic medium needs to be tempered by a sense of, for instance, the hierarchic professional contexts in which it often operates (Ziv 1996), fears about CMC's socially isolating effects need to recognise that 'cyberspace' is a medium for communication between human beings, not robots, and that within virtual communities of practice, there can be, for example, rituals, shared histories, sexual relationships, group norms, regulations and socialisation processes, all of which can help to sustain people in lives they feel to be rich and active (Fernback & Thompson (nd); Kollock & Smith 1996; Deuel 1996; Hall 1996).

Much remains to learnt, then, of the undoubtedly multifarious ways in which CMC relates to the formation, maintenance and decline of community, though written language clearly plays an accentuated role and there is a tendency to emphasise agency and emancipation in the debates about it. In contrast, for the second group that Castells refers to, for those provided only with mass-media products, language often loses its supremacy, and the consequences of this are frequently thought to be deleterious.

Cable and satellite technologies permit a proliferation of channels and choices. This hastens the demise of public service broadcasting, and undermines its contribution to our 'imagining' of national communities (Anderson 1983; Morley & Robins 1995). Mass media channels are much more *deterritorialised* than before, and in the highly competitive markets where programme makers now work, 'exportability' is a major issue. Where potential audiences are much more plural and less known, it is harder to trust the effectiveness of semiotic systems that rely heavily on shared conventions, and exportability is thought likely to be greater for audio-visual rather than for written works, as well as being greater for audio-visual works with less linguistic content than for those with more (Morley & Robins 1995: 63; Wallace and Kovacheva 1996: 190). Language of course often still features, but the product's effectiveness is less likely to rely on semantics and grammar, and instead of being seen as "directly intentional", discourses "may be treated as objects, as typifactions, as local colour" (Bakhtin 1981: 289).[9] And where lexico-grammar and propositional meaning lose ground to the social indexicality of language, there are fears for the public culture which proclaims reasoned argument as one of its cardinal values.

A few steps on from this, the vision emerges of a late capitalist communicative economy where priority is no longer given to the development of members' competence through the closely regulated relay and cultivation of knowledge grounded in a common language, but where instead, aestheticised multi-modal texts are designed to recruit and sustain people in 'life-style' communities which may be more open and inclusive but which can also be construed as 'neo-tribes without socialisation' where centres of authority, inner organisation, platforms or statutes are hard to find (Bauman 1992b: 25), and where entry is a matter of the consumer's desire, personal taste, shopping skills and purchasing power (Bauman 1992b: 25, 1990: Ch. 11). Where advanced capitalism has developed forms of

> control [that] reach...beyond production into areas of consumption, services and social relations [...] a capacity for intervention and transformation which extends beyond the natural environment and exerts an influence on social systems, on interpersonal relations, and on the very structure of the individual. (Melucci 1980: 217, 218)

> new social movements may develop, oppositional 'interpretive communities' (Gilroy 1987) whose principal goal is "the defense of identity, continuity and predictability of personal experience" (Melucci 1980) and the "reappropriation of space, time, and of relationships between individuals in their day to day lives" (Gilroy 1987: 224–5; Habermas 1981; Castells 1997; Rampton 1995a: 9–11, 1995c: 243–5; Gurak 1996). But the success of this resistance is highly unpredictable, particularly if, as some fear, it is not so much "a global village" that we are living in together, but rather a set of isolated "customised cottages globally produced and locally distributed" (Castells 1996: 341).

These, then, are a few of the issues about language, discourse and community that arise with the development of information societies. Sociolinguistics can make a major contribution to our understanding of these processes, though as yet, this has hardly started.

---

9. As in the communities-of-practice perspective, language loses its privileged status, but whereas before, this was due to the semiotic plenitude of an environment shared by producer and receiver, here it results from the unpredictability of the resources they might have in common.

9. Conclusion

Outside the variationist tradition, 'speech community' itself has never been a pivotal analytic tool in sociolinguistics (Irvine 1987: 13), but the argument and unease that have dogged the term suggest that there has been quite a lot at stake in it, and that somehow or other, it has been a sensitive indicator of assumptions that might be as fundamental as they are hard to articulate. Over the course of this article, I have tried to explicate some of these assumptions and uncertainties, and I have pointed to a number of reconceptualisations of how language both does and doesn't connect people, by no means all of them new but most of them gaining impetus with more general developments in the humanities, the social sciences and society.

At the risk of repetition, however, it is worth emphasising at least five reasons why 'community' as a group of people with a sense of shared tradition will continue to be important for sociolinguistics:

i. Communities of practice play an important part in the production, transportation and reception of discourses in circulation.
ii. The idea that the academy is itself a historically specific community, a "communit[y] of scholarly practice" (Eckert & McGonnell-Ginet 1992: 485) plays an important role in its reflexive recognition that there are limits to the neutrality and transcendence of research, and that its own position and responsibility merit careful social, cultural and political analysis (Hymes 1977, 1980; Cameron et al. 1992; Rampton 1997b).
iii. This reflexivity inevitably raises questions about a potentially unsettling congruence between the reconceptualisations of community outlined in this paper and emerging forms of fast, flexible, late-modern capitalism (Gee et al. 1996). In what some see as an enduringly behaviouristic tendency to eschew emotion, desire, alienation, interiority and anything but the external trappings of subjectivity (Hewitt 1992: 38–40; Eckert & McGonnell-Ginet 1992: 485, 486), sociolinguistics may itself be an accomplice to the 'emptying out' of contemporary life and theory, where "various depth models... [are] for the most part" replaced by "a conception of practices, discourses and textual play" (Jameson 1984: 62, though cf. Billig 1995: 134ff). It is partly as a counterweight to this risk of superficiality that community remains important in a third way: where community is associated with long-term fieldwork involvement with (several generations of) people in particular place (Arensberg 1961), there is more scope for the development of relationships with a depth and intimacy that analysts feel confident to talk about (Hewitt 1992: 38).
iv. More than that, 'community-level' studies, understood as long-term engagements with particular groups, also remain essential if we are to try to understand

the changes and intensified inequalities produced by new economic forms (Heath 1995; Zentella 1997; Castells 1983; Harvey 1987; Lash & Urry 1994).

v. This in turn leads into the fifth reason why the concept retains its significance. To the extent that communal life is itself drastically undermined, community grows in importance as a moral value and as a utopian point of critical purchase (Castells 1997). The manner and extent to which community-as-ideal insists on uniformity or builds on social difference is certain to continue as a crucial political and analytic issue (Hymes 1980; Fishman 1982; Gilroy 1987: Ch. 6; Frazer & Lacey 1992; Z. Bauman 1995: 284ff).

References

Abu-Lughod, L. & C. Lutz (1990). Introduction: Emotion, discourse, and the politics of everyday life. In C. Lutz & L. Abu-Lughod (eds.). *Language and the Politics of Emotion: 1–23*. Cambridge University Press.
Anderson, B. (1983). *Imagined Communities: Reflections on the Origin and Spread of Nationalism*. Verso.
Appadurai, A. (1988). Putting hierarchy in its place. *Cultural Anthropology*. 3(1): 36–49.
Appadurai, A. & C. Breckenridge (1988). Why public culture. *Public Culture Bulletin* 1(1): 5–9.
Arensberg, C. (1961). The community as object and sample. *American Anthropologist* 63: 241–264.
Bakhtin, M. (1981). *The Dialogic Imagination*. Texas University Press.
—— (1984). *Problems in Dostoevsky's Poetics*. Minneapolis. University of Minnesota Press.
Barrett, R. (1997). The 'Homo-genius' speech community. In Livia & Hall (eds.): 181–201.
Barth, R. (1992). Towards greater naturalism in conceptualising societies. In A. Kuper (ed.) *Conceptualising Society*: 17–33. Routledge.
Barton, D. (1994). *Literacy*. Blackwell.
Bauman, R. (1986). *Story, Performance and Event: Contextual Studies of Oral Narrative*. Cambridge University Press.
Bauman, R. & C. Briggs (1990). Poetics and performance as critical perspectives on language and social life. *Annual Review of Anthropology* 19: 59–88.
Bauman, R. & J. Sherzer (eds.) (1974). *Explorations in the Ethnography of Speaking*. Cambridge University Press.
Bauman, R. & J. Sherzer (1989). Introduction to the second edition. In Bauman & Sherzer (eds.) *Explorations in the Ethnography of Speaking: Second Edition*. Cambridge University Press.
Bauman, Z. (1990). *Thinking Sociologically*. Blackwell.
—— (1992a). *Intimations of Post-modernity*. Routledge.
—— (1992b). Survival as a social construct. In M. Featherstone (ed.) *Cultural Theory and Cultural Change*: 1–36. Sage.
—— (1995). *Life in Fragments: Essays in Post-modern Morality*. Blackwell.
Bell, A. (1984). Language style as audience design. *Language in Society* 13(2): 145–204.
Bernstein, B. (1973). *Class, Codes and Control Vol. 2: Applied Studies towards a Sociology of Language*. RKP.
—— (1975). *Class, Codes and Control Vol. 3: Towards a Theory of Educational Transmissions*. RKP.
—— (1990). *Class, Codes and Control Vol 4: The Structuring of Pedagogic Discourse*. Routledge.

—— (1996). Sociolinguistics: A personal view. In *Pedagogy, Symbolic Control and Identity*: 147–156. Taylor & Francis.
Billig, M. (1995). *Banal Nationalism*. Sage.
Blommaert, J. (ed.) (1999). *Language Ideological Debates*. de Gruyter.
Blommaert, J. & J. Verschueren (1998). *Debating Diversity: Analysing the Discourse of Tolerance*. Routledge.
Bloomfield, L. (1933). Speech communities. In *Language*: 42–56. Allen & Unwin.
Bolinger, D. (1975). *Aspects of Language: 2nd Ed*. Harcourt, Brace, Jovanovitch.
Bourdieu, P. (1977). *Outline of a Theory of Practice*. Cambridge University Press.
—— (1991). *Language and Symbolic Power*. Polity.
Cameron, D., E. Frazer, P. Harvey, B. Rampton & K. Richardson (1992). *Researching Language: Issues of Power and Method*. Routledge.
Castells, M. (1983). Crisis, planning, & the quality of life: Managing the new historical relationships between space and society. *Environment and Planning Development: Society and Space* 1: 3–21.
—— (1996). *The Rise of the Network Society*. Blackwell.
—— (1997). *The Power of Identity*. Blackwell.
Cazden, C., V. John & D. Hymes (eds.) (1972). *Functions of Language in the Classroom*. Teachers College Press.
Clark, H. (1996). *Using Language*. Cambridge University Press.
—— (1997). Communities, commonalities, and communication. In J Gumperz & S. Levinson (eds.) *Rethinking Linguistic Relativity*: 324–358. Cambridge University Press.
Clifford, J. (1983). On ethnographic authority. *Representations* 1(2): 118–146.
—— (1992). Traveling cultures. In L. Grossberg, C. Nelson, P. Treichler (eds.) *Cultural Studies*: 96–116. Routledge.
—— (1994). Diasporas. *Cultural Anthropology* 9(3): 302–338.
Collins, J. (1998). *Understanding Tolowa Histories: Western Hegemonies and Native American Responses*. Routledge.
Deuel, N. (1996). Our passionate response to virtual reality. In Herring (ed.): 129–146.
Duranti, A. (1988). Ethnography of speaking: Toward a linguistics of the praxis. In F. Newmeyer (ed.) *Language: the Sociocultural Context: Linguistics: The Cambridge Survey IV*: 210–228. Cambridge University Press.
—— (1997). *Linguistic Anthropology*. Cambridge University Press.
Eckert, P. & S. McConnell-Ginet. (1992). Think practically and look locally: Language and gender as community-based practice. *Annual Review of Anthropology* 21: 461–490.
Fairclough, N. (1992). *Discourse and Social Change*. Polity.
Fernback, J. & B. Thompson (n.d.). Virtual communities: Abort, retry, failure? http://www.well.com/user/hlr/texts/VCcivil.html.
Fishman, J. (1972a). *The Sociology of Language*. Newbury House.
—— (1972b). *Language in Sociocultural Change*. Stanford University Press.
—— (1982). Whorfianism of the third kind: Ethnolinguistic diversity as a worldwide asset. *language in Society* 11: 1–14.
Foley, W. (1997). *Linguistic Anthropology*. Blackwell.
Frazer, E. & N. Lacey (1993). *The Politics of Community*. Harvester Wheatsheaf.
Gal, S. (1989). Language and political economy. *Annual Review of Anthropology* 18: 345–367.
—— (1995). Language and the 'Arts of Resistance'. *Cultural Anthropology* 10(3): 407–424.
Gal, S. & J. Irvine (1995). The boundaries of languages and disciplines: How ideologies construct difference. *Social Research* 62(4): 967–1001.

Gal, S. & K. Woolard (1995). Constructing languages and publics: Authority and representation. *Pragmatics* 5(2): 129–138.
Gee, J. (1999). *An Introduction to Discourse Analysis*. London: Routledge.
Gee, J., G. Hull & C. Lankshear (1996). *The New Work Order: Behind the Language of the New Capitalism*. Westview Press.
Giddens, A. (1976). *New Rules of Sociological Method*. Hutchinson.
—— (1984). *The Constitution of Society*. Polity.
—— (1990a). *Social Theory and Modern Sociology*. Polity.
—— (1990b). *The Consequences of Modernity*. Polity.
Gilroy, P. (1987). *There Ain't No Black in the Union Jack*. Hutchinson.
Goffman, E. (1959). *The Presentation of Self in Everyday Life*. Penguin.
Goodwin, C. (1981). *Conversational Organisation: Interaction between Speakers and Hearers*. Academic Press.
—— (1994). Professional vision. *American Anthropologist*. 96(3): 606–633.
Gray, J. (1986). *Liberalism*. Open University Press.
Gumperz, J. (1962). Types of linguistic community. *Anthropological Linguistics* 4: 28–40.
—— (1968). The speech community. In *International Encyclopedia of the Social Sciences*: 381–6. Macmillan.
—— (1982). *Discourse Strategies*. Cambridge University Press.
Gumperz, J. & J. Cook-Gumperz (1982). Introduction: Language and the communication of social identity. In J. Gumperz (ed.) *Language and Social Identity*: 1–21. Cambridge University Press.
Gurak, L. (1996). The rhetorical dynamics of a community protest in cyberspace: What happened with Lotus Marketplace. In Herring (ed.): 265–278.
Habermas, J. (1981). New social movements. *Telos* 49: 33–37.
Hall, K. (1996). Cyberfeminism. In Herring (ed.): 147–172.
Hall, S. (1992). The question of cultural identity. In S. Hall, D. Held & T. McGrew (eds.) *Modernity and its Futures*: 274–316. Polity.
Halliday, M. (1978). *Language as a Social Semiotic*. Arnold.
Hanks, W. (1991). Foreword. In Lave & Wenger (eds.): 13–24.
—— (1996). *Language and Communicative Practices*. Westview Press.
Hannerz, U. (1990). Cosmopolitans and locals in world culture. *Theory, Culture and Society* 7(2–3): 237–251.
—— (1992a). *Cultural Complexity: Studies in the Social Organisation of Meaning*. Columbia University Press.
—— (1992b). The global ecumene as a network of networks. In A. Kuper (ed.). *Conceptualising Society*: 34–56. Routledge.
Harvey, D. (1987). Flexible accumulation through urbanisation: Reflections on 'post-modernism' in the American city. *Antipode* 19(3): 260–86.
Heath, S. (1982). What no bedtime story means. *Language in Society*. 11: 49–76.
—— (1983). *Ways with Words: Language, Life and Work in Communities and Classrooms*. Cambridge University Press.
—— (1995). Ethnography in communities: Learning the everyday life of America's subordinated youth. In J. Banks & C. McGee Banks (eds.) *Handbook of Research on Multicultural Education*: 114–128. Macmillan.
Heller, M. (1999). *Linguistic Minorities and Modernity: A Sociolinguistic Ethnography*. Longman.
Herring, S. (1996). Introduction. In Herring (ed.): 1–12.
Herring, S. (ed.) (1996). *Computer-Mediated Communication*. John Benjamins.

Hewitt, R. (1986). *White Talk Black Talk*. Cambridge University Press.

——— (1992). Language, youth and the destabilisation of ethnicity. In C. Palmgren, K. Lovgren & G. Bolin (eds.) *Ethnicity in Youth Culture*: 27–41. Youth Culture at Stockholm University.

Hill, J. (1993). Hasta la vista, baby: Anglo Spanish in the American Southwest. *Critique of Anthropology* 13: 145–76.

——— (1995). Junk Spanish, covert racism, and the (leaky) boundary between public and private spheres. *Pragmatics* 5(2): 197–212.

Hinnenkamp, V. (1987). Foreigner talk, code-switching and the concept of trouble. In K. Knapp et al. (eds.) *Analysing Intercultural Communication*: 137–80. Mouton de Gruyter.

Hoechsmann, M. (1997). Benetton culture: Marketing difference to the global consumer. In S. Riggins (ed.) *The Language and Politics of Exclusion: Others in Discourse*: 183–202. Sage.

Hudson, R. (1980). *Sociolinguistics*. Cambridge University Press.

——— (1984). *Word Grammar*. Blackwell.

——— (1996). *Sociolinguistics: Second Edition*. Cambridge University Press.

Hymes, D. (1972a). Models of the interaction of language and social life. In J. Gumperz & D. Hymes (eds.) *Directions in Sociolinguistics*: 35–71. Blackwell.

——— (1972b). On communicative competence. In J. Pride & J. Holmes (eds.) *Sociolinguistics*: 269–93. Penguin.

——— (1974). Studying the interaction of languagae and social life. In *Foundations in Sociolinguistics*: 29–66. Tavistock.

——— (1980). *Language in Education*. Washington: Centre for Applied Linguistics.

——— (1987). Short note on publications received. *Language in Society* 16(3): 447.

Irvine, J. (1987). Domains of description in the ethnography of speaking: A retrospective on the 'speech community'. *Working Papers & Proceedings of the Centre of Psychosocial Studies* 11: 13–24. University of Chicago.

——— (1989). When talk isn't cheap: Language and political economy. *American Ethnologist* 16(2): 248–67.

Jameson, F. (1984). Postmodernism, or The cultural logic of late capitalism. *New Left Review* 146: 53–91.

Jones, S. (ed.) (1995). *Cybersociety: Computer-mediated Communication and Community*. Sage.

Kerswill, P. (1994). *Dialects Converging: Rural Speech in Urban Norway*. Clarendon Press.

Kollock, P. & M. Smith (1996). Managing the virtual commons: Cooperation and conflict in computer communities. In Herring (ed.): 109–128.

Labov, W. (1969). The logic of non-standard English. *Georgetown Monographs on Language and Linguistics* 22.

——— (1972a). The reflection of social processes in linguistic structures. In *Sociolinguistic Patterns*: 110–121. Blackwell.

——— (1972b). *Language in the Inner City*. Blackwell.

——— (1980). Is there a creole speech community? In A. Valdman & A. Highfield (eds.) *Theoretical Orientations in Creole Studies*: 389–424. Academic Press.

——— (1981). Field methods used by the project on linguistic change and variation. *Sociolinguistic Working Paper 81*. Austin: South Western Educational Development Laboratory.

——— (1982). Objectivity and commitment in linguistic science: The case of the Black English trial in Ann Arbor. *Language in Society* 11: 165–201.

——— (1989). Exact description of the speech community: Short A in Philadelphia. In R. Fasold & D. Schiffrin (eds.) *Language Change and Variation*: 1–57. John Benjamins.

Lash, S. & J. Urry (1994). *Economies of Signs and Space*. Sage.

Lave, J. (1993). The practice of learning. In S. Chaiklin & J. Lave (eds.) *Understanding Practice*: 3–34. Cambridge University Press.
Lave, J. & E. Wenger (1991). *Situated Learning: Legitimate Peripheral Participation*. Cambridge University Press.
LeCompte, M. & J. Goetz (1982). Problems of reliability and validity in ethnographic research. *Review of Educational Research* 52(1): 31–60.
LePage, R. (1980). Projection, focusing and diffusion. *York Papers in Linguistics* 9.
LePage, R. & A. Tabouret-Keller (1985). *Acts of Identity*. Cambridge University Press.
Leung, C., R. Harris & B. Rampton (1997). The idealised native speaker, reified ethnicities, and classroom realities. *TESOL Quarterly* 31(3): 543–566.
Livia, A. & K. Hall (eds.) (1997). *Queerly Phrased: Language, Gender & Sexuality*. Oxford University Press.
Lury, C. (1996). *Consumer Culture*. Polity.
Lyons, J. (ed.) (1970). *New Horizons in Linguistics*. Penguin.
Marcus, G. (1986). Contemporary problems of ethnography in the modern world system. In J. Clifford & G. Marcus (eds.) *Writing Culture: The Poetics and Politics of Ethnography*: 165–193. University of California Press.
McDermott, R. (1988). Inarticulateness. In D Tannen (ed.) *Linguistics in Context*: 37–68. Ablex.
McDermott, R., K. Gospodinoff & J. Aron (1978). Criteria for an ethnographically adequate description of concerted activities and their contexts. *Semiotica* 24(3&4): 245–275.
McDermott, R. & H. Tylbor (1983). On the necessity of collusion in conversation. *Text* 3: 277–297.
Melucci, A. (1980). The new social movements: A theoretical approach. *Social Science Information* 19(2): 199–226.
Milroy, L. (1980). *Language and Social Networks*. Blackwell.
Milroy, J. (1992). *Linguistic Variation and Change*. Blackwell.
Milroy, L. & J. Milroy (1992). Social network and social class: Toward an integrated sociolinguistic model. *Language in Society* 21(1): 1–26.
Morgan, M. (1994). Theories and politics in African American English. *Annual Review of Anthropology*. 23: 325–345.
Morley, D. & K. Robins (1995). *Spaces of Identity: Global Media, Electronic Landscapes and Cultural Boundaries*. Routledge.
New London Group (1996). A pedagogy of multiliteracies: Designing social futures. *Harvard Educational Review*. 66(1): 60–92.
Nichols, B. (1997). Dislocating ethnographic film: *In and Out of Africa* and issues of cultural representation. *American Anthropologist* 99(4): 810–24.
Pennycook, A. (1994). *The Cultural Politics of English as an International Language*. Longman.
Phillipson, R. (1992). *Linguistic Imperialism*. Oxford University Press.
Pratt, M. L. (1986). Ideology and speech act theory. *Poetics Today* 7(1): 59–72.
——— (1987). Linguistic Utopias. In N. Fabb et al. (eds.) *The Linguistics of Writing*: 48–66. Manchester University Press.
——— (1991). The arts of the contact zone. *Profession* 91: 33–40.
Rampton, B. (1992). Scope for empowerment in sociolinguistics? In Cameron et al. (eds.): 29–64.
——— (1995a). *Crossing: Language and Ethnicity among Adolescents*. Longman.
——— (1995b). Language crossing and the problematisation of ethnicity and socialisation. *Pragmatics* 5(4): 485–515.
——— (1995c). Politics and change in research in applied linguistics. *Applied Linguistics*. 16(2): 233–256.

―― (1997a). Second language research in late modernity. *Modern Language Journal.* 81(3): 329–333.

―― (1997b). Retuning in applied linguistics? *International Journal of Applied Linguistics.* 7(1): 3–25.

―― (1997c). A sociolinguistic perspective on L2 communication strategies. In G. Kasper & E. Kellerman (eds.) *Communication Strategies: Psycholinguistic and Sociolinguistic Perspectives*: 279–303. Longman.

―― (forthcoming a). Sociolinguistics and Cultural Studies: New ethicities, liminality and interaction. *Social Semiotics.*

―― (forthcoming b). Dichotomies, difference and ritual in second language learning and teaching. *Applied Linguistics.*

Reich, E. (n.d.). Virtual community: An annotated bibliography. http://www.amherst.edu/~erreich/vircom.html.

Robins, R. (1979). *A Short History of Linguistics.* Longman.

Safran, W. (1991). Diasporas in modern societies: Myths of homeland and return. *Diaspora* 1(1): 83–99.

Said, E. (1978). *Orientalism.* Penguin.

Sapir, E. (1949 [1931]). Communication. In D. Mandelbaum (ed.) *Edward Sapir: Selected Writings in Language, Culture and Personality*: 104–9. California University Press.

Scollon, R. & S. Scollon (1995). *Intercultural Communication.* Blackwell.

Schieffelin, B. & E. Ochs (1986). Language socialisation. *Annual Review of Anthropology* 15: 163–191.

Sefton-Green, J. (1998). *Digital Diversions: Youth Culture in the Age of Multimedia.* UCL Press.

Silverstein, M. & G. Urban (eds.) (1996). *Natural Histories of Discourse.* Cambridge University Press.

Spitulnik, D. (1997). The social circulation of media discourse and the mediation of communities. *Journal of Linguistic Anthropology* 6(2): 161–87.

Street, B. (1984). *Literacy in Theory and Practice.* Cambridge University Press.

Swales, J. (1990). The concept of discourse community. In *Genre Analysis*: 21–32. Cambridge University Press.

Taylor, T. (1990). Which is to be master? The institutionalisation of authority in the science of language. In J. Joseph & T. Taylor (eds.) *Ideologies of Language*: 9–26. Routledge.

Touraine, A. (1981). *The Voice and the Eye: An Analysis of Social Movements.* Cambridge University Press.

Trudgill, P. (1974). *The Social Differentiation of English in Norwich.* Cambridge University Press.

Trudgill, P. & H. Giles (1983 [1978]). Sociolinguistics and linguistic value judgements: Correctness, adequacy and aesthetics. In P Trudgill *On Dialect*: 201–225. Blackwell.

Trueba, H. & P. Wright (1981). A challenge for Ethnographic researchers in bilingual settings. *Journal of Multilingual and Multicultural Development* 2(4): 243–257.

Turner, T. (1993). Anthropology and multiculturalism: What is anthropology that multiculturalists should be mindful of it? *Cultural Anthropology.* 8(4): 411–429.

Urciuoli, B. (1996). *Exposing Prejudice: Puerto Rican Experiences of Language, Race and Class.* Westview Press.

Urla, J. (1993a). Contesting modernities: Language standardisation and the production of an ancient/modern Basque culture. *Critique of Anthropology* 13(2): 101–118.

―― (1993b). Cultural politics in an age of statistics: Numbers, nations, and the making of Basque identity. *American Ethnologist* 20(4): 818–843.

—— (1995). Outlaw language: Creating an alternative public sphere in Basque radio. *Pragmatics* 5: 245–262.
Volosinov, V. (1973). *Marxism and the Philosophy of Language*. Seminar Press.
Wallace, C. & S. Kovacheva (1996). Youth cultures and consumption in Eastern and Western Europe. *Youth and Society* 28(2): 189–214.
Wardhaugh, R. (1986). *Introduction to Sociolinguistics*. Blackwell.
Werry, C. (1996). Linguistic and interactional features of Internet Relay Chat. In Herring (ed.): 47–64.
Wetherall, M. & J. Potter (1992). *Mapping the Language of Racism*. Harvester Wheatsheaf.
Williams, G. (1992). *Sociolinguistics: A Sociological Critique*. Routledge.
Williams, R. (1977). *Marxism and Literature*. Oxford University Press.
Woolard, K. (1988). Codeswitching and comedy in Catalonia. In M. Heller (ed.) *Codeswitching: Anthropological and Sociolinguistic Perspectives*: 53–76. Mouton de Gruyter. 53–76.
Woolard, K. & B. Schieffelin (1994). Language ideology. *Annual Review of Anthropology* 23: 55–82.
Yates, S. (1996a). English in cyberspace. In S. Goodman & D. Graddol (eds.) *Redesigning English: New Texts, New Identities*. 106–140. Open University & Routledge.
—— (1996b). Oral and written linguistic aspects of computer conferencing. In Herring (ed.): 29–46.
Yeo, E. & S. Yeo (1988). On the uses of 'community': From Owenism to the present. In S. Yeo (ed.) *New Views of Cooperation*: 229–258. Routledge.
Zentella, A. (1997). *Growing Up Bilingual*. Blackwell.
Ziv, O. (1996). Writing to work: How using email can reflect technological and organisational change. In Herring (ed.): 243–264.

Symbolic interactionism

Rod Watson
LIAS, Institut Marcel Mauss, Paris

The approach which came to be known as 'symbolic interactionism' (SI) was first articulated by the philosopher George Herbert Mead at the University of Chicago from 1893 to 1931.[1] Mead elaborated the philosophical underpinnings of a social psychology which was founded both upon earlier and upon contemporaneous behaviorist and pragmatist thought, notably that of John Dewey. This intention is, perhaps, somewhat ironic considering the criticisms by later practitioners in the social and linguistic disciplines that SI was both subjective and unscientific.

In his new philosophy of mind, Mead emphasized that the individual was, *au fond*, a biological organism, part of nature, part of evolution. He built biological concepts into his philosophy of mind, and this is something which has been jettisoned in later SI. For later practitioners of SI, Mead's distinctive contribution was to show the many respects in which individual experience and behavior arose from participation in the social group. The group was seen as a communicative nexus. The acquiring, sustaining and transforming of experience and competence (or competent conduct) was, for Mead, fundamentally a communicative process which could be analyzed developmentally and functionally.

It is this central focus upon communicative interaction which subsequent social scientists and linguists took up, and which renders Mead's writings of particular interest to practitioners in pragmatics. To Mead, language was itself to be seen as actual behavior addressed to practical ends. It was not to be seen as a more transparent conduit to 'other' behavior, nor as a passive representation of the world.

Mead conceived of language as being not just another topic in philosophy but as a generic and all-pervading feature of social life. He therefore turned language into an object of study in its own right. In doing so, however, he did not render language as the kind of object which is readily recognizable by most linguists, or which most conversation analysts might straightforwardly treat as their data.

Language, for Mead, comprised a vast repository of 'significant symbols'. It is these symbols, as 'incarnate' in the language, which so fundamentally set apart human social organization and communication from that of all other animals. Other animals communicate by gestures, behavioral stimuli which are emitted in the course of some

---

[1]. Mead himself, however, never used the term 'Symbolic Interactionism'. It was invented by Herbert Blumer in 1937.

overall act and which elicit a response. This response can itself comprise a further stimulus. Stimuli and responses are unreflectively, 'instinctively', emitted.

Mead's most perspicuous example of what he (rather misleadingly) termed 'a conversation of gestures' was that of a dog fight. Gestures such as growls, the baring of teeth, the firmly-set posture, are part of a broader array of fighting behaviors, often occurring at, and stimulating, the onset of these behaviors. Whilst such an interplay of gestures may re-direct behavior in the course of the dog fight, this interplay is based not upon self-consciousness but upon the involuntary, biologically-based back-and-forth adjustment of behavior. The gesture is also context-bound in the most specific sense, possessing an exclusively 'here and now' character.

Significant symbols, however, differ quite basically from gestures in that they involve a level of self-consciousness on the part of the individual producing that symbol: that is, the person can significantly and self-reflectively take into account his/her own use of that symbol. S/he can orientate towards the projected consequences of that symbol upon others, and can thus anticipate their probable replying act.

The significant symbol is physical gesture, word or term which makes and indicates to the self as well as to the intended recipient(s). The symbol becomes genuinely significant when the recipient imputes the same meaning to this indication as does the producing self. Then a shared scheme of interpretation and the derivative possibility of concerted or joint action are potentiated. Such intersubjectively co-ordinated activities comprise the 'building blocks' of social order.

Consequently, significant symbols which are conveyed vocally are of pivotal importance in Mead's and other SI analyses. The significant vocal symbol is quite distinctive in its capacity to transform human beings from simply being physical organisms merely capable of unreflective biologically-based responses into minded entities who can actively convey and share meanings. The significant vocal symbol is reflexive: it creates in the emitting person the same response as it does in the other (the recipient), thus providing for their actively reciprocal orientation to a given meaning. This, in turn, forms a basis for the mutual alignment of actions and courses of action.

Since this co-ordination of actions is based upon symbolic meanings rather than unselfconscious stimuli and responses, what humans have in common is an immense capacity for subtlety, complexity and abstraction in the organization of their joint conduct. The speaker can hear and take into account what s/he him/herself says and can (a) respond to that utterance in the same way that others may respond, and (b) anticipate the possible or probable response of the other. The speaker can, therefore, treat him/herself as the object of others' orientations. Others are employing the same interpretative process as the speaker. This process of active self-indication is the basis of 'mind', of co-operation and thus of social interaction.

Language, then, is the highest form of symbolization and is the origin of the mind and the self, or, perhaps better put, the self-reflective mind. These, in turn, potentiate shared interpretation and meaning which provide for the complex of interactive responses that form social order. By dint of significant linguistic symbols, human individuals can produce stimuli whose responses can be anticipated in advance, where this anticipation can itself be a factor in guiding the production of the stimulus.

It is through language, or significant symbols in linguistic form, that a given social actor can 'take the role of the other', can prefigure the results of his/her action from the other's standpoint and from that standpoint can treat him/herself as an object, the 'me'. This, in providing for subtly-ordered mutually self-monitoring interaction, presents the notion of social order as a *communicative* order and places language on center-stage in Mead's philosophy.

The 'self' comprises a kind of back-and-forth dialectic between the individuals spontaneously-acting 'I' and his/her talking of him/herself as an object as perceived from the standpoint of other, the 'me'. The notion of 'the other' comprises anyone who is part of the individual's orientational field, but in addition to this there are two orders of other: (a) significant others, (Mead's own term), a child's parents e.g. and (b) the generalized other, the overall attitude, perspective or judgement of the social group. Mead presents a schematic example of how human beings acquire this capacity.

First, the newborn child simply emits unreflective gestures. However, as time passes, the child forms memory images of a result of previous similar acts, begins to adjust to others and begins to copy them, though more or less unreflectively. This is the preparatory or 'imitative stage'. From this, the child moves into the 'play stage', where the child begins to play roles – playing mother, teacher, shopkeeper, etc. This involves the adopting of the perspective of these others, as is attested by the child's burgeoning ability to refer to itself through third-person statements: 'John is a bad boy'. However, moving from one role to another still occurs in a relatively unorganized way. There is still no unitary conception of self. Then, however, the child acquires the third stage, the 'game stage', where the child learns to take account of not just one but a range of standpoints simultaneously. This is the stage of, e.g. team games such as baseball, where the child as a team member has to orientate itself not only to the perspectives of all the specialized role players (shortstop, pitcher, etc.) but those of the opposing team, too. Out of the perspectives of its teammates the child gradually learns how to build a composite perspective. Thus the child learns to orientate to the attitude of the 'generalized other', the common perspective of everyone on that team, learning the standard symbolic meanings which the group attributes to various persons, situations, actions, etc., and to see him/herself as others in general see him/her. Thus the child is a fully-socialized member of the society conceived as a communicative order, possessing the cultural apparatus for taking others into account and acting appropriately. What we have here, then, is Mead's prototypical representation of language and concept acquisition.

It must be said that those who subsequently took up symbolic interactionism have not always made full use of Mead's work, and have often interpreted Mead in divergent ways. The most explicitly faithful of disciples is, perhaps, the sociologist Herbert Blumer (1969). However, even though Blumer makes the crucial point that language is not 'neutral', i.e. it shapes our interpretations (both lay and analytic), he still does not explicitly investigate the role of language *per se* in social interaction. Indeed, it must be said that, with a few notable exceptions, the linguistic side of SI has suffered from the fact that, along with social psychologists, the largest group to take on the approach consisted of sociologists. Sociologists have traditionally tended to treat language as just another topic (and not even a central one at that), rather than according it generic significance. This tendency has, apparently, transmitted itself to most of the SI school of sociology, too, *pace* Mead's focus on language. Perhaps and ultimately, Mead's characterization of language in terms of significant symbols proved to be an insufficiently substantial basis for these studies to accord language a greater centrality. Certainly, later SI came to unduly rely on a simplistic naming theory of language.

Often, symbolic interactionist themes simply operate as a patina on what is otherwise a relatively conventional ethnography. Even the highly influential work of Everett C. Hughes, which inspired so much symbolic interactionist work at the University of Chicago, was only selectively founded upon the concepts introduced by Mead, and certainly did not emphasize the influence of language *per se* upon interaction. Hughes, and (even more so) those working in his tradition tended to restrict their analysis of language to (i) the rendering of an 'insider's' standpoint on his/her occupational or other situation, (ii) the naming or labelling of actions, and, as a corollary of (i) and (ii), (iii) the use of names to confer *identities* onto persons. This concern for the study of the application of names to persons and their deeds has tended to result in symbolic interactionism often being dubbed 'labeling theory'. This is regrettably reductionist.

A classic, and often vivid, ethnographic study in the Hughes/Chicago School tradition is that of Ned Polsky's (1969) chapter on 'The Hustler'. Here he notes that the pool hustler, in his occupational argot, distinguishes between the activities of 'dumping' (the deliberate losing of a match in order to cheat spectators who have made side-bets) and 'lemoning' (where losing is the hustler's means of deceiving his opponent into raising the stakes for a subsequent game). Therefore, what are, to the outsider, two identical cases of a similar activity ('deliberate losing') are accorded different esoteric names and consequently take on very different identification and meaning. Polsky observes that the verb 'dumping' may be nominalized ('the game was a dump') or that the object to which the verb is attached may vary as in 'he dumped on the bettors', 'he dumped on his opponent' or 'he dumped on the game'.

Moreover, Polsky shows how names such as 'hustler' and 'sucker' distribute identities for persons, or even for the same person. For example, a hustler told Polsky: "X has got the heart and he's got the stroke. But he'll never be a good hustler 'cause he's always giving away too many points. He's part sucker, that's what he is". Thus, allocation of identity also allocated the identified person to a status hierarchy amongst his/her colleagues – a favorite theme amongst SI analysts. Through the invocation of esoteric argot, ethnographers seek to 'take the role of the other', to take the standpoint of the actor(s) s/he is studying, and to represent that standpoint to the reader. This gives some SI work something of an exposée character. However, Polsky's restriction of his linguistic considerations to the phenomenon of occupational argot means that his study far from fully espouses Mead's position: interestingly, Polsky never mentions Mead.

One of the relatively rare contemporary SI analyses which – unlike Polsky – examine language extensively and explicitly in 'self' and 'other' terms is Thomas S Weinberg's (1983) study of homosexual identities. Using interview data, Weinberg examines the linguistic construction of the 'self'–'other' dialectic. He notes that this dialectic is open-textured and that the reciprocal determination of that labeling by others and of self-labeling may take place in a variety of ways.

The imputation by others of linguistic labels such as 'homosexual', 'faggot' or 'queer' may occasion a self-suspicion that one is homosexual, or, alternatively, self-suspicion may advert the person to others' view of him, and so on. Whatever the processual specifics, identity construction and transformation is treated by Weinberg as interactional 'work'. This 'work' involves the subject's reciprocal identification of others with whom he interacts – parents, classmates, and the like – as significant others having a greater margin of definitional privilege.

Weinberg thus presents the interactional identification of persons in a dynamic, processual way, as a moving perspective occurring at variable pace, in and through time, in career-like stages (the career is a favored model in SI analysis). Language is seen here, then, more in the social-interactional terms set by Mead himself and this renders Weinberg's study one of the purest recent examples of SI. In particular, it preserves the original Meadian concern with the linguistic constitution of social phenomena.

Weinberg's study shows a strong affinity with the more general observation on language made by the SI analyst Anselm L. Strauss. Strauss (1969, Ch. 1) focuses on how we use names in interaction and how we classify, assess and stratify persons through these names. Persons are defined through the names selected for them, and these definitions prepare others for certain 'appropriate' courses of action vis-à-vis the named subject. They also, and reciprocally, potentiate actions effected by the subject on the basis of his/her anticipation of the name-based actions issued by others.

For Strauss, competing 'naming terminologies', competing definitions of the situation, may be part and parcel of the formation of oppositional courses of action out of which conflict groups may emerge. This study is a particularly persuasive example of the way in which SI takes on the 'actor's perspective', the 'insiders's view'.

Strauss, then, at least treats language as a foundational phenomenon and this allows him to address some Meadian analytic issues such as language acquisition and concept formation during primary socialization (see e.g. Lindesmith, Strauss & Denzin 1977: Ch. 9, 10 and 11). The developmental processes whereby the child acquires a comprehension of symbols, a competent use of concepts, and simultaneously develops a 'self' (i.e. self-awareness including the self conceived as an object from the standpoint of others), are focalized. The phenomena of role-taking, role-playing and role-differentiation, the orientation to significant others and the generalized other, the development of detachment and objectivity are all seen as parts of this development of the child into an accomplished symbolizer of, and competent actor in, his/her social world.

Indeed, to Strauss et al., one important feature of SI is that, by and large, it presents people as competent agents in their world rather than being pushed around like billiard balls by external forces beyond their awareness (but see below for a *caveat*). The work of SI practitioners on how these competencies are acquired is clearly a central requirement and major advantage of their approach and in principle sets it apart from the more traditional sociological and linguistic approaches.

Notwithstanding this distinctiveness, the work of contemporary SI analysts – particularly those dealing with developmental issues – also reveals striking *de facto* features of this approach, namely its absorptive tendencies. It frequently selects from and builds in ad hoc elements of the work of analysts such as Chomsky, Freud, Piaget, speech act theorists and others. This is not to say that SI practitioners are uncritical of these extrinsic approaches – indeed, they are selectively disaffiliative if some proposition appears dissonant with Meadian precepts.

This absorptive tendency of SI finds its mirror-image in that of orthodox North American sociology where, as Goffman observed, Mead's presuppositions came to form (to varying extents) part of its basis, particularly in the sphere of socialization (see e.g. Goffman 1958). The incorporation of these presuppositions was largely tacit, even unrecognized. It must be said, though, that such presuppositions were never exhaustively driven through to the extent where they occasioned a methodological radicalization of the discipline.

A major contributor to the study of communication in social life has been Erving Goffman (see e.g. Verhoeven 1993: 318). His espousal of SI was so ambivalent and allusive that it eludes any formalization by a third party, and I must simply commend to readers Goffman's own avowals on the matter, and perhaps to his fate at the hands of the purists (see e.g. Blumer 1972). Although he always studied communicative conduct, Goffman took a long time to take 'the linguistic turn' *per se*, and it took him at least until mid-career to begin to treat language use as such as a basic element of social life. Indeed, it might be claimed that he never came to fully treat language as foundational. For instance, he preferred to locate the serial organization of talk as having its 'natural home' where talk itself was not necessarily present, i.e. in a more general and generic organization of turn-taking activities. Nonetheless, Goffman is one of relatively few contemporary 'SI' analysts who deals in anything other than rhetorical terms with language as self-contained *social activity*. This is especially clearly seen in his later work (e.g. Goffman 1981).

Goffman's work also exemplifies what has sometimes been termed the 'histrionic' aspects of G.H. Mead's philosophy, and, to be sure, has amplified these aspects by utilizing as a resource Kenneth Burke's 'dramaturgical analysis' (Burke 1965; see also Watson 1989). Part of this extension involved the adoption of what Burke termed the 'perspective by incongruity'. This entailed the (re-)description of social actions in terms of extended similes – predominantly that of theatrical performance but also others such as games, espionage, confidence tricks, etc. These similes are designed to highlight the unacknowledged ways in which persons involve themselves in 'impression management', the reciprocal communication, management and monitoring of (favorable and unfavorable) impressions of the self and others in interaction.

For Goffman, talk was located within a broader interactional context, namely the encounter and the occasion. In this respect, he never entirely abandoned his concern to deal with talk in terms other than 'merely' those of the sequential organization of utterances, as is instanced in his paper *Response cries* (Goffman 1981: 78–123). Whilst he played down the dramaturgical perspective at this later stage in his career, it was never entirely expunged and continued to operate. As a result, Goffman never quite treated language consistently or fully as a self-contained set of activities with its own 'phenomenologial integrity' and as an object of analytic attention in its own right.

It is debatable whether Goffman's approach to communication conduct can properly be subjected to criticisms derived from the SI position *simpliciter*. His use of similes does, certainly, make available for analytic inspection many of the naturally-occurring details of such conduct which would otherwise pass by unremarked, and his dramaturgical analysis has a pleasingly mordant quality which reflects some of the best down-to-earth aspects of SI analysis.

Nonetheless, we might also from an SI standpoint venture to demur from some major features of Goffman's approach. Goffman's notion of the presentation of self to one or more co-present others, cast in terms of the 'performer' – 'audience' simile, captures some aspects of the self-other dialectic in a most compelling manner. Still, the problem with this extraordinary extension of the dramaturgical simile is that it also operates to displace social actors' own orientations to what is for them the 'point' – and often, for them, a highly sincere, serious and consequential point – of the interaction/occasion and to replace this point with the orientation to 'performance values' (Blumer 1972). From a 'purist' SI standpoint, we might, in effect, argue that Goffman downgrades or even relativizes the symbolic meanings in terms of which parties to an interaction conceive of and construct that interaction, and demotes that action in a commonsense hierarchy of sincerity and seriousness.

Goffman, therefore, might be accused of establishing an 'ironic' analytic stance, where, in principle, the stance that SI espouses is a non-ironic one, preserving the endogenous 'phenomenological integrity' of meaningful social activity (cf. Polsky's and Weinberg's analyses). It should be noted, however, that some few examples of SI do, to a greater or lesser extent, become compromised by ironic elements.

As an example of this, Lindesmith, Strauss & Denzin (1975: esp. 46) equivocate at making society-members' knowledge-in-action the sole point of reference in analytically accounting for action. Criticizing some (un-named) versions of ethnomethodology, or their misconstrual of these versions, these authors aver that one cannot analytically account for actions exclusively on the basis of members' knowledge. Lindesmith, Strauss & Denzin apparently seek instead to reserve some measure of 'objective' definitional privilege in analysing actions. In many respects, this claim indicates a retreat from the strong SI program and a first step back into ironic imputations of faulted or inadequate knowledge, and towards conceiving of society-members as cultural or judgemental dopes. This is a stance which has long characterized the conventional sociologies and other disciplines against which the strong SI program has so effectively reacted over many decades.

SI, then, has its strong and weak programmes, and the latter in particular have been semi-permeable vis-à-vis orthodox social science and linguistics. One must, consequently, proceed cautiously in the making of any general statements. However, taking the strong program – i.e. that having an explicit and extensive provenience in Mead's philosophy – we can see many fruitful relevances to pragmatics.

The first set of relevances is that SI is a genuinely praxiological approach to language use. Unlike, say, correlational approaches, it treats language as a built-in, rather than separate-and-added, feature of social action and interaction. The approach treats language use as, *a fortiori*, social, and treats society as a communicative and interpretative order. It treats humans (to modify R.P. MacDermott's phrase) as communicative environments for each other: language use is treated as highly sensitive to social context and to subcultural locations.

An SI analyst studying language use must do so from a culturally indigenous position, from the 'insider's perspective' rather than imposing some *a priori*, externally-derived stipulation of usage, whether this stipulation be derived from some analytic theory or some other lay cultural context. The SI inquirer into language use must consequently submit him/herself to the disciplines of a rigorously naturalistic research method to explicating a given communicative context 'from within'. Such an approach treats language use as an integral, working feature of social life. In this respect, the SI approach to the contextualization of language practices is far richer than many of the orthodox approaches in pragmatics, and is far less formalistic and schematic.

Moreover, SI potentially espouses an explicative rather than an ironic analytic stance to communicative actions and interactions. At its best, this potential is most productively actualized, as in Weinberg's (1983) study. This non-ironic property of SI is part and parcel of a non-positivistic approach to communicative phenomena, one which does not impose a logic of externality. It is an approach – or a family of approaches – which does not depend for its analytic power upon the received distinctions or frameworks of linguistics as found, for example, in semantics. Its power derives in large part from the locating of language as integral to social interaction and organization, and of its conception of social order as being a linguistically-constituted state of affairs. The point of reference is society-members' own definitions of the situation, rather than a scientific (or scientistic) definition stipulated by the analyst.

The best work of SI is typically found in the superbly-crafted intimate empirical explorations of specific (sub-)cultural and occupational settings. Howard S. Becker's classic *Outsiders* (1962) contains several vividly-analyzed cases in point. Others have studied bar-room habitués, Black street-corner groups, religious sects and myriad other collectivities – all studied at 'grass roots' level, through the participation and role-taking of the SI observers. Such participant observation is SI's preferred methodological option.

The programmatic statements by SI practitioners tend to be less secure, especially when they have taken it upon themselves to fight a rearguard action with ethnomethodology[2] and conversation analysis – surely a needless battle from both vantage points, though comparisons can be instructive.

For instance, many have argued that the 'self'–'other' dialectic in language use is nowhere better empirically represented than in the conversation analytic study by Schegloff, Jefferson and Sacks (1977) on self- and other-correction in conversational interaction, and there is some merit in this argument. These and other conversation analysts have produced empirical work of remarkable detail and precision. Unlike many SI Analysts they treat utterances as social actions in themselves and turn talk itself (rather than talk *about* some other activity) into the most explicit datum for analysis. Nonetheless, these conversation analytic studies are not wholly commensurate with those of SI, which espouse a concern with how selves are constituted in the first place, rather than treating 'self' and 'other' as turn-generated categories in talk. There is surely room for debate, but to conceive of one of these approaches in terms of the other is akin to recommending that basketball should adopt tennis's scoring system: after all, these games are both 'ball games' just as conversation analysis and ethnomethodology are both often termed 'interpretative sociologies'.

Consequently, not all dialogue between analytic approaches is fruitless. As I have indicated elsewhere, Blumer's critique of variable analysis in statistical sociology – his 1955 Presidential Address to the American Sociological Association (Blumer 1969: Ch. 7) – has occasioned from positivist sociologists what must be the most

---

2. The battle-lines were drawn up early. The founder of ethnomethodology, Harold Garfinkel made a pre-emptive strike in his doctoral dissertation, *The perception of the other: A study of social order* (1952).

telling four-decade silence in the recent history of academic life. The same may be said of his comments on 'effects' studies on the mass media (Blumer 1969: Ch. 11).

The overriding relevance of SI to pragmatics is that it offers a non-positivistic approach which does not rely upon decontextualized meanings and mentalistic presuppositions. For SI, 'language' and 'mind' are eminently social,[3] available both to lay and professional observation.

References

Becker, H.S. (1962). *Outsiders*. Free Press.
Blumer, H. (1969). *Symbolic interactionism*. Prentice-Hall.
—— (1972). *Action versus interaction*. Society (formerly Trans-Action).
Burke, K. (1965). *Permanence and change*. Bobbs-Merrill Co.
Garfinkel, H. (1952). *The perception of the other*. PhD. Diss. Harvard University.
Goffman, E. (1958). *The presentation of self in everyday life*. Doubleday Anchor.
—— (1963). *Stigma*. Prentice-Hall.
—— (1981). *Forms of talk*. Basil Blackwell.
Gordon, C. & K.J. Gergen (eds.) (1968). *The self in social interaction*. Wiley.
Hughes, E.C. (1974). *The sociological eye*. University of Chicago Press.
Lindesmith, A.R., A.L. Strauss & N.K. Denzin (1975). *Social psychology*, 5th ed. Holt, Rinehart and Winston.
Manis, J.G. & B.N. Meltzer (eds.) (1967). *Symbolic interaction*. Allyn and Bacon.
Marcarino, A. (1988). *Sociologia dell'azione comunicativa*. Guida Editoria.
Mead, G.H. (1934). *Mind, self and society*. University of Chicago Press.
Polsky, N. (1969). *Hustlers, beats and others*. Doubleday Anchor.
Rose, A.M. (ed.) (1962). *Human behavior and social processes*. Routledge & Kegan Paul.
Schegloff, E.A., G. Jefferson & H. Sacks (1977). The preference for self-correction in the organization of repair in conversation. *Language* 53: 361–382.
Strauss, A.L. (1969). *Mirrors and masks* (5th ed.). The Sociology Press.
—— (ed.) (1964). *George Herbert Mead and social psychology*. Phoenix Books.
Trifiletti, R. (1991). *L'identità controversa*. Dott, Antonio Milani.
Verhoeven, J.C. (1993). An interview with Erving Goffman, 1980. *Research on Language and Social Interaction* 26(3): 317–348.
Watson, R. (2009). The Textual Incarnation of Sociological Analysis: The Case of Erving Goffman's Writings, In R. Watson, *Analysing Practical and Professional Texts: A Naturalistic Approach*: 101–120. Ashgate Publishing Ltd.
Weinberg, T.S. (1983). *Gay men, gay selves*. Irvington Publ. Inc. [See also: Cognitive sociology; Ethnomethodology; Social psychology]

---

3. It might be observed, though, that SI's conception of language as 'social' does not mean that its interactional properties *per se* are exhaustively analyzed. In labeling theory, for example, 'labels' are studied without close, explicit reference to the linguistic interaction involved in their conferment.

Index

A

A room of one's own, 154
Abelson, R.P., 117
accent convergence, 21
accent mobility, 21
accommodating elderly, 25
accommodation model, 22–24
accommodation theory, 21–26
accommodation theory, conceptual developments, 23
accommodation theory, definition, 21
accusativity, 37–38
act-constituting, 37
The African Charter on Human and Peoples' Rights, 216
agency, definitions, 28, 34, 36
agency, meta-agentive discourse, 41
agency, role of intentionality, 34–37
agency and praxis, 31
agency and structure, 31
agency as synonym for free will/resistance, 29–30
agency of projects, 36
agency of (unequal) power, 36
Ahearn, L.M., 28–45
Aikio-Puoskari, U., 221
Akinnaso, F.N., 171
Alfonzetti, G., 98
Alim, S., 14
Alonso, A.M., 198
alternational code-switching, 88
Althusser, L., 235
Alvarez Cáccamo, C., 84–85
Amann, K., 117–118
Amazonian languages, 40
American Convention on Human Rights, 216
Ammon, U., 148
Amuzu, E.K., 102

Anderson, B., 179, 203, 242, 289, 294
Andrýsek, O., 217
Angermeyer, P., 98
animacy hierarchy, 39
Anspach, R.R., 117–120
Antaki, C., 51
anthropological approaches to bilingualism and multilingualism, 77–79
Appadurai, A., 288
approximation strategies, 24
Archer, M.S., 31
Arensberg, C., 280, 296
Aron, J., 10, 284
assimilation, 214
Atkinson, D., 49
Atkinson, J.M., 171
Atkinson, K., 25, 249
Atkinson, P., 54, 235
Auer, P., 6, 10, 14–15, 77, 79, 84–107
authoritative validation, 53
authority, example of, 50
authority and gender, 59–61
authority and self, 51–55
authority in (and through) god, 58–59
authority in each other, 55–57
authority in language, 62–64
authority in world, 57–58
automated social cognition, 147
autonomous language, 3
Axelrod, M., 204

B

Backus, A., 103, 106
Bailey, B., 93
Bakhtin, M., 295
Balibar, E., 179
Ballim, A., 171
Bani-Shoraka, H., 98
Barnes, J., 265
Baron, N.S., 64

Barrett, R., 205, 281, 291
Barth, R., 176, 290
Barthes, R., 115
Barton, D., 293
Bateson, G., 29
Baudrillard, J., 235
Bauman, R., 179–180, 200, 202, 243, 256, 276, 279, 281, 283–285
Bauman, Z., 12, 290–292
Baxter, L.A., 56
Baynham, M., 177, 184
Becker, H.S., 312
behavioral confirmation, 23
being accommodative, 25
Bell, A., 277
Bell's audience design theory, 136–137
Benwell, B., 51, 57
Berger, C.R., 22, 56
Berger, P.L., 31, 261–264
Bergvall, V.L., 60–61
Bernstein, B., 235, 277, 280, 283
Berruto, G., 85
Bex, T., 62–63, 179
beyond minoritisation, 254–257
Bhabha, H., 248
Bielby, D., 25
Bierbach, C., 93
bilingual mixed languages, 131
bilingualism and multilingualism, 71–79
Billig, M., 11, 50–51, 282, 288, 296
binding educational linguistic human rights, 223–225
Birken-Silverman, G., 93
Bittner, M., 38
Blackledge, A., 13
Blom, J.-P., 6, 76, 87–88, 95, 194
Blommaert, J., 11–13, 15–16, 64, 78, 85, 90, 179, 181–182, 184, 186–187, 192, 195, 199, 201–202, 249, 256, 288–289
Bloomfield, L., 193, 275, 277

Blumer, H., 304, 307, 309–310, 312
Boas, F., 193, 203
Bobrow, D.G., 117
Bochmann, K., 236
Boden, D., 25, 56, 116, 119
Bogoch, P., 56, 61
Boissevain, J., 265
Bolinger, D., 289
Borker, R., 162
borrowing situations, 86, 130–131
Bott, E., 265
Boumans, L., 102–103
Bourdieu, P., 11, 32–33, 50, 78, 91, 147, 196, 235, 261, 263–264, 283, 286
Bourhis, R.Y., 22–23
Bourne, J., 63
Bradac, J.J., 21–24
Branson, J., 227
Breckenridge, C., 288
bridge system morphemes, 102
Briggs, C., 13, 291–292
Briggs, C.L., 179–180, 196, 198, 200, 202
Brisard, F., 4, 7
Broeder, P., 184
Broom, A., 55
Brown, G., 15
Brown, P., 10, 26
Brown, R., 87, 166
Bruegger, U., 119
Bryant, C.G.A., 31
Bucholtz, M., 14–15, 51–52, 57, 60, 166, 204–205
Bulcaen, C., 192
Bunte, P.A., 203–204, 206
Burke, K., 310
Burnaby, B., 181
Burns, T.R., 31
Butler, J., 164, 251
Butler, Y., 77
Button, G., 171
Buzzelli, C.A., 56
Bychowski, Z., 74

C
Caglar, A., 186
Calvet, L-J., 14–15
Cameron, D., 6–7, 14–15, 49, 57, 59–60, 62–64, 80, 206, 253, 289, 296
Campion, P., 50
Candlin, C.N., 119
Candlin, S., 119

Caporael, L., 25
Capotorti, F., 217
Carter, B., 242
Casanovas, P., 116
Castells, M., 292–295, 297
categorical rules, 145
Cavanaugh, J.R., 205
Cazden, C., 6, 276
Chafe, W., 52–53
Chan, B., 106
Cheshire, J., 23
Chilton, P., 54
Chomsky, N., 3, 143, 156, 228, 277, 309
Chomskyan' linguistics, 2
Chouliaraki, L., 243
Cicourel, A.V., 5, 10, 114–120
Clark, H., 287
Clark, K., 236
Clarke, A., 116, 119
Clarke, S., 160
Clayman, S., 56
Clement, R., 63
Clifford, J., 284, 290
Clyde, M., 265
Clyne, M., 77, 89, 107
Coates, J., 26, 52, 56, 59–61
code-mixing, 86
code-switching, acquisition, 84–85
code-switching, conversational functions, 99
code-switching, conversational structure, 95
code-switching, definition, 85–86
code-switching, development, 107
code-switching, discourse functions, 88
code-switching, early studies, 87–89
code-switching, grammatical constraints on, 101–106
code-switching, interactional analysis, 95–101
code-switching, pragmatic analyses, 87
code-switching, pragmatic uses, 91
code-switching, sequential analysis, 89
code-switching, terminological and methodological issues, 85–87

code-switching research, future directions in, 107
code-switching style, 97
Coe, K., 59
cognition, 115, 117
cognitive sociology, 113–122
cognitive sociology, historical overview, 113–115
Cognitive sociology: Language and meaning in social interaction, 114
cognitive sociology, methodology, 119–120
cognitive sociology, sample analysis, 120–122
Colapietro, V.M., 29
Cole, T.R., 245
collective rights, 216–217
Collier, V.P., 229
Collins, J., 15, 177, 181, 184, 186, 195, 202, 206, 279, 289
Comaroff, J., 11
communicative competence, 4
communities of practice, 284–286
community and discourse, 292–295
community as semiotic sign, 286–287
community speech and speech community, 275–278
Companion to Linguistic Anthropology, 36
competence-related code-switching, 89, 100–101
compound bilinguals, 134
Comrie, B., 37
Conefrey, T., 61
constraint theories, 8
contact, 127
contextualization, 171
contextualization cues, 88, 172
Convention on Human Rights and Fundamental Freedoms, 216
Convention on the Protection and Promotion of the Diversity of Cultural Expressions 2005, 186, 221
convergence, 22
convergence of styles, 24
convergence situations, 131
conversation analysis, 10
conversational interaction and gender, 165

Cook-Gumperz, J., 171, 287
coordinative bilinguals, 134–135
Cornips L., 14
correlational/quantitative sociolinguistics, 5
correlational sociolinguistics, 140–151
correlational sociolinguistics, outlook, 150–151
correlational sociolinguistics, rules, 145–148
Corsaro, W.A., 115–120
Corsican, 198
Costa, A., 107
Couper-Kuhlen, E., 171, 173
Coupland, J., 22, 24–26, 245, 249, 254–255
Coupland, N., 6–8, 10–15, 21–26, 50, 57, 241–257
Cowan, J.K., 188
Coward, R., 235
Crawford, J., 181
Crawford, M., 59–60
Creese, A., 13
Crenshaw, K.W., 251
creoles, 131
Critical Discourse Analysis (CDA), 49, 58
critical ideological analysis, 196
crossing, 93–94
Crowley, T., 179
Culbertson, G.H., 25
Cutler, C., 14
Cutler, C.A., 204
Cutting, J., 170

D
da Silva, E., 186
Daniel, E.V., 29
Dauenhauer, N.M., 205
Dauenhauer, R., 205
Davies, E., 171
De Certeau, M., 32–33
De Groot, A., 74
de Varennes, F., 186, 212, 217, 229
Declaration on the Rights of Persons Belonging to National or Ethnic, Religious and Linguistic Minorities, 1992, 186, 223
DeFrancisco, V., 60
degrees of authority, 53
Delgado, R., 251

Denzin, N.K., 308, 311
Derbyshire, D.C., 40
Derrida, J., 235
Desjarlais, R., 30
Deuel, N., 294
Devlin, B., 226
Dewaele, J.-M., 77
D'hondt, S., 5, 9
Di Luzio A., 172–173
Di Sciullo, A.-M., 106
Dietz, T., 31
difference view of language and gender, 153–155, 158, 162–166
diglossia, 129
Dingwall, R., 56
directionality, 36
Dirim, I., 107
discourse, 45, 116
discourse attuning, 24–26
discourse formations, 50
discourse-related code-switching, 88, 95, 98–99
discursive turn, 12–13
displaying liberalism, 252–253
Dittmar, N., 140–151, 235
divergence, 22
Dixon, J.A., 63
Dixon, R.M.W., 37–40
Dobres, M.-A., 29
dominance view of language and gender, 162
dominant language ideologies, 181–183
Dorian, N., 180, 182–183, 205
double negatives, 196
Drew, P., 171
Dubois, J., 40
Duchene, A., 183, 186
Duck, S., 56
Dunbar, R., 223, 226
Duranti, A., 35–37, 40–41, 172, 277, 280, 283
Durkheim, E., 113

E
early system morphemes, 102
Eats, Shoots and Leaves (2003), 62
Eckert, P., 6, 14, 60, 147, 165, 283–285, 296
Edley, N., 49
Edwards, D., 57
Edwards, J., 24, 62

Edwards, M., 133
Eelen, G., 50, 54, 56
ego-affirming, 37
Ehernberger Hamilton, H., 171
Ehrlich, S., 56
Elite bilingualism, 72
elite closure, 90
Ellis, J., 235
Elster, J., 137
embedded language, 102–106. *see also* matrix language
Emerson, C., 236
Engels, F., 113, 233
English, 198
English with an Accent: Language, Ideology, and Discrimination, 196
Epstein, J.P., 54
equivalence constraint, 101
Erckenbrecht, U., 233
ergative-absolutive, 38
ergative markers, 38
ergativity, 38
Erickson, F., 6, 8, 11, 16, 49–50, 171
Errington, J., 177, 186, 195, 197, 203–204
Escobar, A., 42
ethnography of communication, 5, 194
ethnolinguistic vitality, 132
ethnomethodology, 9–10
European Charter for Regional or Minority Languages, 186, 215
evidentiality, 52
expertise, 118
exploratory code-switching, 97
expressive human rights, 222
expressive *versus* instrumental rights, 222
Extra, G., 184

F
Fabbro, F., 74
Fairclough, N., 49–50, 192, 235, 243, 255, 261, 288–289
family discourse as form of institutional discourse, 266–271
Farnell, B., 32
Ferguson, C., 77, 129
Fernandes, D., 214
Field, M.C., 195, 206
Fillmore, C.J., 116
Finlayson, R., 102

Fisher, S., 115, 117–119
Fishman, J., 3–6, 77, 130, 132, 135–137, 275, 279, 283–284, 289, 297
Fishman, P., 60, 160–161
Fishman's domain theory, 136
Foley, W., 286
Foley, W.A., 39–40
Ford, C.E., 50, 173, 226
Foucault, M., 13, 50, 57, 235
Fowler, R., 261
Framework Convention for the Protection of National Minorities, 215
Frazer, E., 278–279, 282
free morpheme constraint, 101
Freeman, C., 58
French, 198
French-Dutch code-switching, 92
frequent code-switching, 87
From Grammar to Politics: Linguistic Anthropology in a Western Samoan Village, 41

G
Gafaranga, J., 86, 98
Gal, S., 15, 49, 78–79, 81, 91, 176, 179–180, 183, 195, 200–201, 204, 242, 283, 288–289, 291
Galasinski, D., 176, 252
García, O., 229
Gardin, B., 234
Gardner, R., 75–76
Gardner-Chloros, P., 133
Garfinkel, H., 9, 31, 169, 312
Garrett, P., 14, 79
Gastarbeiterdeutsch, 93–94
gay men, 164
Gee, J., 16, 284, 291, 296
Gellner, E., 197
gender, definition, 152
gender, language and authority, 59–61
gender, pragmatic aspects, 153
gender and language, 152–153
gender and language, history of, 155–167
gender and language, prehistory of, 153–155
Genesee, F., 77
Georgakopoulou, A., 14
Gergen, K.J., 24, 51

Gibbons, D., 216
Giddens, A., 11–12, 29, 31–34, 57, 176, 195, 198, 255–256, 278, 282, 292
Giddens' theory of structuration, 31–32
Gilbert, G.N., 58
Giles, H., 21–25, 50, 57, 75–76, 132, 244–245, 248, 256, 277
Gillet, G., 52
Gilman, A., 166
Gilroy, P., 289, 295, 297
Glick Schiller, N., 186
Gobo, G., 120
Goetz, J., 276
Goffman, E, 10, 31, 54, 169, 285, 309–310
Gomez de Garcia, J., 204
Goodrich, P., 50
Goodwin, C., 172, 284–285
Gordon, E., 63
Gospodinoff, K., 10, 284
Graham, E.S., 59
Graham, P., 59
Grainger, K., 25
The Grammar of Consciousness and the Consciousness of Grammar, 195
grammatical encoding of agency, 37–41
grammatical gender, 153
Gramsci, 236
Gramsci, A., 202, 235–239
Gray, J., 279
Green, D.W., 107, 245
Greene, D.L., 59
Grice, H.P., 54, 235
Grillo, R., 13
Grillo, R.D., 71, 176, 178–180, 182
Grimshaw, A.D., 116–119
Grin, F., 229
Groce, S.B., 117–119
Grosjean, F., 74
Grosjean, J., 107
grounding, 12
groupness, 255
Gruber, H., 54
Guerini, F., 98, 100
Gullberg, M., 74
Gumperz, J., 3–7, 10, 12, 76–77, 85, 87–88, 95, 98, 136–137, 194, 275–277, 279, 282, 284, 287

Gumperz, J.J., 5–6, 89, 169–173, 242
Gurak, L., 295

H
Habermas, J., 50–51, 150, 235, 295
habitus, 32
Hague Recommendations Regarding the Education Rights of National Minorities (1996), 224
Hak, T., 238
Hakuta, K., 77
Hale, K., 38
Hall, K., 15, 51–52, 57, 60, 166, 288, 290, 294
Halliday, M., 275, 283
Halliday, M.A.K., 3–4, 116
Hamel, R.E., 229
Hamelink, C.J., 229
Hamilton, H.E., 25
Handler, R., 183
Hanks, W., 283–286
Hannerz, U., 288, 290–291
hard law rights *versus* soft law rights, 221
Harding, E., 129
Harmon, D., 228
Harré, R., 52, 57
Harris, C., 265
Harris, R., 14–15, 49
Harvey, D., 297
Haugen, E., 5, 15, 73, 130
Haviland, J., 206
Heath, S., 176, 179, 297
Heath, S.B., 6
Heller, M., 6, 13, 15, 49, 71–80, 84–85, 88, 89, 92–93, 130, 171, 176–177, 180, 182, 184–186, 264, 279
Helsloot, N., 233–239
Henwood, K., 24
Heritage, J., 8–9, 54, 56, 171
Herman, E.S., 328
Hernandez-Chavez, E., 89
Herriman, M., 181
Herring, S., 293
Herzog, M.I., 4
Heugh, K., 229
Hewitt, R., 94, 183, 287, 296
Hewstone, M., 22, 248, 256
High Religion: A Cultural and Political History of Sherpa Buddhism, 33

Higonnet, P.L.-R., 178
Hilbert, R.A., 114
Hill, J., 78, 105, 130, 195, 254
Hill, J.H., 37, 197, 206
Hill, K., 78, 105, 130, 195
Hinnenkamp, V., 171, 288
Hinrichs, L., 93
Historical Metaphors and Mythical Realities, 33
historiography of language ideologies, 201
Hobsbawm, E.J., 179
Hoechsmann, M., 288
Hoffman, K.E., 203
Holmes, J., 53, 59, 60–61, 170
Holquist, M., 236
Holyoak, K.J., 117
homogenisation, 248–250
Höppe, W., 233
Hopper, P.J., 150
Hopper, R., 21
Hopper P., 56
Houdebine, J-L., 233
Hudson, R., 7, 277, 286
Hughes, E.C., 307
human rights, 212–213. *see also* linguistic human rights
Hutchins, E. K., 117
Hymes, D., 3–6, 15–16, 62–63, 169, 194, 275–276, 279, 283, 289–290, 296–297
Hymes, D.H., 194

I
ideological production, sites of, 199
ideological sites, 198
ideology of contempt, 182
immigrant minorities, 221–222
Indefrey, P., 74
indigenous peoples, 214, 219, 222, 229
individual human rights, 215–216
inequality, 119
Inoue, M., 202
insertional code-switching, 88
institutionalization, 262
instrumental language rights, 222
instrumentalist ideology, 197
integration, 214
intentionality, 34–37
interaction, 116

interactional discourse analysis, 16
interactional sociolinguistics, contributions, 170–172
interactional sociolinguistics, definition, 169
interactional sociolinguistics, program, 173
International Convention on the Prevention and Punishment of the Crime of Genocide (the Genocide Convention), 225
International Covenant on Civil and Political Rights, ICCPR, 216–217
international declarations of rights, 186–188
interpretive procedures, 117–118
intersubjective instruction, 146
intralinguistic rights, 212
Invisible Women: The Schooling Scandal, 162
Irvine, J., 15, 195, 276, 283, 288–289, 291, 296
Irvine, J.T., 44–45, 200–201, 204

J
Jacquemet, M., 171
Jaffe, A., 178, 180, 196, 198, 206
Jakobson, R., 194
Jameson, F., 296
Janulf, P., 225–226
Jarvis, S., 74
Jary, D., 31
Jaspers, J., 1–16, 171
Javanese, 198
Jaworski, A., 200, 252
Jefferson, G., 10, 312
Jewitt, C., 173
John, V., 6, 276
Johnson, P., 23–24, 256
Johnston, A., 56
Johnston, B., 4
Johnstone, B., 4, 19
Jokinen, M., 227
Jones, S., 293
Jonsson, C., 98
Jørgensen, J.N., 14, 87
Joshi, A.K., 106
Journal of Linguistic Anthropology, 202
Jupp, T.C., 171

K
Karn, H.E., 254–255
Karp, I., 31
Karrebæk, M.S., 98
Kasper, G., 77
Kaufman, T., 130
Keane, W., 29, 204
Keating C., 14
Keenan, E.L., 37
Keim, I., 93
Kelly-Holmes, H., 87
Kemal, M., 213
Kerswill, P., 275, 277
Klaus, D., 229
Knorr-Cetina, K., 115–120
Kockelman, P., 29, 35–36
Kollock, P., 294
Kontra, M., 229
Köpke, B., 74
Köppe, R., 107
Kovacheva, S., 294
Koven, M., 77
Kress, G., 242
Kroll, J., 74, 135
Kroskrity, P.V., 192–207
Kubey, R.W., 252
Kulick, D., 6, 78–79, 187
Kushner, T., 251

L
la perruque (the wig), 32
Labov, W., 3–4, 6–7, 136, 143, 145, 147–148, 165, 235
Labov, W.A., 63
Lacan, J., 241
Lacey, N., 278–279, 282, 297
Lachler, J., 204
Laclau, E., 13
Ladd, P., 227
Lakoff, R., 6, 50, 53, 60
Lambert, W., 75–76
Lambert, W.E., 23, 75–76
Lane, H., 227
language, as media of education, 229
Language: its nature, development, and origins, 154
language, numbers, 182, 229
language, oral, 222
language and nationalism, 179–180
'Language and Political Economy,' 195

language and power, 49
language change, 148–150
language change, principle of grammatic inferencing, 150
language contact, bilingual acquisition processes, 129
language contact, causes, processes and outcomes, 127–130
language contact, decision-making in, 135
language contact, definition, 127
language contact, factors contributing to, 127–128
language contact, pragmatics of, 135–138
language contact, theoretical and methodological approaches, 130–135
language creation, 131
language dominance, 176
language genocide, *see* linguistic genocide
language ideologies, awareness, 199–200
language ideologies, constructing, 200, 204
language ideologies, dominant, 202, 206
language ideologies, erasure, 200–201
language ideologies, fractal recursivity, 200–201
language ideologies, future research, 205–207
language ideologies, historical emergence of, 192–195
language ideologies, iconization, 200
language ideologies, Indonesian, 197
language ideologies, Javanese, 193
language ideologies, linguistic differentiation, 200–201
language ideologies, Mexicano, 197
language ideologies, multiplicity, 197–198
language ideologies, multisitedness, 199
language ideologies, recent developments, 201–205

language ideologies, studies of, 197, 202
language ideologies and language standardization, 195
language ideologies and language structure, 192
language ideologies and metapragmatics, 199
language ideologies and production of community, 287–289
language in action, agency in language, 44–45
language maintenance, 79, 127, 130–132, 225, 229–230
language minorization, 183–186
language minorization, role of social categorization, 176
language murder, *see* linguistic genocide
language planning, 64, 187
language policy, 79–80, 213–214
language rationalization, 192
language renewal and linguistic revitalization, 205
language rights, 212–213, 215
language shift, 131–132
Language Shift, 195
language stigmatization, 149
Language Structure and Linguistic Ideology, 192
language subordination process, 196
Language Variation and Cultural Hegemony, 195
Languages in contact, 73
Lanza, E., 77, 107
Lash, S., 297
late modern discourse, language and community, 282–284
late modernity, 12
late system morphemes, 102
Latour, B., 29, 58
Lave, J., 13, 283–284, 285–286
Lawrence, C.T., 251
Layder, D., 8–9, 11
layered code-switching, 85
LeCompte, M., 276
Lee, D., 242
Lemert, C.C., 114
LePage, R., 281, 283, 286, 289, 292
lesbians, 164

Leung, C., 290
Levelt, W.J., 107
Levine, M., 183
Levinson, C., 242
Levinson, S., 10–11, 26
Leyens, J-P., 22
Li Wei, 6, 13, 79, 98–99, 101, 127–138
Lindesmith, A.R., 308, 311
linguistic approaches to bilingualism and multilingualism, 76–77
linguistic capital, 263
linguistic competence, 4
linguistic conservatism, 196
linguistic facts, 143
linguistic false consciousness, 193
linguistic genocide, 225–228
linguistic hierarchy, 178–179
linguistic human rights, 212–213. *see also* human rights
linguistic pragmatics, 5
linguistic rights, 212–213
linguistic structure, 44
linguistic universal, 40
linguistic variables, 143
linguistic variation, 141–144
linguistic variation, application, 144
linguistic variation, description, 143
linguistic variation, explanation, 143
linguistic variation, methodology, 142–143
linguistic variation, tradition and innovation, 142
linguistic variation theory, 143–144
linguistics of community-linguistics of contact, 289–292
Lippi-Green, R., 15, 62, 196, 203, 249
Livia, A., 164
Lo, A., 205
Lo Piparo, F., 236
loanwords, 86
local language ideologies, 198–199, 203
Loether, C., 203, 206
Lowell, A., 226

Luckmann, T., 31, 261–264
Lucy, J.A., 243, 291
Lüdi, G., 107
Lury, C., 288
Lyons, J., 275

M
MacMillan, C.M., 229
Maffi, L., 229
Magga, O.H., 223
Mahmood, S., 30
Makihara, M., 195, 203–204
Makoni, S., 15
Maldidier, D., 238
Maltz, D., 162
Mannheim, B., 37
Mannheim, K., 115
Manning, P., 114
Manzo, J., 56
Mar-Molinero, C., 183
Marcellesi, J-B., 234
Marcellino, W.M., 4
Marian, V., 74
marked code-switching, 96
markedness model, 137
Marr, N.J., 234–235
Marr vs. Stalin, 234–235
Marriott, M., 29
Martin, I., 227
Martin-Jones, M., 107, 182
Marx, K., 31, 113, 233
Marxism, 233
Marxist linguistics, 233–234
Marxist linguistics, recent trends, 235–236
Marxist linguistics today, 238–239
Maryns, K., 15
Maseide, P., 115, 118–119
matrix language, 102–106
Matsuda, M.J., 251
May, S., 6, 79, 181, 183, 212, 229
Maynard, D.W., 54, 171
Mayr, A., 49–50
McClure, E., 88
McConnell-Ginet, S., 6, 40, 60, 285, 287
McDermott, R., 6, 8, 10–12, 16, 171, 284–285
McElhinny, B., 29, 61
McEwan-Fujita, E., 206
McIntosh, J., 203
McMurtry, J., 228
McRae, K.D., 220, 229

Mead, G.H., 50–51, 241, 304, 306–308
Meek, B.A., 203, 205
Meeuwis, M., 4, 7, 15, 85
mega-corpus, 143–144
Mehan, H., 6, 115–120
Meinhof, U.H., 176
Meisel, J., 107
Melucci, A., 295
Mertz, E., 206
Messer-Davidow, E., 28
Messing, J., 205
meta-agentive discourse, 41
meta-agentive discourse, in love letter writing, 42–44
meta-pragmatic discourse, 41
metaphorical code-switching, 88, 95
metapragmatic commentary, sites of, 199
metapragmatics, 171
Mey, J., 62
Mey, J.L., 235
Miller, D., 227
Milloy, J.S., 225
Milroy, J., 6, 62–63, 179, 196, 254, 277
Milroy, L., 62, 77, 101, 179, 196, 254, 265, 277
Minami, Y., 115, 120
Minkowski, M., 74
Misra, G., 227
Mithun, M., 39
Mizrachi, N., 120
modality, 52
Mohanty, A.K., 227
Molinari, L., 116, 119–120
Molotch, H., 116–119
Moore, P., 206
Morgan, M., 165, 280
Morgan, M.J., 202
Morley, D., 282, 294
Morson, G.S., 236
Moscovici, S., 243
mother tongue, 215
Mouffe, C., 13
Moyer, M., 15
Muehlmann, S., 186
Mugglestone, L., 15, 62
Muhamedova, R., 104–105
Muhamedova, R., 102, 105
Mühlhäusler, P., 15
Mulac, A., 23–24
Mulkay, M., 58

multi-dimensional variation, 142
multilingualism, 71–79
multimodal, 23
Muysken, P., 77, 87, 106–107, 133
Myers-Scotton, C., 77, 87, 90, 95–96, 102, 104–107, 133, 137

N
Natale, M., 22
national languages, 180
national minority language, 217, 219–220
Neely, A., 206
negative rights, 213, 219
negative versus positive rights, 219–220
negotiation principle, 137
Nelson, E., 118
neurolinguistic approaches to bilingualism and multilingualism, 73–75
neutral ideological analysis, 196
Nevins, E., 205–206
The New York Times, 167
New Ways of Analyzing Variation, 141
Nichols, J., 52–53
nominative-accusative, 38
non-standard speech, 8
nonce borrowings, 101
Norman, D.A., 63, 117
Nortier, J., 14, 104

O
Oakes, L., 183
Obeyesekere, G., 33
Ochs, E., 41, 173
official languages, 180–181
on representation, 242–243
on 'the other,' 244–248
oppositional agency, 30
organizational activities and materials, 117
organizational constraints, 119
Ortner, S., 8, 12, 16, 31, 33, 35
Ortner, S.B., 7, 28, 34–35, 194
'the other,' 241
overaccommodation, 25
Owens, J., 102

P
Palmer. G. Jr., 206
Paradis, J., 77

Paradis, M., 74
Park, R.E., 246
Parsons, T., 8–10, 113, 143
participant-related code-switching, 88–89, 99
Passeron, J.-C., 264
Patrick, D., 176–188
Paul, H., 84
Pavlenko, A., 6, 71–80
Pavlovitch, M., 72
Pêcheux, 237–238
Pêcheux, M., 235, 237–238
Peirce, C.S., 29, 36, 194
pejoration, 250–251
Pennycook, A., 15, 289
Pentikäinen, M., 221
Peräkylä, A., 171
performance of agency, 36–37
Perley, B., 206
personal *versus* territorial rights, 220–221
Philips, S., 199, 206
Philips, S.U., 44
Phillipson, R., 212, 217, 222, 229, 289
Piaget, J., 117, 309
Pickering, A., 29–30
pidgins, 131
Pigg, S.L., 42
Pitres, A., 74
politics of code-switching, 90–94
Polsky, N., 307–308, 310–311
Pong Sin Ching, 101
Poplack, S., 76, 86, 89, 101, 133, 142
positive rights, 213
Potter, J., 24, 51, 57–58, 251, 288
Potter, M.C., 135
Powesland, P.F., 21, 23
practical consciousness, 34–35
Practice of Everyday Life, 32
practice theory, 31–33
practice theory, anthropological contributions to, 33–34
pragmatics of (real-world) interaction, 5
Pratt, M.L., 7, 12, 15, 281, 289–291
preference-related code-switching, 100
Prevignano, C.L., 173
professional ideologies, 14
professional language ideologies, 202, 206

psycholinguistic approaches to bilingualism and multilingualism, 73–75
Pujolar, J., 84
pure indexicals, 172

Q

quantitative data, 142
Quebec Act of 1774, 185
Queen, R., 203
Quist, P., 87

R

Rampton, B., 6, 10, 13–15, 93–94, 170, 171, 183–184, 198, 204, 242, 254, 257, 274–297
Rational Choice model, 137
Razfar, A., 206
Redish, J.C., 261
refugee minorities, 222
regulative rules, 146
religious authority, 58
Remlinger, K.A., 61
representation devices, 57
representational agency, 36
representations, 241
residential agency, 36
rewrite-rule, 146
Reyes, A., 205
Reynolds, J.F., 206
Reynolds, M., 50
Ribot, T., 74
Ricento, T., 79
Richland, J.B., 206
Rickford, J., 254
Riggins, S.H., 244, 246, 247
Riley, P., 129
Roberts, C., 54, 169, 171
Robins, K., 282, 294
Robins, R., 289–290
Rogers, E.M., 246
Romaine, S., 7, 60, 129
Rönfeldt, B., 100
Ronjat, J., 72
Ronkin, M., 254–255
Rose, K., 77
Rosser, C., 265
Royal Proclamation of 1763, 185
Rubin, J., 49, 87
Rubio-Marín, R., 220, 222
Rumelhart, D.A., 117
Ryan, E., 75, 256
Rymes, B., 13

S

S, A, and O definition, 37
Sachdev, I., 76
Sacks, H., 10, 50, 55, 242, 247, 312
Saer, D., 72
Saferstein, B., 10, 113–122
Safran, W., 290
Sahlins, M., 33
Said, E., 246, 248, 289
Sander, F., 72
Sankoff, D., 89, 142, 150
Sanskrit, 198
Sapir, E., 283
Sarangi, S., 8, 11, 13, 50, 54, 63, 116, 168–169, 261, 264–265
The Satanic Verses, 59
Sayers, P., 171
Schaff, A., 235
Schank, R.C., 117
Schegloff, E., 56, 173, 312
Schegloff, E.A., 10, 114
Schieffelin, B., 78, 176, 204, 206
Schieffelin, B.B., 195–196, 200
Schiffrin, D., 170
Schmid, M., 74
Schmidt, R. Sr., 181
Schrauf, R., 74
Schultz, J., 171
Schumann, J., 76
Scollon, R., 279, 289
Scotton, C., 95
Scotton, C.M., 137
Seabrook Ajirotutu, C., 171
Sealey, A., 242
Searle, J.R., 51, 235
Sebba, M., 93, 98
secondary baby-talk, 25
Sefton-Green, J., 293
Selting, M., 171, 173
semantic roles, 37
semicategorical rules, 145
Sen, A., 227
Sewell Jr., W.H., 31–32
Shankar, S., 203
Shannon, S.M., 181
Shaw, S., 61
Shearwood, P., 187
Sherzer, J., 276, 279, 281, 283
Shotter, J., 24, 51–52, 57
Shuy, R., 54
Silverman, D., 54
Silverstein, M., 15, 39–41, 172, 176–177, 179–181, 187, 192–196, 198, 199, 200, 292

Simmel, G., 246
Simon, D., 117
Simpson, P., 49
Singh, R., 106, 172
situational code-switching, 87–88
situational validity of speech data, 143
Skapoulli, E., 14
Skutnabb-Kangas, T., 6, 186, 212–230
Slembrouck, S., 15, 50, 63, 177, 184, 206–261, 264–265
Small, M.F., 29
Smith, B., 205
Smith, C.A., 59
Smith, M., 294
Smith-Hefner, N.J., 205
social cognition, 147
social cognitive processes, 22
The Social Construction of Reality, 31
social constructivist approach, 262–263
social control, 264–266
social deixis, 147
social gestures, 147
social institutions, 261
social organization, 118–119
social orientation, 147
social perception, 147
social psychological approaches to bilingualism and multilingualism, 75–76
social reproduction and symbolic resource, 263–264
societal pragmatics, 62
socio-historical processes, 44
sociolinguistic approaches to bilingualism and multilingualism, 76–77
sociolinguistic indicators, 145
sociolinguistic validity, 142
sociolinguistic variables, 145
sociological approaches to bilingualism and multilingualism, 77–79
sociology of language, 5
Solovova, O., 14
Soukup, B., 63
Souviney, R., 117, 119
speakers of oral languages *versus* users of sign languages, 222

Speaking Mexicano, 195
speech accommodation theory, 21–23
speech community, 274
speech community, at interface of tradition and modernity, 278–282
speech convergence, 22
speech divergence, 22
speech maintenance, 22–23
Spender, D., 60, 162
Sperber, D., 54
Spitulnik, D., 41, 196, 206, 292
split ergative systems, 39
split grammatical systems, 38
St Clair, R., 132
Stalin, J., 234–235, 239
standard language ideology, 196
Stapleton, K., 6, 49–64
stereotypes, 149
Stevenson, P., 183
Stewart, E., 135
stigmatization, 149
Stoel, M. van der, 219
Stokoe, E., 51, 57
Stolt, B., 87, 104
stratification, 119
Strauss, A.L., 308–309, 311
Strauss, C., 30
Streeck, J., 116
Street, B., 279, 293
Strömqvist, S., 77
Stroud, C., 84, 93
Strydom, P., 115
stylistic code-switching, 85, 98
Su Hwi, T., 64
subject, semantic role of, 37
subordinative bilinguals, 134, 135
subverting tolerance, 253–254
suppression and silencing, 252
Swales, J., 287
Swigart, L., 92–93
symbolic capital, 165, 263
symbolic interactionism, 10, 304–313
syntactic integrity, 89
Szabó, C., 105
Sztompka, P., 28, 31

T
Tabouret-Keller, A., 283, 286, 289
Tajfel, H., 22, 76, 256

Takekuro, M., 166
Talbot, M., 49, 252
Tannen, D., 60–61, 160, 165–166, 171
Tate, S., 93
Taylor, C., 29
Taylor, D.M., 22
Taylor, T., 289
Thakerar, J.N., 23
Thomas, L., 31, 49
Thomas, L.L., 234
Thomas, W.P., 229
Thomason, S., 130, 308
Thompson, S.A., 173
Thornberry, P., 212, 216
Thornborrow, J., 49–50
Thorne, A., 255
Tibbets, P., 57
Timm, L.A., 88–89
Tischreden, 87
Tlen, D., 206
Todorov, T., 236
Tollefson, J.W., 187
Tomaševski, K., 223, 225
Tongan, 199
Torras, M.-C., 86
Tracy, R., 107
transsexuals, 164
Travers, M., 56
Trechter, S., 205
Treffers-Daller, J., 103
Trudgill, P., 7, 22, 147, 165, 277
Trueba, H., 284
Truss, L., 62
Türker, E., 102
turn-external code-switching, 98
turn-internal code-switching, 98
Turner, J., 256
two-dimensional variation, 142
Tylbor, H., 285

U
UN *Convention on the Rights of the Child*, 216
UN *Declaration on the Rights of Indigenous Peoples*, 186, 224
underaccommodation, 25
Universal Declaration of Human Rights, 186, 216, 223
Universal Declaration of Linguistic Rights, 186, 220

Universal Declaration on Cultural Diversity, 221
unmarked code-switching, 88, 95–97
Urban, G., 54
Urla, J., 288, 289
Urry, J., 252, 297
Ury, W., 96
The Use of Vernacular Languages in Education, 186

V
Vaillancourt, F., 229
Van de Walle, J., 3
Van Dijk, T., 192
van Dijk, T.A., 116
Varenne, H., 6, 8, 11–12, 16
variable rules, 144, 146. *see also* variety grammars
Variation theory and language contact: concepts, methods and data, 142
'variety grammar,' 141
Verhoeven, J.C., 309
Verhoeven, L., 77, 309
Vermes, G., 58
Verschueren, J., 5, 11, 13, 15–16, 62, 169, 173, 180, 249, 256, 288
Verwey, N., 50
Vogt, H., 84
Voices of Modernity: Language Ideologies and the Politics of Inequality, 202
Voloshinov, V.N., 4, 11

Vološinov, 236–237
Volosinov, V., 287, 290
Vološinov, V.N., 193, 235–239
voluntaristic theory of action, 8
Vygotsky, L.S., 29

W
Wallace, C., 294
Walsh, C., 61
Wardhaugh, R., 277
Wareing, S., 49
Warren, J., 183
Watson, R., 304–313
Watts, R., 50
Watts, R.J., 62–63, 179, 261–272
Waugh, L.R., 40
Weber, M., 113
Webster, A., 206
Weinberg, T.S., 308, 311
Weinreich, U., 4, 73, 130, 134–135
Wenger, E., 13, 283–285, 286
Werry, C., 293
Wertsch, J.V., 29
West, C., 26, 56, 60, 160
Wetherall, M., 288
Wetherell, M., 24, 49, 51, 57, 251
'When Talk Isn't Cheap: Language and Political Economy,' 195
Whorf, B.L., 192, 242
Widdicombe, S., 51
Widdowson, H.G., 6
Wiemann, J.M., 21

Williams, A., 245
Williams, E., 226
Williams, F., 23
Williams, G., 7–8, 277, 290
Williams, R., 16, 34
Wills, J., 116, 119
Wilson, D., 54
Wilson, J., 49–64, 261
Winford, D., 130, 132–133
Wittgenstein, L., 29, 51
women's language, 162
Woolard, C., 242
Woolard, K., 75, 78, 93, 195–196, 200, 202, 281, 288–289
Woolard, K.A., 1–2, 7, 16, 130, 176, 180, 183, 187
Woolf, V., 154
Wootton, T., 93, 98
Wright, P., 284

Y
Yates, S., 293
Yeo, E., 280
Yeo, S., 280
You Just Don't Understand, 165
Young, L.W.L., 171
Yule, G., 15

Z
Zentella, A., 291, 297
Zentella, A.C., 88, 107, 203–204
Ziamari, K., 102
Zimmerman, D.H., 26, 56
Ziv, O., 294